The Straight State

POLITICS AND SOCIETY IN TWENTIETH-CENTURY AMERICA

SERIES EDITORS

William Chafe, Gary Gerstle, Linda Gordon, and Julian Zelizer

A list of titles

in this series appears

at the back of

the book

The Straight State

⊖

SEXUALITY AND CITIZENSHIP IN
TWENTIETH-CENTURY AMERICA

Margot Canaday

PRINCETON UNIVERSITY PRESS   PRINCETON AND OXFORD

Library of Congress Cataloging-in-Publication Data

Canaday, Margot.
The straight state : sexuality and citizenship in twentieth-century America /
Margot Canaday.
p.   cm. — (Politics and society in twentieth-century America)
Includes index.
ISBN 978-0-691-13598-4 (hardcover : alk. paper) 1. Homosexuality—United
States—History—20th century. 2. Homosexuality—Political aspects—
United States—History—20th century. 3. United States—
Social policy—1980-1993. 4. Political rights—
United States—History—20th century.
I. Title.
HQ75.16.U6C36   2009
323.3'2640973—dc22
2008041020

British Library Cataloging-in-Publication Data is available

This book has been composed in Palatino

Printed on acid-free paper. ∞

press.princeton.edu

Printed in the United States of America

1 3 5 7 9 10 8 6 4 2

For Rachel

Contents

———◯———

Illustrations

———◯———

Acknowledgments

———◯———

I once told a colleague that I decided to become an academic because I wanted to surround myself with smart and unconventional people. She snorted in response, but it really wasn't such a bad call. As I have worked on this project, I have been continually delighted by the wealth of (smart and unconventional) people who have taken time to encourage, mentor, and even offer me their friendship. They have been critical to my development as a historian, and it is my pleasure to be able to thank them here.

This book began as a dissertation at the University of Minnesota, where I was incredibly fortunate to get my own start as well. At Minnesota, I benefited greatly from being in a history department that was not only intellectually dynamic, but also held up feminism, democracy, and kindness to graduate students as core principles. I know that long before I arrived on the scene, my co-adviser Sara Evans played a critical role in imprinting those values on the department, and I thank her especially for creating an environment in which so many of us would thrive. She was, along with co-adviser Barbara Welke, an exquisite mentor, and I thank them both for their distinct but complementary guidance during my years as a graduate student. Elaine Tyler May was essentially a third adviser to the dissertation, and I am grateful for all her generosity and insight. Sally Kenney, Erika Lee, and Kevin Murphy also served on my committee, read dissertation chapters, provided research advice, and moral support. Anna Clark, Mary Dietz, and Lisa Disch each made critical contributions to my graduate education. I also want to thank my friends in American studies (Kim Heikkila, Kate Kane, and Mary Strunk) for inviting me into their terrific dissertation group. I thank as well members of the Comparative Women's History Workshop and those in Elaine and Lary May's dissertation group for their many thoughtful critiques.

The next stop was (and still is) Princeton University, where a postdoctoral fellowship in the Society of Fellows has provided me ample time to write and think. I thank Leonard Barkan, Mary Harper, Carol Rigolot, and Michael Wood for creating the ideal conditions under which to write a book. Graham Jones, Mendi Obadike, Miriam Petty, Sarah Ross, Jennifer Rubenstein, and Gayle Salamon kept a bit of adolescence alive on the second floor of the Joseph Henry House, and I thank them and all the fellows for their camaraderie. I am also grateful for the warm

welcome from many wonderful colleagues in the history department—
Jeremy Adelman, Janet Chen, Angela Creager, Ben Elman, Shel Garon,
Michael Gordin, Tony Grafton, Molly Greene, Josh Guild, Judy Hanson,
Tera Hunter, Bill Jordan, Kevin Kruse, Michael Laffan, Phil Nord, Bar-
bara Oberg, Bhavani Raman, Dan Rodgers, Chris Stansell, Helen Tilley,
Sean Wilentz, Julian Zelizer, and most especially Dirk Hartog, who has
been my friend in New Jersey from day one.

Beyond Minnesota or Princeton, I have been extremely fortunate to
be able to count on the support and mentoring of those more experienced than I. For their kind words and generous deeds over many
years, I thank especially Susan Cahn, John D'Emilio, Linda Kerber, Regina Kunzel, Laura McEnaney, Joanne Meyerowitz, Sonya Michel, and
Chris Tomlins. More generally, I want to acknowledge a broader community of queer historians and a broader community of legal historians
for their respective commitments to nurturing young scholars. In a related but slightly distinct category, Pippa Holloway has been the most
steadfast of professional companions and my favorite person to play
hooky with at annual meetings. In innumerable ways, she has helped
me to keep joy firmly centered in my professional life. (And talk about
smart and unconventional!)

My relationship with Barbara Welke now transcends any institutional
tie (and also merits its own paragraph). Barbara was an amazingly giving dissertation adviser, but her support and friendship have meant
even more to me in the years since graduate school. She reads everything
I write (often multiple times) and consistently asks questions that make
me think about my work in bigger ways. She has fielded questions from
me on every imaginable topic. I call her when things go well, and I call
her when they don't. Her unwavering belief in me and my work has
given me a confidence that I doubt otherwise I would have. Above all, I
appreciate her skepticism about the things in our profession that don't
really matter, as well as her optimism about the things that do.

This book is far better because of those who read it and told me how to
improve it. Individual chapters were read by Mary Anne Case, Andrea
Friedman, Sandy Levitsky, Sonya Michel, Kevin Murphy, Chris Stansell,
members of the Gender and Sexuality Studies Workshop at the University of Chicago, members of the Modern America Workshop at Princeton
University, fellows at the Hurst Institute in Legal History at the University of Wisconsin, and participants at the annual retreat of the Program
in Law and Public Affairs at Princeton University. Brian Balogh, Nancy
Cott, John D'Emilio, Gary Gerstle, Linda Gordon, Dirk Hartog, Beth Hillman, Linda Kerber, Kate Masur, Joanne Meyerowitz, Bethany Moreton,
Claire Potter, Rachel Spector, and Barbara Welke read the entire manuscript (at various stages). All of you were vitally important. Thank you.

This book is also far better because it was supported financially (both as a dissertation and after the dissertation's completion). Thanks to the American Historical Association, the Center for the Study of Sexual Minorities in the Military, the Organization of American Historians, the Philanthrofund Foundation, Princeton University, the Schochet Center, Diane di Mauro and the Social Science Research Council, and the University of Minnesota.

I not only say thank you but also offer here a public apology to a whole myriad of archivists and librarians whose patience I am sure I have tried: Marian Smith, senior historian at Citizenship and Immigration Services; Suzanne Thorpe at the University of Minnesota Law School; Shawn Wilson at the Kinsey Institute; Terence Kissack at the GLBT Historical Society; Joel Wurl at the Immigration History Research Center; David Klaassen at the Social Welfare History Archives; and Daniel Linke at the Seeley G. Mudd Manuscript Library. But no where have I been as irritating as at the National Archives. Thanks to Ed Barnes, Dave Giordano, Suzanne Harris, Michael Hussey, Rebecca Livingston, Lawrence MacDonald, Will Mahoney, Marty McGann, Eugene Morris, Trevor Plant, Rod Ross, Kenneth Schlesinger, Mitch Yockelson, and Barry Zerby.

Since I began this project several years ago, I have been continually awestruck at how much our government has done right in terms of archives infrastructure, records preservation, and open government laws. I want to thank our professional organizations (the American Historical Association, the Organization of American Historians, and the Society of American Archivists) as well as a myriad of open government activists who have worked hard to hold the line against President George W. Bush's efforts to diminish the Freedom of Information Act (FOIA), nullify the Presidential Records Act, slow declassification, and otherwise obscure the historical record. More specifically, I want to express my gratitude to numerous FOIA officers at various federal agencies who did their best to release information to me. Special thanks to Judge Rosemary Collyer of the U.S. District Court for the District of Columbia for her fair and expeditious rulings in a lawsuit I brought against Citizenship and Immigration Services to secure the release of records legally available to me under the FOIA.

At Princeton University Press, I am grateful to the editors of the Politics and Society in Twentieth-Century America series (William Chafe, Gary Gerstle, Linda Gordon, and Julian Zelizer) for believing that this book has a place in their excellent series. Editors Brigitta van Rheinberg and Clara Platter have been extremely supportive and easy to work with. Thanks also to my production editor, Leslie Grundfest, and to Cindy Milstein for expert copyediting.

Portions of chapters 4 and 6 have been published elsewhere in different forms. An earlier version of chapter 6 appeared in *Law and Social Inquiry* 28 (Spring 2003): 351-87; a different version of chapter 4 appeared in the *Journal of American History* 90 (December 2003): 935-57.

A writer is always a burden to her own family, and so my final words of gratitude are for them. I still miss and think often of my dourly Methodist grandmother, Helen Canaday Krippner, who died as I was embarking on this project. Grandma said that to be a good Christian was to finish what you start. Undoubtedly, she would not have appreciated the topic of this book, but she would have been pleased with its completion. My parents, Clarice and Ray Krippner, have taught me to love ideas and learning for their own sake and to be wary of elitism. I cannot imagine a more useful inheritance for an academic career. My quirky older sister, Leah Krippner, and her partner Paul Goddard, have brought us all the joy and buoyancy of little girls, Jemma and Crete. I owe a special debt to my twin sister, Greta Krippner. Anyone who has an identical twin knows what an amazing gift it is. But our bond is even tighter because Greta is also an academic. Although we do not share the same discipline or even subject matter—("We can't all study sex," she snaps. "Someone has to keep an eye on the economy!")—we have for years taken comfort in a (sometimes freakishly) similar approach to intellectual and professional problems. Greta's partner, Sandy Levitsky, has become a very dear friend.

It has been my greatest pleasure to share the last seventeen years of my life with the witty, kind, and insightful Rachel Spector. Rachel's support for my career has been so multifaceted, it's hard to even know how to describe it. I'll try geographically: It was Rachel, after all, who many years ago dropped me off for my GRE exam in San Francisco. Several months later (after she had just passed the California bar exam), she agreed to move with me to Wisconsin so I could establish residency for graduate school there (where she immediately sat for another bar). She did not complain when fairly bad planning on my part required us to head off again for yet another midwestern state (this time, Minnesota). Some years later, Rachel engineered our move to Washington, DC, to put me in daily proximity to the National Archives. And she has patiently tolerated my absence while I have been working in New Jersey these last several years. In every single locale, Rachel has helped me to take risks, embrace change, and otherwise manage the highs and lows of a profession that is usually intoxicating but occasionally toxic. She has also left fresh flowers on my desk more times than I can count. This book is for her.

The Straight State

Introduction

> For all orderly processes, we must in some way
> classify man.
> —Dr. Dahlgren, surgeon, U.S. Public Health Service,
> testifying in *Rosenberg v. Fleuti*

———◯———

Measured against other Western democracies at the dawn of the twentieth century, the American state—slow to develop, small in size, and limited in capability—stood out as distinctive.[1] Fifty years later, a period of expansion had produced a state that was finally European in its heft, but still exceptional in another way: in terms of its homophobia. "There appears to be no other major culture in the world," Alfred Kinsey wrote in 1953, in which homosexual relationships were "so severely penalized."[2] Not only was the United States "the only major power in

[1] See, for example, many of the essays in, and especially the introduction to, Margaret Weir, Ann Shola Orloff, and Theda Skocpol, eds., *The Politics of Social Policy in the United States* (Princeton, NJ: Princeton University Press, 1988); Brian Balogh, "The State of the State among Historians," *Social Science History* 27 (Fall 2003): 456; Meg Jacobs and Julian E. Zelizer, "The Democratic Experiment: New Directions in American Political History," in *The Democratic Experiment: New Directions in American Political History*, ed. Meg Jacobs, William J. Novak, and Julian E. Zelizer (Princeton, NJ: Princeton University Press, 2003), 2. My representation of the early twentieth-century state as a fledgling bureaucracy refers to the federal state. William Novak has argued convincingly that state and local governments were quite vigorous in nineteenth-century America. See William J. Novak, *The People's Welfare: Law and Regulation in 19th Century America* (Chapel Hill: University of North Carolina Press, 1996). I do not find Novak's more recent article applying this notion of a vigorous state more broadly (across all levels of government) as persuasive. William J. Novak, "The Myth of the 'Weak' American State," *American Historical Review* 113 (June 2008): 752–72. Several scholars (Richard John, Jerry Mashaw, and Richard White, among others) have identified pockets of federal authority throughout American history. Yet relative to what existed in Europe at that moment, as well as to what came later, the tools and resources available to the federal state in 1900 were limited.

[2] Alfred C. Kinsey, *Sexual Behavior in the Human Female* (Philadelphia: Saunders, 1953), 483. Kinsey's observation was not unique: "In contrast to England and the United States, the majority of European states do not proscribe homosexual acts between consenting adults. Austria, Germany, and Norway are the only European countries that do so, but in

the world" that excluded homosexuals from its armed services and government employment, the sociologist Donald Webster Cory wrote a decade later, "but the homosexual is the only individual who is punished in this manner, not only for any activities that may be indulged in, but for harboring the desire to perform such activities."[3] Those suspected of homosexuality were purged from the civil service and military in astounding numbers at midcentury. They were also barred from certain federal benefits, faced increased FBI and Post Office surveillance and explicit immigration and naturalization exclusions, as well as the stain of alleged political subversion.[4] It seems a paradox. How did a state that was so late in coming construct such a vast apparatus for policing homosexuality, and why?

Unlike comparable European states, which were well established *before* sexologists "discovered" the homosexual in the late nineteenth century, the American bureaucracy matured during the same years that scientific and popular awareness of the pervert exploded on the American continent. This study examines three of the "engines" of the twentieth-century state—the Bureau of Immigration, the military, and the federal agencies that administered welfare benefits—to demonstrate how federal interest in homosexuality developed in tandem with the growth of the bureaucratic state. In emphasizing the relationship between state formation and homosexual identity, I not only seek to put the history of sexuality into closer dialogue with political and legal history, but to complicate what has now become a standard interpretation within the field of gay and lesbian history as well. Namely, that extreme state repression of sex and gender nonconformity in the mid-twentieth century was a result of the sudden visibility of gays and lesbians during and after World War II.

That explanation is not exactly wrong, but it is incomplete. World War II was a watershed moment in the state's relationship to homosex-

---

Norway the law is not enforced. In Belgium, homosexual conduct is punishable only if there is an assault, if the sexual object is a minor, or if there is a violation of public decency. Similar situations obtain in Denmark, Greece, Italy, the Netherlands, Sweden, and Switzerland. In France, homosexuality between consenting adults has not been a crime since the *Code Napoléon* went into force in 1810" (Thomas S. Szasz, "Legal and Moral Aspects of Homosexuality," in *Sexual Inversion: The Multiple Roots of Homosexuality,* ed. Judd Marmor [New York: Basic Books, 1965], 127–28). See also Institute for Sex Research, "The Challenges and Progress of Homosexual Law Reform," 10–11, vertical file, "Legal Aspects of Homosexuality," Kinsey Institute, Indiana University, Bloomington.

[3] Donald Webster Cory, *The Lesbian in America* (New York: MacFadden-Bartell, 1965), 221.

[4] The earliest study of state homophobia at midcentury was John D'Emilio's *Sexual Politics, Sexual Communities: The Making of a Homosexual Minority in the United States, 1940–1970* (Chicago: University of Chicago Press, 1983). For a recent study that looks exclusively at the civil service purge, see David K. Johnson, *The Lavender Scare: The Cold War Persecution of Gays and Lesbians in the Federal Government* (Chicago: University of Chicago Press, 2004).

uality, yet homosexuality was not a new phenomenon for state officials during and after the Second World War. Rather, federal bureaucrats had been aware of traits and behaviors that were coming to be associated with homosexuality for at least half a century. The regulatory response to this knowledge before the war, however, was fairly anemic. Viewing this period through the McCarthyist lens of what came after, it is hard to understand how federal officials could be both so aware and yet seemingly so indifferent to perversion during these years.

This sluggish federal response loses some of its mystery if we center the processes of twentieth-century state-building, and the way that states must "puzzle before they power."[5] Federal officials were confronted with evidence of sex and gender nonconformity as they did the things that bureaucrats do—whether keeping undesirables out of the country, peopling an army, or distributing resources among the citizenry. But they initially encountered this evidence without a clear conceptual framework to analyze the problem. Even so, they worried about those whose bodies or behaviors seemed perverse to them. Over time, they worked toward an understanding of what this phenomenon was and why it might be significant, and they made some minimal attempts at regulation. Yet when perversion was policed in this early period (treated in part I of this book), it was often through regulatory devices aimed at broader problems: poverty, disorder, violence, or crime, for example.

As the state expanded, however, it increasingly developed conceptual mastery over what it sought to regulate. This itself was part of the work of state-building, part of a longer process of the state coming to know and care about homosexuality. After the Second World War, an increasingly powerful state wrote this new knowledge into federal policy, helping to produce the category of homosexuality through regulation. From the mid-1940s into the late 1960s (the years explored in part II), the state crafted tools to overtly target homosexuality. In contrast to the earlier period, policies were enacted that *explicitly* used homosexuality to define who could enter the country and be naturalized, who could serve in the military, and who could collect state benefits. A homosexual-heterosexual binary, in other words, was being inscribed in federal citizenship policy during these years. Indeed, this study's examination of three of the arenas where the meaning of American citizenship was most sharply articulated over the course of the twentieth century—in immigration, the military, and welfare—reveals the emergence of that binary as one of the organizing categories of federal policy in the postwar United States.

[5] Hugh Heclo, *Modern Social Politics in Britain and Sweden: From Relief to Income Maintenance* (New Haven, CT: Yale University Press, 1974), 305.

Regulation, of course, changed what was regulated. The state did not, I argue, simply encounter homosexual citizens, fully formed and waiting to be counted, classified, administered, or disciplined. This was not, as political theorist Jacqueline Stevens has written in a slightly different context, simply a matter of "pre-constituted groups" either coming into or being blocked from the public sphere.[6] Rather, the state's identification of certain sexual behaviors, gender traits, and emotional ties as grounds for exclusion (from entering the country, serving in the military, or collecting benefits) was a catalyst in the formation of homosexual identity.[7] The state, in other words, did not merely implicate but also *constituted* homosexuality in the construction of a stratified citizenry.

Homosexuality is thus a legal category as much as a medical or psychiatric one. This study not only sets the federal regulation of homosexuality in longer historical view, but also offers an account of the *bureaucratization* of homosexuality—something forged, in short, through legal and administrative processes. To uncover those processes is to challenge the law's own tendency to authorize homosexuality as somehow pregiven or even natural in its constitution. "The power exerted by a legal regime consists less in the force that it can bring to bear against violators of its rules," writes the legal historian Robert Gordon, "than in its capacity to persuade that the world described in its image and categories is the only attainable world."[8]

Before laying out the argument in greater detail, a fuller discussion of three of the main terms that frame this study will be necessary.

The State

The state is notoriously difficult to conceptualize and write about.[9] "The domain we call the state is not a thing, a system, or a subject," political theorist Wendy Brown writes, "but a significantly unbounded terrain of powers and techniques, an ensemble of discourses, rules, and practices, cohabiting in limited, tension-ridden, often contradictory relation with one another."[10] While I appreciate Brown's conception, this is hardly a

---

[6]Jacqueline Stevens, *Reproducing the State* (Princeton, NJ: Princeton University Press, 1999), 56.

[7]On the state's role as an agent that identifies (and a related critique of the concept of identity), see Rogers Brubaker and Frederick Cooper, "Beyond 'Identity,'" *Theory and Society* 29 (2000): 1–47.

[8]Robert W. Gordon, "Critical Legal Histories," *Stanford Law Review* 36 (January 1984): 109.

[9]Stevens, *Reproducing the State*, 57.

[10]Wendy Brown, *States of Injury: Power and Freedom in Late Modernity* (Princeton, NJ: Princeton University Press, 1995), 174–75.

clear recipe for historical research. Historians, for their part, have responded to the vastness and complexity of the state (until fairly recently) by not writing about the state at all. Indeed, it is remarkable how limited the historiography on the U.S. state still is, given the lengthy period of time for which American history *was* political history and vice versa.[11] Yet ignoring the state is less of an option than it once was, largely because social scientists working outside of history have made the case for its significance so powerfully. The state was a "central actor in its own right," historian Brian Balogh observes in his discussion of the work of Theda Skocpol and Steven Skowronek, "an autonomous force and one that had to be reckoned with in writing the nation's history." While those social scientists who advocate "bringing the state back in" have stirred historians' interest, historians have generally not adopted their approach wholesale.[12] The best work on the state by historians takes state institutions seriously, but incorporates rather than jettisons the "society" or "culture" side of the binary, blending social and cultural with legal and political history.[13]

This study, accordingly, takes a "state-building from the bottom up" or "social history of the state" approach. We can see the state through its practices; the state is "what officials do."[14] And by officials, I mean not only top decision-makers but bureaucrats at all levels. This is, moreover, not only a "people" but a "places" approach to the state. In

[11] Despite that long reign, political historian Morton Keller could lament to his colleague William Leuchtenburg in 1986 that there was still "close to *everything* to be learned about the State." William E. Leuchtenburg, "The Pertinence of Political History: Reflections on the Significance of the State in America," *Journal of American History* 73 (December 1986): 594. Of course, it depends who you talk to—where, for example, Brian Balogh saw a paucity of historical scholarship on the U.S. state, William Novak saw an abundance. Both assessments were made in articles written in 2003. In part, these disparate assessments might reflect differences between political (Balogh) and legal (Novak) history. Balogh, "The State of the State among Historians," 455–63; William J. Novak, "The Legal Origins of the Modern American State," in *Looking Back at Law's Century*, ed. Austin Sarat, Bryant Garth, and Robert A. Kagan (Ithaca, NY: Cornell University Press, 2002), 250.

[12] Balogh, "The State of the State among Historians," 458–59. The works that Balogh discusses include Theda Skocpol, "Bringing the State Back In," in *Bringing the State Back In*, ed. Peter B. Evans, Dietrich Rueschemeyer, and Theda Skocpol (New York: Cambridge University Press, 1985), 3–37; Stephen Skowronek, *Building a New American State: The Expansion of National Administrative Capacities, 1877–1920* (New York: Cambridge University Press, 1982). See also Julian E. Zelizer, "Stephen Skowronek's *Building a New American State* and the Origins of American Political Development," *Social Science History* 27 (Fall 2003): 425–41.

[13] William Novak's *The People's Welfare* is an excellent example of this, as are many of the essays in Jacobs, Novak, and Zelizer, *The Democratic Experiment*. Note, however, that almost no attention is paid in this volume to sexuality, the full significance of which I think political history has yet to appreciate. See also George Steinmetz, ed., *State/Culture: State Formation after the Cultural Turn* (Ithaca, NY: Cornell University Press, 1999).

[14] John R. Commons, quoted in Novak, *The People's Welfare*, 8.

locating the places of the state, my method similarly hovers close to the ground. I am as likely to find the state at a Veterans Administration (VA) office in Florida or in an immigration inspector's booth on the border, as in the halls of Congress or before the bar of the Supreme Court. Focusing on these kinds of spaces provides an opportunity to think about the state as not only "intervening" in, but as "intervened" by sexuality as well. The state does not just direct policy at its subjects; various state arenas are themselves sites of contest over sex/gender norms, and therefore structured by those norms.[15] This is, in large measure, what it means to say that we have a "straight state."

In contrast to numerous historical studies that examine one modality of state power over time (the growth of the welfare state or the national security state, for example), my study looks at the state's regulation of one issue (homosexuality) across several venues of federal authority. While I undoubtedly sacrifice some depth for breadth, this broad cross-sectional view illuminates the gradual construction of a legal apparatus to deal with same-sex erotic behavior and gender inversion across state institutions. But despite broad convergence over time, the state is not a monolith, and officials created and implemented policies in ways that were generally sensitive to the needs of the agencies they represented. For instance, an alien discovered to have defective genitalia in the early years of the twentieth century most likely would have been excluded at the border as perverse. The same condition, though, might not have prevented a would-be soldier from being inducted into the army. Across the bureaucracy, sex and gender nonconformity figured in different ways.

An alternative approach might look vertically at local-state-federal interaction rather than horizontally, as I do, across several institutions of the federal state. At a historiographical moment when political and legal historians are turning their attention especially to governance at state and local levels, why shouldn't this be my approach?[16] I focus on the federal government for a simple reason. Numerous commentators at midcentury noted that there was "no crime against being homosex-

---

[15] For a related argument about race, see Michael Omi and Howard Winant, *Racial Formation in the United States: From the 1960s to the 1990s* (New York: Routledge, 1994), 82.

[16] Scholarship exemplifying this approach includes Novak, *The People's Welfare*; Thomas J. Sugrue, "All Politics Is Local: The Persistence of Localism in Twentieth-Century America," in *The Democratic Experiment: New Directions in American Political History*, ed. Meg Jacobs, William J. Novak, and Julian E. Zelizer (Princeton, NJ: Princeton University Press, 2003), 301–26; Laura Edwards, "Status without Rights: African Americans and the Tangled History of Law and Governance in the Nineteenth-Century U.S. South," *American Historical Review* 112 (April 2007): 365–93. Localism has long been the dominant paradigm in LGBT history. See Marc Stein, "Theoretical Politics, Local Communities: The Making of U.S. LGBT History," *GLQ* 11 (2005): 605–24.

ual."[17] This is true. There was no crime. But there was a policy against being homosexual, and it was federal in nature. States and localities generally policed homosexual acts; sometimes the feds did as well. Yet in addition, it was the federal government that gradually developed the tools to target homosexual personhood or status, the condition of *being* a homosexual.[18] The federal government, moreover, never defined homosexual status in the abstract, but always as a part of defining citizenship. Indeed, it is most likely that because citizenship is (since Reconstruction) a national category, the federal government played such an important role in shaping homosexual identity. Now, to take each of the two categories that the federal state filled with meaning in turn:

Citizenship

In contrast to American historical writing on the state, there has been an explosion of historical work on citizenship in recent years.[19] That work—which complements a booming industry in citizenship studies throughout the academy—uses citizenship in a myriad of ways. Citizenship has been long understood as a set of rights, a tradition exempli-

[17] Alfred A. Gross, *Strangers in Our Midst: Problems of the Homosexual in American Society* (Washington, DC: Public Affairs Press, 1962), 93; Edward H. Knight, "Overt Male Homosexuality," in *Sexual Behavior and the Law*, ed. Ralph Slovenko (Springfield, IL: Charles C. Thomas Publishers, 1965), 434.

[18] "The Consenting Adult Homosexual and the Law: An Empirical Study of Enforcement and Administration in Los Angeles County," *UCLA Law Review* 13 (1966): 658.

[19] A sampling of that work includes Linda Gordon, *Pitied But Not Entitled: Single Mothers and the History of Welfare, 1890–1935* (Cambridge, MA: Harvard University Press, 1994); Rogers M. Smith, *Civic Ideals: Conflicting Visions of Citizenship in U.S. History* (New Haven, CT: Yale University Press, 1997); Candace Lewis Bredbenner, *A Nationality of Her Own: Women, Marriage, and the Law of Citizenship* (Berkeley: University of California Press, 1998); Nancy F. Cott, "Marriage and Women's Citizenship in the United States," *American Historical Review* 103 (December 1998): 1440–74; Katherine Franke, "Becoming a Citizen: Reconstruction Era Regulation of African American Marriages," *Yale Journal of Law and the Humanities* 11 (1999): 251–309; Linda K. Kerber, *No Constitutional Right to Be Ladies: Women and the Obligations of Citizenship* (New York: Hill and Wang, 1999); Mary L. Dudziak, *Cold War Civil Rights: Race and the Image of American Democracy* (Princeton, NJ: Princeton University Press, 2000); Alexander Keyssar, *The Right to Vote: The Contested History of Democracy in the United States* (New York: Basic Books, 2000); Alice Kessler-Harris, *In Pursuit of Equity: Women, Men, and the Quest for Economic Citizenship in 20th Century America* (Oxford: Oxford University Press, 2001); Nancy F. Cott, *Public Vows: A History of Marriage and the Nation* (Cambridge, MA: Harvard University Press, 2002); Evelyn Nakano Glenn, *Unequal Freedom: How Race and Gender Shaped American Citizenship and Labor* (Cambridge, MA: Harvard University Press, 2002); Lizabeth Cohen, *A Consumers' Republic: The Politics of Mass Consumption in Postwar America* (New York: Knopf, 2003); Erika Lee, *At America's Gates: Chinese Immigration during the Exclusion Era, 1882–1943* (Chapel Hill: University of

fied by the work of British sociologist T. H. Marshall.[20] More recent
work emphasizes citizenship as obligation.[21] In addition to liberal and
republican paradigms, contemporary scholarship on citizenship also
includes communitarian, social democratic, feminist, and multicultural
critiques.[22] Sociologists Will Kymlicka and Wayne Norman have use-
fully pointed out that this vast scholarship can be broken down into two
broad categories. Some accounts describe citizenship as practice, with
the emphasis on the activity of being a citizen. Other accounts treat citizenship as status, whether defined legally or culturally. Scholarship in
this vein concerns citizenship as identity, seeks to identify the attributes
of good citizens, and to determine the way in which individuals are incorporated into the status of citizenship.[23] While each of my chapters
necessarily touches on the practices of citizenship—soldiering, immi-
grating, or the act of claiming benefits—this project takes its driving
questions from the literature on citizenship as status.

In the American tradition, the legal status of citizenship is simple. According to Linda Kerber, one either is or is not a citizen. In contrast to
some European nations, there are no formal categories here of first- and
second-class citizenship. But the preoccupation of historians in recent
years, including Kerber, has been to examine the "distinctions that were
historically experienced"—how, in Nancy Cott's words, citizenship
"can be delivered in different degrees of permanence or strength."[24]
This study adds sexuality to the ascriptive tradition of American citizenship that Rogers Smith lays out, and makes the case that the trajectory of American citizenship in the twentieth century has not been one
of continual expansion, but is defined rather by the persistent "nexus of
exclusion and inclusion."[25] As the state moved to enfranchise women

---

North Carolina Press, 2003); Mae M. Ngai, *Impossible Subjects: Illegal Aliens and the Making
of Modern America* (Princeton, NJ: Princeton University Press, 2003); Meg Jacobs, *Pocket-
book Politics: Economic Citizenship in Twentieth-Century America* (Princeton, NJ: Princeton
University Press, 2004); Nancy MacLean, *Freedom Is Not Enough: The Opening of the American Workplace* (Cambridge, MA: Harvard University Press, 2006).

[20] Marshall's classic work is "Citizenship and Social Class," in *The Citizenship Debates:
A Reader*, ed. Gershon Shafir (Minneapolis: University of Minnesota Press, 1998), 93–112.

[21] Kerber, *No Constitutional Right to Be Ladies.*

[22] For examples of these various approaches, see Gershon Shafir, ed., *The Citizenship Debates: A Reader* (Minneapolis: University of Minnesota Press, 1998).

[23] Will Kymlicka and Wayne Norman, "Return of the Citizen: A Survey of Recent Work
on Citizenship Theory," in *Theorizing Citizenship*, ed. Ronald Beiner (Albany: State University of New York, 1995): 283–322.

[24] Linda K. Kerber, "The Meanings of Citizenship," *Journal of American History* 84 (December 1997): 834, 837; Cott, "Marriage and Women's Citizenship," 1441.

[25] Ursula Vogel, "Marriage and the Boundaries of Citizenship," in *The Condition of Citizenship*, ed. Bart van Steenbergen (Thousand Oaks, CA: Sage 1994), 77; Smith, *Civic Ideals.*

and dismantle Jim Crow, it was gradually working to construct a boundary in law and policy that by midcentury explicitly defined the homosexual as the anticitizen.[26] What was an inchoate and vague sort of opposition between citizenship and perversion in the early twentieth century became a hard and clear line by midcentury.

Sometimes, as in the case of aliens who were deported because they engaged in homoerotic behavior, homosexuality was defined as outside of citizenship through formal legal expulsion. More often, those suspected of sexual perversion were not formally excluded from citizenship status. One who was denied the right to serve in the military or access to state benefits, for example, would (if not an alien) retain the right to reside in the country.[27] Citizenship is thus best understood through an approach that considers "threshold questions" regarding access to the nation-state (i.e., immigration) alongside, as legal scholar Linda Bosniak writes, "questions about the nature and quality of citizenship as practiced within the political community" (in this study, access to welfare benefits or military employment). Just as few historical studies of the state treat multiple modalities of state power simultaneously, few studies of citizenship consider immigration and naturalization policy in tandem with other aspects of citizenship. In analyzing them together, I hope to show, in Bosniak's formulation, that "citizenship's threshold and its substantive character are interwoven," and to highlight that "political communities exist in a wider world."[28] Indeed, while cer-

---

This is a way of thinking about citizenship historically that has been well articulated by scholars of race and gender.

[26] I am not suggesting here that state-sponsored racism and sexism were eliminated in the twentieth century—only that citizenship expanded to formally include certain groups at precisely the same moments that it contracted to formally exclude others. Moreover, I argue that past exclusions continue to shape the way that those who are newly included experience citizenship.

[27] The right to serve in the military is more accurately understood as *the right to fulfill the obligation* to serve in the military. But fulfilling that obligation is a way to obtain the entitlements (i.e., rights) of full citizenship. So, for instance, military service is a prerequisite for certain government benefits (see chapter 4 on the GI Bill). On the way that the obligations and rights of citizenship are necessarily linked, see Kerber, *No Constitutional Right to Be Ladies*, xxi–xxiii.

[28] Linda Bosniak describes a "division of labor" between immigration scholars who take up the "threshold" issue of access to national citizenship, and political and constitutional theorists who are more interested in the quality and experience of citizenship for those who are already members of the nation-state. "Most political and constitutional theorists presume a bounded citizenry and devote themselves to asking what the nature of relations should be among the already recognized citizens. In contrast, alienage as a category raises questions about the way in which the citizenry's boundaries are constituted in the first instance." See Linda Bosniak, "Universal Citizenship and the Problem of Alienage," *Northwestern University Law Review* 94 (Spring 2000): 964–65, 971. Bosniak's division

tainly not transnational in scope, this study suggests a flow of people, practices, and ideas about sexuality across borders that impacted national belonging for aliens and citizens alike.

Yet whether talking about "threshold" questions of membership or "internal" questions about the way that already-existing citizens actually experienced their citizenship, it is critical to note that many of those who engaged in same-sex erotic practices or expressed gender nonconformity were never vetted by the state at all.[29] Indeed, state policies directed at sex/gender nonconformists have generally not operated by targeting large numbers—and this was especially true for the earlier period. As important as documenting the legal construction of a barrier for sexual minorities in terms of who would be able to immigrate, soldier, and collect benefits, then, is to determine the terms of inclusion within citizenship. The historical evolution of the policies that have over time configured citizenship in relation to homosexuality reveals that, in the words of political theorist Lisa J. Disch, "otherness is immanent to citizenship." Citizenship fosters "internal differentiation and hierarchy," Disch writes, by incorporating some into citizenship in a way that highlights their subordination or "degraded status."[30] And citizenship's mode of incorporation—whether formally inclusionary or exclusionary at any given moment—was not only productive of difference, I argue, but also identity. Over the course of the early to mid-twentieth century, the state crafted citizenship policies that crystallized homosexual identity, fostering a process by which certain individuals began to think of their sexuality in political terms, as mediating and mediated by their relationship to the state.

Homosexuality

Homosexuality is perhaps the most vexing of all, because its meaning changed so much in the years that this study covers, and that change, as I have already suggested, was itself in part a result of the processes of state formation I write about here. Historians of sexuality—critiquing Michel Foucault's assertion that the homosexual had emerged as a "species" by the turn of the century—have argued that the appearance of the

of labor generally holds true for American historians, although some gender historians have bridged the gap. See, for example, Cott, *Public Vows*.

[29] Bosniak, "Universal Citizenship and the Problem of Alienage," 971.

[30] Lisa J. Disch, review of *Being Political: Genealogies of Citizenship*, by Engin F. Isin, *Environment and Planning D: Society and Space* 21 (June 2003): 380–82. Disch asks, "How can inclusion emancipate if those groups who imagine themselves to be outsiders are already necessary to and presupposed by the citizen body—but in a degraded status?"

homosexual as a personality type in medical literature was, in George Chauncey's words, but "one of several powerful (and competing) sexual ideologies."[31] Alongside the medical ideologies were popular frameworks (which Chauncey writes about), and the ideologies of state officials regarding the sexual cultures and types they encountered as their various bureaucracies expanded. Whatever the extent to which Foucault was correct about the invention of homosexuality during these years, Progressive-era officials used the word homosexuality somewhat interchangeably with "pervert," "degenerate," "pederast," and "sodomite." Moreover, these labels generally did not refer to a kind of person who engaged in sexual activity with a member of the same sex. The homosexual was instead a perverted type whose perversion was defined primarily by gender inversion (mannishness in women and effeminacy in men) rather than by sexual behavior per se.[32] And perversion was a fuzzy category, loosely associated with degeneracy, and sometimes manifested as well through morphology (for example, defective genitalia or "poor physique"). Most state authorities in the early twentieth century shared with the populations they policed a notion that men who had sex with perverts (as long as they were masculine and took the "active" role in sexual relations) engaged in immoral behavior (like stealing or whoring), but were not themselves perverse. There was not yet a clear moral axis that cleaved the population into homosexuals and heterosexuals. Rather, a hazier divide existed—something more akin to perverts and normals.

Although "normal" individuals who engaged in sexual relations with persons of the same sex fell outside the moral economy of perversity in early twentieth-century America, they do not fall outside the purview of this history of homosexuality and federal policy. For this is not, actually, a history of federal interest in what homosexuality is at any given moment, but rather a history of federal interest in *what becomes* homosexuality by midcentury. In short, I am writing about a process more than a thing. My approach is, following David Halperin, genealogical. Halperin writes that homosexuality signifies "the effect of a cumulative process of overlay and accretion," in which a variety of "prehomosexual discourses" are held together in an "unstable convergence."[33] Conceptually, I begin with that convergence—homosexuality at midcentury—and follow it backward in time. I follow the threads

---

[31] Michel Foucault, *The History of Sexuality: An Introduction, Vol 1* (New York: Vintage Books, 1978), 48; George Chauncey Jr., *Gay New York: Gender, Urban Culture, and the Making of the Gay Male World, 1890–1930* (New York: Basic Books, 1994), 27.

[32] It was that perverts wanted to be penetrated *like women*, rather than the fact that they had sex with men, that made them perverse.

[33] David Halperin, "How to Do the History of Male Homosexuality," *GLQ* 6 (2000): 90–91.

as they separate; as long as they remain subject to federal policing, they remain part of the story. Or, to put this in another way that follows the chronological movement of this study, I am tracing the "accretion" that over time results in the modern notion of homosexuality as defined by sexual object choice. This was a broadening of the early twentieth-century paradigm—the "normal" man, for example, who was masculine and had sex with other men became a homosexual by midcentury, but the gender invert didn't stop being one. Government policy played a critical role in widening the definitional parameters of what made one homosexual; policing this broader configuration required, in turn, a greater investment of state resources.

The regulation of homosexuality in women was also affected by the overall broadening of homosexuality that state policies had helped to bring about. In the early years of the twentieth century, the emphasis placed on gender difference in defining sexual normativity meant that same-sex eroticism among men and same-sex eroticism among women were seen as distinct kinds of things. As a result, men and women were subject to different forms of policing. Indeed, the federal regulation of male and female sexual deviance occurred on two separate tracks during the first part of the twentieth century, such that state policing of women was almost entirely focused on deviant *heterosexuality*.[34] The new understanding of homosexuality that began to crystallize as midcentury approached was characterized by a binarism between heterosexuality and homosexuality. Everyone was either one or the other, and the defining feature of homosexuality was same-sex sexual activity (whether the act in question concerned two men or two women). In minimizing the definitional importance of gender, this new framework treated sex between men and sex between women as similar acts, and thus subjected women to regulation as *homosexuals*.

Yet it wasn't only that homosexuality came to be seen as pertaining to women as well as men that led to increased policing among women as midcentury approached. Federal officials also had to decide that homosexuality among women was a problem that deserved federal attention. Their slowness to do so (even as government resources for policing expanded) reflects the way that state policies configured citizenship and homosexuality in relation to one another. Gendered ideologies of citizenship, in other words, shaped the gendered regulation of perver-

[34] See Estelle Freedman, "The Prison Lesbian: Race, Class, and the Construction of the Aggressive Female Homosexual, 1915–1965," *Feminist Studies* 22 (Summer 1996): 397–415. For a related point about the development of psychiatry, see Elizabeth Lunbeck, *The Psychiatric Persuasion: Knowledge, Gender, and Power in Modern America* (Princeton, NJ: Princeton University Press, 1994).

sion—male perverts mattered so much to the state because male citizens did.[35] Until almost midcentury, a relatively small regulatory apparatus and genuine state indifference to female perversion meant that women were rarely targeted by legal instruments that were used to vet those who engaged in same-sex sexual behavior or manifested gender inversion. Such tools were deployed against women only as they were more fully incorporated into the arena of first-class citizenship—most visibly, when they were permanently integrated into the military during the early years of the cold war. As women were more completely drawn into citizenship, then, state officials became more focused on lesbianism.

Moving Forward

This study is comprised of two chapters on each of three cases: immigration, the military, and welfare. Thematically, the project is layered. The outer layer, chapters 1 and 6, is immigration. Moving inward, the next layer, chapters 2 and 5, is the military. Finally, the nucleus of the study, chapters 3 and 4, focuses on welfare. The organization of part I of the book (immigration-military-welfare) is mirrored in part II (welfare-military-immigration). The three cases, moreover, each serve two functions in the structure of the project: immigration, military service, and welfare represent major components of citizenship; and, the Bureau of Immigration, the military establishment, and the federal agencies that administered welfare programs all played a major role in the rise of the twentieth-century state. Across several state arenas and over time, then, the six chapters reveal a variety of federal institutions all engaged (but at different stages) in the same enterprise: defining homosexuality and citizenship in relation to one another through the construction of policies that established individuals who exhibited gender inversion or engaged in homoerotic behavior as either outside of or degraded within citizenship.

I proceed throughout by keeping my finger on the arenas where the state was experiencing growth more generally, because the process of state-building itself drew the regulatory eye to sexual/gender deviance. So, for example, I begin with immigration, one of the earliest federal

[35] Despite women's suffrage, citizenship policies defined the typical citizen as male. Women were excluded from military service; naturalization cases from the 1870s through the 1920s concerned men; women's citizenship could be gained or lost based on the alienage or native birth of their husbands; single women were effectively excluded from the 1870s on by immigration provisions barring prostitutes and public charges; and welfare state provision channeled resources toward men as breadwinners. See Cott, "Marriage and Women's Citizenship"; Kessler-Harris, *In Pursuit of Equity*.

bureaucracies, and the first to leave substantial documentation of its response to sexual perversion. The military's adoption of psychiatric and other forms of screening for recruits during World War I led to a growing awareness of sexual "abnormalities" among the troops, so I shift my focus from immigration to the military during this period. (Actual bureaucrats followed this same trajectory, as for example, a Dr. Thomas Salmon, who began his career by inspecting immigrants for the Public Health Service [PHS], and then went on to be the head of psychiatry for the American Expeditionary Forces during the First World War.)[36] The crisis of the Depression inaugurated new experiments with government social provision, and I next examine how New Dealers dealt with rumored and actual homosexuality in work camps for single male transients—the "runaway boys and men." The subsequent chapter focuses on the denial of GI Bill benefits to soldiers discharged for homosexuality during and after World War II. With the dawn of the McCarthy era, I take advantage of the unique opportunity that the 1950s' military provides to examine federal policies on homosexuality that were derived from the regulation of women. My last chapter circles back to immigration policy because it allows me to follow the story from where I began with the Bureau of Immigration to the Immigration and Naturalization Service (INS) and the federal courts. Here especially, I "bring the law back in," as William Novak writes, to political history, considering the courts alongside the administrative agency as just another venue through which the modern state is created.[37]

Readers should be forewarned that in organizing my study by these cases, I do not claim complete coverage of every federal arena where the state acted to define homosexuality. I do not, for example, look at the federal civil service's antihomosexual purge at midcentury because of the comprehensive way this story has been told elsewhere.[38] I also deliberately (if somewhat gingerly) step over World War II.[39] I do not ignore the war but neither do I make it the hub, preferring to engage this

[36] Earl Bond, *Thomas W. Salmon: Psychiatrist* (New York: W. W. Norton, 1950).

[37] Novak, "The Legal Origins of the Modern American State," 272. On the relationship between the courts and the administrative state, see also Reuel Schiller, "'Saint George and the Dragon': Courts and the Development of the Administrative State in Twentieth-Century America," *Journal of Policy History* 17 (2005): 110–24. This point is not meant to suggest that *only* my last chapter involving federal court cases falls within the purview of legal history. The emphasis of the preceding chapters is on the realm of administrative law—for example, the Bureau of Immigration's Boards of Special Inquiry, adjudicative boards within the Veterans Administration, or the investigative arm of the cold war military. Law is, as Robert Gordon notes, "the work of anyone . . . whose task is the administration of public policy" ("Critical Legal Histories," 66).

[38] See especially Johnson, *The Lavender Scare*.

[39] Two extremely skillful accounts that deal with homosexuality and World War II are

story through the World War II–era VA bureaucracy and its implementation of benefits (and hence the welfare-warfare state). I do so because I think welfare has been incredibly understudied in its relationship to sexuality, and because the state was as concerned with using its resources to *settle* men *down* after wartime (think marriage, home, and reproduction) as it was with anything they may have done "over there." Indeed, mobility was a central problematic for the state's regulation of sexuality—the subjects of regulation in this study are all, in one way or another, people on the move. So GI Bill benefits aimed to domesticate men after World War II, but were also a reaction to the memory of so many single men out drifting and "on the bum" during the preceding decade. This inchoate opposition between mobility and settlement evolved into an explicit differentiation between homosexuals and heterosexuals across the temporal span of World War II, and we can see the homosexual-heterosexual binary emerging out of federal welfare policy in this key moment of American state-building. For all these reasons, the state's welfare function makes most sense at the center of this study.

Finally, a note about my semantic choices for the years before homosexuality became a hegemonic term: whenever possible, I try to use the language that federal officials used. Officials not only used a variety of terms, they adopted new terminologies at different rates, depending on the labels they heard used by the sexual cultures with which they came into contact, and on how "up" they were on the current medical literature. State officials also made up terms for bureaucratic usage. So, for instance, immigrants were excluded for a "lack of sexual development," which was closely associated with sexual perversion. "I would first observe that this term in exactly these words will . . . not be found in any of the standard works of medicine," Surgeon General H. S. Cumming wrote to Commissioner-General of Immigration W. W. Husband in 1922. "These words were used by the medical officers [involved] in order to make plain to the non-medical examiners what the condition was which they were certifying."[40] The surgeon general's concern, like that of many of the state officials who will appear in the following chapters, was less technical precision than to find the words and concepts with which to navigate a sex and gender terrain still coming into view.

Allan Bérubé, *Coming Out Under Fire: The History of Gay Men and Women in World War II* (New York: Plume, 1991); Leisa D. Meyer, *Creating G.I. Jane: Sexuality and Power in the Women's Army Corps* (New York: Columbia University Press, 1996).

[40] File no. 55255/070, box 1815, Records of the Immigration and Naturalization Service, RG 85, National Archives, Washington, DC.

PART I

Nascent Policing

CHAPTER 1

IMMIGRATION

"A New Species of Undesirable Immigrant"

Perverse Aliens and the Limits of the Law, 1900–1924

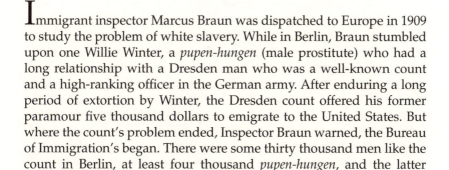

Immigrant inspector Marcus Braun was dispatched to Europe in 1909 to study the problem of white slavery. While in Berlin, Braun stumbled upon one Willie Winter, a *pupen-hungen* (male prostitute) who had a long relationship with a Dresden man who was a well-known count and a high-ranking officer in the German army. After enduring a long period of extortion by Winter, the Dresden count offered his former paramour five thousand dollars to emigrate to the United States. But where the count's problem ended, Inspector Braun warned, the Bureau of Immigration's began. There were some thirty thousand men like the count in Berlin, at least four thousand *pupen-hungen*, and the latter "make it their business to hunt for those unfortunate men who are afflicted with homosexuality and who are known under the Greek name 'Pederast.'" Precisely through such arrangements as those arrived at by the count and Winter, Braun asserted, "we get thousands of them into the United States."[1]

The problem was of even greater magnitude because there were large numbers of "pederasts" not only in Berlin—that city was "honeycombed" with them—but in London, Vienna, and Rome too. There were also many such individuals in the United States, and Braun reported on the existence of "a lively and frequent intercourse between the American and European male prostitutes, as well as among the Pederasts of the two hemispheres." European degeneracy was being exported to the New World as wealthy Europeans like the count of Dresden paid male prostitutes to emigrate, Braun charged, and by transatlantic love affairs as well. American pederasts traveled to Europe, found their "menloves," and "when they leave again they are accompanied by their European

---

[1] File no. 524841/1E, box 594, Records of the Immigration and Naturalization Service (INS), RG 85, National Archives, Washington, DC.

'sweethearts,'" Braun claimed, "to whom they become attached while in Europe." Braun concluded his report by urging that male and female prostitutes as well as "pederasts or sodomites" should be deported from the United States. "If, at the time of their detection," he wrote, "they should be found to have become Citizens of the United States, their Citizenship papers should be declared null and void."[2]

Commissioner-General of the Bureau of Immigration Daniel Keefe read Braun's 1909 report with great alarm, forwarding a copy to his superior, Secretary of the Department of Commerce and Labor Oscar Straus.[3] "The Inspector appears to have discovered a new species of undesirable immigrant not heretofore met with in the enforcement of the immigration law," the commissioner-general noted in an attached memo, "and for whose exclusion no specific provision seems to have been made." What action Secretary Straus may have taken as a result of what Keefe termed "this new development" is unknown, but the response he jotted on the memo indicates his voyeuristic pleasure in reading the report: "Noted with keen satisfaction," Straus scrawled in large, excited lettering.[4] Shortly after Braun's report, the congressionally appointed Dillingham Commission echoed Braun in alerting the government to the "beginning [of] a traffic in boys and men for immoral purposes."[5]

The Braun report is one of the earliest pieces of evidence to document federal-level concern with homosexuality (Braun used the word interchangeably with pederasty), and it demonstrates that federal monitoring of that "affliction" emerged in tandem with the rise of the bureau-

[2] Ibid.

[3] The Immigration Act of 1891 created the Office of the Superintendent of Immigration within the Department of the Treasury. In 1895, the Bureau of Immigration was created. In 1903, the bureau was transferred from Treasury to the Department of Commerce and Labor. In 1913, it was transferred to the Department of Labor. The bureau was renamed the Immigration and Naturalization Service in 1933, and moved to the Department of Justice in 1940. G. T. Kurian, ed., *A Historical Guide to the U.S. Government* (New York: Oxford University Press, 1998), 305–8.

[4] File no. 524841/1E, box 594, Records of the INS, RG 85.

[5] "The same measures employed for the restriction of the traffic in women should be applied with even greater rigidity, if possible, in the case of men," the commission advised. U.S. Congress, Senate, *Importation and Harboring of Women for Immoral Purposes*, 61st Cong., 3rd sess., 1910–1911, S. Doc. 753, 86. Proposed legislation to make the provision barring the importation of any "woman or girl" for immoral purposes gender neutral was most likely a response to the traffic in boys and men. U.S. Congress, Senate, *Regulation of Immigration of Aliens*, 61st Cong., 2nd sess., February 4, 1910, S. Rep. 187, 3–4; U.S. Congress, Senate, *Regulation and Restriction of Immigration*, 64th Cong., 1st sess., December 7, 1916, S. Rep. 352, 4. On the Dillingham Commission, see Robert F. Zeidel, *Immigrants, Progressives, and Exclusion Politics: The Dillingham Commission, 1900–1927* (Dekalb: Northern Illinois University Press, 2004). For an account of the immoral purposes provision of the Immigration Act of 1907 and the way it was used against women, see Ariela Dubler, "Immoral Purposes: Marriage and the Genus of Illicit Sex," *Yale Law Journal* 115 (2006): 756–812.

cratic state. It is no surprise that the Bureau of Immigration, one of the earliest federal agencies, would be the vanguard for such regulation. The need to guard the threshold of the nation-state prompted the development of an administrative apparatus at the border that subsequently moved to the interior. Screening at the border "was among the very first examples of psychological expertise being deployed by the federal government in an important arena of public policy," the historian Ellen Herman writes, arguing that such screening provided a "prototype" for the military during both world wars.[6] Herman's point applies as well to physical screening at the border. And whether one considers immigration, military, or welfare bureaucracies, the federal institutions that most forcefully defined national citizenship during these years were among the first to "see" perversion as they went about counting, sorting, and classifying their subjects.

Yet this new evidence worked its way into the regulatory machinery only gradually. Federal awareness of sex perversion among immigrants preceded by several decades a reliable legal instrument to exclude or deport "sodomites" or "pederasts." Indeed, not until the early 1950s did immigration law explicitly bar aliens alleged to be homosexual from entering or remaining in the country.[7] Despite this, aliens were occasionally excluded or deported for sexual perversion during the early twentieth century, and it is possible to see in such cases the development of a rudimentary apparatus to detect and manage homosexuality among immigrants. That apparatus did not bar immigrants on the basis of perversion per se, but instead relied on the "likely to become a public charge" clause of the immigration law to exclude or deport aliens suspected of sexual deviance. In these types of cases, immigration officials sometimes bolstered the public charge clause with the provision barring immigrants who had committed "crimes of moral turpitude," or later and much more rarely, the prohibition against "constitutional psychopathic inferiors." But it was the public charge clause that was pervasive in state efforts to exclude or deport aliens for sexual perversion.

The use of the public charge clause against aliens suspected of sexual perversion was significant for several reasons. This clause was the most commonly used exclusionary provision in immigration law overall. So it is notable that the state wielded this charge against aliens it considered perverse, because it confirms that the state had no special legal tool for vetting aliens "afflicted with homosexuality" in the early years of the twentieth century. The government had no such tool in part because the immigration bureaucracy was still at a fledgling stage in its devel-

[6] Ellen Herman, *The Romance of American Psychology: Political Culture in the Age of Experts* (Berkeley: University of California Press, 1996), 19.

[7] This was part of the McCarran-Walter Act of 1952. See chapter 6.

opment, but also because homosexuality itself was not yet a meaning-ful category for the Bureau of Immigration. Marcus Braun's use of the term was rare. Immigration officials generally did not conceive of ho-mosexuality as a discrete identity, but instead lumped together aliens who exhibited gender inversion, had anatomical defects, or engaged in sodomy as *degenerates*. Degeneracy was a racial and economic construct that explained "the immorality of the poor," and this helped to give the public charge clause some of its power over sexually deviant aliens.[8]

While the public charge clause was effective against some poor aliens, it was an imperfect tool. Despite the way that the clause both re-flected and reinforced the tightness of a Progressive-era association be-tween poverty and immorality, immigration officials were also slowly awakening to the fact (as with Braun's count, for example) that some-times perverts were not poor.[9] Indeed, an alternative etiology of perver-sion began to circulate during these years that associated perversion with privilege. "Years of luxury and debauchery," reported one medical journal, would lead to gender inversion among the wealthy and even-tually to the most "unnatural acts."[10] Such debauchery was believed more prevalent in the aristocratic Old World than in the United States—a connection that probably offered little comfort to immigration inspec-tors who watched first-class European passengers stream off their boats with minimal inspection.[11] Officials stretched the pliable public charge clause as far as it would go, but in dealing with wealthy immigrants they eventually ran up against the limits of policing perversion by po-licing poverty.

Rich *or* poor, however, it should be said that relatively few aliens were so policed. A systematic search of extant records at the National Archives reveals just thirty-one cases in which aliens who were to be ex-

---

[8] George Chauncey, "From Sexual Inversion to Homosexuality: The Changing Medical Conceptualization of Female 'Deviance,'" in *Passion and Power: Sexuality in History*, ed. Kathy Peiss and Christina Simmons (Philadelphia: Temple University Press, 1989), 100. On degeneration theory and homosexuality, see Jennifer Terry, *An American Obsession: Science, Medicine, and Homosexuality in Modern Society* (Chicago: University of Chicago Press, 1999), especially 37, 43, 48–49, 89. On perversion as a characteristic of primitive races, see Siobhan Somerville, "Scientific Racism and the Emergence of the Homosexual Body," *Journal of the History of Sexuality* 5 (1994): 243–66.

[9] On the increasing "moral register" of dependency during the early twentieth century, see Nancy Fraser and Linda Gordon, "A Genealogy of 'Dependency': Tracing a Keyword of the U.S. Welfare State," in *Justice Interruptus: Critical Reflections on the "Postsocialist" Condition*, by Nancy Fraser (New York: Routledge, 1997), 121–50.

[10] James Weir, "Viraginity and Effemination," *Medical Record* 44 (September 16, 1893), 360.

[11] See Amy L. Fairchild, *Science at the Borders: Immigrant Medical Inspection and the Shaping of the Modern Industrial Labor Force* (Baltimore: Johns Hopkins University Press, 2003), 328.

cluded or deported for perversion in the first quarter of the twentieth century appealed to the commissioner-general of immigration.[12] Certainly, the actual numbers would be somewhat higher; these cases tell us nothing about aliens who were deported or excluded without appeal, nor about those whose records were simply not preserved. Yet even taking this into consideration, data for sex and gender nonconforming aliens mimic patterns established for European, Latin American, and Canadian aliens more generally, only a small percentage of whom were excluded.[13] These thirty-one cases, though, can be read as qualitative as well as quantitative evidence. The weight of quantitative evidence suggests a state that lacked not only an adequate regulatory apparatus but conceptual mastery over what it desired to regulate. Qualitative evidence nevertheless provides the touch and feel of a state as it went about the process of what political scientists call "bureaucratic learning"—"the historical development of the knowledge base on which . . . the public policies of modern governments depend."[14] Small in number, these few cases illuminate (along with congressional and medical texts from this period) a great deal about the development of a federal bureaucracy that was just starting to understand sexual perversion—whether evidenced in sexual acts, gender presentation, or physical anatomy—as inversely related to one's desirability for citizenship.

This was a state that was a long way from being fully mobilized against homosexuality, and yet still beginning to have at least a vague sense of what it was looking for. Its idea was not exactly our idea, but over time, the state's work of discovery and creation would gel into something much more recognizable as homosexuality. It will take six

[12] Of those cases, twenty-eight employed the public charge clause, ten others also relied on the moral turpitude clause (in addition to the public charge provision), and only two employed the constitutional psychopathic inferiority clause (discussed below). Twenty-seven of the cases involved men; four involved aliens whose gender was indeterminate.

[13] Nearly all Asians were excluded by virtue of a series of exclusion laws in the late-nineteenth century and the early-twentieth century. Chinese exclusion was enacted in 1882; most Japanese were barred by the Gentleman's Agreement in 1908; Asian Indians were excluded in 1917. Between 1880 and World War I, by contrast, only 1 percent of the twenty-five million who arrived from Europe were excluded. See Mae M. Ngai, *Impossible Subjects: Illegal Aliens and the Making of Modern America* (Princeton, NJ: Princeton University Press, 2004), 18. Amy Fairchild argues that the medical inspection process resulted in very few exclusions but served to discipline an industrial workforce. Fairchild, *Science at the Borders*, 7–16.

[14] On bureaucratic learning, see chapters 1 and 10 in Michael J. Lacey and Mary O. Furner, ed., *The State and Social Investigation in Britain and the United States* (Cambridge: Cambridge University Press, 1993). Lacey and Furner explain this construct with a passage from Hugh Heclo's work: "Governments not only 'power' . . . they also puzzle. Policy making is a form of collective puzzlement on society's behalf; it entails both deciding and knowing" (3–4).

chapters to lay this entire process out. This chapter begins at the amor-
phous beginning, looking first at the conceptual and legal apparatus that
federal officials started with, its workings and its failures on the slow
but steadily moving conveyor belt that was American state-building.

Vetting Degenerate Aliens

If Progressive-era immigration officials lacked a specific law barring
sexually deviant aliens, there were nonetheless two general provisions
in place before the turn of the century that could be deployed in these
types of cases.[15] First, one provision of late nineteenth-century immigration law prohibited from entry any alien who had been convicted of
a crime of moral turpitude.[16] Later immigration law also provided for
the deportation of aliens who had been sentenced for a term of one year
or more for a crime of moral turpitude within five years after entry, or
who had been sentenced more than once for a crime of moral turpitude
at any time after entry.[17] The Bureau of Immigration defined moral
turpitude as that "which is so far contrary to the moral law, as interpreted by the general moral sense of the community, that the offender
is brought into public disgrace, is no longer generally respected, or is
deprived of social recognition by good living persons."[18] While neither
the bureau nor Congress enumerated the specific crimes that constituted moral turpitude, the charge was sometimes used against aliens
who had committed sodomy.[19]

Then there was also the public charge clause, which mandated the
exclusion of aliens who appeared likely to require public support. This

[15] On the history of immigration law generally, see E. P. Hutchinson, *Legislative History
of American Immigration Policy, 1798–1965* (Philadelphia: University of Pennsylvania Press,
1981); Erika Lee, "Immigrants and Immigration Law: A State of the Field Assessment,"
Journal of American Ethnic History 18 (Summer 1999): 85–114. For discussions of immigra-
tion law and policy that pertains especially to homosexuality, see Shannon Minter, "Sod-
omy and Public Morality Offenses under U.S. Immigration Law: Penalizing Lesbian and
Gay Identity," *Cornell International Law Journal* 26 (1993): 771–818; Robert Poznanski, "The
Propriety of Denying Entry to Homosexual Aliens: Examining the Public Health Service's
Authority over Medical Exclusions," *Journal of Law Reform* 17 (Winter 1984): 331–59;
William B. Turner, "Lesbian/Gay Rights and Immigration Policy: Lobbying to End the
Medical Model," *Journal of Policy History* 7 (1995): 208–25.

[16] This was enacted in 1891. Hutchinson, *Legislative History*, 410–14, 449.

[17] Ibid., 451.

[18] Memo from the Office of the Solicitor, Department of Commerce and Labor, 1908, file
no. 51924/27, box 303, Records of the INS, RG 85.

[19] Even while the federal government was beginning to take more responsibility for
policing sexual deviance, it often intersected with state and local authorities in doing so.
The moral turpitude provision was a key example of this.

provision was initially enacted as part of the Immigration Act of 1882, one of the earliest laws to assert federal control over immigration matters. In 1891, the law was modified to also provide for the deportation of persons who actually became public charges after their arrival.[20] Subsequently, Congress added a financial test—male immigrants were required to possess twenty-five dollars and female immigrants fifteen dollars at the time of entry—and included language that excluded aliens with mental or physical defects that "might affect [the] ability to earn a living."[21]

In contrast to the moral turpitude provision, the public charge clause was a status charge—it required no evidence that a crime had been committed, but only that a person *seem to be something* (likely to be poor). The low evidentiary burden posed by the public charge clause helps to explain its overall popularity in immigration enforcement, as well as its more particular application in cases involving sexually deviant aliens.[22] Only a tiny fraction of public charge cases dealt with immigrants identified as sexually degenerate, but when these aliens were excluded or deported it was almost always as public charges. During congressional hearings on immigration, for example, officials suggested that the public charge clause be used for "persons displaying marked moral indifference or perverseness."[23] The public charge clause was employed in such cases not only because it was difficult to refute and hence effective, but also because of the way it aligned with the Progressive era's ideological melding of moral deficiency and economic dependency.[24] Immigration officials understood this as a bidirectional relationship: a lack of economic resources indicated susceptibility to perversion; perversion was in turn taken as a sign of likely poverty. As important, the public charge clause also connected early twentieth-century ideas about sexual perversion to the particular way that economic dependency was gendered and racialized during these same years.

Most fundamentally, the clause was a feminized provision that was commonly used against women. Single women were almost by defini-

[20] Initially aliens were only vulnerable to deportation if they became a public charge within a year after their arrival. In 1903, this period was expanded to three and then (in 1917) five years. Hutchinson, *Legislative History*, 449.

[21] This language was part of the Immigration Act of 1907. Hutchinson, *Legislative History*, 410–14, 449.

[22] Martha Gardner, *The Qualities of a Citizen: Women, Immigration, and Citizenship, 1870–1965* (Princeton, NJ: Princeton University Press, 2005), 91.

[23] U.S. Congress, House, Committee on Immigration and Naturalization, *To Establish a Bureau of Naturalization, and to Provide for a Uniform Rule for the Naturalization of Aliens throughout the United States, and on the Different Bills Referring to the Subject of Restricting Immigration,* 59th Cong., 1st sess., January 23–March 6, 1906, 170.

[24] See Fraser and Gordon, "A Genealogy of 'Dependency.'"

tion public charge aliens. The charge was also regularly used against women in cases involving immorality, such as adultery, fornication, or prostitution.[25] But if dependency was often linked to immorality for female aliens, dependency for women was also a normative condition.[26] Just as self-sufficiency was a "male prerogative," historian Martha Gardner writes, "dependency continued to delineate what was feminine."[27] For married women dependence was not only normal, it was desirable.[28] So whether it was the stigmatized dependency of the prostitute or the more favorably viewed dependency of the housewife, dependency was the expected outcome of women's true nature. Accordingly, while dependency in women (especially single women) might be associated with immorality, female dependency was not exactly perverse.

This may help explain why there is scant evidence connecting female aliens to sexual perversion at the turn of the century. Because female dependence was considered normal and was almost expected in women, it did not produce or require high levels of scrutiny or suspicion. So, for instance, a Public Health Service (PHS) official working at an entry station in El Paso, Texas, conceded that he did not even bother to examine female aliens.[29] Moreover, the assumption that women traveling with other women were prostitutes probably kept immigration inspectors from seeing sexual connections among women when they may have been in front of them, and reinforced the tendency to deport or exclude women as public charges without first examining their bodies for the physical signs of sexual degeneracy.[30] And because the public charge clause was something of a de facto category for women traveling alone, inspectors were able (and advised) to avoid detailed questioning "along sexual lines." This further circumscribed the information that might have been gathered about female perversion. Nearly the opposite was

[25] See Gardner, *The Qualities of a Citizen*, chapter 3, especially 91–92. On the use of the public charge clause to deport female aliens, see also Ngai, *Impossible Subjects*, 79–80.

[26] Although this was also a racialized construct—dependency was not considered normative for African American women. See, for example, Linda Kerber's discussion of the way that vagrancy laws were used against African American women in the post–Civil War era. Linda K. Kerber, *No Constitutional Right to Be Ladies: Women and the Obligations of Citizenship* (New York: Hill and Wang, 1998), chapter 3.

[27] Gardner, *The Qualities of a Citizen*, 99.

[28] Nancy F. Cott, *Public Vows: A History of Marriage and the Nation* (Cambridge, MA: Harvard University Press, 2000), 143.

[29] Medical Officer-in-Charge to the Surgeon General, January 11, 1939, general classified files, 36–44, general files, 950–56, Records of the Public Health Service (PHS), RG 90, National Archives, College Park, MD.

[30] So, for example, two women who told immigration officials that they were sisters and artists were held for thirty minutes while the board decided "that the artists were no artists, that the sisters were born of two different mothers, and that they came to the United States for an immoral purpose." File no. 52484/1a, box 594, Records of the INS, RG

true with men. The Bureau of Immigration placed no emphasis on avoiding sexual matters in questioning male aliens.[31] The same El Paso official who ignored women conducted "a careful physical examination of all male applicants," reflecting the extent to which men's normative state (independence) required men to be physically robust enough to support not only themselves but others too.[32] A man established his own independence and viability as a good citizen through his relationship to a dependent wife and children (and those men who migrated with families exhibited, according to the 1910 Dillingham Commission, "a stronger tendency towards advancement").[33] Dependency in a man was, on the other hand, as Nancy Fraser and Linda Gordon write, "shameful" and "degrading."[34] In a word, it was perverse.

Just as gendered ideas about dependence sometimes meant that women and men were subject to different inspection procedures, so too did a racialized understanding of dependency affect how aliens were vetted. The public charge clause was used against certain aliens not only because male dependence was considered perverse, but also because perversion itself was seen as a racial characteristic of the lower classes, with perversion as well as poverty arising from the same tainted stock. "Race and ethnicity were important visual clues in the process of discerning [public charge status]," Gardner explains, noting that the clause was disproportionately used against aliens from southeastern Europe and Asia.[35]

The latter were especially targeted—efforts to exclude Chinese aliens began in the late nineteenth century and spread to include other Asians

---

85. A group of five single women who traveled from Hungary to the same town in New Jersey were suspected of prostitution until it was discovered that "these women are all employed as domestic servants in respectable homes." File no. 51698/7-b, box 168, Records of the INS, RG 85. Finally, despite the fact that early twentieth-century sexologists believed many prostitutes were lesbians, this connection seems to have been made by immigration officials only rarely, as in the case of two French prostitutes who also committed "crimes against nature," for example, or a deportation in 1909 of a prostitute who was also a "degenerate." File no. 52503/106, box 611, Records of the INS, RG 85; file no. 52484/8, box 595, Records of the INS, RG 85. On the association between prostitutes and lesbians, see Chauncey, "From Sexual Inversion to Homosexuality," 101.

[31] "Procedure in Inspecting Arriving Aliens," February 13, 1934, file 55855/500B, box 507, Records of the INS, RG 85.

[32] Medical Officer-in-Charge to the Surgeon General, January 11, 1939, general classified files, 36–44, general files, 950–56, Records of the PHS, RG 90.

[33] Quoted in Eileen Boris, "The Racialized Gendered State: Constructions of Citizenship in the United States," *Social Politics* 2 (Summer 1995): 168.

[34] Fraser and Gordon, "A Genealogy of 'Dependency,'" 126–27. See also Nancy F. Cott, "Marriage and Women's Citizenship in the United States, 1830–1934," *American Historical Review* 103 (December 1998): 1451–55.

[35] Gardner, *The Qualities of a Citizen*, 95, 97.

"Another Emergency Project," *Saturday Evening Post* 209 (February 15, 1937). Dependency was perverse in men. Note that there are almost no women in this homoerotic depiction of debauched male immigrants living high on relief rolls—except for that mannish New Dealer, Frances Perkins. Used with permission.

throughout the Progressive period.[36] This special scrutiny may have helped form something of a regulatory template as the association between racial difference and sexual deviance was first and most clearly articulated in the case of Chinese immigrants. The first exclusionary law was the Page Law of 1875, which aimed to exclude Chinese women who were suspected of prostitution. In some measure due to the Page Law and other late nineteenth-century measures prohibiting the immigration of the wives of Chinese laborers, Chinese men immigrated alone (it was the most gender-skewed migration) and lived with other men in bachelor subcultures. These men were further feminized by their work in laundries, restaurants, and domestic service, as well as by the wearing of their hair in a queue.[37] The Alien Land Laws of 1913,

[36] The Chinese Exclusion Act was enacted in 1882. On Chinese exclusion, see Erika Lee, *At America's Gates: Chinese Immigration during the Exclusion Era, 1882–1943* (Chapel Hill: University of North Carolina Press, 2003). Japanese immigration was curtailed in 1908, immigration from India in 1917. The 1924 Johnson-Reed Act completed Asian exclusion, barring Chinese, Japanese, Indians, and other Asians because they were racially ineligible for naturalization. See Ngai, *Impossible Subjects*, 7, 18.

[37] Lee, *At America's Gate*, 26–27; Lisa Lowe, *Immigrant Acts: On Asian American Cultural Politics* (Durham, NC: Duke University Press, 1996), 11–12.

1920, and 1923, which prohibited Asian immigrants from owning land, both reflected the cultural association between Chinese men and effeminacy, and locked them into it. Chinese men would not establish their independence (and hence their manhood) through either marriage or property. Moreover, the application of this law to all Asian immigrants suggests that the particular association between the Chinese, dependency, and perversion had spread to other Asians. The Asiatic Exclusion League declared in 1910, for example, that Asian Indians were "effeminate, caste-ridden, and degraded."[38]

Sexual deviance was linked to racial difference—among Europeans as well as Asians—through the pseudoscience of degeneracy. Early twentieth-century sexology posited a number of contradictory explanations for sexual perversion, but an etiology based on the idea of racial degeneracy seemed to have most captured the attention of immigration officials.[39] Based on the writings of German sexologist Richard von Krafft-Ebing, among others, degeneration theory opposed civilization and sexual morality, and explained perversion, according to historian George Chauncey, as "degeneration to an earlier, lower state of evolution."[40] Degeneration theory associated perversion, in other words, with "primitive" races and lower classes, and poor immigrants and nonwhites were believed to be especially inclined toward perversion.[41]

[38] Quoted in Ian F. Haney López, *White by Law: The Legal Construction of Race* (New York: New York University Press, 1996), 4. Mae Ngai (quoting Robert Lee) writes that "since the time of the anti-Chinese movement in the late nineteenth century, the Oriental threat was cast as an 'ambiguous, inscrutable, and hermophridatic' sexuality, a 'third sex'" (*Impossible Subjects*, 113).

[39] Jennifer Terry describes three etiological frameworks for explaining homosexuality from the later part of the nineteenth century and into the early twentieth century. Degenerationists, discussed in the text above, included Richard von Krafft-Ebing, Jean-Martin Charcot, and Valentin Magnan. Naturalists, such as Karl Ulrichs and Magnus Hirschfeld, treated homosexuality as benign inborn variation. Psychoanalyst Sigmund Freud disagreed that homosexuality was inborn, regarding it as "a psychogenically caused outcome of childhood sexual experiences." By 1909, psychoanalysis was beginning to be important in the United States, but "most medical authorities were less sanguine about the purely psychogenic perspective of psychoanalysts, having invested quite significantly in hereditarian theories which underpinned widely accepted ideas from the eugenics movement." Terry, *An American Obsession*, 43, 106–7. Nicole Rafter confirms Terry's chronology, arguing that while psychopathy emerged around 1915, biological and hereditarian ideas held sway into the 1920s. Nicole Rafter, *Creating Born Criminals* (Urbana: University of Illinois Press, 1997), 6, 167–68. This may explain why immigration officials continued to use the public charge clause against sexually deviant aliens even after the adoption of the law barring constitutional psychopathic inferiors. Rafter also reports considerable blurring of the concepts of degeneracy and psychopathy during the early twentieth century, as commentators frequently used those terms synonymously (174).

[40] Chauncey, "From Sexual Inversion to Homosexuality," 100.

[41] Of sixty-three prisoners listed in the U.S. Census of 1880 for committing crimes against nature, for example, eleven were foreign born and thirty-two were "colored"; only

Perverse bodies as well as perverse acts signified atavism. Hermaphrodism, for example, was considered a kind of reversion to a primitive stage, as was mannishness in women and effeminacy in men.[42] Some degenerationists saw perversion as the result of a "loss of adaptive ability" to the "stresses of modern life"—an explanation that resonated with contemporaneous fears that poor immigrants would not be able to assimilate to American ways.[43]

Furthermore, because degenerationists emphasized racialism and primitivism, their ideas often took on a eugenic character.[44] Degenerates were believed to pass on immoral tendencies, including homosexuality, to their descendants—a situation that led to proposals to sterilize degenerates generally and sex perverts in particular.[45] A less extreme response to the belief that degeneracy was tainting the gene pool was the movement to restrict immigration, which achieved success with the enactment of the Johnson-Reed Act of 1924.[46] The restriction movement was no doubt helped by rhetoric (in this case, in reference to the "traffic in boys and men") decrying the "vilest practices being brought here from continental Europe . . . the most bestial refinements of depravity."[47] It also built on the earlier, successful curtailment of the seemingly

---

one of the prisoners was a woman. Jonathan Katz, *Gay American History* (New York: Meridian Press, 1992), 36–37. The association between perversion and immigrant culture was no doubt reinforced by the vibrancy and visibility of the working-class gay world, as described, for instance, by Chauncey in *Gay New York*, and that world's attachment to a bachelor subculture of immigrant men who rejected the idea that "supporting a family [was] the defining characteristic of both manliness and male respectability." George Chauncey Jr., *Gay New York: Gender, Urban Culture, and the Making of the Gay Male World, 1890–1930* (New York: Basic Books, 1994), 78–79. Homosexuality, according to Terry, was seen as emanating from "outside of the native born white population" (*An American Obsession*, 156).

[42] Somerville, "Scientific Racism and the Emergence of the Homosexual Body," 255; Terry, *An American Obsession*, 46.

[43] Terry, *An American Obsession*, 49.

[44] The eugenics movement "reached its zenith" in the years surrounding World War I. Ian Robert Dowbiggin, *Keeping America Sane: Psychiatry and Eugenics in the United States and Canada, 1880–1940* (Ithaca, NY: Cornell University Press, 1997), 110.

[45] "The ancestors and relatives of homosexuals were assumed to be degenerates and neurotics who passed on their defects to successive generations with cumulative intensity," writes Terry (*An American Obsession*, 47, 93). See also Dowbiggin, *Keeping America Sane*, 77.

[46] In addition to excluding Asians, the Johnson-Reed Act limited the number of immigrants who could be admitted each year from other nations to 2 percent of those already in the United States as of 1890. See especially Mae Ngai, "The Architecture of Race in American Immigration Law: A Re-examination of the Immigration Act of 1924," *Journal of American History* 86 (June 1999): 67–92.

[47] U.S. Congress, Senate, *Importation and Harboring of Women for Immoral Purposes*, Senate Document 753, 61st Cong., 3rd sess., 1910–11, 86.

perverse Chinese, whose exclusion had been mostly accomplished by the Chinese Exclusion Act of 1882 and subsequent acts.[48]

In the years between Chinese exclusion and the Johnson-Reed Act—as testimony on the traffic in boys from Europe indicates—perversion was also seen as emanating from Europe. One congressman blamed gender-skewed immigration ratios rather than the inherent characteristics of certain immigrant groups: "If we see many male immigrants coming here and only a few female," he noted, "the males to a certain extent become degenerate."[49] It was more common, however, to explain perversion in terms of national traits rather than demographic patterns. As Magnus Hirschfeld wrote in 1914, Americans "frequently blame one or the other ethnic group for homosexuality."[50] Thomas Salmon, a psychiatrist who worked as an immigrant inspector for the PHS, remarked, for example, on "the frequency with which we find hidden sexual complexes among Hebrews."[51] Similarly, the 1901 annual report of the Marine Hospital Service (later the PHS) noted a condition, common among Italian men, in which the victim had the "beardless face . . . the high pitched feminine voice, and the general carriage of an old woman . . . with abdomen and pelvis of the female type."[52]

This eugenic and hereditarian view of degeneracy was especially manifest in the belief that perversion—or the "stigmata of degeneration"—was physically visible on the immigrant body.[53] "The true sexual pervert or invert is generally a physical aberration—a *lusus natura*," Dr. G. Frank Lydston wrote in *The Diseases of Society* in 1910.[54] The idea that perversion was visible (along with race and class) was reflected in

---

[48] Erika Lee argues that Chinese exclusion shaped immigration restriction overall, transforming the country into a "gatekeeping nation" (*At America's Gates*, 6).

[49] U.S. Congress, House, Committee on Immigration and Naturalization, *Biological Aspects of Immigration*, 66th Cong., 2nd sess., April 16–17, 1920, 5.

[50] Quoted in Katz, *Gay American History*, 51.

[51] Thomas W. Salmon, "Immigration and the Mixture of Races in Relation to the Mental Health of the Nation," in *Medical Treatment of Nervous and Mental Disease*, ed. W. A. White and S. E. Jelliffe (New York: Lea and Febiger, 1913), 258.

[52] *Annual Report of Marine Hospital Service of the United States* (Washington, DC: U.S. Government Printing Office, 1901), 466.

[53] "Among homosexuals," Terry writes, "Krafft-Ebing claimed to find skull dimensions, postures, gestures, and mannerisms that set them apart from normal people" (*An American Obsession*, 46).

[54] G. Frank Lydston, *The Diseases of Society: The Vice and Crime Problem* (Philadelphia: J. P. Lippincott, 1910), 375. This appears to be a transnational, and even somewhat transhistorical, idea. "There is a remarkably consistent emphasis throughout the history of European sexual representation on the deviant morphology of the invert," David Halperin writes. "Inversion manifests itself outwardly." David M. Halperin, "How to Do the History of Male Homosexuality," *Gay and Lesbian Quarterly* 6 (2000): 104.

procedures for inspecting incoming immigrants. Asian men coming through Angel Island in California and Latino immigrants at the southern border were stripped for examination.[55] Medical inspection at Ellis Island was more cursory, consisting of a line inspection in which as many as five thousand aliens walked by a few PHS doctors each day.[56] Still, inspectors believed that with just a glance, they could identify the most defective of new arrivals. PHS immigrant inspector Salmon instructed examining physicians to single out for closer inspection immigrants with "an oddity of dress" or "unusual decoration worn on the clothing."[57] PHS doctor Howard Knox argued that facial expressions could reveal "sexual habits and relations."[58] Dr. E. H. Mullan urged inspectors to watch for "striking peculiarities in dress, talkativeness, witticism, facetiousness . . . flightiness . . . unnatural actions, mannerisms, and other eccentricities."[59] The *Manual for the Mental Examination of Aliens* further advised examiners that if "the characteristics of one sex approach[ed] those of the other," it might signify "degeneration."[60]

If an alien did catch the attention of a PHS officer, they would be pulled off the line and held for a more detailed inspection—an outcome that occurred for approximately 20 percent of the immigrants coming through Ellis Island.[61] Detention created its own set of problems. Officials sometimes complained about inadequate housing facilities for

[55] Alexandra M. Stern, "Buildings, Boundaries, and Blood: Medicalization and Nation-Building on the U.S. Mexico Border, 1910–1930," *Hispanic American Historical Review* 79 (February 1999): 45, 72. Nayan Shah asserts that Chinese men at Angel Island were completely stripped, but that Chinese women underwent a "less rigorous" physical exam. Nayan Shah, *Contagious Divides: Epidemics and Race in San Francisco's Chinatown* (Berkeley: University of California Press, 2001), 185.

[56] An examination at small stations was generally more thorough, "where each immigrant is given . . . a personal examination by the medical officer." L. E. Coper, "The Medical Examination of Arriving Aliens," in *Medical Problems of Immigration* (Easton, PA: American Academy of Medicine Press, 1913), 31–42. On inspection generally, see Fairchild, *Science at the Borders*; Alan Kraut, *Silent Travelers: Germs, Genes, and the "Immigrant Menace"* (Baltimore: Johns Hopkins University Press, 1994), especially chapter 3.

[57] Salmon, quoted in Kraut, *Silent Travelers*, 71.

[58] Howard A. Knox, "A Diagnostic Study of the Face," *New York Medical Journal* (June 14, 1913): 1226–27.

[59] E. H. Mullan, "Mental Examination of Immigrants: Administration and Line Inspection at Ellis Island," *Public Health Reports* 32 (May 18, 1917): 737. See also C. P. Knight, "The Detection of the Mentally Defective among Immigrants," *Journal of the American Medical Association* 60 (January 11, 1912): 106–7; E. K. Sprague, "Mental Examination of Immigrants," *Survey* 51 (1914): 466–68; L. L. Williams, "The Medical Examination of Mentally Defective Aliens: Its Scope and Limitations," *American Journal of Insanity* 71 (1914): 257–58.

[60] U.S. Public Health Service, *Manual for the Mental Examination of Aliens* (Washington, DC: U.S. Government Printing Office, 1918), 21.

[61] Gardner, *The Qualities of a Citizen*, 6. Virtually all Chinese and Japanese immigrants were detained for further investigation.

aliens held for further exams, involving "scandalous" conditions where the vices of "moral degenerates" were given "free reign."[62] Having spent a night or two in the dormitory, the would-be immigrant's examination then included a thorough physical inspection, and if mental problems were suspected, a barrage of mental tests. Many mental tests were designed to test general intelligence, but aliens might also be asked about their home lives and personal relationships.[63] Examiners, for example, were encouraged to ask aliens such questions as: "Are you married? Do you want to marry? Do you care for the opposite sex? Have you acquaintances of the opposite sex? Are you in love? Have you had any love affairs?"[64] After examination by PHS doctors, a Board of Special Inquiry would decide whether to admit or exclude aliens. Aliens who were excluded were informed of their right of appeal. The appeal then "operate[d] as a stay of deportation, until the entire record [was] submitted through the Commissioner-General of Immigration to the Secretary of the Department of Commerce and Labor." The commissioner-general's decision was final.[65]

Perverse Bodies

So what do the thirty-one extant appeals cases reveal about how the conceptual and legal machinery available to immigration officials actually worked against would-be immigrants? The expanding federal bureaucracy began to exercise more vigorous surveillance of immigrants in general as the twentieth century took hold. As it did so, immigration inspectors usually encountered perversion in one of two ways: perversion was seen as an act, or it was detected on the immigrant's body. The first was more likely to concern the deportation of aliens already in the country; the latter usually involved exclusionary proceedings at ports of entry. Following the order in which immigration inspectors would

[62] File no. 51467/1, box 65, Records of the INS, RG 85.

[63] The Bureau of Immigration employed translators and also used immigrant aid societies to facilitate communication with aliens undergoing examination. See Gardner, *The Qualities of a Citizen*, 7.

[64] *Manual for the Mental Examination of Aliens*, 65.

[65] John J. S. Rodgers, "The Administration of Immigration Laws," in *Medical Problems of Immigration* (Easton, PA: American Academy of Medicine Press, 1913), 29. There was no judicial review for these cases—the success of Chinese immigrants in fighting exclusion in the courts in the late nineteenth century had led to the curtailment of access to the federal courts for immigrants in general. "By 1905," Lucy Salyer writes, "the Supreme Court had endorsed the government's position, greatly restricting judicial review and expanding the authoritativeness and finality of immigration officials' decisions." Lucy Salyer, *Laws as Harsh as Tigers: Chinese Immigrants and the Shaping of Modern Immigration Law* (Chapel Hill: University of North Carolina Press, 1995), 117.

have come across perversion requires starting with perverse bodies at the border, before moving to perverse acts in the interior. In either locale, the public charge clause figured prominently.

A thorough examination of the naked immigrant body was not a routine part of the immigrant screening process at Ellis Island, but if an immigrant appeared frail or strange as they walked the examination line, that alien might be subject to a full examination. Inspectors saw much more in these exams than the signs of physical disease. Inscribed on the immigrant body were also markers that revealed mental defect, propensity for work, as well as abnormal sexual desires or practices.[66] The genitals—more than any other part of the immigrant body—confirmed the vague hints of degeneracy that an inspector might detect in a facial expression, a strange gait, or an unusual physique. Especially illustrative of this phenomenon are numerous cases in which aliens were diagnosed with "lack of sexual development" or "arrested sexual development"—both terms of art that generally indicated an especially small or defective penis.[67] A 1922 letter from Surgeon General H. S. Cumming to Commissioner-General of Immigration W. W. Husband noted that "these individuals are frequently encountered at Ellis Island . . . and are somewhat predisposed to abnormal sexual conduct."[68]

Immigrants diagnosed with arrested sexual development or other related conditions were excluded under the public charge provision because immigration officials associated defective genitalia with perversion, and further viewed perversion as a likely cause of economic dependency. That line of reasoning was sometimes presented in stark terms. Cumming, for example, argued that persons with arrested sexual development "present bad economic risks," because "their abnormality soon becomes known to their associates who make them the butt of coarse jokes to their own despair and to the impairment of the work at hand." As this fact was "recognized pretty generally among employers," Cumming concluded, "it is pretty difficult for these unfortunates to get or retain jobs."[69]

The notion that immigrants with small or defective penises were "bad economic risks" was in many cases bolstered by the fact that many of these immigrants appeared physically weak to inspectors. Donabet

[66] See Fairchild, *Science at the Borders*.

[67] Arrested sexual development figured centrally in the explanation of homosexuality advanced by sexologist Havelock Ellis. As Terry notes of Ellis's theory, "If the body's development was stalled, then its sexual energy remained feeble and was more likely to go . . . towards masturbation or homosexual relationships, since in these situations 'there is no definite act to be accomplished'" (*An American Obsession*, 52).

[68] File no. 55255/70, box 1815, Records of the INS, RG 85.

[69] Ibid.

Mousekian, for example, an Armenian immigrant from Turkey, was certified in 1905 with "feminism," being, in his own words, "deprived of male organs."[70] He is "devoid of every external evidence of desirability," a Bureau of Immigration commissioner wrote in support of the bureau's decision to exclude him as a public charge, adding that "he is weak, emaciated, and really repulsive in appearance."[71] A similar case was that of Francesco Spagliano, a fifteen-year-old Italian immigrant who was certified with arrested sexual development in 1911. The examining surgeon wrote that Spagliano's sexual organs "remain practically like those of a child, in spite of the fact that [he] is full grown." While there was no evidence presented that Spagliano was a sexual pervert, his physical condition made such future behavior likely. "Persons so affected are liable," the PHS official wrote, "owing to inability to satisfactorily perform sexual congress, to become addicted to unnatural practices." An uncle appealed on Spagliano's behalf, stating that he had twelve hundred dollars in the bank and could take care of his nephew. The board ruled for exclusion anyway, justifying its decision not only in terms of the alien's sexual defect, but also because he was frail and small in stature.[72]

The logic of the public charge provision was fairly transparent in cases such as those of Mousekian and Spagliano, where perversion was linked to effeminacy and physical weakness. The likelihood of dependency in these individuals was evidenced by their distance from a notion of independence, and hence capacity for citizenship, that was no longer rooted in property, but inhered, as Nancy Cott writes, "in the self-governing individual who could dispose of his labor profitably."[73] It was an independence that rested on the worker's body itself, and immigrant inspectors could not look at such aliens without seeing the specter of another unmanly type that haunted Gilded Age and Progressive-era Americans: the crippled workingman, reduced by a blight of industrial

---

[70] This usage of the term "feminism" provides an interesting twist on Nancy Cott's etiology, which traces the word's origins to 1880s' France and the French suffragist Hubertine Auclert. The first usage of the term that Cott finds in the United States is a reference in 1906 to the social movement. Nancy F. Cott, *The Grounding of Modern Feminism* (New Haven, CT: Yale University Press, 1987), 14–15. Medical journals were publishing articles on "feminism" around the same time—in that context, however, the term designated men with female characteristics. In a further demonstration of the blurriness of medical and political discourse, the sexologist Havelock Ellis published an essay about feminism and masculinism in 1916. He used the two terms to refer to social movements for female and male supremacy, respectively. Havelock Ellis, *Essays in Wartime* (London: Constable and Company, 1916).

[71] File no. 48599, box 84, Records of the INS, RG 85.

[72] File no. 53248/18, box 351, Records of the INS, RG 85.

[73] Cott, "Marriage and Women's Citizenship," 1453.

accidents, according to the historian John Fabian Witt, "to a 'physically deformed' creature, 'eking out a mere pittance.'"[74]

The public charge provision was also used against more physically robust aliens who were not particularly frail, but whose deformed genitals made perversion seem likely. In the 1912 case of nineteen-year-old Nicolaos Xilomenos, for example, the Greek alien was certified with a lack of sexual development. The PHS's Dr. Stoner wrote in his discussion of the case that those so afflicted "may be sexual perverts." In contrast to Spagliano, Xilomenos, a farm laborer, was a sturdy type. Even so, Xilomenos was rejected as likely to become a public charge. "Aside from the sexual physical defect the individual might appear strong and robust," Stoner concluded, "but it is not thought that this fortunate condition in any way lessens the liability of perversions or mental instability." In light of these liabilities, Commissioner-General William Williams asserted, "the fact that [the alien] possesses $40 is irrelevant."[75]

Similarly, in 1909, the PHS official who certified Irish-born Patrick Eagan with arrested sexual development noted that the alien, like Xilomenos, "looks to be able-bodied." Initially, Commissioner Watchorn observed that the alien "gave a very excellent account of himself as a farm laborer . . . that he has always accomplished the full task of an able-bodied laborer." The commissioner was sufficiently impressed with Eagan to argue that he should be admitted. But the rest of the board overruled the commissioner, stating that the alien was indeed likely to become a public charge, and that persons "effeminately developed" were "undesirable in any community."[76]

Aliens with ambiguous gender were far more perplexing to immigration officials, but again the public charge clause figured centrally in the government's resolution of these cases. Consider, for instance, the case in 1912 of Hungarian Verona Sogan. Sogan arrived in New York dressed in female attire, but medical examiners contended that Sogan was, in fact, a malformed male. She had come from Hungary to meet her mother and stepfather, who "called for the alien as his stepdaughter and said the alien's name [was] 'Mary.'" Sogan was initially diagnosed with "hypospadias" and "arrested sexual development, which affects ability to earn a living." The alien appealed the decision of exclusion, shrewdly maintaining that, if sent back to Hungary, "it [would] be extremely dif-

---

[74] John Fabian Witt, *The Accidental Republic: Crippled Workingmen, Destitute Widows, and the Remaking of American Law* (Cambridge, MA: Harvard University Press, 2004), 82. On the relationship between disability history and queer history, see David Serlin, "Crippling Masculinity: Queerness and Disability in U.S. Military Culture, 1800–1945," *GLQ: A Journal of Gay and Lesbian Studies* 9 (Winter–Spring 2003): 149–79.

[75] File no. 53452/952, box 451, Records of the INS, RG 85.

[76] File no. 52388/158, box 516, Records of the INS, RG 85.

ficult . . . to start my life over again as a male among the people where I have thus far lived as a female." Immigration officials promptly dressed Sogan in male clothing and subjected her to a barrage of questions. When asked why she wore female attire, she answered, "I was baptized as a girl and was always supposed to be a girl, wore girl's clothes and did ladies work." As if looking for another clue to Sogan's true sex, the inspector asked Sogan if she was accustomed to sleeping with the male or female members of the family. "I always slept alone," she cryptically replied.[77]

The inspector then questioned Sogan's stepfather, a poor woodcutter who had been in the country for six years, how he and Sogan's mother would dress the girl if she were released to them. "As a girl," the woodcutter replied. "Did you notice," the immigration official asked Sogan's stepfather, perhaps indicating to the woodcutter that he had given the "wrong" answer and highlighting the broader disciplinary effects of the exclusion process, "that since her arrival she has been placed in male attire?" When again questioned about the sex of his "alleged stepdaughter," the woodcutter replied, "We always considered her a female but every new moon she somehow changes into the other sex." Asked to explain how it was he knew that the alien had changed sex, the stepfather explained that he knew because, "she always appeared sad at such times."[78]

Finally, the board determined that the alien really was a male, and ruled that Sogan was a person likely to become a public charge because the alien's perverse physicality would make employment unlikely. "He is small in stature and presents a poor physical and general appearance," the bureau wrote, adding that "we doubt whether anyone . . . knowing the circumstances would care to employ him." Acting Commissioner F. H. Larned agreed with the decision to exclude Sogan as a public charge: "He is much undersized and rather effeminate in appearance, and I am informed that persons afflicted such as . . . he are prone to be moral perverts."[79]

Just as the seeming compassion of Sogan's stepfather could not save the alien from deportation, so a supportive family also made little difference in the case of a twenty-two-year-old Russian Pole, Helena Bartnikowska. According to the Bureau of Immigration, Bartnikowska was a "hermaphrodite . . . with male type predominating." The bureau reported that the alien had a masculine voice, "considerable beard on the face," and "a well developed penis," but no testicles. Typically, the bureau concluded that "such cases are usually of perverted sexual instincts

[77] File no. 53710/373, box 622, Records of the INS, RG 85.
[78] Ibid.
[79] Ibid.

with lack of moral responsibility." Bartnikowska's aunt and uncle, saloon keepers in Cleveland, filed an affidavit with the commissioner of immigration guaranteeing that they would care for their niece, who they knew was a hermaphrodite yet had no "contagious or loathsome disease." But predictably, Bartnikowska's appeal was rejected on public charge grounds.[80]

The Bureau of Immigration had a more unusual response to the Spanish hermaphrodite José Martinez, who attempted to enter the country at the port of Boston in 1907. Martinez arrived with his manager, who had "the intention of exhibiting him as a curiosity before medical societies." For sixteen years, Martinez had made a living displaying himself as a "phenomenal" throughout Europe. "Every place he has been he has done good," Martinez's manager told the immigration authorities, "so I thought if we came here he would make a good living." Martinez had earned six thousand dollars in just two months in Madrid, his manager reported. Despite this fact, immigration authorities at first ordered Martinez excluded as a public charge. "This man . . . is a hermaphrodite, has very little money," one official concluded, "and as it is the intention to exhibit him to the vulgar gaze of the public, I think it inexpedient to admit this man."[81]

Martinez fared better on appeal. "I do not believe there is any possibility of the alien becoming a public charge," Boston commissioner George Billings told Commissioner-General Larned. Billings conceded his concern that "some Watch and Ward Society might severely criticize us for landing the alien." But there was good reason to think that "the phenomenal" might avoid public opprobrium. Martinez intended to give full exhibitions only to medical societies. The alien appeared "neat and gentlemanly," Commissioner Billings reported. Further, "he states that his exhibitions would be only to the waist line, which would be an interesting exhibition as one arm is like a woman's, the other like a man's, and the breasts . . . one being like a woman's, the other like a man's." A few days later, Larned concurred that there "would seem to be no legal reason for excluding him, other than the possibility of his becoming a public charge." Larned ordered the alien to post a one thousand dollar bond, and the alien was admitted.[82]

In contrast to the preceding cases involving aliens with ambiguous gender, Martinez's anatomy was detached from concerns about his future earning potential precisely because Martinez had found a legitimate (i.e., nonsexual) way to exploit his physical difference in the mar-

---

[80] File no. 51806/16, box 235, Records of the INS, RG 85.
[81] File no. 51787/11, box 228, Records of the INS, RG 85.
[82] Ibid.

ket to make a living, to "dispose of his labor profitably."[83] When "the phenomenal" suggested that displaying his body might have potential scientific value, Martinez only enhanced the legitimacy of his proposed vocation. Yet Martinez's line of work was unusual, and so was the Bureau of Immigration's disposition of the case. More often, immigration officials saw the "stigmata of degeneration" as a reliable indicator of economic hardship, and accordingly, used the public charge clause to exclude aliens they judged to be physically defective.

Perverse Practices

Immigration officials, who regularly asserted that aliens with malformed genitals were prone to perversion, shared with sexologists the notion that a perverted anatomy led to perverse acts.[84] But perverse acts also occurred among those whose bodies were not marked by "physical degeneracy."[85] What connected aliens with degenerate bodies to aliens who engaged in degenerate practices such as sodomy? Immigration officials frequently viewed both types of degeneracy as characteristic of the lower classes, but saw aliens with defective bodies more sympathetically. They expressed skepticism that these "unfortunates" would be able to support themselves as a result of their frail, effeminate physiques or their dim employment prospects once their perversion was known in the community. The logic that made sodomists public charges, by contrast, earned them little sympathy. These aliens were seen as likely economic dependents because their perversion was associated with criminality and vagrancy; they might become public charges because, in a somewhat attenuated argument, they were likely to be arrested, or more simply, because of a willful refusal to work. They failed to establish their independence and their manhood not only because of this refusal to work, but also because they were not "self-governing" individuals—a notion that connected ideas about work to sexual self-discipline as well.[86]

Not surprisingly, sodomists were sometimes deported or excluded under the provision barring aliens who had committed crimes of moral

[83] Cott, "Marriage and Women's Citizenship," 1453.
[84] Krafft-Ebing believed, according to Terry, that "the homosexual's tainted body . . . inclined the individual towards even more degenerate acts and moral dissipation" (*An American Obsession*, 47).
[85] The term "physical degeneracy" is from the 1908 case of Arotioun Caracahian, a Turkish Armenian alien excluded as a public charge for arrested sexual development. File no. 52242/11, box 463, Records of the INS, RG 85.
[86] Cott, "Marriage and Women's Citizenship," 1453.

turpitude, but always in combination with the public charge clause. Typical, then, of these early twentieth-century sodomy cases was the portrayal of sodomists as barely employed bums, drinkers, or vagrants.[87] The immorality of Greek alien Prodromos Smyrneos, for example, was "the talk of the entire Greek colony at sixth and Elm Street" in Saint Louis. Smyrneos was "bumming around the Greek coffee houses doing nothing" when he was arrested on charges that he committed sodomy for pay. The Bureau of Immigration charged that he was "a habitual thief and possessed of immoral tendencies." Smyrneos was, according to the immigrant inspector in charge of his case, "a common bum [who] avoids doing any work." Based on his "habits and tendencies," the bureau concluded that the alien was likely to become a public charge at his time of entry and could be deported.[88] Similarly, the bureau deported another out-of-work Greek alien on public charge grounds after the alien admitted to having sex with a Bulgarian man in exchange for a few drinks. "The alien is a degenerate, by reason of having unnatural intercourse with the male sex," the immigrant inspector wrote in the case, "and from all appearances is a man of very low character and criminal tendencies."[89] In yet another case, an alien who admitted to practicing sexual perversion in both the United States and Canada was deported for crimes of moral turpitude, entering without inspection, and as a person likely to become a public charge. "He claims to be a chicken picker, but evidently does not follow this line very closely," Assistant Commissioner-General of Immigration Alfred Hampton noted dryly.[90]

The association between sodomy and vagrancy is also evident in the case of Daniel Little, a fifteen-year-old boy who emigrated from Canada in 1914. Little, hoping to make it to San Francisco, took a job for a short time on a steamer in Toledo. He reported that the deckhands would come to his bed at night and "stick it in him." After leaving the steamer, Little moved around from Detroit to Chicago, Muscatine to Davenport, and then back to Chicago. Arriving in Chicago again, Little went to Halstead Street, met a Thomas Ryan, and had sex with him for fifty cents—an action that further feminized him in the eyes of immigration officials, who were accustomed to policing female prostitution. Little looked for a job for a short while, but found there was "nothing doing." Finally, he

[87] On vagrancy law, see Kerber, *No Constitutional Right to Be Ladies*, chapter 3; Amy Dru Stanley, *From Bondage to Contract: Wage Labor, Marriage, and the Market in the Age of Slave Emancipation* (Cambridge: Cambridge University Press, 1998), chapter 3.

[88] File no. 53849/037, box 717, Records of the INS, RG 85.

[89] File no. 53429/014, box 436, Records of the INS, RG 85.

[90] File no. 54262/143, box 976, Records of the INS, RG 85.

met a Frank Murray at a restaurant on Halstead. Murray got a job and worked, while Little sat "down with [Murray's] landlady" and read magazines. Little reported that Murray had "played with him three or four times" since they had been together. How exactly Little came to the attention of the immigration authorities is unclear, but his deportation was delayed so that he could provide evidence in sodomy cases against Ryan and Murray. Little was finally deported in 1915 on the grounds that he had entered as a minor unaccompanied by his parents and was likely to become a public charge.[91]

Usually, immigration officials used the public charge clause against aliens suspected of sodomy without much investigation into their actual economic circumstances. The assumption of these officials was that men who were not self-governing in their sexual practices could not be self-governing in their labor. Sexual perversion, linked in this way to crime and vagrancy, would one way or another lead its practitioners to public charge status. In a reversal of this logic, vagrancy charges against a pair of Latin American aliens stood in for actual evidence that sodomy had been committed. "While there is no direct proof . . . that these aliens and their associates have been practicing sodomy or other unnatural crimes in . . . the Mint Hotel," Assistant Commissioner-General Hampton wrote in the 1916 case of Guillermo Castillo and Marcos Cervellos, "the indications are that the aliens are a worthless lot of vagabonds." Castillo, an immigrant to San Francisco from Mexico, met Cervellos in a theater on Market Street soon after his arrival. Savvy about the class dynamics at play, Castillo told immigration examiners that he did not "like Cervellos's looks" or his class of friends. "They had a slangy way and were not educated," Castillo said, and "I was afraid of getting into trouble [by associating] with people lower than me." Still, Castillo visited Cervellos's room three times: "because I am a piano player, I used to like to sit in his hotel and play the piano. That is the only diversion I had." In a remark that revealed how cognizant aliens were of the Bureau of Immigration's fusion of ideas about sexual morality and gainful employment, Castillo then insisted, "I do not like to get into any scandalous trouble. I like to work."[92]

Castillo came to the attention of immigration authorities when William Brosnon, an associate of Cervellos, stole the latter's overcoat while the two immigrants were at a dance at the Mint Hotel. Cervellos persuaded Castillo to go with him to see Brosnon in order to retrieve the coat. Unfortunately, Brosnon's brother George was a police officer, and when trouble started George Brosnon sent for several other officers.

[91] File no. 53839/081, box 712, Records of the INS, RG 85.
[92] File no. 54148/36, box 887, Records of the INS, RG 85.

William Brosnon told his brother George that Cervellos and Castillo solicited on the streets, and that "the younger one was a woman in male attire." Officer Brosnon told his colleagues that he wanted to prove that Cervellos and Castillo were sodomites, and the officers went to find the two men the following day. "[I] had [Cervellos] disrobe to prove his sex, and found that he was a male person," Bronson reported, but that "he was powdered and perfumed the way a woman would do." Both men were then arrested on vagrancy charges.[93]

Immigration officials noted that Cervellos did indeed have cold cream and face powder in his room, and that William Brosnon had been hospitalized for a disease of the rectum. But in the absence of stronger proof that the aliens had committed sodomy, Cervellos's lack of steady work became key evidence for immigration officials. "He admits he has done nothing since his entry," immigration officials wrote of Cervellos. "How much money does it cost you to live in a month?" the immigration inspector grilled Cervellos. "Have you bought any clothes since you came here? How long have you had that suit you are wearing? Did you go to shows, to theaters? How often?" the interrogation continued. Immigration officials also noted that Castillo had only worked "about two weeks since the first of the year and has earned only $20." Predictably, Cervellos was deported on the grounds that he was likely to become a public charge at the time of his entry. The record is silent on the final disposition of Castillo's case. Yet given that he had little in the way of financial assets, it seems unlikely that Castillo's attempt to position himself as a better class of alien who liked to work ultimately prevented his deportation as a public charge.[94] Employed against Cervellos and Castillo, the public charge clause not only reflected the way that immigration officials connected vagrancy to perversion, it provided those officials with a tool to harass and eventually deport two men against whom they had no serious evidence.

Less commonly, immigration officials plied the public charge provision against middle-class aliens, further suggesting how limited the state's antihomosexual arsenal was during these years. Drapery salesman George McBurney and real estate agent Samuel James South shared a night in the Walker House in Toronto prior to their entry to the United States. After entering the country, the two men continued an intimate relationship. This was revealed to immigration authorities when McBurney's landlady provided them with several of the alien's letters that she had found—a move that hints at the state's reliance on accomplices in its regulation of sexuality.[95]

[93] Ibid.
[94] Ibid.
[95] File no. 54134/212, box 871, Records of the INS, RG 85; file no. 54153/140, box 891,

The letters that the landlady turned over were "written in an endearing and effeminate manner," Assistant Commissioner-General Hampton wrote in 1916, "and indicate that both men have been addicted to indecent, unnatural, and immoral practices." Because McBurney denied participating in any sexual activity, his letters to South became a central focus of the subsequent interrogation. "Didn't you write [South] several letters in a very effeminate style?" the immigrant inspector in charge of the case asked McBurney, who acknowledged that he had done so. "Did you and he ever display any signs of affection in an effeminate manner?" the inspector continued. "Well perhaps both of us did give way and say how glad we were to be with one another," McBurney acknowledged. "That explains the statement in your letter," the inspector queried, reading aloud, "'I was lost because [of] . . . the awful long time that stands between us before I can have my dear lover in my arms again'?" "Yes, sir," McBurney conceded.[96]

For his part, South did not deny the sexual encounter, but instead blamed extenuating circumstances. "This young man admits that he is addicted to the use of alcohol, sometimes becomes intoxicated, and that while in an intoxicated condition he committed an unnatural immoral act," Hampton wrote in a memo. An attorney hired by South wrote that his client was "more sinned against than sinning," and that McBurney's letters were "sent without [South's] solicitation or encouragement." In his testimony, South portrayed the tone of the letters as a departure from the otherwise brotherly relationship between the two men. "Has he ever called you his sweetheart?" the inspector asked South. "Just in his letters," South replied. "Did he ever call you his lover?" the inspector queried. "He never did it personally," South responded. But physical evidence of another kind trumped South's attempts to deny or minimize the love affair. The inspector asked South if Mr. McBurney had sent him a ring. South admitted that McBurney had. The inspector then asked how the ring was engraved. "Love finds its way," South admitted. When asked if there was anything else inscribed on the ring, South responded, "From George to Jim."[97]

The two aliens were thus caught in a relationship that had both a physical and an emotional dynamic. "Everything connected with the record tends to indicate that these aliens belong to that class [for] which the English language does not supply a polite term," Assistant

Records of the INS, RG 85. Ngai refers to this as "calling Immigration" (*Impossible Subjects*, 79).

[96] File no. 54134/212, box 871, Records of the INS, RG 85; File no. 54153/140, box 891, Records of the INS, RG 85.

[97] File no. 54153/140, box 891, Records of the INS, RG 85.

Commissioner-General Hampton remarked about the South/McBurney case. But despite the existence of the letters and the ring, Hampton acknowledged that because McBurney did not admit to the sodomy charge and had not been convicted, he could not be deported under the moral turpitude provision. Yet the official wrote, "The evidence would . . . seem to indicate that he is not very well balanced mentally and is also addicted to the use of alcohol." These factors led the bureau to deport him as likely to become a public charge. The bureau also prepared to deport South on the same grounds. South was interrogated as to the "class" of his associates, his financial standing, and asked if "the letters . . . ever caused you any trouble in a business way here in Detroit . . . if you have ever lost a position through them." Perhaps seeing the writing on the wall, the alien left the country voluntarily before the final disposition of his case.[98]

The case of the two Canadian lovers makes clear that the public charge clause was sometimes an effective way to deport aliens when no other charge was available, and also how pliable the charge was—it was used to deport Canadian salesmen as well as Latin American vagrants. In addition to seeing in this evidence how potent the public charge clause could be, its usage in cases like that of South and McBurney might alternately suggest the way that the state's legal apparatus lagged behind as federal officials began to understand perversion in new ways. Perversion was, indeed, not only a kind of degeneracy, it was not limited to the poor, and there were limits as to how far the clause could be stretched. All of this would become much more apparent in cases involving wealthy aliens, where the law's weaving of deviance and dependence into a tight net seemed to loosen and even unravel into a useless mess of thread.

The Limitations of the Law

The numerous cases already explored illuminate how state authorities relied on the public charge provision to deport aliens who either committed perverse acts or had bodies that were considered perverse. The clause was used against these aliens because it was generally effective, and that efficacy was derived, in large measure, from the belief that sexual deviance and economic dependence were intertwined. Extremes of wealth, however, consistently threatened to sever that connection. Giuseppe Delfini, for example, diagnosed with hypospadias, a congen-

[98] Ibid.; file no. 54134/212, box 871, Records of the INS, RG 85.

ital fissure on the surface of the penis, was to be excluded as likely to become a public charge. But then a Tennessee congressman contacted immigration officials and explained that Delfini had wealthy relatives in Memphis, and that one who was worth "more than half a million" would post bond for the alien. Delfini was admitted.[99] Family connections also helped to secure the admission of Anatario Seara, who suffered from "absence of scrotum and testicles," designated both as "arrested sexual development" and "marked feminism." Seara came from a wealthy Brazilian family, and was worth an estimated thirty thousand dollars. Remarkably, the board initially ruled that Seara's condition made him likely to become a public charge, "notwithstanding the fact that he is liberally supplied with funds at this time." The following day, the Brazilian vice consul intervened on Seara's behalf. "I suppose we must admit [him]," Commissioner Williams conceded.[100]

More complex was the case of the Russian alien Andrei de Gurrowski, a longtime resident in the United States who had developed some determined enemies. Apparently, Gurrowski had done some nursing for an elderly patient, who had become attached to the alien. "He seems to have a good deal of influence over her," one immigration official observed, and obtained "some of this widow's money." The elderly woman's heirs worried for their estate and hired a lawyer to get Gurrowski deported. As the alien was returning to the country after a short vacation abroad in the fall of 1911, the lawyer informed the Bureau of Immigration that the alien had been arrested in Geneva for immoral conduct with a man in a urinal just a few weeks before.[101] "I believe him to be a degenerate," the lawyer said in closing his letter to immigration officials. When the alien disembarked at Ellis Island, he was questioned by a Board of Special Inquiry about the arrest in Geneva as well as accusations that Gurrowski had engaged in "degenerate practices" with an insane male patient under his care.[102]

Gurrowski was not just a nurse. He claimed to be a count, and an article in a New York newspaper expressed surprise at the detainment of the "handsome Russian with an aristocratic bearing." The article noted that Gurrowski owned a seven-hundred-acre tobacco plantation in Virginia, and that "the man has been lavish in his hospitality at his coun-

[99] File no. 53625/031, box 566, Records of the INS, RG 85.

[100] File no. 53084/352, box 287, Records of the INS, RG 85. A related case is file no. 52388/6, box 512, Records of the INS, RG 85.

[101] Gurrowski's return from vacation constituted a reentry under immigration law and subjected him to deportation procedures, even though he had long resided in the United States.

[102] File no. 53370/430, box 1409, Records of the INS, RG 85.

try home, having given several costly entertainments there at which champagne flowed like water." In response to press reports, Secretary of the Department of Labor Charles Nagel urged immigration officials to act quickly to determine if the alien had acquired "a right to be in this country." A subsequent hearing determined that in addition to the Geneva arrest, Gurrowski had shown obscene postcards and made suggestive remarks to deckhands aboard the ship on which Gurrowski had recently been a passenger. Despite the fact that further investigation turned up another arrest for "shocking moral conduct . . . with a young man" in Paris, the board finally decided to admit the alien because of his long residence in the United States and because he was "the owner of considerable land in the State of Virginia." The board concluded with a fascinating admission of the state's responsibility for not only policing but perhaps even making perverts: to "deport him to the country from whence he comes," the board wrote, "would be to force him upon a government which had no part in shaping his career." A few days later, Commissioner-General Keefe sent Gurrowski's complete file to the chief of the Division of Naturalization. "While the Board has regarded the evidence as insufficient to warrant exclusion," Keefe advised, "you will find therein facts which may be worthy of grave consideration if and when the alien attempts to complete his naturalization."[103] Immigration officials could not prevent the alien from residing in the country, in other words, but they might be able to prevent him from becoming a citizen.

The case no doubt would have ended there, but the lawyer for the widow's heirs would not give up. He continued to investigate the alien and presented his findings in a lengthy memo to Secretary of Labor Nagel. Because the public charge clause was the department's only hope for deporting Gurrowski, the investigation was as focused on exposing the alien as a class fraud as it was on recounting the Russian's sexual misdeeds. The memo reported the testimony of an acquaintance of the alien who "at first thought he was a gentleman and afterwards came to the conclusion that he was anything but a gentleman and was a worthless sort of person; that he claimed to be of noble family but that she was sure from his actions that he was a vulgar and uneducated person." He was, moreover, "not a professional trained nurse," nor was he a count. "At sometime during his career he has acquired a smattering of both French and German," but his letters in German "were hopelessly illiterate, and were indicative that he had acquired his knowledge of that language in the lowest surroundings." A doctor who had worked

[103] Ibid.

with the alien further reported that "Gurrowski's handwriting in French, German, and Russian was very illiterate," and that the alien "seemed unwilling to make written reports." Most damaging, the lawyer claimed to have evidence that while Gurrowski had indeed purchased between five and six hundred acres of land in Virginia, "the consideration for this purchase was furnished by another person, for whom Gurrowski is a constructive trustee, or to whom . . . he may have given a deed of the property." In sum, the memo concluded that Gurrowski was not a long-time resident with considerable property interests in the United States, but rather a "bird of passage and an adventurer."[104]

Up until that point, the Bureau of Immigration had treated the lawyer investigating Gurrowski as an irritant to be "disposed" of as quickly as possible. But the lawyer's final report clearly changed some minds at the top of the bureaucracy. Attached to this memo was a request that the Bureau of Immigration have the State Department cable the Swiss government for criminal records pertaining to Gurrowski. Secretary Nagel's assistant contacted the lawyer immediately to inform him that the records had been requested. Nagel then issued a memo stating that the bureau had made a mistake in the case, and in fact, the alien's misconduct "was in no sense the result of our own institutions." That determination was based not only on the fact that Gurrowski had spent some unspecified amount of time in Europe during his twenty-seven-year residence in that United States, but as well by the fact that the Virginia plantation apparently belonged to someone else. Gurrowski was then ordered deported on the grounds that he had committed moral turpitude prior to his entry and was likely to become a public charge.[105]

It is striking that the disposition of the fake Russian count's case rested as much on his finances and aristocratic bearing as on his alleged sexual misconduct. Because the state apparatus to vet degenerate immigrants depended on the public charge clause, the count's misdeeds were somewhat irrelevant until his fraudulent wealth and lineage were exposed. Once the fake count rejoined the ranks of immigrants of ordinary means, the machinery to remove him from the country could be set into action. Gurrowski's fate illustrates how for wealthy aliens as well as poor ones, for depraved aristocrats as well as feminized wretches, the public charge clause was all the state had. And despite Marcus Braun's warning several years prior, the Immigration Law of 1917 added little to the state's arsenal for policing homosexuality, as one final case reveals.

[104] Ibid.
[105] Ibid.

A Perverse Priest

It began in February of 1916, when Secretary of Labor William Wilson issued a warrant for the arrest of Reverend Parthenios Colonis, a Greek immigrant and the priest of the Greek Orthodox Church in Wheeling, West Virginia. Colonis was arrested on the ground that he had been a person likely to become a public charge at the time of his entry to the United States in 1904. Sexual scandal had plagued Colonis in each of his pastoral assignments in the United States and was finally threatening to tear the Greek community in Wheeling apart. Colonis had been an outstanding priest—this no one denied. "It is admitted, without question," the immigration official in charge of the case wrote, "that the Priest has been very active in building the church in Wheeling." Colonis's attorneys claimed that his wonderful work on behalf of the church, "having done more than any other minister in Wheeling," entitled him "to a peculiar consideration not usually accorded aliens."[106]

Colonis's trouble began in Wheeling as a result of his relationship with two young men who lived in his rooming house. Colonis frequently invited the young men to his room, where he had allegedly made improper advances. George Lucas testified that he had been able to resist the reverend. "When I saw he was that kind of a man," he said, "I did not associate with him anymore." But then the reverend "got friendly" with Lucas's cousin, Cristos Sotiropulos, who told Lucas that the reverend had given him a dollar to play with his penis. Colonis later returned to Sotiropulos's room, ostensibly to talk about the church. Then, Sotiropulos told investigators, the reverend had opened the young Greek's pants and began "monkeying" with him. The reverend stripped to his underwear and climbed on to the young man's lap, and "start[ed] to jump up and down," telling Sotiropulos to "bugger him." When Sotiropulos replied that he did that "to girls," the reverend allegedly asked, "How about me?" Sotiropulos told his cousin what had transpired with the reverend, but Lucas did not believe him. So Sotiropulos arranged for Lucas to hide in a cupboard in his room, "where he could see everything." Lucas testified that he then "saw them feeling one another and acting that way."[107]

When rumors about the reverend's behavior began to circulate around town, the Greek community split over the reverend's innocence or guilt. The reverend's enemies in town contacted immigration officials, who commenced an investigation. After conducting extensive in-

[106] File no. 54134/62A, box 869, Records of the INS, RG 85.
[107] Ibid.

terviews into the allegations in Wheeling, the Bureau of Immigration declared that it seemed likely that Colonis was a "moral pervert," and ordered that investigations be done in the other communities where the reverend had worked. An investigation into the Milwaukee parish yielded a letter in which a community member had urged an investigation to "see what is concealed under the vestments," as a well as a letter that Colonis had purportedly written to a boy in Greece. The substance of the letter, Commissioner-General Anthony Caminetti wrote, "strongly indicates that the Priest had, prior to entry, sustained immoral relations with the [boy]."[108]

After the scandal broke in Milwaukee, Colonis had moved to Haverhill, Massachusetts. An investigation in that community revealed that the reverend had only been in town for a few weeks before trouble arose. The reverend had been spending time in the poolroom in Haverhill. One afternoon when the proprietor was absent, he began to fondle a young man he had met there. "Later the Priest invited [this man] to his room [and] attempted to induce the witness to have unnatural relations," according to the bureau's report. The youth became angry and threatened the reverend with a knife. The bureau also questioned another young man from Haverhill who accepted the reverend's invitation to come to his house for a cognac. When the reverend tried to kiss his guest, the man punched him and ran out of the house. Following these advances, these two young men assembled a gang to beat up the reverend. Colonis sought help from a respected community member, who helped the reverend flee Haverhill. When asked by immigration officials if Colonis was guilty, this man replied that the reverend "practically admitted it . . . and said 'what shall I do now?'" The Bureau of Immigration also turned up rumors of a sexual assault by the reverend against a steward on board the vessel that brought him to the United States.[109]

But Colonis was not without extraordinary resources to fight the charges—and unlike the Russian count's, his were authentic. A West Virginia congressman corresponded with the bureau about the investigation; the reverend was alleged to have friends in the Holy Synod in Athens who destroyed damaging documents; and Colonis hired a lawyer, who filed a writ to stay the deportation charges.[110]

Whether or not Colonis had actually made the alleged sexual advances—or was, as he claimed, the victim of an elaborate blackmail scheme—is less interesting than the discussion that ensued among

[108] Ibid.
[109] Ibid.
[110] Ibid.

government officials about how to handle the case. After its extensive investigation, the Bureau of Immigration recommended that Colonis be deported. Because Colonis was a moral pervert, the bureau opined, and hence likely to run into trouble with the authorities, "it logically follows that he was a person likely to become a public charge at the time of his last entry into the United States." But the attempt to deport Colonis *as a public charge* seemed somewhat illogical, and Assistant Secretary of Labor Louis Post asked the solicitor's office for an opinion on the case.[111] His query is evidence that the bureau was indeed venturing into new regulatory territory, confronted with a different kind of evidence than that presented by effeminate laborers or degenerate vagabonds. "Assuming, for the purpose of this memorandum only," the solicitor wrote, summarizing the central issue, "that the alien is a moral pervert, does that fact bring the alien within the exclusion provisions of the Immigration Act [of 1917]?"[112]

The answer was not as simple as the Bureau of Immigration had hoped. "Moral perverts are not specifically excluded by any of the provisions of that act," the solicitor's memo asserted. "It is impossible to avoid the presumption that the real ground for desiring to deport this alien is that the immigration authorities consider him an undesirable acquisition to this country, whose class, unfortunately, is not excluded by the immigration laws." Yet, the memo continued, there *was* the public charge clause. "But this alien has no physical disabilities, holds a remunerative position, and . . . 'has plenty of money and is backed by influential friends.'" Given this, was there support for the Bureau of

---

[111] The Bureau of Immigration became part of the Department of Labor in 1913.

[112] File no. 54134/62A, box 869, Records of the INS, RG 85. The solicitor's query may have referred to the 1917 law's inclusion of a new provision barring constitutional psychopathic inferiors from entry. Because the related psychopathic personality provision of the McCarran-Walter Act of 1952 was clearly used against homosexual aliens, historians and legal scholars have sometimes assumed that the constitutional psychopathic inferior provision was similarly used in the early twentieth century. My own review of immigration records suggests that this is an erroneous assumption. (Indeed, the charge was not used against Reverend Colonis.) The usage of the psychopathic inferiority provision might have changed somewhat in the 1930s, when the PHS mentioned "sexual perverts" in its discussion of constitutional psychopathic inferiority, but evidence of the provision's actual usage is sparse. *Regulations Governing the Medical Examination of Aliens* (Washington, DC: U.S. Government Printing Office, 1930), 13. Revealingly, a debate continued into the 1940s and 1950s as to whether Congress had intended psychopathic inferiority to include perversion, and was one of the reasons that Congress changed the law (from psychopathic inferiority to psychopathic personality) in the 1950s. Moreover, in the 1940s and early 1950s, aliens suspected of homosexuality were deported under moral turpitude provisions of the law, as reflected in published opinions of the Board of Immigration Appeals (BIA). See chapter 6.

Immigration's position that "the alien is likely to be arrested and imprisoned on account of his immoral habits," and was therefore likely to become a public charge at the time of his entry? The memo noted that the Bureau of Immigration was in the practice of deporting persons with "habitual criminal propensities" on this very theory. But the solicitor found this practice problematic because the phrase "habitual criminal propensities" had no fixed meaning. To be a criminal was to be someone convicted of a crime. The Greek reverend had never been convicted of anything; he had, in fact, been acquitted of criminal charges in Wheeling. It was "far-fetched," the memo concluded, to think that the reverend's habits, however distasteful, would render him a public charge.[113]

Colonis's lawyers had already threatened to file a writ of habeas corpus if a warrant of deportation was issued, and the Bureau of Immigration canceled its warrant against the reverend. Assistant Commissioner-General Alfred Hampton warned that the reverend's time would come—he only had to be convicted of a crime of moral turpitude within five years of his last entry or be convicted twice at any time after admission, and his deportation could be achieved. "There is considerable likelihood that a man of Colonis's apparent moral makeup will eventually fall under one of . . . these provisions," he wrote. Nevertheless, the bureau was troubled by the broader implications of the solicitor's memo. "There can scarcely be any doubt," Hampton concluded, "that a moral pervert is a person likely to become a public charge within the meaning of the statute."[114]

Hampton could make such an assertion because in numerous cases the Bureau of Immigration did indeed successfully wield the public charge clause against aliens considered to be perverse. But as the Office of the Secretary of Labor made clear in the exceptional case of the Greek reverend, there was no law preventing the immigration of sexual perverts, and moreover, no legal connection between sexual perversion and the provision barring aliens who were likely to become public charges. It was not the law that gave the clause its power in these cases but rather an ideological framework that treated perversion as a class attribute. Yet the saga of Colonis was probably not unique in suggesting to officials the inadequacy of using an antipoverty provision to police perversion. The public charge clause was simply not targeted enough to cover all the undesirable types who were beginning to cause the Bureau of Immigration discomfort.

[113] File no. 54134/62A, box 869, Records of the INS, RG 85.
[114] Ibid.

From Degeneracy toward Homosexuality

The reverend's advantage of course was not just ideological—*that he made no sense as a public charge*—but also quite literally material. Like other aliens with ample financial resources and powerful friends, Colonis avoided deportation because he could hire a lawyer, call in favors with a congressman, and otherwise return some of the heat that immigration officials were directing at him. This too is an important part of the story—by the 1950s, material resources would offer far less protection to immigrants suspected of homosexuality who sought to enter or remain in the country. Which is not to deny that there were "genetic traces" of this older framework in place; immigration lawyers defending aliens facing deportation for homosexuality during the 1950s and 1960s, for example, frequently cited the positive work histories and/or economic resources of their clients in arguing against deportation.[115] But such strategies rarely worked.[116] They failed because immigration law had been revised in the early 1950s to reflect the idea that homosexuality was a discrete identity—one that was distinct from class and race, and posed a unique threat to the state.

Certainly, though, the reverend's case was a harbinger of the 1950s. After all, the state was far from indifferent to Colonis: it recognized him as a moral pervert, and devoted considerable resources (separate investigations in three different communities) trying to deport him. Yet while immigration officials were beginning to identify certain aliens as moral perverts separate from their class position, the legal apparatus to remove such aliens from the country lagged behind this process of identification. Marcus Braun's report on homosexuality was written in 1909, for example, but his warning about the "new species" of undesirable immigrant seemed to have little impact on the provisions of the Immigration Act of 1917. Even after the 1919 case of the Greek reverend—involving considerable bureau personnel, taking up the better part of three years, and probably quite an event in what was still a small federal agency—state authorities waited more than thirty years to enact an explicit antihomosexual provision in immigration law.

Bureaucracy is not known for the speed of its operations, and yet this delay warrants some further explanation. On the one hand, state authorities did not enact an antihomosexual provision in immigration law until the 1950s simply because they could often get by without one. Be-

[115]On the "genetic traces" of "pre-homosexual discourses" and traditions, see Halperin, "How to Do the History of Male Homosexuality," 90.

[116]For an analysis of immigration cases involving homosexuality decided under the McCarran-Walter Act of 1952, see chapter 6.

cause most immigrants were poor, it was usually easy to invoke the public charge clause to exclude or deport those who were suspect. Moreover, by the 1920s, immigration restriction had vastly reduced the number of aliens coming into the country, taking pressure off of exclusion and deportation procedures in general.[117]

But there is another, perhaps more important reason as to why the state's apparatus for vetting homosexual aliens was so measly until the 1950s. Before the state could equip itself with a provision barring homosexual aliens, the *homosexual* had to appear to immigration officials. Some officials were vaguely aware of the medical literature on homosexuality (Braun, for example), but the homosexual type was far from hegemonic.[118] Instead, frail and underdeveloped creatures, hermaphrodite phenomenals, vagrant sodomites, and pederast priests were points on their map of perversion. If these figures seem to have some vague resonance with homosexuality, that is only because, as David Halperin has recently argued, homosexuality signifies the "effect of [a] cumulative process of historical overlay and accretion," in which a variety of "pre-homosexual discourses" are projected onto an unstable figure.[119] The hazy outlines of that figure were only beginning to emerge in the eyes of Progressive-era immigration officials, only beginning to overturn an older notion that tethered perversion to racial and economic typologies as a marker of the degenerate.

Homosexuality, moreover, did not simply become visible to immigration authorities. Federal regulation instead involved a complex dialectic of discovery and creation, such that there was at first neither chicken nor egg. (As in: What came first? Homosexuality, or its regulation?) State-building itself was instrumental in helping to produce the category that an expanding state would then see as its function to police. Such dynamics were at work as officials constructed an apparatus to screen incoming aliens, and then began to flag sex and gender deviance among them; similarly, as the bureau hired a small staff of investigators who could go into the field to follow up on neighbors' calls, police reports, or other rumors that circulated about immoral conduct by alien vaga-

[117]Immigration restriction also undermined the immigrant bachelor subculture that provided a foundation for a vibrant working-class gay world in early twentieth-century New York. The bachelor subculture "began to disappear in the 1920s," Chauncey writes, "when the sex ratios of immigrant communities started to stabilize after the strict new immigration laws passed in that decade made it difficult for immigrant workers to enter the United States for brief periods of work" (*Gay New York*, 78).

[118]So, for instance, an incredibly detailed list from the 1909 *Annual Report on the Medical Examination of Aliens* (which included mental and physical conditions such as hypospadias, frostbite, and tumor of the eyeball, among many others) had no listing under homosexuality. File no. 52572/8, box 689, Records of the INS, RG 85.

[119]Halperin, "How to Do the History of Male Homosexuality," 90–91.

bonds and other ne'er-do-wells. But if attention to the nation's border spurred an impulse to scrutinize the population more broadly—if it began to affect the way that other federal actors saw their own clientele—this was still a slow process of bureaucratic learning, and one that was delayed by the gradual rise of the bureaucracy itself.[120]

Inchoate things can still be studied, however. Indeed, just as political theorist Wendy Brown has observed that an investigation of the masculinism of the state does not require the existence of a coherent female subject, so too this investigation of the growth of a straight state need not await the arrival of a coherent homosexual identity.[121] The next chapter proceeds without one, turning to the World War I–era military.

[120] Lacy and Furner, *The State and Social Investigation*.

[121] Wendy Brown, "Finding the Man in the State," in *States of Injury: Power and Freedom in Late Modernity* (Princeton, NJ: Princeton University Press, 1995), 166–96.

CHAPTER 2

MILITARY

"We Are Merely Concerned with the Fact of Sodomy"

Managing Sexual Stigma in the World War I–Era Military, 1917–1933

———◦———

Berlin was "known by connoisseurs as one of the most immoral cities in the world," reported an American military intelligence officer in Germany in the early 1920s. It had, the officer continued, "regular centers for perverse practices."[1] His impression of the German capital mirrors that of the immigrant inspector Marcus Braun (described in chapter 1), who had sent a similar dispatch to his superiors in the Bureau of Immigration after coming across the same scene more than a decade earlier. It is not a coincidence that the earliest sites of federal interest in sex perversion (the Bureau of Immigration and the World War I–era military) were also sites that connected the American state to Europe. Just as immigration officials worried about the entry of perverse aliens into the country, so too were military officials concerned that U.S. soldiers serving in Europe would be contaminated by continental depravity.[2] Indeed, European degeneracy was a common and long-lasting trope among American officials. More than twenty years after the intelligence officer's Berlin memorandum—in the midst of the Second World War—another generation of officials worried that soldiers abroad, "exposed to standards of morality at variance with our own," were succumbing to "unnatural relations."[3]

[1] "Subject: Germany—Sexual Perversion," January 24, 1921, file no. 2656-B-32, box 1610, Military Intelligence Division, 1917–1941, Records of the War Department General Staff (Army), RG 165, National Archives, College Park, MD.

[2] This was a contamination that sometimes superseded the merely sexual. For example, during World War I, a soldier named Harry Gerber discovered German movements for homosexual emancipation and came home to found the first such organization in the United States (the Society for Human Rights, chartered in 1924). Jonathan Katz, *Gay/Lesbian Almanac: A New Documentary* (New York: HarperCollins, 1983), 418–21, 553–66.

[3] Memorandum W615-4-43, "Sodomists," January 10, 1943, file no. 250.1, box 379,

Europe was not the only thread connecting early twentieth-century immigration officials to their military counterparts, however, and neither group had to cross an ocean to learn of immorality. Immigration and military vice investigators alike encountered more "homegrown" varieties of perversion in the saloons, dance halls, and brothels that the foreign born shared with soldiers and sailors on leave. Moreover, as certain key officials left the immigration service to join in the military's effort, these two bureaucracies passed information back and forth.[4] The army adapted Bureau of Immigration methods of mass examination to identify undesirable recruits. "As the patient approaches the examiner, his gait is noted," one army captain wrote, describing a technique that paralleled that used by immigrant inspectors. "A rapid glance is made for stigmata."[5] The Bureau of Immigration also turned over its facilities for mental examination to the army and navy during the war. When the conflict was over, the military in turn suggested ways that it could assist immigration officials with the psychological examination of aliens.[6] One military doctor, for example, noted how military statistics broken down by ethnicity provided an instrument with which to forecast the incidence of psychiatric disorder among immigrant populations more broadly.[7]

With their personnel, methods, and missions so intertwined during the war years (aliens also earned their citizenship by serving in the armed forces), it is perhaps not surprising to find in the military's re-

decimal file 1918–1942, Records of the Judge Advocate General (Army), RG 153, National Archives, College Park, MD.

[4] The most notable case was that of Thomas Salmon, who left his work with the Bureau of Immigration to become the head of psychiatry for the American Expeditionary Forces during the First World War. Earl Bond, *Thomas W. Salmon: Psychiatrist* (New York: W. W. Norton, 1950).

[5] File no. 51490/19, Records of the Immigration and Naturalization Service (INS), RG 85, National Archives, Washington, DC; K. M. Bowman, "Report of the Examination of the ——— Regiment, U.S. Army, for Nervous and Mental Diseases," *American Journal of Insanity* (April 1918): 555–56.

[6] This did not occur without causing some offense, however. "As is often the case . . . with the most tender of well meant suggestions," the surgeon general wrote to the commissioner-general of immigration in response to a letter from the army offering its services, "the authors apparently are not well informed as to the present agencies provided by the Government for securing the objects in which they are interested. The officers of the Public Health Service, for many years, have been greatly interested in the mental examination of arriving aliens and, especially at Ellis Island, they have carried out research work as well as the routine performance of their duties." Surgeon General Rupert Blue to Anthony Caminetti, Commissioner-General of Immigration, October 9, 1918, file no. 53139-13A, box 1147, Records of the INS, RG 85.

[7] Pearce Bailey, "A Contribution to the Mental Pathology of Races in the United States," *Mental Hygiene* 6 (1922): 370; Captain Walter S. Hunter to the Surgeon General of the Army, "Psychological Examination of Immigrants," September 17, 1918, file no. 53139-13A, box 1147, Records of the INS, RG 85.

sponse to perversion the same administrative lag that characterized the reaction of the Bureau of Immigration in the years before immigration restriction.[8] In the army and navy—as among immigration officials— the awareness of perversity was far ahead of a reliable apparatus to handle the condition among soldiers and sailors. Indeed, even more than is evident from the extant records of the Bureau of Immigration, army and navy records during and after the First World War prodigiously reveal a military establishment that was becoming well-versed in the problem of perversion. This is important because historians have usually treated World War II as *the* war when the military "uncovered" sexual perversion as a large-scale problem for the institution.[9] But World War II is, in fact, only the war in which military officials developed and implemented a policy solution to deal with what they learned about perversion during World War I: that "the presence of sexual perverts among the commissioned and enlisted personnel [was] common," as one report from 1919 concluded.[10] This was official knowledge that continued to expand in the interwar period. Until World War II, though, when it came to homosexuality, the military "puzzle[ed]" rather than "power[ed]," hesitating for many years to explicitly bar the perverted soldier from service.[11]

As the military puzzled, it came to see perversion less as a marker of degeneracy (as immigration officials had) and more as behavior associated with a psychopathic type. In recognizing the pervert as a distinct type, the military was falling into step with European sexology, and the way that it was beginning to impact medical and scientific opinion more generally in the United States. But the new "type" also exposed

[8] On the naturalization of alien soldiers during this period, see Lucy E. Salyer, "Baptism by Fire: Military Service and U.S. Citizenship Policy, 1918–1935," *Journal of American History* 91 (December 2004): 847–76. Immigrants made up 18 percent of the military during the war. Gary Gerstle, *American Crucible: Race and Nation in the Twentieth Century* (Princeton, NJ: Princeton University Press, 2001), 18.

[9] See especially Allan Bérubé, *Coming Out Under Fire: The History of Gay Men and Women in World War II* (New York: Plume, 1990).

[10] "Report of Sexual Perverts among Commissioned and Enlisted Personnel at Camp Jackson," April 9, 1919, decimal 250.1, box 528, decimal file 1917–1925, Records of the Adjutant General's Office, RG 407, National Archives, College Park, MD.

[11] This is political scientist Hugh Heclo's formulation of state social investigation. See Hugh Heclo, *Modern Social Politics in Britain and Sweden: From Relief to Income Maintenance* (New Haven, CT: Yale University Press, 1974), 305. On state "social investigation," see also Michael J. Lacey and Mary O. Furner, "Social Investigation, Social Knowledge, and the State: An Introduction," in *The State and Social Investigation in Britain and the United States*, ed. Michael J. Lacey and Mary O. Furner (Cambridge: Cambridge University Press, 1993), 3–62. They use the term social investigation to denote "an ongoing process of public inquiry into social conditions, especially problematic ones, with the intention of bringing knowledge to bear on the decisions and functions of governance" (11–12).

the military to increasing disgrace, as illustrated by several naval scandals that became public during the early 1920s. Those scandals not only reflected but further broadened official knowledge about perversion. They also made salient that, in contrast to the Bureau of Immigration, the military represented an institution (even an actual physical space) that could itself be tainted by the stigma of homosexuality. If the Bureau of Immigration failed to detect perverts, it might look ineffective; when the military failed, it looked queer.

That lesson sunk in over time. Proceeding without a reliable instrument to exclude or remove perverts from the service during these years, military officials focused on managing this stigma in two ways. First, they blamed the immoral scourge on civilians, emphasizing the extent to which perversion was a civilian disease and a civilian incursion—one that was no doubt associated with a (much-resented) wartime takeover of military planning by civilian officials.[12] They also continued to rely on the military's traditional criminal procedure: court-martialing soldiers who engaged in sodomy. An examination of 120 court-martial trials from this period reveals, however, that what the court-martial punished most often was not homosexuality per se, but rather publicity and violence.[13] Indeed, these trials reveal many instances in which soldiers who were assaulted by other men in their companies for being perverts were returned to their units rather than sent home.

In the mid-1920s and again in the early 1930s, the military briefly considered the adoption of a new policy that would shift the emphasis from court-martialing soldiers for sodomy to administratively discharging perverts (policing homosexual status rather than acts alone). In both instances, military officials declined to add the administrative discharge to the state's regular antihomosexual arsenal, and it is easy to see that decision solely in the draconian terms that some military decision-makers used to explain their preference for harsh punishment. Yet more was at play: policing the pervert as an individual as well as sodomy as

[12] Robert D. Cuff, "War Mobilization, Institutional Learning, and State Building in the United States, 1917–1941," in *The State and Social Investigation in Britain and the United States*, ed. Michael J. Lacey and Mary O. Furner (Cambridge: Cambridge University Press, 1993), 388–426.

[13] This represents a small, random sample of the available courts-martial records during this period. I looked at both trials for sodomy and assault to commit sodomy. Before 1920, "assault with attempt to commit any felony" was under Article of War 93, while sodomy was under Article of War 96. In 1920, sodomy was moved to Article of War 93, where it was thought to "more properly belong, with the other felonies." See the memo from the Adjutant General to the Judge Advocate General, September 25, 1931, "Disposition of Sex Perverts," decimal 253, box 1259, central decimal file 1926–1939, Adjutant General's Office, RG 407. I also looked at courts-martial for "lewdness" and "conduct unbecoming an officer and a gentleman."

an act involved not merely a reactive but also a proactive and preemptive kind of policing. It required much more sophisticated screening and surveillance mechanisms, as well as a full complement of psychiatrists and military police to implement and maintain them. The early twentieth-century military was one that still had to deploy its limited resources carefully, and in these years it mostly dealt with perversion by responding to loose proxies (sex in the open or sexual assault) that brought negative attention to the service. As midcentury approached, however, the gap between knowing that perversion existed and deciding that something definitive must be done about it would be closed—aided, of course, by the greater resources that state-building made available for various federal endeavors.

The Emergence of the Sex Pervert as a Type

The growth of the state that occurred during the *First* World War, however, was not insignificant, and expanded wartime functions did have the effect of making federal officials more cognizant of sex and gender nonconformity. While dwarfed by the scale and permanence of state-building produced by the Second World War, mobilization for the Great War nonetheless led to the creation of several new federal agencies, and it finally gave Progressive reformers a stage on which to enact their varied agendas.[14] Progressivism during the war, as during peacetime, had a coercive edge. This was perhaps most evident in the disciplinary aims of the draft, which went beyond simply attaining bodies to fight the war. Mass conscription would, reformers hoped, "aid in disciplining a selfish and inefficient workforce."[15] Draft boards, as the historian

[14] In addition to expanding the army and navy, some of the federal agencies created during World War I include the War Industries Board, the U.S. Railroad Administration, the U.S. Food Administration, the U.S. Fuel Administration, and the Committee on Public Information. See Robert H. Zieger, *America's Great War: World War I and the American Experience* (Lanham, MD: Rowman and Littlefield Publishers, 2000), chapter 3. On World War I and the growth of the federal state, see also Gerstle, *American Crucible*, 91–92.

[15] The draft would also, according to Zieger, "teach unruly immigrants the stern lessons of patriotic Americanism." While immigrants were encouraged to "abandon old world ethnic identities" and help prove General John Joseph Pershing's theory that "America had developed a type of manhood superior" to Europe's, African Americans continued to be seen as especially prone to perversion. The latter were allowed to serve, but given menial work and not allowed in combat positions. The exclusion of black soldiers from combat feminized them, reinforcing the view, as a 1929 study of neuropsychiatry during the war put it, "that the colored show a higher percentage of sexual psychopathy than the whites." Zieger, *America's Great War*, 34, 95–96, 103–6; Pierce Bailey et al., *The Medical Department of the United States Army in the World War: Neuropsychiatry in the United States* (Washington, DC: U.S. Government Printing Office, 1929), 230.

Gerald Shenk has shown, especially targeted unmarried men without gainful employment, as did the federal agencies that partnered with the military to meet the needs of a wartime state.[16] The Department of Justice (DOJ), for example, conducted massive "slacker raids" that subjected to "gender ridicule" those "emasculated" men loitering on city streets whom federal officials suspected were evading the draft.[17]

Quasi-state institutions were also inaugurated to aid in the war effort. As Progressives launched a series of attacks on the urban vice that could pollute soldiers, Secretary of War Newton Baker created the quasi-military Commission on Training Camp Activities (CTCA) in 1917 to spearhead an antiprostitution campaign. The CTCA was charged with carrying out the provisions of the Draft Act that prohibited alcohol and vice in "moral zones" around the military camps. In order to keep these zones "clean," the CTCA sent inspectors into these areas to identify threats to troop morals.[18] Just as immigration officials encountered homosexuality while investigating "white slavery," so too did the effort to keep prostitutes away from U.S. soldiers result in increased awareness of the problem of sex perversion on and around military bases.

In brothels and cabarets, rooming houses, and on street corners across the urban landscape, then, CTCA investigators found that it was not only women and girls who pandered to the sexual needs of sailors

[16] Gerald E. Shenk, *"Work or Fight!" Race, Gender, and the Draft in World War One* (New York: Palgrave Macmillan, 2005), 155–56.

[17] Peter Beattie, "Conflicting Penile Codes: Modern Masculinity and Sodomy in the Brazilian Military, 1860–1916," in *Sex and Sexuality in Latin America*, ed. Donna Guy and Daniel Balderston (New York: New York University Press, 1997), 78. Given the association between vagrancy and perversion discussed above in chapter 1, Zieger's assertion that DOJ agents "publicly humiliated" men whose "appearance and demeanor" indicated "working-class status," raises the possibility that gender traits and sexual behavior may have helped federal agents pick out slackers among the urban crowds (*America's Great War*, 63). On the gendered traits of the "slacker," see also Shenk, *"Work or Fight!"* Michael Willrich's documentation of the use of the Progressive-era term "home slacker" to refer to men who did not support their families—who did not live up to their roles as men, in other words, and who were a drag on the success of marital heterosexuality—further suggests the gender/sexual content of the word "slacker." Michael Willrich, "Home Slackers: Men, the State, and Welfare in Modern America," *Journal of American History* 87 (September 2000): 460–89. Important too is the association of homosexuality with conscientious objectors in the World War II era. See Timothy Stewart-Winter, "Not a Soldier, Not a Slacker: Conscientious Objectors and Male Citizenship in the United States during the Second World War," *Gender and History* 19 (November 2007): 528.

[18] Allan M. Brandt, *No Magic Bullet: A Social History of Venereal Disease in the United States since 1880* (New York: Oxford University Press, 1987), 59, 71–74. See also Nancy K. Bristow, *Making Men Moral: Social Engineering during the Great War* (New York: New York University Press, 1996). Vice investigations aimed at prostitution frequently mentioned sexual perversion. See, for example, Chicago Vice Commission, *The Social Evil in Chicago: A Study of Existing Conditions* (Chicago: Gunthorp-Warren Printing Company, 1911), 295–98.

and soldiers. "From 9th Street at the Post Office Building to Juniper Street, the corners contain from one to five male perverts, or 'fairies,' waiting for the street cars coming with their loads of sailors from the Navy Yard," reported a CTCA investigator in Philadelphia. "These degenerates take the sailors into alleyways . . . also into the lavatories of the cheap saloons, and occasionally into their own rooms."[19] The CTCA also learned about perversion through the cooperation of vice societies, even as the latter remained primarily focused on female prostitution.[20] In New York, for example, the Committee of Fourteen investigated camp conditions and reported to CTCA Secretary Raymond Fosdick a case "in connection with sailors and soldiers," involving "a pervert [who] took two men . . . to his room for immoral purposes."[21] The general secretary of the same society similarly informed a lieutenant from the CTCA that a clerk in a Brooklyn establishment had admitted "a male pervert" into rooms with men in uniform.[22]

Other vice reports warned of female impersonators in the cabaret shows that soldiers attended. Acting on information from vice investigators, military police raided a club on Long Island where "alleged female[s]" performed. "I believe this place should be out of bounds and no soldiers permitted," the investigator opined, "as the entire atmosphere is degrading. . . . To my mind the male performers are actually a far greater menace than the female performers."[23] A report from Providence, Rhode Island—"as wide open a town as there is"—stated that intoxicated soldiers shared the streets and saloons with perverts of both sexes. "Was also told there are a lot of muff-divers (men that practice perversion)," the investigator wrote, "and also women pervertors in Providence."[24] Another report described male and female perverts in Fall River, Massachusetts, noting that "even the charity girls are practicing perversion."[25] While it is

[19] CTCA Report on Philadelphia, sent from Raymond Fosdick to Secretary of the Navy Josephus Daniels, July 10, 1917, reel 1, container 458, navy subject file, Josephus Daniels Papers, Library of Congress, Washington, DC.

[20] On the suppression of gay life in New York by vice societies (such as the Committee of Fourteen and the Society for the Suppression of Vice) during World War I, see George Chauncey, *Gay New York: Gender, Urban Culture, and the Making of the Gay Male World, 1890–1940* (New York: Basic Books, 1994), 141–49.

[21] General Secretary to Raymond Fosdick, December 6, 1917, Brooklyn folder, box 25, Committee of Fourteen Records, New York Public Library, New York.

[22] General Secretary to Lieutenant Timothy Pfeiffer, March 5, 1918, Local Camp Conditions folder, box 25, Committee of Fourteen Records.

[23] "Investigation of Hempstead, Long Island," July 31, 1918, in Hempstead, L.I., folder, box 25, Committee of Fourteen Records.

[24] "Investigation Report," November 16, 1918, in Special New England Towns folder, box 24, Committee of Fourteen Papers.

[25] "Investigation Report," November 21–23, in Special New England Towns folder, box 24, Committee of Fourteen Records. Other than these vice reports, I found no evidence

unclear from these dispatches if these charity girls and women "per-vertors" were women who engaged in homoerotic practices with other women, their mention adds another layer to the depiction of gender chaos in these urban scenes. The use of "muff-diver" to refer to men rather than women suggests that investigators not only viewed such chaos as a threat to soldiers' morality, but were themselves somewhat disoriented by what they saw on their nightly forays.

The reform crusade to keep soldiers morally and physically clean was not the only aspect of the military campaign that brought the issue of sex perversion to the fore, however. Just as the requirement that immigration authorities examine incoming aliens drew the inspector's eye to sexual defect, so too did the need to screen recruits establish another administrative apparatus on the border of national citizenship that led to greater awareness of sex/gender nonconformity. Military screening guidelines from the war years warned that "the degenerate male physique as a whole is often marked by diminished stature and inferior vigor." Examiners were advised to watch for male recruits who "present the general body conformation of the opposite sex, with sloping narrow shoulders, broad hips, excessive pectoral and pubic adipose deposits, with lack of masculine [hair] and muscular markings."[26]

Such instructions were, however, inconsistently administered—"it was not until March 1918" that local draft and medical advisory boards were provided with the revised 1917 instructions barring the "psychopathic character, including the homosexual," from the service. As a result, such boards "continued to forward to Army cantonments men they would have rejected under . . . revised standards."[27] Even after the new standards were distributed, the ratio of examiners to recruits meant screening at local draft boards and army or navy induction stations was cursory at best. So one Ohio recruit was inducted, for ex-

that military officials were concerned with perversion among women during the World War I–era. Susan Zeiger argues in her study of women workers with the American Expeditionary Force, however, that "the popularity of the YWCA's network of woman-only clubs, restrooms, and leave areas for over-seas war workers suggests that many women wished to spend their leisure time with other women. . . . It seems likely that the army and auxiliary agencies' insistence on heterosocial sociability and careful control of women's leisure time reflected in part anxiety over the possibility of lesbian liaisons in the AEF." Susan Zeiger, *In Uncle Sam's Service: Women Workers with the American Expeditionary Force, 1917–1919* (Ithaca, NY: Cornell University Press, 1999), 66.

[26] Special Regulations no. 65, Physical Examination of Recruits, decimal 342.15, box 795, central decimal files 1917–1925, Records of the Adjutant General, RG 407.

[27] Albert G. Love and Charles B. Davenport, *Defects Found in Drafted Men* (Washington, DC: U.S. Government Printing Office, 1920), 63; WWI Physical Standards (SSS Special Monograph, no. 15, vol. I, 1947), in World War II Project Records 95–16, box 15, GLBT Historical Society, San Francisco.

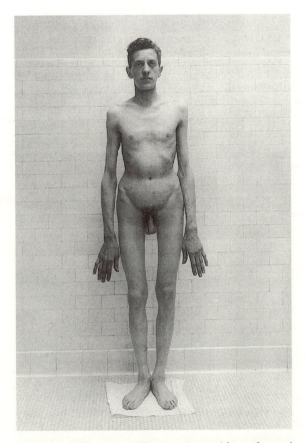

Screening soldiers (as well as immigrants) brought sex/ gender difference to the attention of federal officials. One army major, for example, wrote in 1917 to a medical doctor about certain "abnormalities" and was sent this photo in return. The man in the picture was described as having "feminine pelvis and waistline, feminine distribution of pubic hair, great muscular weakness, no hair on lips or chin." Courtesy of the National Archives.

ample, even though he had no testicles.[28] Another soldier told officials, "that he or she has been repeatedly examined by all kinds of doctors . . . and that he or she is still in doubt as to whether he is male or female." The Texan was inducted anyway. "This individual possesses in his

[28] Case of Harry Bright, July 15, 1918, file: Ohio 42-11, box 237, states file 1917–1919, Records of the Selective Service System, RG 163, National Archives, College Park, MD.

physical makeup one penis, two testicles, and a prostate," a colonel from the medical corps concluded. "This is fairly good evidence that he can be classified under male gender."[29] Yet another inductee with "large well developed breasts . . . feminine pelvis, small male genitalia, testicles size of beans, large hips . . . [and] high pitched voice" was examined twice. The examination board wanted to photograph him. Clearly, his defects were not overlooked, but he was passed anyway.[30] That these inductions appear to be guided by far less stringent standards than those employed by immigration officials in the preceding years undoubtedly had something to do with disparate screening objectives—bringing individuals into the military as opposed to keeping them out of the country. But they also evidence the way that sexual perversion was increasingly seen less in physical morphology and more within the realm of the mind.

This shift was related to the rise of the psychological and psychiatric professions in general, each given something of a boost by the war itself.[31] Indeed, before the United States had even entered the war, a group of psychologists led by Robert Yerkes and Lewis Terman had convened to develop intelligence tests that would be used during the conflict.[32] The primary function of the intelligence test was to sort recruits into job classifications according to ability, but they were also intended to eliminate "defective" or "undesirable" recruits from the service.[33] Mil-

[29] Case of Harvey Devereaux, July 27, 1918, file: Texas 32-21, box 283, states file 1917–1919, Records of the Selective Service System, RG 163.

[30] Case of John Sheridan, November 17, 1917, file: Illinois 16-1, box 117, states file 1917–1919, Records of the Selective Service System, RG 163.

[31] Herman Adler, "The Broader Psychiatry and the War," *Mental Hygiene* 1 (1917): 364–76; Ben Shephard, *A War of Nerves: Soldiers and Psychiatrists in the Twentieth Century* (Cambridge, MA: Harvard University Press, 2001); Robert M. Yerkes, "Psychology in Relation to the War," *Psychological Review* 25 (March 1918): 85–115. For an account that looks at the relationship between psychology and the military in the postwar period, see Ellen Herman, *The Romance of American Psychology: Political Culture in the Age of Experts* (Berkeley: University of California Press, 1995).

[32] Interestingly, Yerkes went on to head the National Research Council's Committee for Research in Problems of Sex, which existed from 1922 until 1947. Terman, Thomas Salmon, Frankwood E. Williams, and William A. White were some of the other military psychiatrists and psychologists who were associated with the work of that committee. The military played an important role in producing the first generation of American sex researchers. See Sophie D. Aberle and George W. Corner, *Twenty-five Years of Sex Research: History of the National Research Council Committee for Research in Problems of Sex, 1922–1947* (Philadelphia: W. B. Saunders Company, 1953).

[33] On the development of intelligence testing in the World War I–era military, see Robert M. Yerkes, ed., *Psychological Examining in the United States Army*, vol. 15, *The Memoirs of the National Academy of Sciences* (Washington, DC: U.S. Government Printing Office, 1921); Franz Samuelson, "Putting Psychology on the Map: Ideology and Intelligence Testing," in *Psychology in Social Context*, ed. Allan R. Buss (New York: Irvington Publishers,

itary psychologists drew some connection between low intelligence and moral defect. The army tested the intelligence of prostitutes, for example.[34] After completing work on the IQ test, moreover, Terman went on to develop a test to measure masculinity and femininity in soldiers imprisoned for sodomy.[35]

Yet the association that psychologists made between immorality and low mentality was only tenuous, a barely surviving corollary of a late nineteenth-century theorem that sexual perversion signaled the declining quality of the population overall.[36] Navy officials soon questioned the premise that the intelligence tests would have any effect in screening out sex perverts "who may have a relatively high intelligence." The navy warned that detecting such types "when on good behavior at the recruiting office" was a "matter of great difficulty."[37] Another navy official dismissed the usefulness of intelligence tests as "a psychopathic individual may be homosexually inclined," and still "score a high percentage in the required psychometric tests."[38]

This suspicion—that a sex pervert might be intelligent—reflected the shift away from degenerationist theories of homosexuality. Although the etiological frameworks continued to be messy and overlapping, by the 1920s military psychiatrists most often understood sexual perversion not as a kind of biological atavism but as one of the most common markers of a psychopathic personality.[39] "Homosexuals," stated a report

1979), 103–68; Stephen Jay Gould, *The Mismeasure of Man* (New York: W. W. Norton, 1981), 146–233; Daniel J. Kevles, "Testing the Army's Intelligence: Psychologists and the Military in World War I," *Journal of American History* 55 (December 1968): 565–81.

[34] On the mental testing of prostitutes, see Brandt, *No Magic Bullet*, 91–92; Major Frank E. Leslie to Division Surgeon, Camp MacArthur, Texas, June 13, 1918, decimal 730, box 429, general decimal file, 1917–1927, Records of the Surgeon General, RG 112, National Archives, College Park, MD.

[35] On Terman and the development of the masculinity-femininity test, see Henry L. Minton, *Lewis M. Terman: Pioneer in Psychological Testing* (New York: New York University Press, 1988), 172–77; Jennifer Terry, *An American Obsession: Science, Medicine, and Homosexuality in Modern Society* (Chicago: University of Chicago Press, 1999), 169–72; Lewis M. Terman and Catherine Cox Miles, *Sex and Personality: Studies in Masculinity and Femininity* (New York: McGraw-Hill, 1936).

[36] See Robert A. Nye, "The Medical Origins of Sexual Fetishism," in *Fetishism as Cultural Discourse*, ed. Emily Apter and William Pietz (Ithaca, NY: Cornell University Press, 1993), 13–30.

[37] E. K. Stitt to Bureau of Navigation, December 29, 1920, file no. 126588, General Correspondence 1912–1925, Records of the Bureau of Medicine and Surgery, RG 52, National Archives, Washington, DC.

[38] Lieutenant H.A.N. Bruckshaw to the Surgeon General, U.S. Navy, "Opinion, Relative to the Use of Psychometric Tests, as Applied to Recruits," January 18, 1922, file no. 126588, General Correspondence 1912–1925, Records of the Bureau of Medicine and Surgery, RG 52.

[39] It was not uncommon for the military, in Bérubé's words, "to encase these new psychiatric concepts in the theory and language of degeneration" (*Coming Out Under Fire*,

on neuropsychiatry during the First World War, "constitute a more or less typical group" of psychopaths.[40] Vague and indefinite, the category of psychopathy was constituted by those strange types who inhabited the "vast borderland" between "sanity and insanity," as frequently brilliant as they were feebleminded.[41] They were attracted to the "excitement, idleness, and male companionship" of military life.[42] But unlike the sexual degenerate, the sexual psychopath often did not stand out. They could occasionally be detected, noted one military investigator, by the "sway of their hips" and their "lavish use of powder, paint, rouge, and lipstick."[43] Just as often, though, as Dr. Albert Abrams warned in his 1918 tract on the military menace of homosexuality, "the homosexualist may [appear] like a normal individual."[44]

Recognizing that intelligence tests were of little use, the military began to work on screening devices that emphasized personality or character rather than IQ to identify this enigmatic figure. A lieutenant commander from the Medical Corps of the navy urged that undesirables be eliminated by a "brief study of the personality of each applicant . . . for the purpose of determining . . . any abnormal, unstable, or asocial tendencies."[45] Thus, both the army and navy designed questionnaires that delved into sexual matters. Instructions for the army's mental test advised examiners to ask, "Did you ever have any fears? Ideas that haunted you and which you could not control?" Examiners were then advised to "inquire into sex habits, using familiar slang."[46] Similarly, the navy's mental test included such questions as, "Were you ever shy with boys? Do you have too many sexual dreams? Have you ever hurt yourself by masturbation (self abuse)? Did you ever make love to

13). The induction standards in 1921, for example, listed both "anatomical stigmata of degeneration" and "sexual psychopathy" as grounds for rejection.

[40] Bailey et al., *The Medical Department of the United States Army in the World War*, 230.

[41] Heber Butts, "Further Observation on the Insane of the Navy," *United States Naval Medical Bulletin* 6 (April 1912): 202; Elizabeth Lunbeck, *The Psychiatric Persuasion: Knowledge, Gender, and Power in Modern America* (Princeton, NJ: Princeton University Press, 1994), 64–71.

[42] John W. Visher, "A Study of Constitutional Psychopathic Inferiority," *Mental Hygiene* 6 (1922): 733.

[43] Camp Inspector to Inspector General, March 29, 1919, "Report of Sexual Perverts among Commissioned and Enlisted Personnel at Camp Jackson, S.C.," decimal 250.1, box 258, central decimal file 1917–1925, Records of the Adjutant General, RG 407.

[44] Albert Abrams, "Homosexuality—A Military Menace," quoted in Jonathan Katz, *Gay and Lesbian Almanac* (New York: Harper and Row, 1983), 382.

[45] J. G. Ziegler to Commander H. W. Smith, "Mental Examination of Applicants for Enlistment," June 9, 1922, file no. 126588, General Correspondence 1912–1925, Records of the Bureau of Medicine and Surgery, RG 52.

[46] "Instructions to Line Recruiting Officers," decimal 341.41, box 1784, central decimal files (bulky files) 1917–1925, Records of the Adjutant General, RG 407.

a girl? Did you ever think you had lost your manhood?"[47] Company commanders also were instructed by psychiatrists to report "abnormal sex practices," "distinct feminine types," or any "queer, peculiar behavior" among their men.[48]

The numbers snared by such screens were invariably quite small. When the Ohio State Board of Charities wrote to the secretary of war asking for the names of all Ohio residents refused induction for psychological reasons, a fifteen-page, single-spaced typewritten list yielded 1 sexual pervert.[49] Out of 1,787 neuropsychiatric rejects at Camp Devens, Massachusetts, 4 were sexual psychopaths.[50] Of more than 24,400 men subjected to routine examination at an undesignated camp (routine meaning cases that were not referred because of observed problems), 2 were described as sexual psychopaths.[51] Similar statistics were presented for Camp Shelby, Mississippi. At the bottom of the page, the major compiling the data wrote the words "one sexual pervert only referred."[52] The way this particular statistic was separately denoted and the officer's wording—"only"—is a little curious. Did he expect a larger number? Or did he intend the statistic as evidence in support of a call for a program of more intensive screening?

The latter explanation is quite plausible—military psychiatrists and psychologists routinely complained about inadequate resources to carry out their work during and after the war. One navy doctor reported in 1918, for example, that he was performing psychiatric examinations on as many as seventy-five recruits per hour.[53] Another who devoted ninety seconds to each recruit groused that as psychologists at his camp had not been assigned to a building, examinations had to be conducted "here, there, and everywhere." There was also the general hostility of the regular officers to psychology and psychiatry, which were considered "unnecessary from the standpoint of an organization commander,"

---

[47] "Mental Test," December 1919, file no. 124957, box 371, General Correspondence 1912–1925, Records of the Bureau of Medicine and Surgery, RG 52.

[48] L. E. Bisch, "A Routine Method of Mental Examinations for Naval Recruits," *United States Naval Medical Bulletin* 13 (April 1919): 200.

[49] The Adjutant General of the Army to the Surgeon General of the Army, April 16, 1918, file no. 702, box 1090, central decimal files 1917–1925, Adjutant General's Office, RG 407.

[50] Bailey et al, *The Medical Department of the United States Army in the World War*, 78.

[51] John F. W. Meagher to Surgeon General of the Army, "Comparison of Work in Different Camps," March 10, 1918, decimal 702.2, box 383, general decimal file 1917–1927, Records of the Surgeon General, RG 112.

[52] "Summary of Work of Nervous and Mental Board at Camp MacArthur, Texas," December 15, 1917–July 10, 1918, decimal 730, box 429, general decimal file 1917–1927, Records of the Surgeon General, RG 112.

[53] Albert Warren Stearns, "The Psychiatric Examination of Recruits," *Journal of the American Medical Association* 70 (January 26, 1918): 230.

and "hobb[ies] saddled upon the army."[54] And the first line of defense against the defective recruit—the local draft board—did little to shore up the admittedly weak showing by the military's own examiners. Local boards usually passed defectives without question, opined one man who served on Portland's draft board. "These defectives say nothing," he reported, "and the examiner commonly lacks sufficient neurological training to himself suspect defects."[55] If anything, the situation deteriorated as psychiatric and psychological testing was further scaled back after the war. Additional guidelines for screening sexual perverts were issued in 1921, but according to the historian Allan Bérubé, rarely implemented.[56] In 1925, one medical officer complained to the adjutant general that the army still had no procedure for a "systematic and sustained inquiry as to the mental and moral condition of applicants for enlistment."[57]

The small number of psychopathic personalities identified thus reflected, as one official put it, the problem of "non-recognition" rather than an actual absence of perverted types among military personnel.[58] As time wore on, for much of the officer corps, this nonrecognition was more likely a failure to *detect* than it was a failure to *know*. "Sex offenses," stated one colonel in the plainest of terms, are "generally committed by *a social category of persons*, sexual perverts, [who form] a class."[59] However clear this formulation—and however quickly the idea of the pervert as a kind of person may have taken hold among the top brass—it did not immediately yield a firm response among military officials, but instead only the hazier declaration that such types were "a troublesome group in the army."[60]

Blaming Civilians

Sex perverts were problematic not only because they were considered unfit to associate with other soldiers, but also because they stigmatized

[54] Colonel R. J. Burt to the Chief of Staff, "Report of Psychological Tests in the Army," June 1918, decimal 702, box 1090, central decimal files 1917–1925, Records of the Adjutant General, RG 407.

[55] Doctor William House to Colonel Pierce Bailey, September 24, 1918, decimal no. 702.2, box 383, general decimal file 1917–1927, Records of the Surgeon General, RG 112.

[56] Bérubé, *Coming Out Under Fire*, 14.

[57] Major M. A. Ashford to the Adjutant General, November 13, 1925, decimal 342.15, box 795, central decimal file 1917–1925, Records of the Adjutant General, RG 407.

[58] Stearns, "The Psychiatric Examination of Recruits," 231.

[59] Pearce Bailey, Memorandum for General Munson, December 20, 1918, decimal 250.1, box 128, general correspondence, Records of the Surgeon General, RG 112 (emphasis added).

[60] Major Frank E. Leslie, "The Constitutional Psychopath, as Found in the Army," 1918, file no. 700.7-1, box 364, Records of the Surgeon General, RG 112.

the army and navy. Even before the First World War, commanding officers had worried that the military's "filthiness" might become public knowledge.[61] But official concern that "moral degenerates" would "bring discredit upon the military service" intensified at the war's end.[62] In part this was due to the military's own stated goal of attracting a better class of recruit after the suspension of the draft. "We cannot expect to attract good men to the Service," a navy board concluded in 1920, "if the Navy is going to be known as a haven for . . . degenerates."[63] There was also the fact of a press hungry for salacious details— as sexological concepts began to seep into American popular culture— constantly threatening to bring this or that sex scandal to the public's attention.[64] So the mother of a lieutenant discharged for perversion appealed for help to the secretary of the navy. His interest was no doubt piqued when she wrote that "the *Chicago Tribune* was most desirous of taking it up . . . and making the whole affair public."[65] Sometimes the warnings came too late. "There is one thing I do want to mention right here," Assistant Secretary of the Navy Franklin Roosevelt lamented after a particularly damaging scandal erupted: "The charge is made in the *Register* and the *Journal*."[66]

Such press coverage helped to feed a broader suspicion that there might actually be a *causal* relationship between martial culture and perversion. Some observers expressed this notion in the most general of terms, wondering if the "congregation of large masses of men with restricted liberties," as Dr. Samuel Kahn wrote about armies and prisons, was "the culture medium in which the bacillus homosexualis . . . flourishes."[67] Was perversion to be expected, another psychiatrist asked,

[61] See numerous cases in file no. 20615, box 115, document file 1894–1912, Records of the Judge Advocate General (Army), RG 153, National Archives, Washington, DC; file no. 20615, box 22, Records Cards (1894–1912), Records of the Judge Advocate General (Army), RG 153.

[62] Commanding General, Camp Devens, to the Adjutant General, February 17, 1920, decimal 220.8, box 105, Adjutant General file 1917–1938, First Corps Area, Records of the U.S. Army Commands, RG 394, National Archives, Washington, DC.

[63] Medical Examining Board to Commandant, "Report on Recruit Material," February 15, 1920, file no. 26288-951, box 1863, General Correspondence 1916–1926, Records of the Secretary of the Navy, RG 80, National Archives, Washington, DC.

[64] Relevant here is George Chauncey's argument that Prohibition (enacted in 1920) made gay life more visible than it had previously been (at least in New York, but presumably elsewhere) (*Gay New York*, 301). Likewise, Sigmund Freud's emergence on the American continent surely helped to popularize sexological constructs.

[65] Mrs. Chas E. Smith to the Secretary of the Navy, May 25, 1921, file no. 26283-299, box 1752, General Correspondence 1916–1926, Records of the Secretary of the Navy, RG 80.

[66] File no. 26288-944, box 1863, General Correspondence 1916–1926, Records of the Secretary of the Navy, RG 80.

[67] Samuel Kahn, *Mentality and Homosexuality* (Boston: Meador Publishing Company, 1937), 5.

anytime "men or women must be grouped alone for prolonged periods . . . in army camps [or] aboard ships?"[68] Perhaps it was not only the
lack of a "normal" sexual outlet that promoted perversion, but also the
homoerotic quality of life in the army or navy: "Being so robustly male,
there is no place in a soldier's heart or sexual impulse for anything not
vehemently manly." Such hypermasculinity could actually be feminiz-
ing as, this same writer observed, "the naval and military atmosphere
are highly aesthetic. They are full of color, romance, life, grace, symme-
try." This martial aesthetic connected visual pleasures to emotional and
perhaps even physical ones: "Beauty of body, the effective uniforms that
enhance the physique in constant appeal to masculine good looks, the
free and often tender intercourse, intimacies of specially fine psychic
fiber between men."[69] Or was there something about the circumstance of
this *particular* war? Men and women had been separated "into masses of
their own sex," there were "ten million men" missing in Europe, and
there was "a great outbreak of [male] hysteria" (itself a kind of psychopathy), recently given the name "shell-shock."[70] American troops
had been exposed to perversion in Europe, some military and government officials speculated. Were they bringing it back home with them?[71]

As these various hypotheses—which suggested that military life created the conditions for perversion to thrive—gained currency, even ineffective and/or rarely implemented screening guidelines served a purpose in symbolically highlighting perversion as a civilian disease.
Military life did not produce perversion—these standards seemed to
say—rather it was imported from the outside such that military officials
had to be on guard against the incursion of civilian perverts. This assertion seems more rhetorically than actually true (as the weak screening
apparatus indicates), but the limited military policing that did exist in
these years was, in fact, often directed against civilians. The army conducted, for example, a nationwide investigation into perversion among
YMCA personnel because of the work that the organization did with
soldiers.[72] More generally, military officials found the discourse of civil-

[68] Edward J. Kempf, *Psychopathology* (Saint Louis: C. V. Mosby, 1921), 477.

[69] Xavier Mayne, *The Intersexes: A History of Similisexualism as a Problem in Social Life*
(1908; repr., New York: Arno Press, 1975), 187–88. The notion that militarism was connected to effeminacy has a long history. Kerber reports that Mary Wollstonecraft "sneered
at standing armies, likening uniformed soldiers who were admired for their status and attire to frivolous women, brought up to be deferential and to please their superiors by their
manners and their dress" (*No Constitutional Right to Be Ladies*, 242).

[70] Constance Long, "A Sign of the Times for Those Who Can Read Portents," 1919, in
Jonathan Katz, *Gay and Lesbian Almanac* (New York: Harper and Row, 1983), 385. On shell
shock, see Shephard, *A War of Nerves*.

[71] Bulletin no. 1480, box 88, Committee of Fourteen Records.

[72] File no.10656-7, box 3729, Military Intelligence Division Correspondence, Records of
the War Department, RG 165.

ian contamination a useful way to defend the moral integrity of the institution whenever the public seemed ready to call that integrity into question.

Military officials, in other words, directed as much attention to the other side of the civilian-military border as they could. "Our men were being preyed on by perverts from Baltimore [and] Washington," noted the commanding officer of the USS *Reina Mercedes* in one such commonly used formulation that portrayed soldiers as victims of civilians. The *Reina*'s commander described how civilian musicians first began to appear in the recreation room at the naval hospital in Annapolis. "Using this as a base," he reported, "they gradually obtained a hold on the enlisted men." After these soldiers left the hospital, they were transferred to various stations. And this was how "such a large number of men" began to visit "the haunts of perverts," including a house in Baltimore called "the Garden of Allah"—the name undoubtedly a reference to the "eastern male loving zone" of Turkey, Persia, and Arabia.[73]

The navy moved to stop this cancer-like spread of perversion, offering undesirable discharges (rather than prison sentences) to sailors who had consorted with the perverts and agreed to turn "state's evidence." As a result of the soldiers' testimony, five civilian perverts were sentenced to up to five years in the state penitentiary. One man fled and was never apprehended, and another, a Baltimore doctor, committed suicide.[74] As the relatively lenient treatment of the soldiers involved in this incident demonstrates, military officials were not particularly concerned with protecting *civilians* from immoral soldiers. This was the case even when it was clear that it was soldiers who were in fact the "predators." In one such episode, an effeminate soldier who was known down on the corner as "Dutch Kate" and a "feminist" was court-martialed for fellating several civilians. Initially found guilty, the sergeant's sentence was remitted on the findings of a medical board that he was a sexual psychopath, and hence "could not be held responsible for his abnormal sexual desires and practices." It perhaps helped his case that army officials were able to blame the soldier's behavior on his own civilian past. Dutch Kate had admitted "indulgence in abnormal sexual practices for many years," one colonel observed, and that his condition "existed prior to enlistment."[75]

Just as Dutch Kate was being discharged to civilian society "without danger to self or others," navy officials laid the blame for one of the

[73]File no. P13-7/1, box 845, General Correspondence 1925–1940, Records of the Bureau of Naval Personnel, RG 24, National Archives, Washington, DC; Mayne, *The Intersexes*, 75.

[74]Memo from Commanding Officer to the Bureau of Navigation, April 30, 1928, file no. P13-7/1, box 845, General Correspondence 1925–1940, Records of the Bureau of Naval Personnel, RG 24.

[75]Court-Martial file no. 121216, 1919, Records of the Judge Advocate General, RG 153.

largest sex scandals in naval history on civilians in and around the navy training station at Newport, Rhode Island.[76] In 1919, a naval machinist's mate named Earvin Arnold first observed a perversion ring that centered around the Newport YMCA, especially around a civilian minister, the Reverend Samuel Kent. Arnold told a naval doctor named Erastus Hudson of his discovery, and together they approached various naval officials, warning that "acts of perversion were being committed on men of the navy by certain civilians."[77] As a result, the two men obtained approval to conduct an entrapment operation in which enlisted men allowed civilians to perform sexual acts on them. Several civilians were imprisoned and tried, but when Arnold and Hudson went after Reverend Kent, there was an outcry from Newport ministers and a backlash ensued. This group of local ministers, allied with the local newspaper editor, protested that the navy had made its men "perverts by official order" and foisted indignities on the citizens of Newport. The scandal finally resulted in a congressional investigation that held Josephus Daniels, the secretary of the navy, and especially his assistant secretary, Franklin Delano Roosevelt, responsible for exposing young navy recruits to perversion.[78]

As they dealt with the political fallout, naval officials defended their actions by referencing the threat posed to their men by civilian perverts. "There was no intention to be immoral," said one captain in defense of the entrapment scheme. "It was only the work that we thought . . . necessary to save the young boys who were going into the service."[79] In-

---

That the sergeant was described as a feminist is intriguing. The exact passage is: "On several occasions I have heard people making remarks to me to the effect that I was a feminist, stuck up." The term could refer to effeminacy, or perhaps it is being used as "feminism" was in immigration cases about ten years earlier, to refer to men with defective genitalia. (As early as 1911, the navy included "feminism in men" on a list of "stigmata of degeneration." See Heber Butts, "The Mental Examination of Candidates for Enlistment in the Navy and Marine Corps," *United States Naval Bulletin* 5 [1911]: 38.) Because "stuck up" does not really suggest a physical condition but an attitude (and because there is no other indication in this file of physical defect), the first interpretation is more likely.

[76] Court-Martial file no. 121216, 1919, Records of the Judge Advocate General, RG 153.

[77] Testimony of Captain Leigh, January 22, 1920, case no. 10821-3, box 256, Proceedings of the Court of Inquiry, Records of Judge Advocate General (Navy), RG 125, 1540, National Archives, Washington, DC.

[78] The Newport scandal has received considerable attention from historians. See Lawrence R. Murphy, *Perverts by Official Order: The Campaign against Homosexuals by the United States Navy* (New York: Harrington Park Press, 1988); George Chauncey Jr., "Christian Brotherhood or Sexual Perversion? Homosexual Identities and the Construction of Sexual Boundaries in the World War One Era," *Journal of Social History* 19 (Winter 1985): 189–211.

[79] Testimony of Captain Leigh, January 22, 1920, case no. 10821-3, box 256, Proceedings of the Court of Inquiry, Records of Judge Advocate General (Navy), RG 125, 1785.

deed, even the mayor of Newport admitted that a group of civilian perverts—"floaters," as he called them, using a term associated with vagrants—followed the naval fleet up and down the coast. "In times gone
by we used to say, summer after summer," the mayor explained, that
"when a boy passed down the street with his straw hat cocked to one
side of his head, [that] he had followed the fleet up from Norfolk." But,
the mayor continued, the problem of perversion was not with New-
porters themselves. "I felt that Newport was clean of that type," the
mayor asserted, "and if those cases took place, it was simply men who
came in to Newport to spend a short period of time, perhaps because
there was a great gathering of men in the service here, due to the war."[80]

It was precisely this attitude on the part of the mayor—that "it was
all a sailor matter"—that had forced the navy, according to Secretary
Daniels, to take its own action to clean up civilian perversion in Newport.[81] As early as 1917, CTCA chairman Raymond Fosdick told Secretary Daniels that he was worried about vice in Newport. "The civil
government is a muddy, spineless affair," Fosdick reported to Daniels.
"All hope lies in the Navy Department, none in the Mayor or Council."[82] It was not only the mayor who was apparently looking the other
way on perversion cases, though. During the navy's own investigation into the scandal, the Newport chief of police told an incredulous
court of inquiry that he knew of no sex perverts in Newport. "You
want this court to believe," the chief was asked, "that you knew of no-
body residing in Newport . . . [whom] you [suspected] of being a moral
pervert?"[83]

The navy thus blamed immoral conditions in Newport not only on
civilian perverts but also on city officials, from whom the military expected help in handling perversion. (Around the same time, the navy
expressed frustration at the reluctance of Norfolk officials to police perversion around the naval training station there.)[84] And not only local
but federal officials were held responsible, including the attorney general, whom Assistant Secretary Roosevelt had asked to "send [his] most
skilled investigators" to "protect . . . [the navy's] men from such con-

[80] Testimony of Mayor Jeremiah Mahoney, January 22, 1920, case nos. 10821-2 and
10821-3, box 255, Proceedings of the Court of Inquiry, Records of the Judge Advocate General (Navy), RG 125, 691–94.

[81] Ibid., 715.

[82] Raymond Fosdick to the Secretary of the Navy, May 10, 1917, reel no. 1, container 458,
navy subject file, Josephus Daniels Papers.

[83] Testimony of Chief of Police John Tobin, January 22, 1920, case nos. 10821-2 and
10821-3, box 255, Proceedings of the Court of Inquiry, Records of Judge Advocate General
(Navy), RG 125, 1158.

[84] File no. 26262-2203:1, box 1151, General Correspondence 1897–1915, Records of the
Secretary of the Navy, RG 80.

taminating influences."[85] The Department of Justice, according to Roosevelt, sent an agent to Newport but "failed utterly to stop the trouble."[86] That agent asserted that the whole matter was "exaggerated," and "on account of so many navy men being involved . . . it was a navy matter." Moreover, he said, the issue would fall under DOJ jurisdiction only if authorities found a liquor or cocaine violation or a house of prostitution.[87] The problem of homosexuality, in other words, did not come under the purview of the Department of Justice, which was, by its own admission, too busy with Bolsheviks to be troubled with the matter anyway.[88]

It was only after the secretary of the navy had, then, "exhausted every one of the regular channels in an effort to clean up conditions," that he became convinced that the "navy itself [had to] take steps to secure the wholesome environment for youths sent to Newport."[89] Roosevelt further defended his (and Daniels's) role in the sordid investigation by pointing out that Hudson and Arnold (who originally exposed the perversion ring) were, after all, not so far removed from the corruption of civilian life themselves. Arnold had spent nine years working as a state detective in Connecticut who "ran down perverts."[90] Furthermore, as both men were just "out of civilian life," they "did not know and had no opportunity of becoming inculcated with navy traditions."[91] But Roosevelt's opponents took a page out of this same playbook as the attempt to blame civilians backfired somewhat: "The terrible abuses we have been subjected to were authorized," a group of Newport ministers told the Senate Naval Committee, "not by any subordinate officer or enlisted man in the navy, but by the civilian authorities [Roosevelt and

---

[85] Franklin D. Roosevelt to Attorney General A. Mitchell Palmer, March 22, 1919, case no. 10821-3, box 258, Proceedings of the Court of Inquiry, Records of the Judge Advocate General (Navy), RG 125.

[86] Statement of Franklin D. Roosevelt, July 18, 1921, Papers Pertaining to Family, Business, and Personal Affairs, box 80, RG 14, Franklin Delano Roosevelt Library, Hyde Park, NY.

[87] George E. Rowe to Tom Howick, May 17, 1919, exhibit 97, and Report Made by Agent Daly, exhibit 88, case no. 10821-3, box 257, Proceedings of the Court of Inquiry, Records of the Judge Advocate General (Navy), RG 125; Testimony of Agent Daly, January 22, 1920, case nos. 10821-2 and 10821-3, box 255, Proceedings of the Court of Inquiry, Records of the Judge Advocate General (Navy), RG 125.

[88] Murphy, *Perverts by Official Order*, 16–17.

[89] The Secretary of the Navy to the Bureau of Navigation, March 3, 1921, file no. 26283-2591, box 1776, General Correspondence 1916–1926, Records of the Secretary of the Navy, RG 80.

[90] Murphy, *Perverts by Official Order*, 209.

[91] Roosevelt to Daniels, March 1, 1921, reel 59, container 94, Special Correspondence, Josephus Daniels Papers.

Daniels] responsible for the department."[92] Young men in the navy were vulnerable, opined the editor of the *Providence Journal*, not to the civilian perverts of Newport, but rather to the civilian officials of the navy who had employed "the most bestial and dishonorable methods known to man."[93]

In a second well-publicized incident, navy men blamed civilian officials within the military for fostering the spread of sexual depravity among enlisted men. As with the Newport scandal, implicating civilian authority enabled military officials to depict perversion in opposition to martial citizenship—as a contagion introduced by outsiders rather than as a product of the military's own institutions. Thomas Mott Osborne was a particularly easy target. The notorious prison reformer had recently been under grand jury investigation for sexual improprieties with prisoners as the warden of Sing Sing Prison in New York when Secretary Daniels appointed him the commanding officer of the Portsmouth Naval Prison.[94] Osborne had been brought on because Daniels believed the warden's innovative penology would improve conditions at the Portsmouth facility. Daniels miscalculated. A civilian had never been placed in charge of a military prison before, and naval officers resented Osborne and his assigned rank of lieutenant commander.[95]

Osborne's approach was to give prisoners a great deal of responsibility for running the institution, in the hopes of rehabilitating them and returning them to duty. But prison officials protested that the warden made life too soft for the prisoners, some of whom reportedly wrote letters to shipmates telling them how easy life at Portsmouth was, that they were "in a home so good that they would not even try to escape." There were also complaints that Osborne had "pets" among the prison-

[92] Testimony of Dr. Stanley Hughes, March 8, 1919, case no. 10821-1, box 254, Proceedings of the Court of Inquiry, Records of the Judge Advocate General (Navy), RG 125.

[93] Telegram from John Rathom to Franklin Roosevelt, January 22, 1920, file no. 26288-944, box 1863, General Correspondence 1916–1926, Records of the Secretary of the Navy, RG 80.

[94] The charges against Osborne at Sing Sing were eventually dropped. It is somewhat remarkable that Osborne was appointed by Daniels under such circumstances—perhaps evidence of partisan loyalty or the way that elite men may have been protective of homoerotic class privilege. On Osborne, see Kevin P. Murphy, *Political Manhood: Red-Bloods, Mollycoddles, and the Politics of Progressive Era Reform* (New York: Columbia University Press, 2008); Regina G. Kunzel, *Criminal Intimacy: Prison and the Uneven History of Modern American Sexuality* (Chicago: University of Chicago Press, 2008). On homosexuality and prison culture more generally, see Kunzel, *Criminal Intimacy*; Chauncey, *Gay New York*, 91–96; Estelle Freedman, *Maternal Justice: Miriam Van Waters and the Female Reform Tradition* (Chicago: University of Chicago Press, 1996).

[95] Ted Morgan, *FDR: A Biography* (New York: Simon and Schuster, 1985), 219–20.

ers, and some speculation that perversion was widespread at Portsmouth. The most damning charge, however, was that Osborne had sent sexual perverts back to the fleet from Portsmouth. "To return a man who has been convicted of . . . indecent and unnatural practices to duty among the honorable and decent men of the naval service," a captain wrote to Secretary Daniels, "[will] result in the contamination and . . . demoralization of the men of the navy."[96] Another officer wrote in an editorial in the *Army and Navy Journal* that ship captains "shuddered" when naval prisoners were returned to ships, as it forced the "good men of the navy" to associate with "moral perverts."[97] The service would be "embarrassed" by the return of Portsmouth inmates to the fleet, one officer stated.[98]

While personally bruised from the recent events in Newport, Assistant Secretary Roosevelt defended the reformer Osborne. Roosevelt asserted that only two out of forty men convicted of sodomy had been restored to duty, and after making a trip to the prison, the assistant secretary denied reports that immorality was a common practice at the Portsmouth prison. Osborne soon resigned anyway.[99] "The experiment of turning over the naval prison . . . to a civilian prison reformer has been a failure," concluded the commander of the USS *Rochester*.[100] Osborne was—as his critics had requested—replaced with a "regular line officer" of the navy.[101]

[96] File no. 26288/951:13, box 1863, General Correspondence 1916–1926, Records of the Secretary of the Navy, RG 80.

[97] Morgan, *FDR*, 220.

[98] Bureau of Navigation to Judge Advocate General, September 25, 1918, file no. 26288/951:13, box 1863, General Correspondence 1916–1926, Records of the Secretary of the Navy, RG 80. On Portsmouth, see also file no. 26288-944, box 1863, General Correspondence 1916–1926, Records of the Secretary of the Navy, RG 80.

[99] Memorandum for the Assistant Secretary, January 21, 1920, file no. 26288-944, box 1863, General Correspondence 1916–1926, Records of the Secretary of the Navy, RG 80; Board Appointed to Report on General Conditions at Portsmouth Prison to the Secretary of the Navy, February 26, 1920, case no. 10604, box 242, Proceedings of the Court of Inquiry, Records of the Judge Advocate General (Navy), RG 125.

[100] Commanding Officer, U.S.S. Rochester to Secretary of the Navy, January 17, 1920, file no. 26288-951, box 1863, General Correspondence, Records of the Secretary of the Navy, RG 80.

[101] Captain J. K. Taussig to the Assistant Secretary of the Navy, February 24, 1920, file no. 26288/951:13, box 1863, General Correspondence 1916–1926, Records of the Secretary of the Navy, RG 80; Frank Freidel, *Franklin D. Roosevelt: The Ordeal* (Boston: Little, Brown and Company, 1952), 45–46. Portsmouth, however, remained plagued by the association between its facility and sexual perversion. In 1937, a senator created a big splash in the papers when he demanded that allegations of sodomy at the prison be investigated. File no. NF1/p13-7 (370316) P, box 3229, General Correspondence 1926–1940, Records of the Secretary of the Navy, RG 80.

Policing Publicity and Violence

The military's tendency to blame civilians for perversion was a key institutional strategy for managing stigma. The scandals that produced this form of damage control, moreover, themselves reveal the extent of official knowledge about the problem of sexual deviance among soldiers and sailors during the interwar period. Incidents at Portsmouth and Newport were not isolated events: "My God, now it's Newport!" one admiral exclaimed on hearing of the situation there, indicating that he "was receiving reports of similar conditions from many other places in the United States," including the Great Lakes and Norfolk training stations.[102]

Yet for all the military knew about perversion, as well as the negative consequences that followed when that information was exposed to the public, it is somewhat remarkable that the military did not regularly purge or punish sexual perverts. This may seem hard to believe, especially given that between 1917 and 1930, the army court-martialed between fifty and one hundred soldiers each year for sodomy.[103] When these soldiers were found guilty, they served prison terms before being dishonorably discharged from the military.[104] However, a close reading of these sodomy trials reveals that the army mostly used the court-martial to punish overt displays and (especially) violence with regard to sexual acts. The court-martial was another tool to manage the stigma associated with perversion—but not to actually remove perverts from the force. The military was still many years away from constructing such an instrument.

Consensual and private encounters were, of course, less likely to be uncovered anyway, yet their irregular appearance on court dockets also

[102] Testimony of Captain Hibbs, January 22, 1920, case nos. 10821-2 and 10821-3, box 255, Proceedings of the Courts of Inquiry, 1886–1940, Records of the Judge Advocate General (Navy), RG 125. At the Norfolk training station, naval authorities blamed immoral conditions on civilian authorities and threatened to withhold ships from the vicinity unless they cleaned up the town. File no. 26262-2203:1, box 1151, General Correspondence 1897–1915, Records of the Secretary of the Navy, RG 80. There was also a naval investigation during these years into perversion at the Mare Island Prison. See case no. 10892, box 262, Proceedings of the Court of Inquiry, Records of the Judge Advocate General (Navy), RG 125.

[103] On the history of the court-martial more generally, see David A. Schlueter, "The Court-Martial: An Historical Survey," *Military Law Review* 87 (1980): 129–66. Elizabeth Hillman's study of the cold war court-martial also contains some useful background material on this period. See Elizabeth Lutes Hillman, *Defending America: Military Culture and the Cold War Court-Martial* (Princeton, NJ: Princeton University Press, 2005).

[104] The sentences generally ranged from one to five years. The sentencing procedures were not entirely uniform. Generally anal and oral sex were considered sodomy; mutual masturbation was punished under the crime of "Lewdness."

suggests that military courts were less likely to convict men involved in discreet relationships. This was true even in cases where male-male intimacy was publicly expressed, as long as that intimacy could be deemed nonsexual. In one such episode, a lieutenant was investigated for an allegedly inappropriate relationship with a sergeant. It was known around the unit that several times the two men had stayed out together all night, at least once at a Turkish bath. On another occasion, they spent the night behind the locked door of the room of another lieutenant who was away on leave. The two men, moreover, had been seen lying in bed together around the unit on various occasions, with their faces just three or four inches apart, or with one man's head resting on the other's arm. But witnesses testified that there was nothing terribly unusual about the pair holding each other. "I have seen some of the lieutenants lying in bed together and have done the same thing [myself] lots of times in the same way," one lieutenant testified. The commanding officer explained that "the friendship" between the two men "was of such a quiet, unassuming, and genuine nature" that he did not "deem disciplinary action necessary."[105]

Other officers testifying in this case stated that what was unusual about the relationship was only its cross-rank character, suggesting the extent to which a nineteenth-century tradition of romantic friendship persisted among officers into the early twentieth century. Yet even cross-rank intimacy was somewhat tolerated within the military's homosocial tradition—"it was a custom of the service," one commanding officer reported, to have an enlisted man from his company sleep with him. It was only when this commander attempted one night to sodomize his bedmate that he was court-martialed.[106] This degree of prosecution was itself unusual. Officers who were caught engaging in sexual relations with enlisted men were rarely tried and, if anything, "quietly ushered out of the service." It was enlisted men who bore the brunt of military justice.[107] This was the case not only because military courts were inherently biased in favor of officers, but also because the more public nature of enlisted men's sexual culture meant that the latter were more vulnerable to prosecution in the first place.[108]

[105]Memorandum for the Chief of Staff, April 19, 1919, decimal: 250.17, box 531, central decimal file 1917–1925, Records of the Adjutant General, RG 407.

[106]Court-martial file no. 133259, 1919, Records of the Judge Advocate General, RG 153.

[107]Major General Johnson Hagood to the Adjutant General, September 3, 1931, decimal 253, box 1258, central decimal file 1926–1939, Records of the Adjutant General, RG 407.

[108]For an argument that "wealthier men tended to be more discreet" during these years, see Matt Houlbrook, *Queer London: Perils and Pleasures in the Sexual Metropolis, 1918–1957* (London: University of Chicago, 2005), 140. On the visibility of the working-class gay world, see Chauncey, *Gay New York*.

Working-class cultures during these years, as George Chauncey has argued, defined sexual normativity not in terms of sexual-object choice but rather in terms of gender.[109] The masculine soldier or sailor who sought sexual gratification and the effeminate pervert who received him were seen as distinct types, in other words, and only the latter was subject to the scorn of enlisted men. Gender did not only define these relationships, but (for the partner playing the masculine role) it also legitimized them. One case illustrative of this point involved a private O'Dell, who was in bed, apparently rocking back and forth. Soldiers in the barracks told O'Dell to stop the noise. When he did not, they turned on the light and found him on top of another man. "I am doing nothing wrong . . . Johnson is my punk," he explained, using the term that designated (along with "chicken") one who would "lift his skirts" to the boys, or who could be used by another "as a girl."[110]

As O'Dell's assertion makes clear, some soldiers saw sex with effeminate partners as a prerogative of their manhood. Sexual banter and a rough culture of sexual play were thus—at least as evidenced through the window of court-martial records—quite common. On one base, the immorality taking place among soldiers at a nearby ball diamond "was all plain talk."[111] In another instance, one soldier bragged about having a "nice ass," to which another replied that, "if the soldier had such a nice ass," then he should join him in bed. When the latter soldier was asked during court-martial proceedings why he had said such a thing, the man responded that it was "a common occurrence for men to fool that way."[112] Men propositioned each other, another man told the court, "practically every day." When asked to elaborate, he explained that one man would say, "'How would you like to suck my cock?' or something like that, just as a joking matter, and the [other] guy says 'I'll suck you' and goes away, and that is all there is to it."[113]

There was more to it. Courts didn't convict soldiers for talking about sex but for performing it, especially in front of an actual audience.[114] Indeed, sex in the barracks frequently occurred in the presence of other men. Two men, for example, climbed onto a bunk not four feet away

[109]Chauncey, *Gay New York*, especially chapter 4. The 1910s and 1920s are years when certain middle-class men were more likely to claim an identity as queer based on their sexual relationships with other men (rather than gender traits).

[110]Court-martial file no. 107603, 1917, Records of the Judge Advocate General, RG 153; Court-martial file no. 154609, 1922, Records of the Judge Advocate General, RG 153; Court-martial file no. 137715, 1920, Records of the Judge Advocate General, RG 153.

[111]Court-martial file no. 153989, 1922, Records of the Judge Advocate General, RG 153.

[112]Court-martial file no. 147300, 1921, Records of the Judge Advocate General, RG 153.

[113]Court-martial file no. 186085, 1929, Records of the Judge Advocate General, RG 153.

[114]Conviction for sodomy rested on penetration, although "circumstantial evidence" of

from another soldier's bed, and witnesses heard one ask the other if "papa love[s] mama?" With the streetlight shining in through a nearby window, the two men's lovemaking was "just as plain as a man having intercourse with a woman."[115] In another instance, a witness reported seeing men come to one soldier's bunk in two-minute intervals while a group of soldiers stood around the bed asking, "is he taking it?"[116] Sexual "horseplay" was also common, as for example, several men who had their penises out "kidding each other" in "a sort of public exhibition." One man claimed that he took his penis out "because all the rest of the boys were playing," and ended up lying down on a bunk with another man who had "his pants down."[117]

This kind of public stunt, as one prosecutor remarked during the sodomy trial of an enlisted man (who "with a rifle and ammunition, in full uniform . . . in broad daylight took out his penis"), was "a very serious offense to the U.S. Army."[118] Indeed, enlisted men were dangerous because their distinctive sexual culture threatened to expose a much broader world of male intimacy inside the military. Courts thus applied military law as a counter to the sexual mores of enlisted men—especially the notion that men who played the penetrative role in sexual relations did "nothing wrong." So despite his testimony that he was "normal" because he never himself "dropped down," one private who was fellated by another was sentenced to a year in prison. In justifying the sentence, the judge advocate general explained that there was "no distinction between the active and passive partners so far as the law is concerned."[119] This sometimes came as a surprise to enlisted men, as in the case of two soldiers who testified that they committed sodomy on a "degenerate" in their unit "without knowing that" by their testimony, they also had "incriminate[d] themselves."[120]

Often, military courts tried both sex partners together and routinely gave them the same sentence.[121] In one such case, the court ruled that two men involved in an act of consensual sodomy were "equally guilty," despite the fact that the man who took the "feminine" part "was

---

the latter "may be sufficient." *Digest of Opinions of the Judge Advocate General of the Army* (Washington, DC: U.S. Government Printing Office, 1931), 15.

[115] Court-martial file no. 154887, 1923, Records of the Judge Advocate General, RG 153.

[116] Court-martial file no. 135154, 1919, Records of the Judge Advocate General, RG 153.

[117] Court-martial file no. 118357, 1918, Records of the Judge Advocate General, RG 153.

[118] Court-martial file no. 175963, 1927, Records of the Judge Advocate General, RG 153.

[119] Court-martial file no. 114884, 1918, Records of the Judge Advocate General, RG 153. "Both parties are liable as principals if each is an adult and consents." *A Manual for Courts-Martial* (Washington, DC: U.S. War Department, 1920), 439.

[120] Court-martial file no. 107667, 1919, Records of the Judge Advocate General, RG 153.

[121] Court-martial file no. 154887, 1923, Records of the Judge Advocate General, RG 153; Court-martial file no. 156641, 1923, Records of the Judge Advocate General, RG 153; Court-martial file no. 154887, 1923, Records of the Judge Advocate General, RG 153.

a habitual offender."[122] In another trial, a doctor confirmed for a judge that the "active party in a case of sodomy is just as much a pervert as the person who permits it."[123] Military judges and prosecutors in such cases sometimes tried to inculcate offenders into their own sexual norms. "Didn't you feel you were as bad as Murphy after you'd done it?" the court asked an enlisted man who was fellated by another. "No, sir," the soldier said, but when the judge asked again, the man admitted to being "disgusted" with himself about his behavior.[124] "Do you know that anyone who takes part or gives their permission in the act of sodomy is as guilty as the other?" another soldier was asked in court. "I guess they are," he replied halfheartedly.[125] In contrast to these enlisted men, military officials stated that it made no difference to them whether or not the accused was a sexual pervert: "We are merely concerned with the fact of . . . sodomy."[126]

That focus directed military policing away from effeminacy and toward sex. Yet this approach—in which sexual acts but not gender inversion triggered a court-martial proceeding—sometimes meant retaining perverted types in the military. So many perverts had joined a particular unit in one year, for example, that the troop had "a majority of men of that class."[127] In another case, a man known in his unit as "Tessie" and "fairy Sonnenshein" was teased for being effeminate and "perhaps a little queer." Soldiers would call out to him, "Sergeant Sonnenshein, I want my cock sucked." They reported that Sonnenshein "did not resent it," but would instead smile in response. Sonnenshein was tried for purportedly attempting to fellate a man in the latrine who then used his knee against Sonnenshein's jaw. The sergeant was initially found guilty, despite the fact that the credibility of his accuser was said to be compromised by the latter's willingness "to submit to Sonnenshein's alleged obscene proposals and manipulations." Significantly, while the prosecution argued that the sergeant was "just such an effeminate type as is ordinarily associated with this crime," the judge advocate general declined to find, in the absence of other evidence, that the man's effeminacy proved the occurrence of fellatio. Tessie's sentence was overturned, and he was returned to duty.[128]

[122] Court-martial file no. 1198038, 1918, Records of the Judge Advocate General, RG 153.
[123] Court-martial file no. 154190, 1922, Records of the Judge Advocate General, RG 153.
[124] Court-martial file no. 169960, 1926, Records of the Judge Advocate General, RG 153.
[125] Court-martial file no. 171934, 1926, Records of the Judge Advocate General, RG 153.
[126] Court-martial file no. 153989, 1922, Records of the Judge Advocate General, RG 153.
[127] Court-martial file no. 157044, 1923, Records of the Judge Advocate General, RG 153.
[128] Court-martial file no. 123252, 1918, Records of the Judge Advocate General, RG 153.
This was not an isolated incident. In another case, for example, a soldier was initially sentenced to two years for fellating men in his unit. "For some time there has been a rumor around the Company that Private Cook was committing sodomy by way of mouth," a witness stated. Because the evidence was later judged insufficient, the private was re-

Tessie's case also suggests that violence may have brought attention to encounters that otherwise might have gone unnoticed. This is part of what made sexual violence especially troubling to officials concerned with protecting the military's reputation, and it also may help explain why the passive/effeminate partner would participate in public displays that often led him to be ostracized from his unit, "that ma[de] him into a thing to be shunned."[129] Routinely, although certainly not in every instance, that participation was coerced. "This case is practically identical with that of every sodomy case we have in the service," a prosecutor stated during one trial that involved force, thereby testifying to the frequency of sexual assault.[130] It was almost always the "pathic" type who was targeted—weak, young, or effeminate.[131] For example, one sixteen-year-old recruit had been on his way to the shower when an older man grabbed him. At first it looked as though the two soldiers were "scuffling," witnesses said, but "afterwards" (with blood on the attacker's penis) it "looked as though" the older man had "put his penis into" the young recruit.[132] In another case, a man who was known as "punk-boy" and "sister" was "hounded" for sex by men in his unit. Two men took him to the coal pile and told him to "put out" or they would "smash his face."[133] "Catch[ing] up with a cock-sucker" was how another man justified his rape of a fellow soldier.[134]

Violence put attackers into greater legal jeopardy (forcible sodomy carried a more severe sentence), but it also served to separate them from the "weaklings," "degenerates," or "perverts" they assaulted by establishing one party as dominator, and the other as dominated. Soldiers sodomized such men, they said, because they "did not want . . . punk[s] around." One court asked if this "wasn't a peculiar way" to separate oneself "from a punk?"[135] But such a question ignored the way that brutality could sever the connection that sex implied. "How about it, chicken?" one man said to another soldier before assaulting him on a troop train, later bragging to a third soldier that "he was not a cock-sucker and he would kill any son of a bitch that thought he was. He could fuck a boy before he got his pants down," he said, "and

stored to duty. Court-martial file no. 165459, 1925, Records of the Judge Advocate General, RG 153.

[129] Court-martial file no. 178440, 1927, Records of the Judge Advocate General, RG 153.

[130] Court-martial file no. 177310, 1927, Records of the Judge Advocate General, RG 153.

[131] Pathic is used in these cases to mean "passive," but it seems likely that it is also a derivation of psychopathic.

[132] Court-martial file no. 140880, 1920, Records of the Judge Advocate General, RG 153.

[133] Court-martial file no. 154190, 1922, Records of the Judge Advocate General, RG 153.

[134] Court-martial file no. 148066, 1921, Records of the Judge Advocate General, RG 153.

[135] Court-martial file no. 162863, 1925, Records of the Judge Advocate General, RG 153.

would just as soon knock a boy in the head and fuck him before he got cold."[136]

Force existed on a continuum—and this was obviously its far end—but even those men who were brutally assaulted were condemned by their fellow soldiers. "Get away, boy," one soldier reported telling another who had been raped, and then added that "we chased him away."[137] In the eyes of enlisted men, then, it was weakness rather than will that mattered. But military courts cared about the issue of will, reasoning by analogy that if a pervert was like a woman, sodomy was legally (by the judge advocate general's own order) like rape.[138] As in rape cases, when judges were presented with evidence that victims had flirted with their attackers—evidence that pointed to consent—they were likely to go easier on those charged or to prosecute both men. During the trial of two men who were court-martialed for forcibly sodomizing a private, for instance, it came out that in the past, the victim had laid on a bunk with the two men, and "they used to call me their boy and once in a while I would call them daddy." The court suggested that the private's actions had shown that he was "the sort of man upon whom these men could commit sodomy." Despite the fact that the soldier declared that on the night in question he did not "voluntarily lay on the bunk," the court sentenced the accused to a mere five months in prison.[139]

Similarly, military courts treated soldiers who appeared interested in sex with other men as having consented to sex with *any* man. Men charged with sexually assaulting other men thus commonly defended themselves by claiming that their victims were perverts. "Stewart's reputation was that of a fluter," stated the defense in one such case. "It [was] generally understood in his company what he [was]."[140] In another case, Private Smith, a man believed to be a "moral pervert," "was monkeying around with everybody" one night in the camp stockade. He approached two different prisoners who each warned him that "he had better get away from [their] bunk[s]." Prisoner Frisby called out to Smith and asked him to come over to Frisby's bunk. Smith said no, but Frisby took Smith by the arm and pulled him to his bunk. In view of the other men, Frisby penetrated Smith, who appeared to be in considerable pain, saying, "[Y]ou don't know how it hurts." In court-martialing

[136] Court-martial file no. 117037, 1918, Records of the Judge Advocate General, RG 153.
[137] Court-martial file no. 143190, 1921, Records of the Judge Advocate General, RG 153. I saw a number of cases in which men who reported being sodomized were not allowed to eat with other men. "I didn't want to eat off the same plate that he did." Court-martial file no. 148066, 1921, Records of the Judge Advocate General, RG 153.
[138] *A Manual for Courts-Martial*, 439.
[139] Court-martial file no. 147300, 1921, Records of the Judge Advocate General, RG 153.
[140] Court-martial file no. 175963, 1927, Records of the Judge Advocate General, RG 153.

Frisby, the court ruled that Smith had consented to the act and was "therefore . . . a principal with Frisby." Both men were sentenced to five years in the federal penitentiary.[141]

In cases where military courts saw consent as completely lacking, however, they acted to protect the men who were judged to be so-called perverts in their units. One private was "half crying," when he reported that three men in his unit held him down while two of the men raped him. Despite the fact that his attackers claimed that the private "was used to doing it," the man's assailants were found guilty and sentenced to five years in prison.[142] In another case, one soldier in the guardhouse found out that a soldier named Piedmont "was a degenerate," and forced the man to fellate him. Piedmont, laughing witnesses told the court, made "this funny noise . . . 'ghrr' . . . 'ghrr' . . . like he was being choked." Despite Piedmont's reputation as a degenerate, the court found his attacker guilty of assault.[143] In still another instance, Private Neuse told a man named Shandor that he had better "come across."[144] Neuse struck Shandor and then raped him. Shandor was in pain, and asked Neuse not "to stick it in so far." In response, Neuse struck Shandor again. With many witnesses around, Shandor cried out, "Mama, help me." The men nearby did nothing to assist him, but Neuse was later sentenced to five years in the penitentiary.[145] Not infrequently in these types of assaults, male victims referenced their gendered position in the attack to call forth the state's protection: "They ravished me like they would a woman," one cried.[146] "I was raped," said another, "like a bad woman."[147]

This brutality is breathtaking but also distorting. Such cases can make it seem that most sex between soldiers during and after the First World War was violent. Rather, much of the sex between soldiers *that was policed* was violent. These cases are a window less into sexual culture than into sexual regulation. They help make sense of the puzzle that confronted psychologist Lewis Terman's 1936 study of forty-six army prisoners serving sentences for sodomy. Terman "reported that in practically every case the prisoners [had] . . . played the active part."[148] Where

[141] Court-martial file no. 138877, 1929, Records of the Judge Advocate General, RG 153.
[142] Court-martial file no. 143190, 1921, Records of the Judge Advocate General, RG 153.
[143] Court-martial file no. 144568, 1921, Records of the Judge Advocate General, RG 153. The man's six-month sentence in this case was, however, rather light.
[144] "Come across" is common World War I–era vernacular and means roughly the same thing as "put out." Another variation of this is to "come cocoa."
[145] Court-martial file no. 144764, 1921, Records of the Judge Advocate General, RG 153.
[146] Court-martial file no. 143190, 1921, Records of the Judge Advocate General, RG 153.
[147] Court-martial file no.154265, 1922, Records of the Judge Advocate General, RG 153.
[148] Terman, *Sex and Personality*, 241.

were all the pathics? Quite a few—if court-martial cases from a few years earlier are any measure—were still in the service.

What is remarkable here is not the army's prosecution of violent and public sexual acts. Disparate sexual cultures were an obvious lightning rod for simmering class tensions between enlisted men and officers, as was the push and pull about who would control the exercise of state violence.[149] Moreover, encounters that were out in the open and/or violent were the exchanges most likely to come to the army's attention, and court-martialing soldiers who committed acts of sodomy was a long-standing practice. What is notable instead is the blend of traditional and modern at work here, as illustrated, for example, by the way that military lawyers increasingly began to bring psychiatrists and sexologists into sodomy trials to provide testimony about sexual perversion. (Yes, one such doctor testified, he'd read the "the standard works" on "psychopathic sexualis" in medical school.)[150] Occasionally, court-martial boards also began to include statements that one or the other party in the case was a sexual psychopath whose condition "existed prior to enlistment" and was not "caused by military service."[151] In the bastion of traditional military justice, then, military officials demonstrated their appreciation of perversion as "a nervous affliction rather than a criminal offense," as one naval officer put it in 1924.[152] Even if they were not yet ready to respond administratively to that new knowledge, military officials were becoming fluent in sexology, and increasingly interested in more than the fact of sodomy.

Debating Change

Indeed, the appropriateness of a criminal framework for treating what was coming to be seen as a psychological disorder was taken up briefly by the navy in the mid-1920s, and more extensively by the army in the 1930s. In the navy, in response to one officer's assertion that he believed punishing perversion to be ineffective and irrational, the chief of the Bureau of Medicine circulated a memo that differentiated among sexual

[149] World War I marked the high point of vigilantism and violence in U.S. political culture more generally. See Christopher Capozzola, "The Only Badge Needed Is Your Patriotic Fervor: Vigilance, Coercion, and the Law in World War I America," *Journal of American History* 88 (March 2002): 1354–82.

[150] Court-martial file no. 154190, 1922, Records of the Judge Advocate General, RG 153.

[151] Court-martial file no. 193200, 1930, Records of the Judge Advocate General, RG 153.

[152] R. T. Whitten to Commanding Officer, February 27, 1924, "Punishment of Offenses Involving Sexual Offenses," file no. 127574 (34), box 528, General Correspondence 1912–1925, Records of the Bureau of Medicine and Surgery, RG 52.

offenders. Some who were "normally heterosexual" would behave homosexually under the influence of alcohol, he noted, but he also provided a psychoanalytic account of homosexuality in some as a failure to progress beyond a certain developmental stage. He thus recommended more flexibility in the navy's approach to the problem and that "the individual should first be studied by a competent psychiatrist before being brought to trial."[153] But the navy didn't have the resources to adopt a more flexible approach; instead, the chief of the Bureau of Navigation responded to the medical officer's recommendation with pragmatism. *"As competent psychiatrists are not available,"* he wrote, "it is felt that the best interests of the service would be met by continuing the usual practice of trying such cases by court-martial."[154]

Army policymakers—beginning in the 1930s—also asked whether it made more sense to discharge perverts than to imprison sodomists. (Navy policy had not changed in the intervening years.) In part, army commanders worried about the issue of housing men convicted of sodomy with other military offenders. "There is a case at Ft. Leavenworth," one general wrote, "where the post commander constrains the man in a separate cell to keep him from performing."[155] The influence of such men on others whose avenues for "normal gratification" were suddenly "cut off" was thought to be pernicious.[156] ("To keep sex perverts as integers of a general prison population [was] like keeping rotten apples in a barrel of sound ones.")[157] Even the benefits of imprisonment seemed nebulous. So one memorandum—which medicalized perversion for both active and passive partners by defining each as psychopathic—declared prison futile.[158] There was no deterring a pervert, and certainly no curing one.

---

[153] E. R. Stitt to the Chief of the Bureau of Navigation, March 26, 1924, file no. 127574 (34), box 528, General Correspondence 1912–1925, Records of the Bureau of Medicine and Surgery, RG 52.

[154] R. H. Leigh to Commanding Officer, April 4, 1924, file no. 3711-175, box 219, General Correspondence 1913–1925, Records of the Bureau of Naval Personnel, RG 24 (emphasis added).

[155] Major General Hagood to the Adjutant General, "Disposition of Sex Perverts," September 3, 1931, decimal 253, box 1258, central decimal file 1926–1939, Records of the Adjutant General, RG 407. On the debate over imprisonment more generally, see many of the documents filed under decimal 253, boxes 1258 and 1259, central decimal file 1926–1939, Records of the Adjutant General, RG 407.

[156] G. E. Hesner, Medical Corps, to Commandant, Pacific Branch of the Disciplinary Barracks, "Sexual Perverts," November 12, 1930, decimal 253, box 1259, central decimal file 1926–1939, Records of the Adjutant General, RG 407.

[157] E.L.M., "Punishment, Enlisted Men—Homosexuality," November 25, 1930, decimal 250.1, box 116, Adjutant General's file 1935–1943, 9th Corps Area, Records of the U.S. Army Commands, RG 394.

[158] George A. Skinner to the Commanding General, September 3, 1931, decimal 253, box 1258, central decimal file 1926–1939, Records of the Adjutant General, RG 407.

Hard-liners, though, had a difficult time letting go of the penitentiary. They noted that all forty-eight states had laws against homosexual offenses (a unanimity that "appear[ed] to cease," others countered, in the lax enforcement of these laws).[159] They worried that men who were not perverts would claim to be in order to get out of the service. Mostly, they seemed to concur with a naval officer who had declared that it would be a "pity" for perverts to "entirely escape punishment."[160] But one wonders—as with the navy's assertion that it lacked the necessary psychiatrists to adopt a new procedure—what to make of a handwritten scribble on stationery from the War Department's general staff that it was "too busy to handle the issue."[161]

Fast-forwarding ahead, the military finally changed its course in the midst of the Second World War. After a debate that followed precisely the contours of the discussion that had been occurring in the army and navy for twenty years, officials decided to continue to court-martial violent sex offenses, but to administratively discharge those who admitted to or were caught engaging in consensual encounters. Adding the administrative discharge to the state's regular antihomosexual apparatus, however, did not just give the state a new way to process homosexual offenses. The new policy also provided for the administrative discharge of soldiers who confessed to having homosexual desires or to being homosexual (regardless of sexual acts). It thus shifted the fulcrum of military law, as Allan Bérubé has argued, from acts to status. It would no longer be homosexual behavior alone that the army and navy penalized, but homosexual people.[162]

Still, that shift should not be understood as an expedient substitution whereby a modernizing military traded in a Byzantine legal contraption for a sleeker administrative process. Administrative boards could move more quickly than a court-martial, but the court-martial nonetheless remained a constant part of military justice. (Around 275,000 courts-martial were conducted for all offenses in 1918, but that number approached nearly 750,000 in 1944.)[163] Indeed, because many of the sodomy cases that ended up in military courts during and immediately after World War I involved violence, they most likely would have been

[159] Brigadier General Andrew Moses to Chief of Staff, "Punishment of Sexual Perverts," January 11, 1938, decimal 253, box 1259, central decimal file 1926–1939, Records of the Adjutant General, RG 407.

[160] Commanding Office, U.S. Naval Training Station, Hampton Roads, VA, February 28, 1924, file no. 127574(34), box 528, General Correspondence 1912–1925, Records of the Bureau of Medicine and Surgery, RG 52.

[161] Adjutant General, "Memorandum for General McKinley, January 22, 1932, decimal 253, box 1259, central decimal file 1926–1939, Records of the Adjutant General, RG 407.

[162] Bérubé, *Coming Out Under Fire*, chapter 5.

[163] This statistic covers all service branches. Hillman, *Defending America*, 139–40.

resolved in the same venue had they been committed after 1944 as before. The military's adoption of the administrative discharge was, in other words, not a paring down but a building up of state machinery.

That was true not only because the administrative discharge supplemented rather than replaced the court-martial, but also because of the way that shifting the emphasis from penalizing acts to people involved a more preemptive and proactive kind of operation. During and after World War I, "psychopaths," as one officer conceded, "only [came] to [our] attention when they [got] into trouble."[164] After 1944, by contrast —with its new policy in place and virtually all army hospitals equipped "to process suspected homosexuals"—the military stopped waiting for criminal acts to occur and went out to look for those abnormal persons unfitted for military service. In order to detect homosexuals in the ranks, the military inaugurated much more aggressive vice patrols, and the numbers impacted grew from hundreds to thousands. Suspected homosexuals were sent to hospitals where they were interviewed by psychiatrists, observed by hospital staff, inventoried by the Red Cross, interrogated by military intelligence, and ultimately adjudicated by a board of officers. Finally, an expanded and empowered cadre of army and navy psychiatrists pushed for and got the kind of intensive screening of recruits that some of their colleagues had been clamoring for since 1917. They were able to ask all recruits point-blank if they were homosexual, strip them naked to look for feminine body traits (and expanded rectums), and pursue clues, such as occupational choices and teachers' impressions, for indications of effeminacy. Such techniques led the army to reject roughly five thousand soldiers for homosexuality during World War II at the point of induction—a number that dwarfed the tiny handful refused induction for similar reasons during World War I.[165]

So why not earlier? Some part of the timing has to do with simple wherewithal. World War I was not a war that built new state structures in quite the same way that World War II did. After the conclusion of that earlier conflict, the size of the U.S. Army fell from roughly 846,000 to remain under 200,000 until 1940, and as Michael Sherry writes, the Great War's "jerry-manded machinery to mobilize men and material was soon in shambles."[166] These were not the most propitious years, in other

[164] Stearns, "The Psychiatric Examination of Recruits," 231.

[165] Bérubé, *Coming Out Under Fire*, especially chapter 1 and chapter 5.

[166] Cuff, "War Mobilization, Institutional Learning, and State Building in the United States," 399. By the mid-1920s, the U.S. armed forces were 10 to 20 percent of the size of forces maintained by nations such as France and Britain, and "national defense claimed only a minor part of the nation's resources." Michael S. Sherry, *In the Shadow of War: The United States since the 1930s* (New Haven, CT: Yale University Press, 1995), 5–6, 9. By con-

words, for new state initiatives (initiatives that required more psychiatrists, more military police, more hospital orderlies, and more administrators with more time to "handle the issue"). But the delay was
not only a matter of resources. As political scientists contend, policymaking entails both *knowing* and *deciding*.[167] Certainly the evidentiary
record makes clear that military officials during the interwar period
were becoming more aware of perversion as a phenomenon as well as
its apparent prevalence among soldiers. Indeed, as compared to their
Progressive-era counterparts in the immigration bureaucracy, military
officials in the 1920s and 1930s were a good deal less befuddled about
homosexuality. Yet figuring out that something exists is not the same as
determining that it is the thing that matters. Military officials worried a
great deal during these years about questions of institutional disorder,
violence, and reputability, but they hadn't yet come to agreement that
queer men didn't belong in the service. There isn't even consistent evidence to suggest that they took great offense at consensual and discreet
relationships.

The irony is, of course, that this was in no way a kinder world for sex
and gender nonconformists, as court-martial records well illustrate.
Neither does the absence of an administrative apparatus to deal explicitly with the queerness of these soldiers mean that the period should be
dismissed as a regulatory dead spot. The military channeled its expanding knowledge about perversion through its traditional disciplinary
machinery, the court-martial. If that instrument turned out to be imper-
fectly fitted for the task—if it tended to penalize publicity and violence
much more than perversion per se—the way it was used during and
after World War I nonetheless paved the way for the paradigm shift that
came later. As military courts established the equal guilt of both parties
in an act of sodomy, they pushed the state's regulatory apparatus closer
to the way that homosexuality would come to be identified at midcentury, by sexual-object choice rather than gender inversion alone. Here
then, in the World War I–era courts-martial, is an early tip-off that legal
authorities would be as important as their medical counterparts in making that norm hegemonic.

Finally, the way that wartime and interwar courts-martial highlighted connections between psychopathy and violence may have reflected and encouraged a tightening association between perversion,

---

trast, "after the defeat of France in June 1940," Lizbeth Cohen writes, "Congress appro-
priated at one stroke more than the nation had spent in total on World War I." Lizbeth
Cohen, *A Consumers' Republic: The Politics of Mass Consumption in Postwar America* (New
York: Alfred A. Knopf, 2003), 63. On the permanency of state structures after World War
II, see chapter 5.

[167] Heclo, *Modern Social Politics in Britain and Sweden*, 305.

danger, and social instability in the immediate aftermath of the war. The notion that psychopaths were roving sex predators was, indeed, an idea that caught fire in the 1930s, and as we will see in the next chapter, fixed itself especially to the figure of the Depression-era transient who was "unattached" from home and family. Before and after the Depression, however, social commentators blamed more than just economic downturn for this troubling population of unattached men. The national government, one sociologist complained, encouraged this "social evil . . . by appealing to youth to enter . . . the army and navy."[168] Was it perhaps in the nation's service, then, that these young men acquired their taste for a womanless life of mobility sweetened by the rough intimacy of their fellows?

[168] Albert M. Shulman, "Social Attitudes of Transients with Particular Reference to Their Personal Problems" (PhD diss., University of Southern California, 1928), 78.

CHAPTER 3

WELFARE

"Most Fags Are Floaters"

The Problem of "Unattached Persons"
during the Early New Deal, 1933–1935

———⊖———

T he early years of the Depression were not especially kind to the veterans of the First World War. Hard times threw them, like millions of
other Americans, on to their last resources and finally pushed them to
desperate action. In the case of some twenty thousand veterans, such
measures involved demanding early payment of their service bonus,
and when refused, heading to Washington, DC, to set up an encamp-
ment to protest from the banks of the Potomac. There, during the angry
summer of 1932, they stayed for weeks, in the words of historian William
Leuchtenberg, "homeless, jobless, and aimless." Opposed in their crusade not only by Veterans Administrator Frank Hines, but also by President Herbert Hoover himself, the "Bonus Army" was finally dispersed
by four troops of cavalry, six tanks, and a "column of steel helmeted in-
fantry with fixed bayonets" led by General Douglas MacArthur.[1]

The event is usually chronicled as sealing Hoover's loss in the 1932
election, but the issues the Bonus Army raised did not go down with his
defeat. Immediately upon taking office, the Roosevelt administration
would have to deal on an even greater scale with the way that the Depression unmoored desperate people from their communities, and set
them out wandering across the nation in search of a way to live. Many
of these transients were veterans; some were boys, and a few were women
or girls. Because the majority were people who had left home and family behind, federal officials called them "non-family people," or the
"unattached." (The mass family migrations like the one symbolized by
John Steinbeck's Joad family were more a hallmark of the later 1930s.)[2]

---

[1] William E. Leuctenberg, *Franklin D. Roosevelt and the New Deal* (New York: Harper and
Row, 1963), 14–15.

[2] Joan M. Crouse, *The Homeless Transient in the Great Depression: New York State, 1929–
1941* (Albany: State University of New York, 1986), 191; John Steinbeck, *The Grapes of
Wrath* (New York: Viking Press, 1939).

As states and municipalities clamored for help with the drifting hordes arriving daily, New Dealers implemented two federal programs to address the problem. In 1933, the Federal Transient Program (FTP) was established as part of the Federal Emergency Relief Administration (FERA). The program created a national system of camps and shelters for mostly male migrants. That same year, the quasi-military Civilian Conservation Corps (CCC) set out to *prevent* transiency among young unemployed men by placing them in camps to carry out conservation projects.

The FTP and the CCC were closely related in strategy and outreach, yet the results of the two programs were remarkably different. The story of the CCC is more familiar (and therefore less elaborately told in this chapter). It was one of the most successful of the New Deal programs, lasting a full decade, and enrolling roughly 2.5 million young men during those years. It was so popular, in fact, that Congress seriously considered making it a permanent agency. By contrast, the FTP was one of the most disparaged of all the New Deal programs, and despite the troubling persistence of transiency, the program was abruptly terminated in 1935. Another striking difference, not unrelated to each program's popularity and life span, was the way that the problem of sexual perversion figured in each setting. One notes a glaring absence in this regard in the records (and historiography) of the CCC, while the FTP was perpetually shadowed by concerns about perversion among its clientele.

This chapter explores these differences between the FTP and the CCC, focusing on the failure of the former program (in part by contrasting it with the success of its better-known counterpart). Both camp programs were gender-segregated institutions where men worked, ate, recreated, and slept together. But the transient in particular was associated with the distinctive sexual subculture of hoboes and bums in which homosexuality featured prominently. So the FTP was burdened from its inception by the image of the depraved bindle stiff.[3] FTP officials responded by attempting to distinguish the virtue of the Depression-era transient from the hobo of old, suggesting that youthful migrants in particular needed to be protected from sexual advances by the latter type. This discourse of sexual vulnerability, however, did not mitigate but rather attached greater stigma to the program. Moreover, the FTP's promoters were unable to overcome the moral suspicion aroused by single, able-bodied men on relief. Indeed, while federal aid for unattached men was clearly not the same thing as federal support for homosexuality, what is strik-

---

[3] "Bindle stiff" is a slang term for a hobo (who carries a bedroll); bindle is derived from bundle.

ing in the FTP records is the discursive linkage between them: critics of the FTP felt that the program not only enabled men to walk out on the dull responsibility of wife and family, but simultaneously established a state-sponsored haven for sex perverts. The CCC avoided such charges. The program's militarism created the (false) impression that enrollees were soldiers-in-training rather than reliefers. What they were, in reality, was more akin to breadwinners-in-training, as members were required to allot most of their monthly income to a "dependent." While the definition of who counted as a dependent was incredibly loose, this policy enabled CCC officials to claim that its camps for single men were really supporting families, thereby distancing the program from the conjoined stigma of the transient and the pervert.

The CCC's attempt to disguise the extent to which it also served the unattached was belied by the requirement that CCC enrollees be unmarried. The dependency allotment helped to conceal the significance of that fact; it also sheds light on how the FTP's unabashed support for single men without families quickly led the program into disrepute. The FTP program merits attention as distinct from other, more commonly studied welfare state programs because it was *nonfamilial* in its approach. It was aimed not at shoring up breadwinners or helping needy mothers, but rather at addressing the severe economic needs of individuals considered apart from family units.[4] The transient program thus illustrates how the economic crisis of the Depression, "with its widespread dislocation of men, women, and children from their 'normal' location," opened up radical possibilities for the structuring of American social provision.[5] That radicalism was of course limited by the programmatic focus on men—whose neediness alarmed policymakers in a way that women's did not—and its fleeting nature. With the demise of the FTP and eventually the CCC (which was despite the rhetoric a program for the unattached), generous federal-level programs

[4]On the gendering/familialism of welfare policy more generally, the historiography is voluminous. See especially Linda Gordon, *Pitied But Not Entitled: Single Mothers and the History of Welfare, 1890–1935* (Cambridge, MA: Harvard University Press, 1994); Alice Kessler-Harris, *In Pursuit of Equity: Women, Men, and the Quest for Economic Citizenship in 20th Century America* (Oxford: Oxford University Press, 2001). The history of laws/policies pertaining to the unmarried has been understudied. But see Ariela R. Dubler, "In the Shadow of Marriage: Single Women and the Legal Construction of the Family and the State," *Yale Law Journal* 112 (2003): 1641–1715.

[5]Ellen C. Potter, "Brief of Statement Made in Re: Transients and Homeless by Representatives of the National Committee of Transients and Homeless to the Federal Emergency Relief Administrator, Mr. Hopkins," June 27, 1933, box 82, Old General Subject Series, FERA central files 1933–1936, Records of the Works Progress Administration (WPA), RG 69, National Archives, College Park, MD.

specifically aimed at "nonfamily" people would vanish from the steadily expanding American welfare state.[6] The FTP in particular not only reveals an alternative vision of social provision, but offers as well a unique glimpse into the way that a discourse of perversion helped to undermine that alternative.

This occurred despite the fact that homosexuality and heterosexuality were not yet categories that organized federal welfare policy in explicit ways. As with the Bureau of Immigration during the Progressive era and the World War I–era military, examining an arena of the state as its authority expanded reveals that the process of state-building itself increased federal awareness of the problem of perversion. Different arenas of the state, moreover, were not isolated laboratories—various bureaucracies transferred their knowledge even as the specific mission at hand changed. The superintendent of one FTP camp, for example, "remembered his army experience and [was] very alert to the development of abnormal relationships" among transients.[7] And a group of social work professionals who worked for the FTP commented in 1934 on "the significant and appalling situation of homosexuality which has been manifest *since the war*."[8]

Yet just as their predecessors in the Bureau of Immigration and the military had been slow to react to perversion among aliens and soldiers, so too the response of New Deal officials to homosexuality in transient and CCC camps was characterized more by frustrated resignation than active hostility. New Dealers most often thought of perversion as something to be quietly contained rather than violently purged from early welfare state programs. Those attitudes would gradually begin to shift after 1935: first, with the termination of federal aid for the unattached during the "second" New Deal, and later, via more explicit prohibitions against homosexuality in postwar social provision.

But for now the problem is to understand that initial failure to act—a failure that owes something to the "fits and starts" quality of state expansion during these years, as well as to lingering confusion surrounding the category of homosexuality.[9] Indeed, it is impossible to cull the

[6]Some "unattached" today receive meager benefits from state-run general assistance programs for able-bodied adults without dependents.

[7]Robert S. Wilson and Dorothy B. de la Pole, *Group Treatment for Transients* (New York: National Association for Travelers Aid and Transient Service, 1934), 72.

[8]Committee on Care of Transient and Homeless, Minutes of Meeting, May 1, 1934, folder 82, National Social Welfare Assembly, Social Welfare History Archives, Minneapolis, MN (emphasis added).

[9]On the "pattern of state growth in America [as] one of fits and starts," see Meg Jacobs and Julian Zelizer, introduction to *The Democratic Experiment: New Directions in American Political History*, ed. Meg Jacobs, Julian Zelizer, and William Novak (Princeton, NJ: Princeton University Press, 2003), 2.

taint of perversion from all of the other factors that led to the public's condemnation of the transients: their dependency, their potential criminality, and above all, their mobility. The state, likewise, made only rhetorical but no actual attempts to sort relief recipients as deserving or undeserving according to their sexuality. Yet rather than struggle against this murkiness, it must be embraced as historically important and itself part of the story. For this is still the prehistory of a federal policy cleaved by a sharp homosexual-heterosexual binary. Meanwhile, the FTP and the CCC are the perfect locations—state-created enclaves of male intimacy—to see murky categories begin to come into focus, and to watch the state as it gathered even more information on homosexuality, filing it away for future action.

On the Road

The first evidence collected by both federal officials and their allies in social work and sociology, however, pointed to the *heterosexual* family in crisis. Numerous reports were written at the Depression's onset about young married couples who could not afford to set up their own households, and so stayed with parents or moved into small, shabby apartments with one or two other couples. Some marriages were indefinitely postponed. And when that happened, as one contemporary noted, "the normal longing of these individuals for intimate companionship with the opposite sex [was] thwarted or turned into illicit channels."[10] The Depression, the Rabbi Sidney E. Goldstein concluded during congressional hearings in early 1933, was "a menace to . . . moral life."[11]

Most troubling of all was what unemployment seemed to do to American men. Psychologists and social workers believed that unemployment created neurosis among men. Laid-off workers were compared to the shell shock patients of the Great War, although unemployment inflicted psychological damage more gradually.[12] For a while,

[10] "Youth Comes of Age," pamphlet, June 1938, box 611, Smith-Melvin file, General Administrative Correspondence and Data, Records of the Research Project, 1935–1942, Records of the WPA, RG 69.

[11] U.S. Congress, Senate, Committee on Manufacturers, *A Bill to Provide for Cooperation by the Federal Government with the Several States in Relieving the Hardship and Suffering Caused by Unemployment, and for Other Purposes*, 72nd Cong., 2nd sess., January 3–17, 1944, 143.

[12] George K. Pratt, *Morale: The Mental Hygiene of Unemployment* (New York: National Committee for Mental Hygiene, 1933), 15. Shell shock was considered, Elaine Showalter argues, a kind of male hysteria, and "when military doctors and psychiatrists dismissed shell shock patients as cowards, they were often hinting at effeminacy or homosexuality." See Elaine Showalter, *The Female Malady: Women, Madness, and English Culture, 1830–1980* (New York: Pantheon Books, 1985), 172.

many workers remained optimistic, leaving the house each day to look for work, believing that a break might come tomorrow or next week. But protracted failure eventually broke them. "I guess we'll all be wearing skirts pretty soon," one unemployed man told the economist E. Wight Bakke. Finally going to the relief office to apply for assistance was the "last resort in a losing battle to remain normal."[13]

Yet a trip to the relief office also meant, one citizen fretted in a letter to the president, "a total surrender of manhood."[14] A man who asked for relief "admitted failure in his attempt to be independent and self supporting." Not just the fact of relief but also the way it was delivered (often a grocery order) was reported to be humiliating. So was the requirement that a man applying for relief put himself under the authority of a caseworker, who was most likely a woman. In some cases, men were sidelined altogether. "The investigators are chiefly women and deal . . . with the women in the family," Bakke wrote in his study of unemployment, and "this is a further blow."[15] The degradation of male unemployment was complete when husbands began to assume feminine responsibilities around the house. "His failure was underlined by this transgression of sex boundaries," wrote one social scientist. "Some men took so easily to their new work that one must suspect that it fulfilled an inner need." Finally, wives started to resent and even deride their husbands. One man told an interviewer that his wife now "wore the pants" in the family and refused him sex. "She keeps repeating, 'F.D.R. is the head of the household since he gives me the money.'"[16] Under such conditions, Secretary of Labor Frances Perkins warned, the wage earner (going "around to the relief agencies twice a week to get the [food] basket") was in danger of "becoming detached from his family through desertion."[17] The secretary hinted at what others would say

[13] E. Wight Bakke, *The Unemployed Worker: A Study of the Task of Making a Living without a Job* (New Haven, CT: Yale University Press, 1940), 363.

[14] Alathea Briggs to Franklin D. Roosevelt, box 4, General Correspondence 1933–1942, Division of Selection, Records of the Civilian Conservation Corps (CCC), RG 35, National Archives, College Park, MD.

[15] Bakke, *The Unemployed Worker*, 363, 354.

[16] Sol Weiner Ginsburg, "What Unemployment Does to People: A Study in Adjustment to Crisis," *American Journal of Psychiatry* 99 (November 1942): 444; Eli Ginzberg, *The Unemployed* (New Brunswick, NJ: Transaction Publishers, 2004): 76–77 (orig. pub. 1943). Women withholding sex from out-of-work husbands was a commonly remarked on phenomena during the Depression years. See, for example, Michael Kimmel, *Manhood in America: A Cultural History* (New York: Free Press, 1996), 200.

[17] U.S. Congress, House and Senate, Senate Committee on Education and Labor and House Committee on Labor, *Joint Hearings on a Bill for the Relief of Unemployment through the Performance of Useful Public Work and for Other Purposes*, 73rd Cong., 1st sess., March 23 and 24, 1933, 27.

more directly: out-of-work husbands were hitting the road to escape their dominating wives and the feminization of housework.[18] Some married men would, one report warned, "never return to claim the family relationship."[19]

As much as going on the dole may have created strife between married couples, though, it was single men, often unable to secure any form of state or local relief, who were on the road in the greatest numbers. "The young and unmarried have been left out of the calculation by most of the relief agencies," Perkins remarked during congressional hearings.[20] One destitute widower testified that he had "been to relief boards, and they all say, 'nothing for single men.'"[21] So vicious was the prejudice cultivated against single persons in relief administration circles, wrote a social welfare official in Wisconsin, that even high school–age children could threaten a family's relief check: "Parents were criticized for having able-bodied sons and even daughters living in the household on supplies furnished by the public, and withdrawal of assistance was threatened if these children did not 'get out and find a job.'"[22]

Relief practices that were at best indifferent and sometimes hostile to the unmarried thus led many of the unattached to leave home in search of work. (Approximately 395,000 single men—and a trickle of single women—were estimated to be on the road by the mid-1930s, as compared to 16,000 family groups.[23]) The overall numbers were large enough for the transient problem to have attracted significant national attention even before Roosevelt took office. So many transients hopped freight trains—as many as 1,500 passed through one midwestern hub in a single day in 1932—that railroad officials were often powerless to stop them from riding.[24] They traveled south and west, looking for the occa-

[18] One probation and parole officer, for example, worried about "men who have been driven from home by neurotic wives and suffered demoralization from unemployment." Gordon D. Shipman to W. Frank Persons, April 15, 1936, box 889, General Correspondence 1933–1942, Records of the CCC, RG 35.

[19] Report on Transient Youth in the State of Illinois, April 1933, box 4, General Correspondence 1933–1942, Division of Selection, Records of the CCC, RG 35; Ellery F. Reed, *Federal Transient Program: An Evaluative Survey* (New York: Committee on Care of Transient and Homeless, 1934), 93.

[20] U.S. Congress, House and Senate, *Joint Hearings on a Bill for the Relief of Unemployment*, 22.

[21] U.S. Congress, House, Committee on Banking and Currency, *Hearings before Subcommittee to Amend the Emergency Relief and Construction Act of 1932*, 72nd Cong., 2nd sess., February 2–3, 1933, 41.

[22] Fred Wilcox to Ellen C. Potter, June 20, 1934, box 79, Old General Subject Series, FERA central files 1933–1936, Records of the WPA, RG 69.

[23] Differences in statistical estimates of the transient population are discussed in Crouse, *The Homeless Transient in the Great Depression*, 182–83.

[24] "Memorandum on the Transient Boy," U.S. Children's Bureau, 1932, box 4, General

sional odd job, begging food from farmwives, and sleeping in huge "jungles" along the railroad tracks or in cheap "flophouses" in town.[25] Most cities—overwhelmed with their own needy citizens—had nothing to give the newcomers and, moreover, no obligation to help the nonresident poor who lacked a legal settlement.[26] Thus, an encounter with local officials usually ended with a night in jail or a shelter (and hopefully a meal), followed by a ride out of town the next morning. Social workers decried the "passing on" policy as merely encouraging mendicancy. "About a million-and-a-half men and boys and a smaller number of women, girls, and drifting families are thus being passed along throughout this country," one relief official wrote.[27]

Local communities not only lacked the resources to help the transients, they were afraid of them. Ragged and dirty, "among the moving population," it was difficult to tell the good "from the vicious."[28] Mobility was to some degree problematic in itself, but the apprehension that mobility caused was never fully separate from its sexual and gendered content. Settlement law (rules for belonging legally to a community that enabled an individual to claim poor relief) was, for example, gendered in that a woman's domicile followed her husband's. (One California report told of a San Francisco woman who lost her right to relief because she married a transient without legal settlement.)[29] And the literal cessation of movement was only a precondition for *settling down*, which implied not only steady employment and property ownership, but marriage and reproduction as well.

Transients, by contrast, were said to have an "urge" that had to be gratified or "wanderlust"—a term that quite literally connected their

---

Correspondence 1933–1942, Division of Selection, Records of the CCC, RG 35. "The railroads have practically thrown up their hands as to the problem," social reformer Grace Abbott told Congress early in 1933. U.S. Congress, Senate, Committee on Banking and Currency, *Hearings on Further Unemployment Relief through the Reconstruction Finance Corporation*, 72nd Cong., 2nd sess., Feb 2–3, 1933, 94.

[25] On the prevalence of "perverts" in flophouses, see David Scheyer, "Flop-House," *Nation* 139 (August 22, 1934): 216–18. Jungles were large camps where transients congregated (usually at railroad crossings, and also referred to as "stems"); for a dime, a transient could get a "flop" in a seedy rooming house.

[26] Settlement laws (which date to the colonial period) varied from place to place, but most required at least one year's residence to be eligible for relief.

[27] Clarence King to Sumner Simpson, December 21, 1933, box 80, Old General Subject Series, FERA central files 1933–1936, Records of the WPA, RG 69.

[28] U.S. Congress, House, Select Committee Investigating National Defense Migration, *Analysis of Material Bearing on the Economic and Social Aspects of the Case of Fred F. Edwards vs. the People of the State of California*, 76th Cong., 1st sess., 1939, 54.

[29] M. H. Lewis, *Transients in California* (San Francisco: State Relief Administration of California, Special Surveys and Studies, 1936), 40. On settlement law, see Philip E. Ryan, *Migration and Social Welfare* (New York: Russell Sage Foundation, 1940), 49–61; Harry M.

movement with unrestrained sexuality.[30] "This habit of shifting about gratifies the natural inclination called lust," opined one medical authority, "and serves as an outlet for unstable emotions."[31] Physical and "moral freedom" went together for those who were driven to "satisfy sexual desire" apart from "a stable home life."[32] Transiency was not only associated with nonmarital sexuality in general, but with sexual perversion in particular. Since at least the turn of the century, homosexuality was considered a defining characteristic of vagrants, tramps, and hoboes who "promenade[d] unashamed on the public highways," preferring "rough-hewn male camaraderie" over a "normal" life of work and family.[33] In the "womanless state of transiency," one Ohio caseworker concluded, the "perverted sex instinct" and "lack of ambition . . . were one."[34]

The belief that perverts were to be found among the transient population was thus widely held and sometimes even promoted. The small town of Britt, Iowa, ballyhooed itself as the nation's hobo headquarters by staging an annual pageant in which the Hobo King was given for his queen "a local lad, chosen for his youthful beauty."[35] Dr. Samuel Kahn was less celebratory in his assessment that "most fags are floaters," as he wrote in 1937, "and move from town to town."[36] Kahn's assertions referenced a predominantly same-sex sexual culture in which homosex-

---

Hirsch, *Compilation of Settlement Laws of All States in the United States* (Chicago: American Public Welfare Association, 1939); Harry M. Hirsch, *Our Settlement Laws: Their Origin; Their Lack of Uniformity; Proposed Measures of Reform* (Albany: State of New York Department of Public Welfare, 1933). For the way that the law of domicile/settlement pertains to marriage, see Hendrik Hartog, *Man and Wife in America: A History* (Cambridge, MA: Harvard University Press, 2002). On the relationship of settlement, poor relief, and citizenship more generally, see Kunal M. Parker, "State, Citizenship, and Territory: The Legal Construction of Immigrants in Antebellum Massachusetts," *Law and History Review* 19 (Fall 2001): 583–644.

[30] John Nye Webb, *The Migratory Casual Worker* (Washington, DC: U.S. Government Printing Office, 1937), 90.

[31] P. R. Vessie, "The Wanderlust Impulse," *Medical Journal and Record* 120 (July–December 1924): 20.

[32] Edwin H. Sutherland and Harvey J. Locke, *Twenty Thousand Homeless Men: A Study of Unemployed Men in the Chicago Shelters* (Chicago: J. B. Lippincott, 1936), 24.

[33] Vessie, "The Wanderlust Impulse," 20; Kenneth L. Kusmer, *Down and Out, on the Road: The Homeless in American History* (Oxford: Oxford University Press, 2002), 141.

[34] William G. Downs, "Statistical Study of 373 Clients in Transient Camp #3," July 16, 1934, box 32, Records of the Transient Division 1933–1936, Records of the WPA, RG 69; George Henry and Alfred Gross, "The Homosexual Delinquent," *Mental Hygiene* 25 (1941): 425–30.

[35] Kenneth Allsop, *Hard Travellin': The Hobo and His History* (London: Hodder and Stoughton, 1967), 224–25.

[36] Samuel Kahn, *Mentality and Homosexuality* (Boston: Meador Publishing Company, 1937), 127.

ual activity probably was quite common. A 1928 study of the social problems of transients included a report from the Midnight Mission, for example, where two "wolves" routinely invited "young boys to a room for immoral purposes."[37] Such instances were not anomalous, according to Josiah Flynt's account of life on the bum: "Every hobo in the United States," he wrote in 1907, "knows what 'unnatural intercourse' means."[38]

This may have been especially true during the Depression, when survival on the road sometimes led men and boys (as well as women and girls) to trade sexual favors for food or money. One Los Angeles transient declared, for instance, that he could "get by all right" by living "off . . . the queers."[39] Similarly, Tom Kromer's fictionalized account of his own experiences as a vagrant during the Depression—*Waiting for Nothing*—included a scene in which the homeless protagonist allows himself to be picked up in a park by a perfumed and rouged man, who "twists and wiggles with mincing steps." The narrator is repulsed when "the queer" touches his leg, commenting, "These pansies give me the willies, but I have got to get myself a feed." The two agree to meet later in the park, and while the narrator waits he learns that his date is quite wealthy and known around town as "Mrs. Carter." The park is full of "queers," as well as the "stiffs" who are jealous of the narrator's new meal ticket. As Mrs. Carter comes "frisking" down the walk, the stiffs wink and whistle as she passes. When she starts to leave with Kromer's narrator, "the stiffs scowl" at him. He follows Mrs. Carter back to her apartment and finally into her bed, because "you can always depend on a stiff having to pay for what he gets." "I am ashamed of this," he says. "I am sick in the stomach, I am so ashamed of all this. What can I do? . . . A stiff has got to live."[40]

Kromer's account sheds interesting light on a statement by Secretary Perkins that the Depression had "forced people to the most unfortunate practices, things that they did not want to do."[41] Whether or not she had in mind a scenario like the one that transpired between Kromer's stiff and Mrs. Carter, there is good evidence that New Deal officials were well-informed of the particular sexual culture of the road, and that such

---

[37] Albert M. Shulman, *Social Attitudes towards Transients with Particular Reference to Their Personal Problems* (PhD diss., University of Southern California, 1928), 97.

[38] Josiah Flynt, "Homosexuality among Tramps," in *Studies in the Psychology of Sex, Volume I*, by Havelock Ellis (New York: Random House, 1940), 360 (appendix A in part 4).

[39] Lewis, *Transients in California*, 225.

[40] Tom Kromer, *Waiting for Nothing: And Other Writings* (Athens: University of Georgia Press, 1986), 43–53.

[41] U.S. Congress, House and Senate, *Joint Hearings on a Bill for the Relief of Unemployment*, 22.

awareness helped condition the federal response to the transient problem. For example, New Dealers read Carlton Parker, the agricultural
economist whose classic 1920 essay, "The Casual Laborer," suggested
that living conditions among itinerants bred a perversion "as developed and recognized as the well known similar practice in prisons and
reformatories."[42] The New Deal's own Nels Anderson had also written
a 1920 study of hoboes that elaborately detailed their sexual practices.
"I knew," he said most pointedly, "that hobohemia had its homos."[43]
Moreover, government officials were privy to the reports of vice investigators as they expanded their traditional beat from the urban red-light
districts and army cantonments to search out moral dangers along
highways and railroad tracks. ("The 'wolf' and 'pansy' are there," read
one commission's report on a Saint Louis jungle that made its way to
FTP officials.)[44] Knowledge of the moral dangers of the road most likely
came to government officials as well through many of the same channels by which it was reaching the general public. Accounts like Kromer's—including many memoirs of life "on the bum"—were becoming
a staple of Depression literature.[45] There were, moreover, so many social workers, academics, and other journalists "slumming" as transients
and writing journalistic exposés about their experiences, that *Harper's*
magazine suggested there were as many undercover bums out riding
the rails as real ones.[46]

It was thus both expert advice and "persistent rumors"—especially
about the number of young men and boys on the road—that prompted
the U.S. Children's Bureau to undertake its own study of transiency in
1932. The resulting memorandum on the "Transient Boy" outlined the
risks of the current epidemic, including "degenerates and perverts [who
were] eager to initiate new boys into evil habits and teach them how they
can pick up a few odd dollars in any big city."[47] That report "most effec-

[42]Carlton H. Parker, *The Casual Laborer and Other Essays* (Seattle: University of Washington Press, 1920), 73–74.

[43]Nels Anderson, *On Hobos and Homelessness* (Chicago: University of Chicago Press,
1999), 203.

[44]Saint Louis Community Council, September 20, 1933, box 32, Records of the Transient Division 1933–1936, Records of the WPA, RG 69; Letter from Harry W. Butz, High-
way Investigator, December 11, 1933, box 80, Old General Subject Series, FERA central
files 1933–1936, Records of the WPA, RG 69.

[45]Two Depression-era works that describe young jobless men engaging in sex with
"perverts" for food or money include John Worby, *The Autobiography of a Tramp* (New
York: Lee Furman, 1937); Clifford R. Shaw, *The Jack Roller: A Delinquent Boy's Own Story*
(Chicago: University of Chicago Press, 1966). The latter was originally published in 1930.

[46]Joseph Fulling Fishman, "Bum's Rush," *Harper's* 168 (May 1934): 750–51.

[47]"Memorandum on the Transient Boy," U.S. Children's Bureau, 1932, box 4, General
Correspondence 1933–1942, Division of Selection, Records of the CCC, RG 35.

tively dramatized the situation for the country," generating a "wave of popular articles" with titles like "Boys on the Loose" and "Uncle Sam's Runaway Boys."[48]

As a result of such publicity, congressional hearings held during 1932 and 1933 devoted considerable attention to problems of the nonresident poor. When the Federal Emergency Relief Act of 1933 established the FERA to administer $500 million in matching grants to states for general relief spending, it thus also set aside federal monies for the care of "needy persons who have no legal settlement in any one state or community."[49] In order to qualify for federal transient funds, each state had to establish a transient bureau that was run under the FERA's oversight. Within months, the FTP had taken form: the program had a national staff (led initially by social worker Morris Lewis, but soon run by Lewis's assistant, Elizabeth Wickenden), and forty states had set up shelters and camps for those persons who had been within the boundaries of a state for less than twelve months. There were even camps for transient veterans run in partnership with the Veterans Administration. By 1935, more than three hundred thousand transients would be receiving care under the program.[50] Significantly, the FTP was the only FERA program that had 100 percent federal funding.[51] Policymakers had prioritized transients in relief spending because of overlapping concerns

[48] Around this same time, the Family Welfare Association of America and the National Association of Travelers Aid Societies also conducted special studies on transiency. U.S. Congress, House, Select Committee to Investigate the Interstate Migration of Destitute Citizens, *Hearings on Interstate Migration, Part I. New York City Hearings*, 76th Cong., 3rd sess., July 29–31, 1940, 52; Philip E. Ryan, *Migration and Social Welfare: An Approach to the Problem of the Non-Settled Person in the Community* (New York: Russell Sage Foundation, 1940), 8; A. Wayne McMillen, "An Army of Boys on the Loose," *Survey* 68 (September 1932): 389–93; O. R. Lovejoy, "Uncle Sam's Runaway Boys," *Survey* 69 (March 1933): 99–101; R. Carter, "Boys Going Nowhere," *New Republic* 74 (March 1, 1933): 77; J. F. Healey, "Boys on the Loose," *Commonweal* 17 (March 22, 1933): 574–76.

[49] Crouse, *The Homeless Transient in the Great Depression*, 132–33; Ryan, *Migration in Social Welfare*, 8; Reed, *Federal Transient Program*, 32–35. The Federal Emergency Relief Act's provision of grants to states for direct relief was a sharp departure from previous federal relief policy. Under President Hoover, the federal government had first provided only advice and eventually loans to the states for relief purposes (under the auspices of the Reconstruction Finance Corporation). On the history of the FERA generally, see Harry L. Hopkins, *Spending to Save: The Complete Story of Relief* (New York: W. W. Norton, 1936); Charles F. Searle, *Minister of Relief: Harry Hopkins and the Great Depression* (Syracuse: Syracuse University Press, 1963); William R. Brock, *Welfare, Democracy, and the New Deal* (Cambridge: Cambridge University Press, 1988); Nancy E. Rose, *Put to Work: Relief Programs in the Great Depression* (New York: Monthly Review Press, 1994).

[50] Crouse, *The Homeless Transient in the Great Depression*, 182.

[51] Interview with Elizabeth Wickenden by Blanche D. Coll, May 28, 1986, New York City, box 2 (M99-098), Elizabeth Wickenden Papers, Archives Division, State Historical

about the threat that a large population of wanderers posed to social stability, as well as the threat that the culture of the road posed to them. It was not uncommon for both sets of fears to be conceptualized and articulated in terms of perversity.

Transients Are Normal People

The goal of transient care was to feed, clothe, and house the migrant population, so eventually they could be stabilized, returned, and reintegrated into their home communities. Initially, some state transient bureaus tried to accomplish this task by either establishing city shelters or contracting with existing congregate facilities (such as those run by local charitable associations). Situated in rough areas, these shelters seemed more alike than distinct from the flophouses and rooming houses to which they sat adjacent. After FERA administrator Harry Hopkins sent out a bulletin proclaiming camps, "the most satisfactory method of meeting the problem of the unattached male transient population," a majority of states shifted their emphasis to building camp programs. By July 1934, 189 camps had been created (usually in the countryside) to put men to work in a wholesome and controlled environment. Yet townspeople were often unhappy about the establishment of these federally sponsored transient camps a few miles outside of town. FTP officials labeled such attitudes toward the "needy stranger" as "provincialism," and encouraged Americans to "begin to think in terms of our national responsibility for all our fellows."[52] So as transients set to work to build barracks and dig latrines to make their new homes, FTP officials simultaneously embarked on a public relations campaign. That campaign had one simple message: transients were normal people in danger of being corrupted on the road.[53]

Cognizant of the "adverse publicity" that equated transients with "degenerates, vagrants, and bums," relief officials underscored in all their communiqués with the public the difference between the Depression transient and the hobo or bum of old.[54] "The public does not yet realize that the present problem is, in many respects, something new,"

Society of Wisconsin, Madison; Crouse, *The Homeless Transient in the Great Depression*, 133. See also Brock, *Welfare, Democracy, and the New Deal*, 178.

[52] Ellen C. Potter, "Mustering out the Migrants," *Survey* 69 (December 1933): 412.

[53] Reed, *Federal Transient Program*, 58. On the differences between shelter care and camp care, see Crouse, *The Homeless Transient in the Great Depression*, chapters 6 and 7.

[54] H.A.R. Carleton to William J. Plunkert, December 28, 1934, box 27, State Series (California), FERA central files 1933–1936, Records of the WPA, RG 69.

Transients at work setting up a Pennsylvania camp. Courtesy of the National Archives.

one administrator wrote.[55] Bums and hoboes—the confirmed, chronic, or habitual wanderers—had been "with us during [all] the eras of history" in "little or no relation to the fluctuations of our economic conditions."[56] These were the criminals, perverts, and psychopaths, those with antisocial traits and moral quirks, who were on the road to avoid the sacrifices in life that stability (marriage, children, employment) required.[57] "The Federal Government would not have committed itself to an emergency relief program for unemployed transients," stated a report on the Pennsylvania transient program, "if the traditional pre-Depression vagrant alone were being considered."[58]

[55] Edward J. Webster to Howard B. Myers, undated, box 79, Old General Subject Series, FERA central files 1933–1936, Records of the WPA, RG 69.

[56] "A Program for Transient Education and Rehabilitation," undated, box 52, State Series (DC), FERA central files 1933–1936, Records of the WPA, RG 69.

[57] Webb, *The Migratory Casual Worker*; Nels Anderson, *Men on the Move* (Chicago: University of Chicago Press, 1940), 88.

[58] "Transients (Report for 16 Counties in Southeastern Pennsylvania)," box 32, Records of the Transient Division 1933–1936, Records of the WPA, RG 69.

By contrast, the new transient was "a product of the [current] economic order," on the road by necessity rather than choice.[59] This new variety of tramp, officials opined, had little in common with the 15 to 20 percent of the wandering population who were confirmed hoboes.[60] The typical Depression transient was not the usual outcast or misfit, but rather a young man who simply could not stand to go on the dole or loaf around town without work. "The more venturesome and the more ambitious take to the road," General Glassford told Congress during hearings on transiency. "Those without ambition, content to remain in their communities unemployed, idle and hanging around street corners and pool rooms . . . are not in any way comparable with the young men who are traveling the road today."[61] The new group, it was said again and again, were "not hoboes but pioneers."[62] Elaborating on such sentiments, one administration publication was called *Depression Pioneers*. "Most of these people are on the road," the inset read romantically, "for the same reason that kept the covered wagons rumbling across the prairies for the better part of the century."[63] The pioneer trope was, of course, a racialized one that negated the presence of African Americans and Latinos on the road. "Transiency was predominantly the migration of native white persons," one New Dealer concluded.[64]

Drawing a boundary between old and new transients—in a way that referenced the whiteness of the latter—was thus a critical way in which FTP officials established the deservingness of their charges. The new transient was represented as not merely normal, but as the archetypal pioneering American. Yet justifying the enormous expenditure of fed-

[59] Narrative Report, undated, box 32, Records of the Transient Division 1933–1936, Records of the WPA, RG 69.

[60] Anderson, *Men on the Move*, 28.

[61] Ibid., 126, 145.

[62] U.S. Congress, House, *Hearings on Interstate Migration, Part I*, 56.

[63] David Cushman Coyle, *Depression Pioneers* (Washington, DC: U.S. Government Printing Office, 1939).

[64] Of the total number of unattached (transients apart from families), 7 to 12 percent were African American, according to this same source. Despite the great migration of African Americans from the South during and after World War I, this writer concluded, "In view of the long tradition of population mobility in this country . . . it was not surprising to find that the transient population was composed mainly of native white persons." John N. Webb, *The Transient Unemployed: A Description and Analysis of the Transient Relief Population* (Washington, DC: Works Progress Administration, 1935), 33–34. Outside the South, FTP facilities were usually not racially segregated, but a survey of the program suggested that "many concessions can be made to community feeling without complete segregation." Reed, *Federal Transient Program*, 28. See also *Negroes on the Road: A Survey of the Transient Negro in New Jersey* (Trenton: New Jersey Emergency Relief Administration, 1935).

eral relief dollars (at a time when the unemployment rate reached 25 percent) also involved establishing the vulnerability of the population to be served, and this threatened to blur the distinctions so carefully articulated between the chronic hobo and the Depression pioneer. The "depression transients" had not yet become "chronic vagrants," FTP officials warned, but were in "great danger of becoming such."[65] Wandering was said to be "habit-forming"; it was drawing "a goodly portion away from the mores of our social structure," one study of a transient shelter in Buffalo concluded. These transients had only been outcasts for a few years, the study warned. But what would "they be like when they have had a score [more years] in which to develop their unusual habit patterns and form their new allegiances?"[66] It was frequently remarked that it was already too late for the older men. "All we can do for those adults," Eleanor Roosevelt's intimate Lorena Hickok wrote to FERA administrator Hopkins, "is to keep them off the road for a little while." Maybe the young, however, had been "caught in time to prevent their becoming professional tramps," she reported optimistically from her tour of the western camps. "We're making honest-to-God citizens out of those kids!"[67]

It was this mixture of hope and vulnerability that made youths the symbol of what the transient program was most trying to accomplish. "Little was written on the older transients and homeless, the bums, the hoboes, and the migratory workers, except to hold them up as the awful examples of what was in store for this 'army of youth,'" John Webb explained in his study of the transient program. Older men on the road alone were, after all, especially suspicious. If not the traditional bindle stiff, then they were either lifelong bachelors or men who had already deserted their wives, or were at risk to do so. (One FTP survey estimated that a mere 6 percent of transients were married.)[68] Accordingly, "public opinion and legislative support would be more readily influenced by the dramatic aspects of youth on the march," and FTP officials sometimes justified the camp program by raising the specter of a generation so far knocked off the track of marriage, work, and family that it might never get back.[69] When good times returned, a typical query

[65] "Transients (Report for 16 Counties in Southeastern Pennsylvania)," box 32, Records of the Transient Division 1933–1936, Records of the WPA, RG 69.

[66] Herman J. P. Schubert, *Twenty Thousand Transients: A One Year's Sample of Those Who Apply for Aid in a Northern City* (Buffalo: Emergency Relief Bureau, 1935).

[67] Richard Lowitt and Maurine Beasley, *One Third of a Nation: Lorena Hickok Reports on the Great Depression* (Urbana: University of Illinois Press, 1981), 300–301. Hickok (formerly a reporter for the Associated Press) was hired by the FERA to travel the country, and be Hopkins's eyes and ears regarding how Americans were faring during the Depression.

[68] Webb, *The Transient Unemployed*, 35.

[69] Ibid., 17.

went, would the young nomads, corrupted by experiences on the road, confirmed in "antisocial habits," be "able to stick?" Would the transient camps have made boys who longed for "companionship, home, and family," who wanted to "settle down?"[70] Or would the "wanderlust, with its evils," remain strong, such that the boy "is not the same as when he went away?"[71] Not surprisingly—as mention of wanderlust and its evils suggests—nothing more dramatically signified the ruin of this potentially "lost generation" than sexual seduction by hoboes and bums.

This was not just good copy, but a genuine concern on the part of federal officials. There was by the early 1930s both sociological and journalistic evidence that boys on the road were in fact at risk of being exploited sexually by older men, and some of that evidence had been turned up by the same social reformers who served in the Roosevelt administration. Nels Anderson's 1920 study of hoboes described in detail the relationships between "wolves" or "jockers" (older men) and young men or boys referred to as "chickens," "punks," "kids," or "lambs." The wolves, Anderson wrote, "put themselves into the position of a protector, or they may win favor by making presents."[72] Numerous accounts from the 1930s portrayed the threat to boys in terms analogous to those used by Anderson. "I have seen wolves and their little 'lambs' or 'fairies,'" Thomas Minehan explained in his 1934 exposé, *Boy and Girl Tramps of America*. "The man and the boy were pals. The older man got clothes and food for the boy, later teaching the boy how to get for himself."[73] Another writer described "the unfortunate youngster who has come under the control of some pervert" as a common sight on the road.[74] And an article published in the *Survey* (a flagship journal of reform since the Progressive era) by an FTP adviser warned that transient youths were in danger of "becoming the prey of degenerates."[75]

So just as the original plea of the Children's Bureau for federal services was in part prompted by concern over the sexual degeneration of boys, once the FTP was established, the idea of youthful vulnerability

[70] "A Manual for Superintendents of Transient Relief Camps," November 1, 1934, box 31, Records of the Transient Division 1933–1936, Records of the WPA, RG 69; "Transients (Report for 16 Counties in Southeastern Pennsylvania)," box 32, Records of the Transient Division 1933–1936, Records of the WPA, RG 69.

[71] U.S. Congress, Senate, Committee on Manufactures, *Hearings on Relief for Unemployed Transients*, 72nd Cong., 2nd sess., January 13–25, 1933, 32; Franklin F. Newcomb, "Transient Boys," *Family* 14 (April 1933): 58.

[72] Anderson, *On Hobos and Homelessness*, 110–15.

[73] Thomas Minehan, *Boy and Girl Tramps of America* (New York: Grosset and Dunlap, 1934), 143.

[74] Towne Nylander, "Wandering Youth," *Sociology and Social Research* 17 (1933): 62. For memoirs, see also Worby, *The Autobiography of a Tramp*; Shaw, *The Jack Roller*.

[75] McMillen, "An Army of Boys on the Loose," 392.

continued to motivate reformers. Program officials liked to point to the success of their endeavor by harkening back to the time "before the establishment of transient bureaus and camps," when older men taught youths to beg, to steal, and "the perversion of sex."[76] "Without adequate facilities for caring for the better types," men and boys had mingled in flophouses, where "degenerates and perverts" initiated boys "into evil habits."[77] But the "picture brighten[ed]," one partisan of the program wrote, "when we consider the steps taken by the Federal Government to remove the boys from this unwholesome influence."[78]

Such statements not only expressed the transient camps raison d'être, but they had what one New Dealer called "propaganda" value.[79] Yet there was always the risk of overplaying it. At what point did corruptible youths become merely corrupted in the public's eye? Calling attention to sexual danger, in other words, made hazy whatever distinctions might otherwise be drawn between the young pioneer and the predatory hobo; the lamb lost some of its innocence once taken by the wolf. And while FTP officials insisted that (regardless of what happened on the road) "the old time, professional hobo" would keep his distance from the transient facilities because of his dislike of "investigation, routine, and work," public doubts certainly followed the drifters right into camp.[80]

In the Camps

Whether the rhetorical emphasis on saving "normal" boys on the road helped justify the transient program or merely reinforced the idea that the "floating population" was degenerated, there is no doubt that the program's claim of protection was undermined by any suggestion of perversion within the actual camps.[81] Much as FTP officials had en-

[76] "A Program for Transient Education and Rehabilitation," May 15, 1935, box 52, State Series (DC), FERA central files 1933–1936, Records of the WPA, RG 69.

[77] "New Mexico Transient Relief Service," December 6, 1933, box 193, State Series (New Mexico), FERA central files 1933–1936, Records of the WPA, RG 69; U.S. Congress, House, Select Committee to Investigate the Interstate Migration of Destitute Citizens, *Hearings on Interstate Migration, Part VII. Los Angeles Hearings*, 76th Cong., 3rd sess., September 28, 1940, 2871.

[78] Raphael Konigsberg, "Social Factors in the Transiency of Boys" (master's thesis, Ohio State University, 1935), 143.

[79] Webb, *The Transient Unemployed*, 17.

[80] Elizabeth Wickenden to Eugene Willard, January 15, 1935, box 79, Old General Subject Series March 1933–January 1935, FERA central files, Records of the WPA, RG 69.

[81] Lorenzo Wilson to Harry Hopkins, box 80, Old General Subject Series, FERA central files 1933–1936, Records of the WPA, RG 69.

deavored to distinguish the old-time hobo from the Depression pioneer, they also attempted to differentiate sexual vice on the road from the moral purity of the camp environment. The camps were, officials insisted, not just a convenient resting place for bums on their way to the next destination. Rather, an explicit willingness to leave the road and "settle down" was said to be a prerequisite to enter the camp program.[82] Once in a camp, those who had gotten "into the stream of hoboism through the Depression" were to "sublimate transiency" through an orderly program of education, recreation, and work.[83] The latter was most important. Although the transient program was, like most other FERA initiatives, direct relief (a dole rather than a job), it was designed to resemble work relief as much as possible. Camp residents were not paid a wage in relation to the work performed, yet they were required to work about thirty hours a week at either camp maintenance or community projects. In exchange, residents received room and board along with a small weekly allowance of roughly $1 to $3.[84] The work program was designed not only to restore the manhood of those long unemployed, but also to deter work-adverse hoboes (and their perverse culture) from entering the camps.

Apart from the rhetoric, how well did the program succeed in keeping perversion at the camp's gate? Probably not very well: "The effect of the bad apple upon the rest of the barrel," one student of the camp program stated in a discussion of the unfortunate moral effects of mixing boys and older men, "is one of the great problems of the Federal Government in handling the transients."[85] The 1934 handbook of the National Association for Travelers Aid and Transient Services more directly conceded that homosexual activity in the camps was to be expected.[86] That resigned attitude was reflected in the very mechanics, to back up a bit, of getting into a camp in the first place. A transient's first step in entering the camp system was usually a night at an urban FTP shelter, which was generally considered something of a temporary way station and referral bureau. From there, officials aspired to send degenerates to state institutions and local almshouses, and direct the younger and more hopeful types to their own facilities. But in practice, registration and intake were

[82] "Transients (Report for 16 Counties in Southeastern Pennsylvania)," box 32, Records of the Transient Division 1933–1936, Records of the WPA, RG 69.

[83] William Rupert Holloway to Ellen Potter, August 8, 1933, box 82, Old General Subject Series, FERA central files 1933–1936, Records of the WPA, RG 69; Thomas Hudson McKee to Elizabeth Wickenden, October 16, 1934, box 32, Records of the Transient Division 1933–1936, Records of the WPA, RG 69.

[84] Crouse, *The Homeless Transient in the Great Depression*, 155–59.

[85] Konigsberg, "Social Factors in the Transiency of Boys," 144.

[86] Wilson and de la Pole, *Group Treatment for Transients*, 70.

haphazard—mainly focused on establishing whether one was a state or federal transient or a local homeless person—and this goal "was only partly realized." Registrars, medical examiners, and caseworkers were all underpaid, hugely overworked, and usually insufficiently trained—hardly the ideal conditions for any sort of elaborate screening or classification.[87] Somewhat pragmatically, they were advised to be tolerant and not be shocked by what the transients told them.[88]

Newspapers and magazines produced by camp residents provide additional evidence that the sexual culture of the camps was not as sharply distinguished from that of the jungle and the flophouse as FTP promoters claimed. One candid editorial asserted that men in the camps did not have a normal sexual life, and that most men would be "slaves" to the "habit" rather than "go hungry."[89] More common than such frank admissions, gender inversion was a regular source of humor in camp publications. "Professor, what's the Latin for pansy?" one rather ambiguous-looking "co-ed" was shown asking in a cartoon in one camp's paper. (The heading at the top of the page is "Passing Show.")[90] Another newspaper featured a cartoon that shows an effete gentleman trying to decide between the men's or women's restroom. The caption reads: "'She' tosses a coin to decide."[91]

Some contributors, moreover, used the camp magazines to express homoerotic desires through double entendre. At about the same time as some men in New York were, according to historian George Chauncey, using the word "gay" as code to signal their interest in other men, one transient wrote a personal ad in his camp paper that began: "I am a tall, handsome, and gay brute. My friends are surprised at the things I say."[92] A similarly themed personal was written by two men who had, as they said, "had varied experiences."[93] Another provocative cartoon, captioned "Camp Foster Pajamas," shows a man who is naked from the waist down climbing into bed. "Good night, fellows," he says. His

[87] Reed, *Federal Transient Program*, 32–65.
[88] George E. Outland, *A Suggested Manual of Procedure for the Federal Transient Program for Boys in Southern California*, pamphlet, California Social Welfare Archives, Los Angeles, CA.
[89] *Pioneer*, box 1, Records of the Transient Division 1933–1936, Records of the WPA, RG 69.
[90] *Nomad*, box 1, Records of the Transient Division 1933–1936, Records of the WPA, RG 69.
[91] *Oriole Round Up*, box 1, Records of the Transient Division 1933–1936, Records of the WPA, RG 69.
[92] *Capital News*, box 1, Records of the Transient Division, Records of the WPA, RG 69. One would ask, "Are there any gay spots in Boston?" or remark to a stranger that one was "having a gay time." This use of the word "gay," according to Chauncey, "served to alert the listener familiar with homosexual culture." George Chauncey, *Gay New York* (New York: Basic Books, 1994), 17–18.
[93] *Capital News*, box 1, Records of the Transient Division, 1933–1936, Records of the WPA, RG 69.

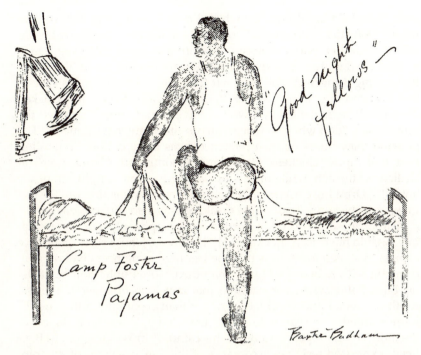

"Good night fellows!"

Camp Foster
Pajamas

An example of the homoerotic content that was common in transient newspapers. This one is from Camp Foster in Florida. Courtesy of the National
Archives.

skimpy sleepwear may have been a statement about inadequate clothing supplies, but it also left its readers wondering: What exactly was a
good night at Camp Foster?[94] Tellingly, one camp's rules prohibited excessive nakedness as well as "lounging" on another man's bed.[95]

Perhaps the clearest evidence that transients brought the sexual
mores of the road with them into the camps was the frequent reference
to jockers, wolves, kids, chickens, and lambs, the vernacular terms used
in hobohemia to refer to predatory men and the boys/young men who
serviced them. One paper's poetry section printed a poem titled, "A
Jocker to His Preshun." The poem is an adaptation of "Hard Rock
Candy Mountain," a traditional poem that, according to historian Clark
Spence, describes a preshun's (or boy's) seduction by a tramp.[96] "With

[94] *Pioneer*, box 1, Records of the Transient Division 1933–1936, Records of the WPA, RG
69.

[95] "Conduct," undated, box 27, State Series (California), FERA central files 1933–1936,
Records of the WPA, RG 69.

[96] Clark C. Spence, "Knights of the Tie and Rail—Tramps and Hoboes in the West,"
Western Historical Quarterly 2 (1971): 8.

likely kids I do big things, for which I'm not accountin'," this version reads. "You stick with me and you shall see the big rock candy mountain."[97] Another paper's gossip column was potentially suggestive when it used wolves, chickens, and lambs to describe camp life. "Now that the big hungry WOLF [has] left the lodge who will be his successor? . . . Send in your answers . . . and receive a free ticket to a chicken dinner." "Who is the big bad wolf at the infirmary now?" queried the same writer, "and where, o where can our little lamb have gone?"[98] The potential bawdiness of such references was more oblique in another post that "most chickens like corn." It continued, "Some prefer it shelled off the cob, while others are willing to drink it right out of the bottle."[99] Drinking corn from the bottle refers to moonshine, but the fact that it is a chicken who does the drinking may also suggest fellatio.

Neither these more coded nor the most graphic of such representations would have been shocking to FTP officials, whose correspondence expressed a keen awareness that the Depression pioneers had more in common with hoboes and bums than their more public statements let on. Ellen Potter wrote, for example, that transients often left home as a result of mental and psychiatric (rather than economic) difficulties.[100] More pointedly, one camp director acknowledged "several instances of the more common perversions" in his camp.[101] In Washington, FTP officials expressed resigned acceptance of the "sex problems of the transients" as "one of the most unfortunate things about a camp program." "I hardly know what to say about [it]," the FTP's director Wickenden wrote. "Every effort is made to provide for a complete program of work, education and recreation, but I am not one to maintain that this is completely adequate as a substitute."[102] Also at a loss, Dorothy Wysor Smith,

[97] *Contact*, box 1, Records of the Transient Division 1933–1936, Records of the WPA, RG 69.

[98] *Transvues*, box 1, Records of the Transient Division 1933–1936, Records of the WPA, RG 69.

[99] *Midwest Breeze*, box 1, Records of the Transient Division 1933–1936, Records of the WPA, RG 69.

[100] Ellen C. Potter to Miss Christine Robb, box 80, August 3, 1933, Old General Subject Series, FERA central files 1933–1936, Records of the WPA, RG 69.

[101] "Statistical Study of 373 Clients in Transient Camp," July 16, 1934, box 32, Records of the Transient Division 1933–1936, Records of the WPA, RG 69.

[102] Elizabeth Wickenden to Miss Viola Ilma, December 6, 1934, box 79, Old General Subject Series, FERA central files 1933–1936, Records of the WPA, RG 69. After Morris Lewis and his successor William Plunkert were replaced at the FTP, Wickenden was put in charge (she actually ran the program for most of its tenure). While her formal title was never changed from assistant director, she was in every respect but title the director. I refer to her as the director of the program to avoid the impression that there was someone positioned above her in the organization. See interview with Elizabeth Wickenden by Blanche D. Coll, May 28, 1986, New York City, box 2 (M99-098), Elizabeth Wickenden Papers.

the director of California's transient program, wrote to the national office to ask, "[W]hat advice can you give us as to the handling of homosexuals?" Her letter revealed both pragmatism and tolerance. "It seems to me that in the case of the majority of boys the homosexuality is accidental or incidental and should not be made too much of," she remarked. "We should not throw [an offender] out of camp or rush him into jail." There were, Smith conceded, those "thoroughly deviated persons whom we cannot have in congregate housing." But Smith said that it would not do "to boot them out and have them on the road from camp to camp, city to city." "What else," she asked her supervisors, "can you suggest?"[103]

That there was, in fact, not much to do was reflected in the absence of any formal policy on perversion within the FTP, whose incentive in this regard was far less than that of the Bureau of Immigration or the military. The overly vigorous policing of men (like the overly intensive screening of camp registrants) only threatened to put destitute men back out on the bum (where desperation might make them dangerous), as well as draw public attention to the already suspect sexuality of the transient population. "If rumors get into the community that such practices exist," the National Association for Travelers Aid and Transient Services warned, "it is a menace to the good name of the camp." FTP officials thus tried to minimize the problem—homosexuality did not occur, they said, with any greater frequency than in construction camps or army barracks—and quietly contain it.[104] The only guideline put into place within the FTP was not a national one. Some camp directors began to separate men from boys in the barracks. "The warped social outlook which frequently results when transient boys and men are mingled over a long period is often accompanied by definite physical dangers," wrote George Outland, Smith's colleague in the California transient program. "Sex perversion is the worst of these, with cases frequently found where a boy has been bought, or forced, or led into degeneracy."[105] Significantly, Outland made no mention of removing from the camps those who were leading boys to degeneracy.

Rather than exert a heavy disciplinary hand, most transient program officials seemed to encourage keeping negative information under wraps. An official with the Arizona camp system wrote to Washington to complain of a social worker with particularly loose lips who had discussed

[103] Dorothy Wysor Smith to William J. Plunkert and H.A.R. Carleton, September 12, 1934, box 31, Records of the Transient Division 1933–1936, Records of the WPA, RG 69.

[104] Wilson and de la Pole, *Group Treatment for Transients*, 70.

[105] George E. Outland, "The Federal Transient Program for Boys in Southern California," in *Boy Transiency in America: A Compilation of Articles Dealing with Youth Wandering in the United States* (Santa Barbara: Santa Barbara State College Press, 1939), 65.

the "moral situation" with "absolute strangers." "She seems to be 'hipped' to the idea of sex," the official remarked angrily. "When you have a group of seven hundred men, this is bound to occur. It certainly doesn't make it better to have a member of the staff telling the world at large how rotten the situation is."[106] And when the educational director of the New Mexico program wrote to White House adviser Louis Howe to complain about the "absolute perversity prevailing" in the camps, FTP director Wickenden hinted at his removal: "It does not seem to me that the attitude which this gentleman expresses towards transients fits him to successfully carry out an educational program for this group."[107]

Indeed, it appears that FTP social workers and staff were more likely to be monitored for signs of gender or sexual deviance than were camp inmates. This was not only because social workers had something to lose that their clients did not—a job—but also reflects the way that both male social workers (working in a traditionally female field) and female social workers (of whom "too many" were "*in charge* of transient bureaus") troubled normative gender roles.[108] Social work appears to be one of those rare professions that "queered" both genders.[109] Casework was, on the one hand, said to be "effeminate"; on the other hand, there was, as one New Dealer complained to Wickenden, that regrettable "*something* in social work that [made] women . . . masculine."[110] So part of the FTP's strategy for quietly containing the stigma of perversion in the camps was to occasionally remove those employees whose appearance or behavior might attract suspicion—those mannish social work-

[106] It is unclear from the passage if the "moral situation" refers to men seeking female prostitutes or other men, or perhaps both. F. M. Warner to Mr. Morris Lewis, February 13, 1934, box 11, State Series (Arizona), FERA central files 1933–1936, Records of the WPA, RG 69.

[107] Endre Gregor to Louis Howe, December 13, 1934, box 193, State Series (New Mexico), FERA central files 1933–1936, Records of the WPA, RG 69; Elizabeth Wickenden to Riley Mapes, January 2, 1934, box 193, State Series (New Mexico), FERA central files 1933–1936, Records of the WPA, RG 69.

[108] Charles K. Sisler to Harry Hopkins, box 79, Old General Subject Series, FERA central files 1933–1936, Records of the WPA, RG 69. Regarding complaints about the authority of women social workers, see William J. Plunkert to Mrs. Dorothy Wysor Smith, October 27, 1934, box 27, State Series (California), FERA central files 1933–1936, Records of the WPA, RG 69. Ellery Reed's evaluative study of the FTP noted the "prominent position occupied by women" within the organization. Reed, *Federal Transient Program*, 39.

[109] Magnus Hirschfeld argued that homosexuals compensated for their anemic family ties through their "absorption in . . . social welfare." (He also noted their passion for both military life and vagabondage.) Magnus Hirschfeld, *The Sexual History of the World War* (New York: Falstaff Press, 1937), 137.

[110] Outland, *A Suggested Manual of Procedure for the Federal Transient Program*, 14; J. P. Mestrezat to Miss Wickenden, September 5, 1934, file no. 420, box 287, State Series (Texas), FERA central files 1933–1936, Records of the WPA, RG 69.

ers and their "cissie type" male colleagues.[111] For example, one regional director recommended discharging a male caseworker who was "the 'city slicker' type, most sartorially correct, and too sophisticated to get the confidence of the men."[112] It was the proximity of male caseworkers to young men or boys that made officials even more anxious than the "physical dangers" of contact between older and younger transients. One "pervert," for instance, who had been in charge of the Verdi Boys Camp, was dismissed "for incompetency and other obvious reasons."[113] Smith, the California official who recommended looking the other way in most cases of perversion among transients, regretted not calling sooner for the resignation of a social worker "who had stated his intention of taking three of our transient boys to live with him." She added that "every boy's worker I know would fully appreciate the danger of scandalous charges against the Federal Transient Service . . . if it ever permitted its employees, particularly young unmarried men, to remove boys from the care of the Federal Service to their own homes."[114]

Despite their efforts to dampen sexual rumors surrounding the program's personnel, "scandalous charges" were not uncommon, especially from those who had spent time in transient camps. One seaman who had been under the care of the Transient Bureau in New Orleans complained about a social worker who was "one of those persons with a male body and a woman's soul." Moreover, he protested that there were a "galaxy of those freaks on the second floor" (presumably the administrative offices), and that "these creatures are allowed to rule and govern decent men of moral habits." He called angrily for an "investigation of the moral character of these social case workers."[115] In a separate incident, a father wrote in to complain about a male social worker whom he suspected of infecting his son with venereal disease, always had "younger boys around him," and did "not mix with company of his own age."[116] The social worker responded by placing the blame on the

[111] J. P. Mestrezat, "My Experiences in a Federal Relief Job," September 5, 1934, box 287, State Series (Texas), FERA central files 1933–1936, Records of the WPA, RG 69; W. T. Hawley to H. B. Levin, June 5, 1934, box 78, Old General Subject Series, FERA central files 1933–1936, Records of the WPA, RG 69.

[112] Helen C. Mawer to Gay B. Shepperson, November 17, 1934, (report on Atlanta Transient Center), box 31, Records of the Transient Division 1933–1936, Records of the WPA, RG 69.

[113] George O. Smith to William J. Plunkert, August 22, 1934, box 31, Records of the Transient Division 1933–1936, Records of the WPA, RG 69.

[114] Dorothy Wysor Smith to J. E. Mills, September 5, 1934, box 31, Records of the Transient Division 1933–1936, Records of the WPA, RG 69.

[115] S. J. Smith to Harry Hopkins, May 2, 1935, box 116, State Series (Louisiana), FERA central files 1933–1936, Records of the WPA, RG 69.

[116] W. T Hawley to H. B. Levin, June 5, 1934, box 78, Old General Subject Series, FERA central files 1933–1936, Records of the WPA, RG 69.

existence of the camp system and the way it encouraged "young men to seek a life which is a disgrace to the nation as well as family and self," so that "sex perversion is gaining the widest influence." The young man in question had become, the social worker asserted, "a common prostitute, passed from one bum to another." In short, the transient program itself was creating, as the man charged, "sex pervert[ed] wanderlustful undesirable citizen[s]."[117]

Others whose own self-interest seemed less directly at stake also complained that it was not just a few social workers but the transient program as a whole that was "confirming vagrants" by encouraging (rather than stopping) both the spread of transiency and the expression of "suppressed desire."[118] "I could tell you dirt immoral," one former resident wrote in a letter to the Department of Justice regarding his time in a Texas transient camp.[119] Another complained of his experience in Pensacola's transient facilities where he was assigned to share a bed with a naked man. "There is the possible angle of moral degeneracy to be considered," he warned.[120] But even where sleeping accommodations were more spacious, the charge spread that the program's goals of restoring men to "more normal living habits," and then teaching them to again desire women, home, and family, were failing.[121] "It is hard to see how it is possible to prepare people for normal living," a 1934 article in the *Nation* puzzled, "by adjusting them to the abnormal . . . life in a congregate camp."[122] FTP director Wickenden conceded the point when she looked back on the program after its early termination in 1935. Transients were removed from "contact with women and normal family relationships . . . [in] the segregated, adolescent barrack life," she reflected. "In this way transients came to be associated in the minds of

[117] E. J. Wheeler to Franklin D. Roosevelt, May 1, 1934, box 80, Old General Subject Series, FERA central files 1933–1936, Records of the WPA, RG 69.

[118] Fred Wilcox to Ellen Potter, June 20, 1934, box 79, Old General Subject Series, FERA central files 1933–1936, Records of the WPA, RG 69; E. J. Wheeler to Franklin D. Roosevelt, May 1, 1934, box 80, Old General Subject Series, FERA central files 1933–1936, Records of the WPA, RG 69.

[119] Arthur Johnson to U.S. Department of Justice, February 1934, box 287, State Series (Texas), FERA central files 1933–1936, Records of the WPA, RG 69.

[120] William P. Gillis to Federal Transient Relief Administration, July 31, 1934, box 58, State Series (Florida), FERA central files 1933–1936, Records of the WPA, RG 69. These sleeping arrangements may not have been uncommon. A report from transient facilities in Montana stated that "the men are sleeping in rooming houses, two in a bed." Irving Richter to Mr. Plunkert, December 21, 1934, box 31, Records of the Transient Division 1933–1936, Records of the WPA, RG 69.

[121] U.S. Congress, House, Select Committee to Investigate the Interstate Migration of Destitute Citizens, *Hearings on Interstate Migration, Part VII. Los Angeles Hearings*, 76th Cong., 3rd sess., September 28, 1940, 2872.

[122] James P. Mitchell, "Coddling the Bums," *Nation* 139 (August 22, 1934): 216.

the men as well as of the public with the tradition of hoboism," and "men, too long segregated . . . came to exhibit certain characteristic maladjustments."[123]

Yet it wasn't only the abnormality of the camp setting that made it impossible for the transient program to escape the stigma of some of the very problems it had tried to solve. The CCC—the New Deal's other major initiative to deal with unattached persons—also relied on a camp program, but was far more successful at convincing the general public that gender-segregated facilities were not necessarily perverting. Its success is a prism through which to see the FTP's failure.

The CCC

Although they were rarely considered together at the time, the CCC was closely related to the FTP. Congress created the CCC in 1933 to prevent transiency among young men before they were "forced into the anti-social group, productive of juvenile delinquency, and ne'er-do-wells."[124] Like the FTP, the CCC thus saw its mission as saving young unemployed men from ruin, including sexual degeneration, and the CCC was regularly credited with keeping boys off the road. "Remember what it was like," Ellen Potter urged in a 1937 speech praising the accomplishments of the CCC, "when 250,000 boys were on the road" and "in moral danger?"[125] As with the FTP, the CCC was designed around a residential camp program, and CCC camps were intended almost exclusively for unmarried men (ages seventeen to twenty-eight) as the "separation of married men from their families would be undesirable."[126] Most of the enrollees were under twenty-one, and therefore the CCC was far less intergenerational than the FTP.[127] The CCC was also distinct from the transient program in that members were selected for six-month enrollments, and then required to remit a monthly allot-

---

[123] Elizabeth Wickenden, "Transiency = Mobility in Trouble," *Survey* 73 (October 1937): 308–9.

[124] Address by Robert Fechner, January 26, 1938, box 1, General Letters 1937–1939, Division of Selection, Records of the CCC, RG 35.

[125] Dr. Ellen Potter, "New Youth for Old," box 1, General Letters 1937–1939, Division of Selection, Records of the CCC, RG 35.

[126] Letter to Robert Fechner, October 13, 1936, box 26, Office of the Secretary 1933–1941, General Records of the Department of Labor, RG 174, National Archives, College Park, MD. An exemption allowed up to five married men to enroll in each camp. See "If You Get Married," in *CCC: A Handbook for Enrollees*, box 6, General Correspondence 1933–1942, Division of Selection, Records of the CCC, RG 35; Bruce L. Melvin and Elna N. Smith, *Rural Youth: Their Situation and Prospects* (Washington, DC: U.S. Government Printing Office, 1938), 102.

[127] Melvin and Smith, *Rural Youth*, 102.

ment to dependents (often but not always their parents). Moreover, the CCC camps were run by the army, and the conservation work that the CCC performed was a more visible part of its program. Corps members were also better paid than transients—around $30 a month as compared to $1 to $3 a week for residents of transient camps—and the "opportunity to go to camp carrie[d] a certain prestige which shows plainly [in] the reaction . . . of the community as a whole."[128] The CCC was, as this passage illustrates, vastly more popular than the FTP, and in existence much longer (until 1943), enrolling approximately 2.5 million while the FTP probably provided services to less than 500,000 during its life span.[129] Still, the two programs were enough alike that historian Todd Depastino could refer to them together as "zones of regeneration for defeated white men."[130]

Despite many similarities, the most obvious comparison—between sexual activity in transient and CCC camps—is one that government officials never made. (The University of Chicago sociologist Ernest Burgess suggested, however, that such a comparison would be fruitful.)[131] Indeed, given that both the FTP and the CCC relied on gendersegregated camps, it is remarkable how differently homosexuality figured in each setting. The FTP seemed plagued by the stigma of perversion; such a stigma was almost wholly absent from public discussions of the CCC. "One striking aspect to the records of . . . the CCC," notes the historian Eric Gorham, "is how little homosexuality is mentioned."[132] Especially noteworthy in this regard is the fact that it was the army—which had already developed a certain expertise on the issue—that administered the conservation program. And while military officials had just renewed (in 1933) their commitment to punish homosex-

[128] W. R. Dyess to W. Frank Persons, July 14, 1934, box 4, State Procedural Records 1933–1942, Division of Selection, Records of the CCC, RG 35.

[129] Numbers for the FTP are somewhat uncertain—one estimate of the peak receiving care at any given time is 300,460; another estimate is 395,384 unattached persons and 16,232 family groups. See Crouse, *The Homeless Transient in the Great Depression*, 182–83.

[130] Todd Depastino, *Citizen Hobo: How a Century of Homelessness Shaped America* (Chicago: University of Chicago Press, 2003), 207. On the history of the CCC generally, see John A. Salmond, *The Civilian Conservation Corps, 1933–1942: A New Deal Case Study* (Durham, NC: Duke University Press, 1967). Also useful is chapter 6 (on the CCC) in Desmond King, *In the Name of Liberalism: Illiberal Social Policy in the USA and Britain* (Oxford: Oxford University Press, 1999), 180–215. There were segregated camps for African Americans in the CCC—but the majority of the clientele served by the program (as with the FTP) were white. "Negro enrollment," concludes Salmond, was "an obvious blot on the record of the CCC" (99).

[131] Ernest Burgess, "Sociological Aspects of the Sex Life of the Unmarried Adult," in *The Sex Life of the Unmarried Adult: An Inquiry into and an Interpretation of Current Sex Practices*, ed. Ira S. Wile (New York: Vanguard Press, 1940), 152.

[132] Eric Gorham, "The Ambiguous Practices of the Civilian Conservation Corps," *Social History* 17 (May 1992): 242.

uality within the army harshly (with the court-martial and prison sentences), the "very mild" discipline within the CCC in general was said to depend on "moral suasion."[133] The CCC was "not like the army," one official opined during a conference of state CCC directors. "You cannot throw a man in the guard house when he disobeys. He has a lot of freedom, in many ways more than he has at home."[134] Besides docking a man's pay, about all that the CCC could do with an unruly charge was to kick him out of the corps. Yet because a dishonorable discharge was said to entrench an "unsocial or anti-social attitude," as well as jeopardize future employment prospects, CCC officials were urged to keep disciplinary discharges to a minimum. Punishment was "not mandatory," and a "punitive system" was not "in accord with the nature and purpose of the CCC and the President's instructions relative to the rehabilitation of unemployed youth."[135] The discharges that did occur were rarely for sexual offenses, and mostly for refusal to work or desertion—the latter more often attributed to "homesickness" rather than the pathological "wanderlust" of the transient.[136]

Such disciplinary discharges led CCC officials to urge a "more careful job of selection," but here too the army's administrative practices did not seem to transfer very well to the CCC camps.[137] "The physical standards for acceptance to the Civilian Conservation Corps are less exacting in many respects than those governing enlistment in the regular army," a major in the Medical Corps wrote to the army's adjutant general, and "do not meet the standards for military service."[138] The CCC examination, one official declared, "was not anything like the physical examinations that an officer or private received upon being accepted during the War."[139] This was quite an admission given the widespread

[133] U.S. Congress, House, Committee on Labor, *Hearings to Make the Civilian Conservation Corps a Permanent Agency*, 75th Cong., 1st sess., April 14 and 15, 1937, 99; U.S. Congress, House, Committee on Labor, *Hearings to Make the Civilian Conservation Corps a Permanent Agency*, 76th Cong., 1st sess., February 9, 23, and 24, 1939, 39.

[134] Conference of State Directors of CCC, December 9, 1940, box 858, General Correspondence 1933–1942, Records of the CCC, RG 35.

[135] R. E. Miles to FERA District Relief Director and Deputy CCC Selecting Agents, March 11, 1936, box 9, Policy file 1933–1942, Division of Selection, Records of the CCC, RG 35; Brigadier General to the Director, CCC, June 10, 1940, box 860, General Correspondence 1933–1942, Records of the CCC, RG 35; CCC Letter Number 3, August 19, 1937, box 2, State Procedural Records 1933–1942, Division of Selection, Records of the CCC, RG 35.

[136] Colonel Clark Lynn to the Commanding General, April 23, 1937, box 38, CCC General Administrative files, Records of the Adjutant General, RG 407.

[137] CCC Letter Number 11, April 1, 1938, box 2, State Procedural Records 1933–1942, Division of Selection, Records of the CCC, RG 35.

[138] Major L. L. Gardner to the Adjutant General, box 8, Division of Selection, General Correspondence 1933–1942, Records of the CCC, RG 35.

[139] Mr. Martin to Mr. West, May 10, 1933, box 5, General Correspondence 1933–1942, Records of the CCC, RG 35.

dissatisfaction with military screening during these years. The ratcheting downward of standards was true not only generally but in terms of homosexuality as well. Even if rarely implemented, screening standards for enlistment in the army at least barred both "homosexuals" and "sexual psychopaths." The War Department's list of conditions barring enrollment in the CCC listed only "hermaphroditism," and made no mention of homosexuality or sexual psychopathy.[140]

Character requirements were equally vague. The minimum eligibility requirements called for men of "good character and stability of purpose."[141] A more elaborate "interpretation of eligibility requirements for young men" mandated only that enrollees be "clean-cut, purposeful, and ambitious."[142] The closest the CCC came to alluding to homosexuality in selection standards was the organization's decision to bar young men on probation and parole from entering the corps because they would "tend to demoralize normal boys in camp." Judge Charles Taylor put it more bluntly when he found out that one parolee had been accidentally accepted into a CCC camp. "It is a well known fact that sexual perversion is frequently found among ex-convicts," he groused. CCC officials lamented the "poor publicity" of the judge's statement (which ended up in the newspapers), but some remained ambivalent about the policy.[143] "Practically everything that the captured juvenile delinquent does has been done by a great many of the boys in the camps," the Chicago reformer Ben Reitman (who had worked with hoboes since the 1890s) pointed out to CCC director Robert Fechner, including "sex crimes."[144]

Reitman was correct—common sense and even fragmentary evidence suggest that homosexual activity probably occurred in CCC camps as frequently as it did in the transient program. Robert Wilson and Dorothy de la Pole's 1934 guide for transient care—which included a section on homosexuality—was, they said, equally applicable to the CCC.[145] A study of the CCC conducted by Harvard psychiatrist John Dynes noted that the "close herding together of men tended to precipi-

---

[140] See chapter 2; U.S. War Department, *Civilian Conservation Corps Regulations* (Washington, DC: U.S. Government Printing Office, 1937), 146.

[141] Civilian Conservation Corps, *Standards of Eligibility and Selection for Junior Enrollees* (Washington, DC: Office of the Director, 1939).

[142] "Interpretation of Eligibility Requirements for Young Men," box 874, General Correspondence 1933–1942, Records of the CCC, RG 35.

[143] Gordon D. Shipman to Charles H. Taylor, November 8, 1937, box 890, General Correspondence 1933–1942, Records of the CCC, RG 35; "Judge Scores CCC as Criminal Haven," July 13, 1937, box 890, General Correspondence 1933–1942, Records of the CCC, RG 35.

[144] Conference Proceedings, and Ben L. Reitman to Robert Fechner, November 30, 1938, box 890, General Correspondence 1933–1942, Records of the CCC, RG 35. On Reitman's own past as a hobo, see Christine Stansell, *American Moderns: Bohemian New York and the Creation of a New Century* (New York: Henry Holt and Company, 2000), 135–36, 295.

[145] Wilson and de la Pole, *Group Treatment for Transients*, preface.

tate latent homosexual trends," resulting in "definite homosexual acts."[146] Dynes's account suggests that the CCC camps were intensely erotic spaces. The typical member of the "tree army" was usually described as a bare-chested, tan, and well-chiseled man, and CCC officials bragged about the "fine physical specimens" in the camps.[147] One woman wrote to Frances Perkins to complain about the "half-naked perspiring bodies" of the CCC enrollees in her community. When they walked into town, she harped, "it is in this same un-clad condition."[148] But not everyone was so appalled—one man's flirtatious comment about the tan of one such shirtless enrollee led to a sexual rendezvous, according to a document later sent to the sexologist Alfred Kinsey that detailed a myriad of similar trysts among men in the CCC camps.[149] And a letter from CCC director Fechner acknowledging that men in the camps were at risk to pass venereal disease to one another indicates that CCC authorities were not oblivious to such activities.[150]

Disciplinary files are rare, but they do exist for cases of forcible sodomy—when, for example, groups of enrollees were dishonorably discharged for raping other men in their camps. In contrast to the military, CCC officials often appeared ill–equipped to handle even these violent cases, and rape victims routinely went to civilian authorities, rather than the company commander, for help.[151] A "boys will be boys" attitude is further indicated by a corps decision that "hazing" was not moral turpitude, even when it involved, say, shellacking the penis and anus of a young enrollee.[152] "Camp razzing [is] just one of the things that people enjoy," advised one CCC guidebook merrily, and enrollees should "learn

[146] John B. Dynes, "Mental Disorder in the C.C.C. Camps," *Mental Hygiene* 23 (1939): 364.

[147] U.S. Congress, House, Committee on Labor, *Hearings to Make the Civilian Conservation Corps a Permanent Agency*, 76th Cong., 1st sess., February 9, 23, and 24, 1939, 39.

[148] Edith Bowdoin to Frances Perkins, July 15, 1933, box 26, general subject file 1933–1941, Office of the Secretary, General Records of the Department of Labor, RG 174, National Archives, College Park, MD.

[149] "The New Deal: Sex in the CCC Camps," in *About Time: Exploring the Gay Past*, by Martin Duberman (New York: Meridian, 1991), 151.

[150] Robert Fechner to Colonel Louis Howe, August 25, 1933, box 610, General Correspondence 1933–1942, Records of the CCC, RG 35.

[151] See, for example, "Disciplinary Discharges," November 1, 1939, box 203, general administrative files of the CCC, Records of the Adjutant General, RG 407, National Archives, College Park, MD; "Discharges for Commission of Crimes Involving Moral Turpitude," March 28, 1941, box 205, general administrative files of the CCC, Records of the Adjutant General, RG 407; "Dishonorable and Administrative Discharge among Junior Enrollees," February 15, 1939, box 202, general administrative files of the CCC, Records of the Adjutant General, RG 407; "Group Discharges," July 16, 1941, box 206, general administrative files of the CCC, Records of the Adjutant General, RG 407.

[152] "Report of Concerted Action by Enrollees," November 12, 1940, box 204, general administrative files of the CCC, Records of the Adjutant General, RG 407.

to take it."[153] Sexual hazing was in fact routine enough that a 1939 study of mental disorders among sixty-six CCC enrollees stated that many of the subjects were "sissies" or "weak sisters," who were the victims of "direct homosexual approaches" by "aggressive individuals in the camp [who] took great delight in tormenting them."[154] Such evidence suggests that CCC enrollees were as likely to be degenerated by other enrollees as lambs were to be seduced by wolves in the transient program. The CCC, one young enrollee declared, "was a good place to ruin a chap."[155]

Most likely, then, the sexual cultures of transient and CCC camps were not that distinctive. Neither was the response of New Deal officials who, in each setting, tried to minimize the homosexual problem and avoid drawing attention to it. That strategy was far more successful in the CCC—"not a breath of scandal has touched it," one journalist wrote—for several reasons.[156] Perhaps most significantly, the CCC's quasi-military character provided a group of men living apart from women with a frame of normalcy. Although the CCC was not technically a military organization, it was said to be "run very much as the army." "The objective of the War Department is national defense," opined one CCC guidebook, "the objective of the CCC is national conservation."[157] CCC enrollees wore green uniforms, lined up in formation once a day, addressed officers as "Sir," and stood "erect with head up, chest out, arms by the side."[158] Like military recruits, Director Fechner reported, CCC enrollees were "taught proper respect for constituted authority" and were "built up physically to a splendid standard."[159] ("All that soft appearance gone," another commented.)[160] Moreover, men in the CCC were being trained to "live together, work together, and exert their energies as a team"—skills that would come in handy should the nation mobilize for war.[161] Thus, while the "womanless state" of

[153] Ned H. Dearborn, *Once in a Lifetime: A Guide to the CCC Camp* (New York: Charles E. Merrill Company, 1935), 217.

[154] Dynes, "Mental Disorder in the C.C.C. Camps," 365.

[155] Irene C. Phillips to Norma Y. Queen, box 8, State Procedural Records 1933–1942, Division of Selection, Records of the CCC, RG 35.

[156] "Politicians Trying to Grab CCC; Labor Urges McEntee as Director" [clipping from January 16, 1940, issue of *Labor*], box 124, Office of the Secretary general subject file 1940–1945, Records of the Department of Labor, RG 174.

[157] Dearborn, *Once in a Lifetime*, 234.

[158] "Instructions to Corps Area Commanders Relative to Daily Formations . . . for CCC Enrollees," November 24, 1937, box 26, Office of the Secretary general subject file 1933–1941, Records of the Department of Labor, RG 174.

[159] U.S. Congress, House, Committee on Labor, *Hearings to Make the Civilian Conservation Corps a Permanent Agency*, 76th Cong., 1st sess., February 9, 23, and 24, 1939, 9.

[160] W. R. Dyess to Frank Persons, July 14, 1934, box 4, State Procedural Records 1933–1942, Division of Selection, Records of the CCC, RG 35.

[161] U.S. Congress, House, Committee on Labor, *Hearings to Make the Civilian Conservation Corps a Permanent Agency*, 76th Cong., 1st sess., February 9, 23, and 24, 1939, 39.

transiency was viewed as a kind of "dispossession," it was celebrated in the CCC as fitting young men for military service.[162]

The CCC also disavowed perversion by disavowing transients—a move that it justified in terms of the "widespread public disapproval" of drifters and nomads.[163] (One journalist contrasted, for instance, the voluminous praise "concerning the Civilian Conservation Corps and its accomplishments" with the "decidedly adverse" information that "has appeared concerning the transient program.")[164] Although they did similar work among similar populations, CCC officials resisted a suggestion to merge with the FTP because of the likely "effects on public opinion" that would result from any perceived partnership between the two organizations. Transients were, opponents of the merger wrote, not seen as reflecting "the same personal and physical qualities" as CCC men. "The transients [were] accustomed to a roving life, in most cases they do not have close family ties [and] they do not look forward to a permanently established vocational adjustment in their own home community."[165] And when the two programs were occasionally *forced* together—for example, the president's order placing in CCC camps the transient veterans who gathered seasonally in Washington to demand bonus payments—CCC officials advised that the plan be kept "entirely confidential so that it will not become generally known."[166]

The CCC further differentiated its men from transients (and kept the latter out of the conservation program) by requiring enrollees to make an "allotment" of $22 each month to a dependent. "I can't get into the CCC because I have no dependents," one young transient explained.[167] This regulation allowed the CCC to depict its enrollees (young unmarried men) as those with "family responsibilities"; transients, by con-

[162]"Statistical Study of 373 Clients in Transient Camp," July 16, 1934, box 32, Records of the Transient Division 1933–1936, Records of the WPA, RG 69.

[163]"Merging FERA Transient Camps with the Civilian Conservation Corps," January 28, 1935, box 654, General Correspondence 1933–1942, Records of the CCC, RG 35.

[164]Lewis Rohrbaugh, "A Brief for the Transient," *Commonweal* 23 (February 7, 1936): 404–5.

[165]"Merging FERA Transient Camps with the Civilian Conservation Corps," January 28, 1935, box 654, General Correspondence 1933–1942, Records of the CCC, RG 35.

[166]Conrad Van Hyning to Robert Fechner, September 20, 1935, box 619, General Correspondence 1933–1942, Records of the CCC, RG 35. President Roosevelt signed an executive order in 1933 mandating that twenty-five thousand veterans (regardless of age) be enrolled in the CCC, and gave priority to the "resurgent Bonus Armies that formed each spring" (Depastino, *Citizen Hobo*, 206).

[167]Minehan, *Boy and Girl Tramps of America*, 20. In later years, this requirement was loosened somewhat, and enrollees without dependents were allowed to make a savings deposit rather than an allotment. But preference was still given to enrollees with dependents over those without dependents, and provisions governing the enrollment of the unattached usually specified "not transients." T. B. to D. S., March 27, 1936, box 1, Division of Selection policy file 1933–1942, Records of the CCC, RG 35.

trast, were those who desired "to escape such responsibilities."[168] "Unattached, homeless, transient men were not selected," wrote Director Fechner, "because it was believed that the enterprise would be of more benefit to whole families than single individuals."[169] CCC officials were unmoved by arguments that it was boys without any family ties who needed the program most. One man's plea that such boys be admitted to the corps because they "are an easy prey to pernicious influences," most likely only shored up official resistance.[170]

Ironically, while CCC officials saw the dependency allotment as a way to avoid "get[ting] the transient youth," they simultaneously defined dependents in incredibly broad terms.[171] Dependents could be, according to the policy, by blood or obligation. The latter included persons, whether or not they were legal dependents or relatives, whom the enrollee felt "morally obligated to help."[172] "For example," the eligibility guidelines explained, this could include "a young man who has been living with an unrelated family for some years and who is considered a member of the family and feels an obligation to contribute to its support."[173] A family was defined not in terms of marriage and reproduction, in other words, but as an "economic group."[174] "When naming allottees of obligation," the Secretary of Labor's office informed the War Department, "the designations of relationship are likely to be in terms of 'foster parent,' 'friend,' and . . . 'guardian.'"[175]

In practice, many enrollees did name "friends" (often other men) as their dependents of obligation. While decisions regarding the acceptability of named allottees were generally left in the hands of state CCC

[168] Frank Persons to Robert Fechner, January 28, 1935, box 654, General Correspondence 1933–1942, Records of the CCC, RG 35.

[169] "Report of the Director of Emergency Conservation Work," April 1933–June 1935, box 26, Office of the Secretary general subject file 1933–1941, Records of the Department of Labor, RG 174.

[170] J. Fred Kurtz to W. Frank Persons, September 2, 1936, box 4, Statistical Reports on Enrollees 1933–1942, Division of Selection, Records of the CCC.

[171] Advisory Council, Emergency Conservation Work, June 18, 1935, box 1, Minutes of the Advisory Council, Records of the CCC, RG 35.

[172] Ernest W. Goodrich, Office of the Solicitor, Department of Labor, to Mr. Snyder, November 9, 1937, box 1, Division of Selection policy file 1933–1942, Records of the CCC, RG 35.

[173] "Handbook for Agencies for Selecting Men for Emergency Conservation Work," box 1, Directives to State Directors of Selection 1933–1942, Division of Selection, Records of the CCC, RG 35.

[174] Civilian Conservation Corps, *Standards of Eligibility and Selection for Junior Enrollees* (Office of the Secretary of the Department of Labor, 1938), box 124, Office of the Secretary general subject file 1940–1945, Records of the Department of Labor, RG 174.

[175] W. Frank Persons to General E. T. Conley, November 30, 1936, box 1, Division of Selection policy file 1933–1942, Records of the CCC, RG 35.

officials, the designation of a friend was regularly deemed an accept-able dependent of obligation.[176] Occasionally, officials explained their rationale: "The allottee, William Fisher, is dependent by obligation upon the enrollee because the enrollee made his home with Mr. Fisher a good deal of the time since 1929." The same official approved another relationship of dependency between two men because "the enrollee made his home with Mr. Klinger."[177] That this official spoke of these men as making their homes together is striking language that suggests something like domestic partnership—and reveals another layer of New Deal pragmatism about the way that the Depression had dis-rupted "normal" family relationships. But even as the CCC's allotment policy stretched the definition of family, the contrast between the ex-alted CCC and the disreputable transient program exposes the way that "familialism" was becoming more deeply entrenched in New Deal so-cial policy.[178] Gender-segregated camps were less stigmatized than the perversity of the state providing resources to single unattached men without dependents. That stigma helps to explain the early termination of the transient program, as well as the overall move away from relief for "nonfamily people" in the transition from the first to the second (post-1935) New Deal.

Liquidation

The CCC survived for so long and with such broad popularity because it resembled less relief for needy men than a kind of training program. Most obviously, CCC enrollees were not merely residents of a camp but also members of a junior "corps" whose minds as well as bodies were being hardened by military-style discipline. But CCC boys were in "training" to be breadwinners in addition to soldiers. The requirement that corps members allot most of their monthly income to a dependent supposedly kept the unattached out of the program; it also helped nur-ture cultural linkages between emergent manhood and the provider role even in the midst of a depression. For the resources that the govern-ment had poured into two-and-a-half million CCC boys, as Director

[176] See, for example, the list of CCC enrollees from Michigan and Wisconsin, box 1, Di-vision of Selection policy file 1933–1942, Records of the CCC, RG 35.

[177] Helen McKnight to W. Frank Persons, February 17, 1937, box 1, Division of Selection policy file 1933–1942, Records of the CCC, RG 35.

[178] On familialism as an alternative to maternalism as a framework for understanding political culture (especially in the context of welfare state formation), see the introduction to *Families of a New World: Gender, Politics, and State Development in a Global Context*, ed. Lynne Haney and Lisa Pollard (New York: Routledge, 2003), 1–14.

James McEntee put it, "two-and-a-half million girls will get better hus-bands."[179] Federal social provision, as numerous welfare state histori-ans have observed, was less about meeting absolute need than about se-curing the gendered underpinnings of certain familial arrangements.

How else to explain the *absence* of a federal program "for the care of the unattached woman," assuredly as vulnerable a population as any other on the road?[180] ("Homeless women are tragic," asserted the monthly bulletin of the National Association of Travelers Aid Societies, "of all the transient groups, they seem to be the most hopeless.")[181] While the numbers of single transient women did not match the num-bers of single men, there were enough of them (as well as mothers with children) to merit some mention by federal officials. A 1933 survey con-ducted by the U.S. Women's Bureau found, for example, "9,769 women moving from one place to another, unattached, jobless, and home-less."[182] Moreover, during the period in which the number of boys on the road decreased due to federal services, there was a "decided in-crease in the number of girls on the road." Some observers speculated that the consequences of bumming "were more severe for girls than boys."[183] Both women and girls were in fact subject to an astounding level of sexual violence—"She has been attacked and raped on several occasions, and given in on several more," read one profile of a transient woman—and many female transients wore overalls, and either passed as men or adopted a stance as toughies to protect themselves.[184] "Sev-eral times gals have come in here in men's clothing," wrote one ob-server of a municipal shelter, "and raised hell with the place before morning."[185] This strategy led to press portrayals of the "lady hobo" as an "angular-bodied, flint-eyed, masculine-minded travesty upon her

[179] James J. McEntee, *Now They Are Men: The Story of the CCC* (Washington, DC: Na-tional Home Library Foundation, 1940), 69. McEntee succeeded Fechner as head of the or-ganization.

[180] Ellen S. Woodward to Anne Carter, April 10, 1935, box 88, New General Subject Se-ries, FERA central files 1933–1936, Records of the WPA, RG 69.

[181] Bulletin No. VII, National Association of Travelers Aid Societies, February 1933, box 82, Old General Subject Series, FERA central files 1933–1936, Records of the WPA, RG 69.

[182] *Nation* 137 (August 9, 1933): 143.

[183] Boys' Work Division, First Methodist Church, "Transient Boys of the Road," 1934, folder 5, box 1, California Migrant/Homeless Populations Collection, California Social Welfare Archives.

[184] Walter C. Reckless, "Why Women Become Hoboes," *American Mercury* 31 (February 1934): 176, 179. Many reports mention "overalled girls." See, for example, Saint Louis Community Council, September 20, 1933, box 32, Records of the Transient Division 1933–1936, Records of the WPA, RG 69. On women transients passing as men for safety, see "Lady Hoboes," *New Republic* 61 (January 1930): 164–69.

[185] Lewis, *Transients in California*, 73.

sex," and helped to fortify "the popular belief" that there was something "unnatural" about a girl who "set out for herself."[186]

Despite the occasional call for attention—"there has been too little said about homeless transient women," Nels Anderson testified before Congress—female transiency was not a problem that the federal government felt it had to solve.[187] There was "more sympathy" for men and boys. "Possibly there is an element of fear in this," explained Dorothy Wysor Smith, who ran transient services in Los Angeles, "that is, fear that the men and boys will commit crimes or be destructive to property."[188] The problem of women and girls on the road, opined the report of another transient bureau, was "not yet serious enough to merit . . . major consideration." Rather, the same writer continued, female transiency would "automatically be solved when the boy and young man problem is solved."[189] The logic was obvious: if unattached men could be restored as providers and potential husbands (taught again to *want* home and family), the small number of women on the road would also be able to resume normal roles as wives.[190] As a result of this derivative approach, there were almost "no rehabilitation centers for women."[191] Unattached women and girls were mostly returned to their home communities, or sent to the YWCA or other local care facilities whose ser-

[186] Cliff Maxwell, "Lady Vagabonds," *Scribner's* 85 (March 1929): 292; Robert C. Myers, "Some Observations on Transient Girls," *Social Forces* 21 (1942–1943): 189. Also hinted at in transient records is an association between perversion among women and prostitution. "In the San Joaquin Valley, I found two women, abnormal types, who followed the road and men," wrote one investigator for the Emergency Relief Administration in California in 1933. "Hobo Journeys," July 1933, box 31, Records of the Transient Division 1933–1936, Records of the WPA, RG 69.

[187] U.S. Congress, Senate, *Hearings on Relief for Unemployed Transients*, 67. Elaine Abelson has also found homeless (nontransient) women during the Depression to be largely invisible and not well provided for by social services. Homelessness was represented as a male phenomenon. Elaine S. Abelson, "Women Who Have No Men to Work for Them: Gender and Homelessness in the Great Depression," *Feminist Studies* 29 (Spring 2003): 104–27. Joanne Meyerowitz reports a declining interest in women adrift (single women living apart from family) by the 1930s. Joanne J. Meyerowitz, *Women Adrift: Independent Wage Earners in Chicago, 1880–1930* (Chicago: University of Chicago Press, 1988).

[188] U.S. Congress, Senate, *Hearings on Relief for Unemployed Transients*, 74.

[189] "Report on Transient Youth in the State of Illinois," April 1933, box 4, General Correspondence 1933–1942, Division of Selection, Records of the CCC, RG 35.

[190] This logic was not unique to the transient problem but has instead undergirded twentieth-century social policy in a myriad of ways. See, for example, Anna Igra's discussion of the use of antidesertion reform as a tool to contain female poverty by enforcing male breadwinning. Anna R. Igra, "Likely to Become a Public Charge: Deserted Women and the Family Law of the Poor in New York City," *Journal of Women's History* 11 (Winter 2000): 59–81.

[191] "Six Months with the Transient Program," box 32, Records of the Transient Division 1933–1936, Records of the WPA, RG 69.

vices varied, but even there "for girls there [were fewer] accommodations than [for] boys."[192] Likewise, the paltry number of CCC-type camps that were designated for women were incredibly short-lived, with FERA administrator Hopkins declaring them too expensive for use with women.[193] The government's best investment of rehabilitation dollars was to be made in men; through them, homeless women could be rehabilitated as well.

Which is perhaps why some federal officials were so keenly disappointed by the results of the transient program—rather than stabilizing men to find employment, settle down, and marry, some worried that the camp and shelter program was actually having a destabilizing effect. "These fellows go [on the road] because they get a bed," the New Dealer Aubrey Williams asserted, "and [freedom] from responsibilities."[194] Hopkins concurred that reintegration was failing. Transients did not seem to want to leave the camps, but rather "hoped, like certain soldiers, that the war would never end."[195] Furthermore, the program had never achieved community support.[196] "We are getting buried by complaints of all types and varieties about the transient order," Frank Bane of the Chicago office told Williams, who replied that Hopkins and others felt that the FTP had "started something that had to be stopped."[197] In late 1935, Hopkins abruptly sent telegrams to all transient bureaus announcing the liquidation of the FTP. Those who argued against termination—even those who warned about the return to "conditions as they existed in

[192] Minehan, *Boy and Girl Tramps of America*, 75. "Mass shelter facilities" were not considered "desirable" for women and girls. "Report of Program and Standards of the Committee on Care and Transient and Homeless," April 12, 1933, box 82, Old General Subject Series, FERA central files 1933–1936, Records of the WPA, RG 69. "The facilities and projects of the Federal Transient Program were used almost exclusively for unattached men," writes Crouse. "Families and unattached women were generally treated on an individual basis, often with no distinction being drawn between them and the local homeless" (*The Homeless Transient in the Great Depression*, 178). Because the FTP was a federal program, and hence better funded than most state and local relief projects, this meant that single male transients usually received better care and more generous allowances than transient families. Harold Schultz to Franklin Roosevelt, January 4, 1934, box 115, State Series (Louisiana) FERA central files 1933–1936, Records of the WPA, RG 69.
[193] Harry L. Hopkins to Dr. M. Matheson Poole, August 18, 1933, box 82, Old General Subject Series, FERA central files 1933–1936, Records of the WPA, RG 69. See Anthony J. Badger, *The New Deal: The Depression Years, 1933–1940* (New York: Hill and Wang, 1989), 206.
[194] Transcript of telephone call from Frank Bane, Chicago, September 26, 1935, box 9 (Mss 800), Elizabeth Wickenden Papers.
[195] Hopkins quoted in Crouse, *The Homeless Transient in the Great Depression*, 169.
[196] U.S. Congress, House, *Hearings on Interstate Migration, Part VII. Los Angeles Hearings*, 2900.
[197] Transcript of telephone call from Frank Bane, Chicago, September 26, 1935, box 9 (Mss 800), Elizabeth Wickenden Papers.

1933" with men "accepting or . . . condoning degeneracy"—could do little to save a program that had become so unpopular.[198]

Without their own program, transients were somewhat uniquely stranded when the FERA was also ended in 1935. (The FTP had been something of a lightning rod for the FERA, attracting negative attention to it.) Under the new system, "unemployables" were to be "turned back" to the states for relief, while "employables" were to be given jobs on the newly created Works Progress Administration (WPA).[199] General relief for the needy—provided by state and local governments—was restricted to the "locally settled," and WPA jobs, while technically available to transients, were administered by local relief boards that also preferred "home town men and boys."[200] "Cases of migrants who are assigned to WPA employment," noted the New Dealer Nels Anderson, were "so rare as to be conspicuous."[201] "These people continued to be labeled nonresidents," concurred Charles Alspach, the state director of the transient program in Pennsylvania, "and it was fairly simple for the [WPA] clerk not to pull this group of cards for placement, because these people were 'a little different.'"[202]

The closing of transient intake in fall 1935 thus produced "a major crisis." Each day, an average of 30 transients in Memphis, 180 transients in Philadelphia, and 200 transients in Atlanta were being refused care. In Jacksonville, police reported a "marked increase in the number of transients sleeping in box cars, riding freight trains, and panhandling near the railway station."[203] Relief officials throughout the country "reverted to the old practices of exclusion and passing on."[204] Reports again surfaced that young boys were "sleeping in flop houses, all-night theaters, and jungles," and even frequenting the taverns where the "degenerate men hang out," hoping "to get a bed and about $1.50 for a date."[205] In

[198] 193 Enrollees of Camp Haledon to Franklin D. Roosevelt, September 16, 1935, Records of the Transient Division 1933–1936, Records of the WPA, RG 69.

[199] James T. Patterson, *America's Struggle against Poverty, 1900–1985* (Cambridge, MA: Harvard University Press, 1986), 59.

[200] Ryan, *Migration and Social Welfare*, 54; U.S. Congress, House, *Report of the Select Committee to Investigate Migration of Destitute Citizens* (Washington, DC: U.S. Government Printing Office, 1941), 603.

[201] Quoted in Crouse, *The Homeless Transient in the Great Depression*, 212.

[202] U.S. Congress, House, *Report of the Select Committee to Investigate Migration of Destitute Citizens*, 602.

[203] "Transient Population," November 9, 1937, 1935, box 9 (Mss 800), Elizabeth Wickenden Papers; "FERA Reports concerning Closing Transient Intake," 1935, box 9 (Mss 800), Elizabeth Wickenden Papers.

[204] U.S. Congress, House, *Report of the Select Committee to Investigate Migration of Destitute Citizens*, 607.

[205] U.S. Congress, House, *Hearings on Interstate Migration, Part VII. Los Angeles Hearings,*

California—the state most burdened by transiency—frustration over the end of the federal program led the State Relief Administration to send an employee undercover to determine conditions on the road after liquidation. His "Journal of a Transient" resurrected the pre-1933 themes of sexual danger and degeneration. During a night in a flophouse, for example, the "transient" noted that among the obscene pictures and verse adorning the walls was "a list of locations in various cities throughout the country ... where degenerates might be contacted." More ominously, he observed several instances of degenerates "moving among" crowds of transient men and boys. Most transients walked away from the perverts, he said, but not the "youngest and the hungriest."[206]

Queering the Welfare State

With transiency unabated, the end of the FTP clearly signaled a foreclosure in the landscape of American social provision.[207] Not only would the federal government surrender its responsibility to care for the country's most destitute, but less and less assistance would be delivered outside the family economy. The moment in which social workers could envision the creation of a more lasting federal "Department of Services to Unattached Persons" had passed.[208] One transient so much more accurately captured the wave of the future when he declared, "I will get married and go on relief."[209] Indeed, WPA jobs were regularly reserved for married men, designed to put a "brake on women's eagerness to be the family breadwinner," and to direct federal assistance away from single men who were swept off the WPA rolls on several occasions.[210] The FTP had been conceived "almost exclusively in terms of single

---

2894; Margaret Cochran Bristol, "Transients in Recent Reports," *Social Service Review* 10 (June 1936): 317.

[206] Lewis, *Transients in California*, 171, 189, 225, 226.

[207] Ryan, *Migration and Social Welfare*, 10.

[208] Reed, *Federal Transient Program: An Evaluative Survey*, 94.

[209] Sutherland and Locke, *Twenty Thousand Homeless Men*, 129.

[210] Howard, *The WPA and Federal Relief Policy*, 279; "Beiter Assails WPA Failure to Hire Single Men," *Buffalo Courier Express*, July 8, 1938, 13; "WPA Evils," *Boston Post*, August 17, 1938, 10; "City to Weed Out WPA Careerists," *Cleveland Plain Dealer*, June 18, 1939, 7. Despite its efforts to bar single men, the WPA did not entirely escape the gendered and sexualized stigma of relief programs more generally. Especially telling are state policies barring from the WPA those who were unable "to adjust themselves socially," the "antisocial," and the "abnormally troublesome" (Howard, *The WPA and Federal Relief Policy*, 458).

men."[211] The WPA, by contrast, contained a "relative needs amendment" that was "passed with the sole intent to get rid of single men," as one unemployed bachelor complained. "[It] is vicious in intent and vicious in results."[212]

The Social Security Act of 1935 more permanently cemented the same biases into the structure of the welfare state. It also made migrants ineligible for benefits, and even more than the WPA, was simultaneously designed to shore up men as family breadwinners by creating a generous system of unemployment and old-age insurance for workers in certain industries.[213] That unemployed (and later retired) men could justify relief (or pensions) "as benefits from a fund to which they have contributed through deductions," wrote the economist Bakke, helped to "reinstate the husband and father to his functional place."[214] The act also created a miserly public assistance program for single mothers whose inadequate benefits made living outside of marriage intentionally difficult.[215]

The Social Security Act's social insurance and public assistance programs thus created a "two-track" system of "entitled" male breadwinners and "pitied" single mothers.[216] The gendered imbalance of the welfare state was further skewed in 1939 when accumulating contributions generated a surplus in Social Security funds that needed to be spent to prevent deflation. Congress's solution was to amend the Social Security Act to include dependents' and survivors' benefits for the wives and widows of those breadwinners who were already covered by the law's social insurance programs. "The added benefit did not belong to the wife," notes the historian Nancy Cott. "The check . . . was sent to the husband, recognizing his [role] rather than the service of his wife."[217] In

[211] U.S. Congress, House, Select Committee to Investigate the Interstate Migration of Destitute Citizens, *Report of the Select Committee*, 77th Cong., 1st sess., 1941, 600.

[212] U.S. Congress, House, *Hearings on Interstate Migration, Part VII. Los Angeles Hearings*, 3033.

[213] Old-age insurance excluded farmworkers and casual laborers (many of whom were migrants), and "old-age and other assistance rendered through the Social Security Board permitted the states to maintain or erect lengthy residence requirements." U.S. Congress, House, Select Committee Investigating National Defense Migration, *Supplement to Brief of John H. Tolan, Amicus Curiae, Edwards v. California*, 77th Cong., 1st sess., undated, 22. The exclusion of farmworkers, casual laborers, and domestics also meant that benefits were heavily skewed toward white workers as well as men.

[214] Bakke, *The Unemployed Worker*, 397.

[215] Gordon, *Pitied But Not Entitled*.

[216] On the welfare state's two tracks, see ibid.; Barbara J. Nelson, "The Origins of the Two-Channel Welfare State," in *Women, the State, and Welfare*, ed. Linda Gordon (Madison: University of Wisconsin Press, 1990): 123–51.

[217] Nancy F. Cott, *Public Vows: A History of Marriage and the Nation* (Cambridge, MA:

this way, the 1939 amendments further deepened women's dependence on male providers.

The decision to use the Social Security surplus to beef up benefits to (settled) married men should be weighed against some of the other ways that the surplus could have been spent. Most obviously, resources could have been directed to women themselves. Transiency, moreover, was still recognized as "one of the nation's most serious welfare problems." Officials continued to insist that the problem of the transient would only be met through federal action, and headlines late in the decade echoed conditions at the beginning: "Depression's Transients Still Creating Problems," for example, or "Lost Generation Still on the Move."[218] In the wake of the FTP's termination, a federal program of general relief would have helped the transients by spreading "a net under various categories of relief so as to catch those who are not provided for specifically," New Dealer Charles Alspach explained. "Among those [uncovered] people, the transients [can] be found." Despite the plea of Alspach and others who had worked with transients that "the federal government should [thus] go further in its Social Security provisions," general relief was left out of Social Security.[219]

In the debate over general relief, the transient population represented the worst-case scenario of who might be taken care of, in FTP director Wickenden's words, by "undifferentiated relief with no real standards": not only single, young, able-bodied men, but also chronic drifters who were suspected of secretly relishing their freedom from work and family.[220] (Wickenden blamed "sadistic" feelings toward the transient on the resentments of those who had "settled down" to the "drudgery" of

---

Harvard University Press, 2000), 177. For the most thorough exploration of the gendered effects of the amendments of 1939, see Kessler-Harris, *In Pursuit of Equity*, 117–70.

[218] Excerpt from "Transient Program Legislation," 1936, and "The Problem of Transiency," 1937, box 9 (Mss 800), Elizabeth Wickenden Papers; "Depression's Transients Still Creating Problems," *Macon Telegraph*, May 26, 1937, 2; "Lost Generation Still on the Move," *San Francisco News*, June 22, 1937, 1. In 1940, Congress appointed a select committee to investigate transiency. The Tolan Committee conducted an extensive two-year investigation into the interstate migration of destitute persons and produced a ten-volume report.

[219] Charles H. Alspach to Miss Emily C. Chew, December 5, 1935, box 55, Records of the Transient Division 1933–1936, Records of the WPA, RG 69. Moreover, as Thomas Sugrue notes, "in 1940, many states did not offer general relief, and those that did put stringent barriers on the condition and length of receipt." Thomas J. Sugrue, "All Politics Is Local: The Persistence of Localism in Twentieth-Century America," in *The Democratic Experiment: New Directions in American Political History*, ed. Meg Jacobs, William J. Novak, and Julian E. Zelizer (Princeton, NJ: Princeton University Press, 2003), 310.

[220] Interview with Elizabeth Wickenden by Blanche D. Coll, May 28, 1986, New York City, box 2 (M99-098), Elizabeth Wickenden Papers.

employment and found "family life perhaps a little dull.")[221] That those types would be banished from federal welfare provision demonstrates not only anxiety about men's potential resistance to marriage, but sheds light on the ways that the welfare state (and citizenship policy more generally) was both gendered and (hetero)sexualized as well. Men were the beneficiaries of marital perks but also the targets of marital imperatives. The latter could be quite punitive, but both types of incentives were necessary to make heterosexuality work as a system that was even more binding for women.[222]

Historians have seen the gendered structure more clearly than the overall heterosexual matrix of welfare state provision. This is what focusing on the unmarried and childless makes visible. So if the "family wage norm was a dead weight crushing the imagination of welfare reformers," as Linda Gordon astutely observes, it has also crushed the imagination of historians who have not been able to fully break from the familial categories of the Social Security Act itself.[223] Male breadwinners and single mothers did not comprise the entire universe of social provision in the 1930s. In between the masculine and feminine tiers of entitlement and pity was a more androgynous one of emergency relief.[224] Here (in the FTP and the FERA more generally) relief sometimes flowed outside the channels of both marriage and reproduction to single men (and a few unattached women), degraded for their dependence, judged for their solitude, and feared for their desperation. These understudied programs are the historical prologue to state/local general assistance, which with its miserly provision for able-bodied adults without dependents—*it was almost on the tip of Elizabeth Wickenden's tongue!*—is surely the queer side of the welfare state. It is also the losing side, hav-

---

[221] Elizabeth Wickenden, "The Problem of Transiency," box 9 (Mss 800), Elizabeth Wickenden Papers.

[222] In understanding the welfare state, we "have come up on the limits of focusing on women alone," Ann Orloff writes. See Ann Shola Orloff, "Markets Not States? The Weakness of State Social Provision for Breadwinning Men in the United States," in *Families of a New World: Gender, Politics, and State Development in a Global Context*, ed. Lynne Haney and Lisa Pollard (New York: Routledge, 2003), 217. Also relevant are Michael Willrich, "Homeslackers: Men, the State, and Welfare in Modern America," *Journal of American History* 87 (2000): 460–89; Anna R. Igra, *Wives without Husbands: Marriage, Desertion, and Welfare in New York, 1900–1935* (Chapel Hill: University of North Carolina Press, 2007).

[223] Gordon, *Pitied But Not Entitled*, 291.

[224] For the notion of an androgynous tier of the welfare system, see Nancy Fraser, *Unruly Practices: Power, Discourse, and Gender in Contemporary Social Theory* (Minneapolis: University of Minnesota Press, 1989), 150–51. Chad Allan Goldberg applies that concept specifically to relief policies in "Contesting the Status of Relief Workers during the New Deal: The Workers' Alliance of America and the Works Progress Administration, 1935–1941," *Social Science History* 29 (Fall 2005): 335–71.

ing remained the "weak link in the . . . welfare system."[225] Its suppression, its invisibility, its *abnormality*, may be a critical part of the story of how a welfare policy organized around breadwinners and caregivers—the straight side of the welfare state—came to be seen as so natural, so inevitable.

Talking about the welfare state in terms of its "queer" and "straight" sides suggests a binary. It was there in the early 1930s, but only in an inchoate form: *mobility/settlement*. State concern about sex perversion was still being articulated in terms of these broader issues, and there was no formal prohibition against homosexuality in 1930s' social provision. But FTP camps—which did not become a permanent fixture in the modern state—were nonetheless another arena of state-building where government officials were schooled in perversion. So when a homosexual-heterosexual binary was explicitly written into federal welfare/citizenship policy at the end of the Second World War, it should come as no surprise that it was in the context of fears about "roving armies of jobless veterans," and concerns that "the army had created a generation of bums" who would be "unwilling or unable to assume positions as family breadwinners." In the GI Bill's extension of "the family breadwinning model of the second New Deal," both the carrot and the stick would be applied to encourage veterans to settle down to home and family.[226]

[225]Patterson, *America's Struggle against Poverty*, 63. "From any standpoint, America needed a nationally financed program of general relief" (ibid). Jason Scott Smith discusses the way that the relief stream has been neglected in welfare state historiography in *Building New Deal Liberalism: The Political Economy of Public Works, 1933–1956* (New York: Cambridge University Press, 2006). General assistance usually refers to state/local programs —relevant in that state-administered programs are feminized. On this point, see especially Suzanne Mettler, *Dividing Citizens: Gender and Federalism in New Deal Public Policy* (Ithaca, NY: Cornell University Press, 1998).

[226]DePastino, *Citizen Hobo*, 220, 223.

PART II

Explicit Regulation

CHAPTER 4

WELFARE

"With the Ugly Word Written across It"

Homo-Hetero Binarism, Federal Welfare Policy,
and the 1944 GI Bill

———◯———

Transiency during the World War II years took a form in some ways
new and in some ways familiar. Even more people were said to be on
the move than during the Depression, with a good number of them
heading for jobs in war-production centers. Social workers worried
about conditions in the dormitories set up for war workers (many of
them young men and boys) where "homosexuality was being practiced."[1] Some reformers noted as well how much "the veteran of today
remind[ed] them of the Depression migrant."[2] Indeed, the sheer number of veterans among the transients was striking, as the transient problem increasingly came to be seen as a major veterans' issue.[3] Social service agencies like Travelers Aid directed their services toward veterans
and pleaded for federal help with this large population of unattached.[4]
They eventually got an answer of sorts when Congress enacted the GI
Bill in 1944. This was major legislation directed at settling men down

[1] Margaret Blenkner and Jeannette M. Elder, "Migrant Boys in Wartime as Seen by
U.S.O. Travelers Aid," *Social Service Review* 29 (September 1945): 335.
[2] See "Travelers Aid Services to Veterans," Migrant Boys in Wartime folder, box 21,
Travelers Aid Association Records, Social Welfare History Archives, Minneapolis, MN.
[3] Margaret Creech, "Travelers Aid Service in Wartime," in *Social Service in Wartime*, ed.
Helen R. Wright (Chicago: University of Illinois Press, 1944), 106–32; National Committee
on Service to Veterans, *Veterans on the Move: Report on Transient Veterans*, Veterans no. 3
folder, box 98, USO Administrative files, YMCA Archives, Minneapolis, MN. A full third
of transients in California, for example, were veterans. California Committee for the
Study of Transient Youth, *Transient Youth in California: A National, State, and Local Problem*,
1948, folder 3, box 1, California/Migrant Homeless Collections, California Social Welfare
Archives, Los Angeles, CA.
[4] "Travelers Aid Services to Veterans." For a history of Travelers Aid, see Grace Eleanor
Kimble, *Social Work with Travelers and Transients: A Study of Travelers Aid Work in the United
States* (Chicago: University of Chicago Press, 1935); "Milestones in the History of Travel-
ers Aid," Misc. folder, box 25, Travelers Aid Association Records.

after wartime. It provided soldiers with home and business loans, employment services, college or vocational training, and unemployment compensation. Yet while extremely generous for some, not all veterans could access the help. In 1945, the Veterans Administration (VA) issued a policy barring GI Bill benefits to any soldier who had been administratively discharged as undesirable "because of homosexual acts or tendencies."[5] These undesirably discharged soldiers were then the ones most likely to become "drifters" after the war—cut off from federal support for "readjustment," sometimes unwelcome back home, and holding separation papers that hurt their chances in the labor market.[6]

In the years between the Federal Transient Program (FTP) and the GI Bill—years in which early experimentation blossomed into a full-blown welfare state—a vague opposition between mobility and settlement hardened into a clear line between homosexuality and heterosexuality in federal citizenship policy. So sharply was that line drawn—and so quickly did the impetus to police homosexuality explicitly rather than by proxy begin to spread across the federal bureaucracy—that it might seem as though a switch was suddenly thrown during the World War II period. And indeed, the war did make vast resources available for all kinds of new federal endeavors during these years.[7] But the shift in policy also picked up on earlier debates that had taken place in the 1920s and 1930s. Within the military, this was a discussion about whether to administratively discharge homosexual personnel in addition to court-martialing soldiers for violent and public sexual acts; within the welfare bureaucracy, it was a debate about the relative merits of channeling social provision to single individuals in need or male breadwinners in families. Not the circumstances of wartime alone, then, but an expanding state's steady accretion of tools, knowledge, and experience finally culminated in a decision to act.

The federal regulation of homosexuality during the World War II era thus seems a bit different if one keeps an eye out for linkages to earlier policymaking, rather than assuming a sudden step into utterly unfamiliar territory. So, too, the picture of antihomosexualism during the war years is altered when the emphasis is tilted away from the military, where historians have tended to look, and toward the welfare state by

[5] Excerpts from "VA Instructions," quoted in Donald Webster Cory, *The Homosexual in America: A Subjective Approach* (New York: Greenberg, 1951), 278–79.

[6] "Travelers Aid Services to Veterans"; Jules V. Coleman, "When People Move—Motives, Meanings, and Problems," in Professional Papers folder, box 24, Travelers Aid Association Records.

[7] On the impact of World War II on state-building, see Bartholomew H. Sparrow, *From the Outside In: World War II and the American State* (Princeton, NJ: Princeton University Press, 1996).

focusing on veterans' benefits.[8] This is only a tilt, of course, because care for veterans is the point at which the military meets the federal welfare bureaucracy. The former (an especially potent space of same-sex eroticism) and the latter (empowered to decide which *sorts* of individuals would benefit from state largesse) made for a combustible mix. The result was the first federal policy to directly exclude persons identified as homosexual from the benefits of the welfare state. And it was actually the VA, with its memory of being saddled with the care of psychiatric discharges after the Great War, rather than the military, which occasionally looked on queer soldiers as a necessary reserve, that was the most zealous gatekeeper. Congress, believing the VA had usurped its authority, was even more ambivalent about the agency's policy. But eventually all major parties fell into line. Once they did, this was not a trivial or symbolic kind of exclusion. Along with Social Security, the GI Bill comprised the largest portion of welfare state expenditure at midcentury.[9]

If the last chapter was about the losing side of the welfare state, this one concerns the winning side where entitlement and masculinity come together. What is important about moving across that border (losing to winning, queer to straight, single to married, on the move to settled down) is that the suggestive and symbolic removal of the sexually deviant from federal relief (via termination of support for the unattached) has morphed into the *actual removal* of homosexuals from programs for veterans' benefits. In examining this latter case, this chapter again draws on the powerful feminist historiography on the welfare state, and also urges more attention to sexuality alongside gender. Feminist historians have already shown that embedded in the GI Bill, as in other welfare state social provision, was a heterosexual norm that positioned male heads of households as the most deserving citizens.[10] Yet this conclusion

[8]See especially Allan Bérubé, *Coming Out Under Fire: The History of Men and Women in World War II* (New York: Plume, 1990); Leisa D. Meyer, *Creating G.I. Jane: Sexuality and Power in the Women's Army Corps during World War II* (New York: Columbia University Press, 1996).

[9]See Edwin Amenta and Theda Skocpol, "Redefining the New Deal: World War II and the Development of Social Provision in the United States," in *The Politics of Social Policy in the United States*, ed. Margaret Weir, Ann Shola Orloff, and Theda Skocpol (Princeton, NJ: Princeton University Press, 1988), 120. For a consideration of the military as a welfare state institution, see Brian Gifford, "The Camouflaged Safety Net: The U.S. Armed Forces as Welfare State Institution," *Social Politics* 13 (Fall 2006): 372–99.

[10]See, for example, Susan M. Hartmann, *The Home Front and Beyond: American Women in the 1940s* (Boston: Twayne Publishers, 1982); Nancy F. Cott, *Public Vows: A History of Marriage and the Nation* (Cambridge, MA: Harvard University Press, 2000); Gretchen Ritter, "Of War and Virtue: Gender, American Citizenship, and Veterans' Benefits after World War II," *Comparative Study of Conscription in the Armed Forces* 20 (2002): 201–26. Also, Lizabeth Cohen provides a compelling account of exclusions from GI Bill benefits based on

about the heterosexual bias of the GI Bill (and welfare state programs more generally) has been reached by analyzing how state benefits were filtered through marriage.[11] Historians have focused, in other words, on one-half of the binary (heterosexuality) while leaving the other half (homosexuality) mostly in the shadows. Casting a light on those shadows reveals that soldiers discharged for homosexuality were not just inadvertently excluded from the economic benefits of the GI Bill because they did not fit into the normative heterosexual family model through which benefits were primarily channeled. Rather, homosexual exclusion was deliberate, built into the very foundation of the welfare state.

This is not the origin story about the GI Bill that is usually told. It complicates (along with the feminist critique) the celebratory way in which the GI Bill is often understood, as democratizing citizenship by opening up education and home-ownership, thereby providing "a modicum of economic welfare and security."[12] The GI Bill—one of the most far-reaching pieces of social policy legislation in the twentieth century—did have this effect. By 1948, the program represented a staggering 15 percent of the federal budget, and veterans constituted nearly

race, class, and gender. See Lizabeth Cohen, *A Consumers' Republic: The Politics of Mass Consumption in Postwar America* (New York: Knopf, 2003): 137–43, 156–60, 166–70.

[11] This statement most closely describes Cott's work on the GI Bill in *Public Vows*, but see also Hartmann, *The Home Front and Beyond*; Cohen, *A Consumers' Republic*. Some other important feminist works that clarify this relationship between welfare state benefits and marriage more generally are Linda Gordon, *Pitied But Not Entitled: Single Mothers and the History of Welfare, 1890–1935* (Cambridge, MA: Harvard University Press, 1994); Alice Kessler-Harris, *In Pursuit of Equity: Women, Men, and the Quest for Economic Citizenship in 20th-Century America* (Oxford: Oxford University Press, 2001). Linda Kerber's research on women's access to veterans' preference points (while not actually a part of welfare state benefits) is related and significant. Linda K. Kerber, *No Constitutional Right to Be Ladies: Women and the Obligations of Citizenship* (New York: Hill and Wang, 1998), chapter 5.

[12] The GI Bill was a classic example of what British sociologist T. H. Marshall called "social citizenship"—the notion that citizenship would become truly democratic when all citizens had the socioeconomic resources to participate to the fullest extent in the social and political life of the nation. Marshall formulated his ideas about social citizenship in the context of mid-twentieth-century Britain. While the U.S. welfare state was more miserly than its British counterpart, some American policymakers hoped that the GI Bill would inaugurate social citizenship in the United States. T. H. Marshall, "Citizenship and Social Class," in *The Citizenship Debates: A Reader*, ed. Gershon Shafir (Minneapolis: University of Minnesota Press, 1998), 94; Edwin Amenta, *Bold Relief: Institutional Politics and the Origins of Modern Social Policy* (Princeton, NJ: Princeton University Press, 1998). Some examples of the celebratory literature on the GI Bill include Michael J. Bennett, *When Dreams Came True: The G.I. Bill and the Making of Modern America* (Washington, DC: Brassey's, 1996); Suzanne Mettler, *Soldiers to Citizens: The G.I. Bill and the Making of the Greatest Generation* (New York: Oxford University Press, 2005); Theda Skocpol, "Delivering for Young Families: The Resonance of the G.I. Bill," *American Prospect* 7 (September–October 1996): 66–72.

one-half of the student body in colleges and universities across the country.[13] "No other New Deal initiative," the political scientist Ira Katznelson concludes, "had as great an impact on changing the country."[14]

Yet close attention to the Veterans Administration's use of homosexuality to restrict veterans' benefits also demonstrates that the trajectory of American citizenship in the twentieth century was not simply expansionary. Rather, the GI Bill resulted in a simultaneous expansion and contraction in citizenship—making education and home-ownership available to many working- and middle-class Americans at the same moment that it explicitly prevented soldiers discharged for homosexuality from taking advantage of those same benefits. Even as citizenship was supposedly becoming more democratic, then, the status of citizenship did not confer a shared set of benefits. Rather, benefits were selectively distributed to differentiate first- and second-class citizens—a differentiation that not only set soldiers above civilians, but as VA policy makes clear, simultaneously relied on ascriptive characteristics such as sexual identity to separate the deserving from the undeserving.

The case of federal welfare policy also shows how citizenship operated through inclusion as well as exclusion. While approximately nine thousand World War II–era soldiers and sailors were denied GI Bill benefits because they were undesirably discharged for homosexuality, a much greater number of soldiers who experienced and even acted on homosexual desires were able to use the GI Bill.[15] Some did so because the military judged them "casual offenders" who it either returned to

[13] Samantha Sparks, "The G.I. Bill: The Rites of Its Passage" (master's thesis, Duke University, 2001), 20–24, 96; Kathleen Jill Frydl, "The GI Bill" (PhD diss., University of Chicago, 2000), 201.

[14] Ira Katznelson, *When Affirmative Action Was White: An Untold History of Racial Inequality in Twentieth-Century America* (New York: W. W. Norton, 2005), 113. "Study after study," Cohen writes, "has documented that World War II veterans achieved substantially higher median incomes, educational attainments, home ownership rates, and net worths than non-veterans of comparable age" (*A Consumers' Republic*, 138).

[15] For an estimate that between 1941 and 1945, more than four thousand sailors and five thousand soldiers were so discharged, see Bérubé, *Coming Out Under Fire*, 147. On the greater number who might have been considered eligible for such discharges but were not, see ibid., 245. According to Alfred C. Kinsey's midcentury reports, roughly 4 percent of adult men and 2 percent of adult women were exclusively homosexual in their sexual behavior. By those estimates, perhaps five hundred thousand or more of the sixteen million men and women who served during World War II would have been exclusively homosexual—a number that dwarfs the nine thousand undesirably discharged for homosexuality. See Alfred C. Kinsey, Wardell B. Pomeroy, and Clyde E. Martin, *Sexual Behavior in the Human Male* (Bloomington: University of Indiana Press, 1948), 610–66, especially 651; Alfred C. Kinsey et al., *Sexual Behavior in the Human Female* (Philadelphia: Saunders, 1953), 446–501.

the service or honorably discharged. Profoundly domesticating legislation, the GI Bill helped some of these "casual" or "situational" offenders transition from the homosociality of the World War II military to the heterosexual and familial imperatives of postwar America. Yet the more explicit demarcation between homosexuality and heterosexuality led not only to the category of the casual homosexual (who was really a salvageable heterosexual), but to the construction of a closet in federal welfare policy as well. That closet enabled many soldiers who experienced homosexual desire during the war to claim benefits because they were undetected. The World War II policy on homosexuality thus provided not only for formal exclusion, in other words, but also for a degraded kind of inclusion in citizenship. And the stakes of being included—on any terms at all—were only made higher by the magnitude of the GI Bill programs.

Congressional Enactment of the GI Bill

Veterans had received some assistance after previous wars, but the scope of GI Bill support was unprecedented.[16] The GI Bill was a cornerstone of postwar planning—a "model . . . welfare system" for recipients—and the generosity of the program was based on gratitude to returning veterans who had suffered severe disruption and hardship during the war.[17] It was also based on a broader cultural fear of the possibility of another depression and the social instability that sixteen million unemployed veterans might provoke, of "a military group returning to find their services no longer needed, [of] a working class without jobs," as veteran Charles G. Bolte put it in 1945.[18] Legislators remembered the World War I veterans who had formed a Bonus Army and marched on Washington, DC, to demand their bonuses, as well as the veterans among Depression-era transients. They worried that a new generation of World War II veterans would wander the country aimlessly if not directed in some way. The country would have "a lot of

[16] Veterans from the Revolutionary War, the Civil War (not including Confederate soldiers), the Spanish-American War, and World War I all received some form of compensation from the federal government—typically land grants, cash bonuses, or pensions. Sparks, "The G.I. Bill," 57. See also Theda Skocpol, *Protecting Soldiers and Mothers: The Political Origins of Social Policy in the United States* (Cambridge, MA: Belknap Press, 1992).

[17] Sar Levitan and Karen A. Cleary, *Old Wars Remain Unfinished: The Veterans Benefit System* (Baltimore: Johns Hopkins University Press, 1973), 27; U.S. Congress, Senate, Committee on Finance, *Providing Federal Government Aid for the Readjustment in Civilian Life of Returning World War II Veterans*, 78th Cong., 2nd sess., March 18, 1944, 2.

[18] Charles G. Bolte, *The New Veteran* (New York: Raynal and Hitchcock, 1945), 49.

trouble," Senator Harley Kilgore warned, if soldiers were not given some way to "cool . . . off."[19] These images of angry, anchorless men counterposed the strongly domestic thrust of the legislative initiatives under consideration, which treated marriage and family life as critical to the veterans' rehabilitation. Stressing education, employment, and home-owning, veterans' benefits were intended to tame soldiers into husbands, to stop the ex-serviceman who was "drifting" and help him "to make long[-term] plans."[20]

Support for the GI Bill gained momentum as it moved through Congress, despite the initial opposition of some New Dealers (including Roosevelt) to the exclusion of civilians from the extensive benefits of the bill. The New Dealers had by the late 1930s trimmed veterans' benefits programs because they believed, according to social scientists Edwin Amenta and Theda Skocpol, "that the needs of ex-soldiers should be met chiefly through programs directed at the entire population."[21] And Roosevelt had bravely gone to an American Legion convention to tell veterans that "no person, because he wore a uniform must thereafter be placed in a special class of beneficiaries over and above all other citizens."[22] Such sentiments led Roosevelt to prefer a competing version of the GI Bill that distributed benefits to civilians as well as veterans.[23]

The VA, under the leadership of the anti–New Deal Republican Frank Hines, was committed to a different set of principles. First, the VA should be designated as the agency to provide *all* services to returning veterans, and second, civilians should in no way be brought into programs for returning veterans.[24] "Whenever the opportunity arose to win benefits for veterans that would be denied to other citizens," Amenta writes, "the VA jumped at it."[25] Closely allied with the VA, the American Legion drafted the numerous proposals for programs for veterans into a single omnibus bill. The resulting legislation expressed the commitment of the American Legion and the VA to the idea that civilians not join veterans in collecting benefits. Indeed, the historian Kathleen Frydl notes that the American Legion continued to fight against civilian benefits long after the GI Bill was enacted; it opposed not only

[19] U.S. Congress, Senate, Committee on Military Affairs, *Hearings on S. 1730 and S. 1893*, 78th Cong., 2nd sess., June 14, 1944, 343.

[20] Alfreda Stanley, "A Study of the Moving Person in War-time: A Sampling of Clients Known to the USO-Travelers Aid Service in New Orleans" (master's thesis, Tulane University, 1947), 32 in box 24, Travelers Aid Association Records.

[21] Amenta and Skocpol, "Redefining the New Deal," 85–86.

[22] Frydl, "The G.I. Bill," 47.

[23] Ibid., 23.

[24] Ibid., 75.

[25] Amenta, *Bold Relief*, 243.

the "intermingling of civilians and veterans" but also "the granting of any greater benefits to civilians than those granted to veterans."[26]

With an increasingly conservative Congress committed to abolishing New Deal reforms and with growing popular support for a veterans' bill, the VA's vision of postwar reform triumphed over Roosevelt's.[27] Conservatives supported the bill, in the historian Alan Brinkley's words, "precisely because the program was limited to veterans," directing benefits to an especially deserving segment of the citizenry. New Deal liberals initially opposed the legislation, but they eventually signed on in the hope that, according to Brinkley, the GI Bill would become the basis of a "broader network of programs aimed at the whole population." Even Roosevelt changed his position on benefits for veterans, stating that soldiers had "been compelled to make a greater . . . sacrifice than the rest of us."[28]

The version of the bill that Congress passed was generous in that it offered full benefits to all who had served a minimum of ninety days and received a discharge "under conditions other than dishonorable."[29] The implicit rationale behind the eligibility policy was that while military service was an obligation of citizenship, such service deserved to be rewarded when faithfully rendered. "Basically, every citizen has a duty to serve in the armed forces," noted a navy report (which conflated "citizen" and "man"), but the GI Bill was "passed by a grateful Congress for the benefit of persons who served . . . during World War II."[30] From the outset it was clear that dishonorably discharged soldiers, regardless of their length of service, had not earned entitlement to GI Bill benefits, whereas soldiers who were separated with honorable discharges after even brief service had.

[26] Frydl, "The GI Bill," 150, 402.

[27] The elections of 1942 brought a conservative coalition into power that began dismantling New Deal programs. The pendulum swung back a bit in 1944 when the election returned twenty-four seats to the Democrats, but the overall culture in Congress remained conservative. Brian Waddell, *The War against the New Deal: World War II and American Democracy* (De Kalb: Northern Illinois University Press, 2001), 132.

[28] Alan Brinkley, *The End of Reform: New Deal Liberalism in Recession and War* (New York: Knopf, 1995), 259. "Veterans' benefits were a bargain for conservatives who feared increasingly high taxation and the extension of New Deal national government agencies," writes Amenta, explaining conservative support for the GI Bill. "Veterans' benefits would go to a small group without long term implications for others, and programs would be administered by the VA, diverting power from New Deal bureaucracies" (*Bold Relief*, 247).

[29] Servicemen's Readjustment Act of 1944 (GI Bill of Rights), Public Law 78-346, *U.S. Statutes at Large* 58 (1944) 284.

[30] Commander-in-Chief Atlantic and U.S. Atlantic Fleet to Secretary of Defense, June 1946, decimal 292, box 800, decimal file G-1 Personnel, Records of the War Department General Staff, RG 165, National Archives, College Park, MD.

Yet all branches of the service awarded a series of discharges that ranged between honorable and dishonorable. The commonest of the in-between discharges was called a "blue" (later an "undesirable") discharge because the document was printed on blue paper. The blue discharge was an administrative discharge that involved neither a court-martial nor a prison sentence. It had been in existence since World War I, when approximately twenty-four thousand such discharges were issued.[31] But it came into much greater usage during the Second World War, when it was often employed for the quick removal from the service of a soldier whose offenses did not merit a court-martial or whose case lacked sufficient evidence.[32]

The proposed legislation made undesirably discharged soldiers—whether separated for homosexuality or other forms of "inaptitude"—eligible for the GI Bill by declaring that all soldiers who were discharged "under conditions other than dishonorable" could claim benefits. Army and navy representatives objected to this terminology, and urged the Congress to limit the extension of benefits to soldiers discharged "under honorable conditions." Without that limitation, the navy's Admiral Jacobs warned one senator, "benefits will be extended to those persons who will have been given . . . undesirable discharges [and] might have a detrimental effect on morale."[33] Various members of Congress disagreed, arguing that the legislation should distribute benefits broadly. Presented with the objections of the military to the more generous terminology, Congresswoman Edith Nourse Rogers commented, "I would rather take the chance so that all deserving men get their benefits."[34] During hearings on the GI Bill, chairman John Rankin of the Committee on World War Veteran's Legislation declared, "I am for the most liberal terms."[35] The Senate report on the proposed GI Bill legislation noted that many blue discharges—released for "minor offenses"—had served faithfully and with distinction. "It is the opinion of the com-

---

[31] World War I records show that there were 24,260 discharges issued that were in-between honorable and dishonorable. File no. 211, box 37, AGO Legislative and Policy Precedent file 1943–1975, Records of the Adjutant General, RG 407, National Archives, College Park, MD.

[32] Bérubé, *Coming Out Under Fire*, chapter 5.

[33] Quoted in *Congressional Record*, 78th Cong., 2nd sess., March 24, 1944, 3077. Whether benefits would be distributed to soldiers discharged "under honorable conditions" or under conditions "other than dishonorable" was one of the main points of controversy during Senate debate on the GI Bill. Roland Young, *Congressional Politics in the Second World War* (New York: Columbia University Press, 1956), 214.

[34] Quoted in *Congressional Record*, 78th Cong., 2nd sess., June 13, 1944, 5890.

[35] U.S. Congress, House, Committee on World War Veteran's Legislation, *Hearings on H.R. 3917 and S. 1767*, 78th Cong., 1st sess., March 30, 1944, 419.

mittee," the report concluded, that "such offenses should not bar entitlement to benefits."[36]

Accordingly, when Congress finally enacted the veterans' legislation,
it authorized benefits to all who had been discharged "under conditions
other than dishonorable." The military itself interpreted the new legislation as granting benefits to soldiers with undesirable discharges: "The
recently enacted 'G.I.' legislation," explained the army's adjutant general, "contains provisions under which it appears that [those with blue
discharges] are eligible for . . . benefits."[37]

The VA and Homosexual Exclusion

The VA would nonetheless distort the terms of the eligibility requirements in administering the new law. The agency opined that although
distinct from a dishonorable discharge (which required a court-martial
conviction), an undesirable discharge could take place *under honorable
or dishonorable conditions*. A soldier with an undesirable discharge would
receive benefits, the VA declared, only if the agency determined that
they had been discharged under "honorable conditions."[38] "The matter
of definition is left to . . . the Veterans Administration," stated one VA
official, asserting that the agency would make that determination on a
case-by-case basis.[39]

Many soldiers accused of homosexuality during World War II were
caught in this limbo between an honorable and a dishonorable discharge. Shortly after the war broke out, the military "tightened . . . antihomosexual screening standards" for induction as part of a push for
greater screening of recruits (for which with "due modesty, the Veterans' Administration claim[ed] credit").[40] The military also began to rely
on the blue discharge to separate soldiers for homosexuality as the re-

[36] U.S. Congress, Senate, Committee on Finance, *Providing Federal Government Aid for the
Readjustment in Civilian Life of Returning World War II Veterans*, 78th Cong., 2nd sess.,
March 18, 1944, 15.

[37] Adjutant General to James Burke, District Attorney, September 28, 1944, file no. 211,
box 36, AGO Legislative and Policy Precedent file 1943–1975, Records of the Adjutant
General, RG 407.

[38] Frank T. Hines, "Legal Bars under Section 300, Public No. 346, 78 Cong., and Character of Discharge under Public No. 2, 73 Cong., as Amended, and Public No. 346, 78
Cong.," October 30, 1944, Policy Series 800.04, volume 2, Records of the Department of
Veterans Affairs, RG 15, National Archives, Washington, DC; U.S. Congress, House, Committee on Military Affairs, *Blue Discharges*, 79th Cong., 2nd Sess., January 30, 1946, 9.

[39] Luther Ellis to Mr. Hiller, October 30, 1944, Policy Series 800.04, volume 2, Records of
the Department of Veterans Affairs, RG 15.

[40] See "Neuropsychiatric Problems of the Veterans Administration," May 1944, Corre-

sult of a determined effort by military psychiatrists and other officials at the outbreak of the war. The new policy relied on a three-part typology for dealing with homosexuality in the service. First, there was the violent offender who committed sodomy by force and was subject to court-martial. In cases involving violence, military policymakers thus treated homosexuality as an act. But in the majority of the cases, the military had begun to process homosexuals as a class of people. "Homosexual proclivities and acts," the assistant chief of naval personnel wrote in 1942, "represent . . . the habitual performances of persons actually homosexual in their respective inclinations."[41] This "true" or "confirmed" homosexual was to be discharged undesirably. The military's belief in a true homosexual who was "attracted only to members of his own sex"—a correlate of the notion that persons were defined by their desire for same- or opposite-sex partners—reflected a growing binarism in the way that policymakers understood sexuality.[42] (The pervert had no precise opposite, but the homosexual clearly did.) That binarism was also evident in the final class in the typology—the "casual" homosexual who was actually "a normal young man" who "through curiosity or intoxication submits to the practice . . . without being by nature homosexual."[43] This last type—really a "salvageable" heterosexual—was to be treated and returned to duty.[44]

---

spondence and Papers folder, 1944, box 5, Social Work Service of the United States Veterans Administration, Social Welfare History Archives; "Release of Information Records in Connection with Program for Screening Men Inducted into the Army to Determine Those Mentally or Emotionally Unfit for Service," February 26, 1944, Correspondence and Papers folder, 1944, box 5, Social Work Service of the United States Veterans Administration, Social Welfare History Archives. Bérubé describes screening regulations from 1942 that "for the first time defined both the homosexual and the normal person . . . and clarified procedures for rejecting gay draftees." The procedures "listed three possible signs for identifying male homosexuals . . . 'feminine bodily characteristics,' 'effeminacy in dress and manner,' and a 'patulous [expanded] rectum.'" See Bérubé, *Coming Out Under Fire*, chapter 1. For an account that focuses on the Women's Army Corps, see Meyer, *Creating G.I. Jane*.

[41] Chief of Naval Personnel to Commandant, U.S. Marine Corps, "Proposed Procedure for the Disposition of Cases of Homosexuality," July 22, 1942, file no. P13-7, box 845, General Correspondence 1925–1940, Records of the Bureau of Naval Personnel, RG 24, National Archives, College Park, MD.

[42] "Notes on Homosexuality and Suggestions concerning Its Control and Punishment," circa 1943, decimal 000.51, box 5, decimal file 1918–1942, Records of the Judge Advocate General, RG 153, National Archives, College Park, MD.

[43] Memorandum from Colonel John M. Weir to Director of Military Personnel, "Sodomists," December 17, 1942, decimal 250.1, box 438, G-1 Personnel decimal file 1942–1946, Records of the War Department General Staff, RG 165.

[44] The policy was revised slightly and reissued as "War Circular # 3" in 1944. See documents in decimal 250.1, box 438, G-1 Personnel decimal file 1942–1946, Records of the War Department General Staff, RG 165.

The policy shift—which emphasized discharge over court-martial and imprisonment—had been debated since the mid-1920s. It finally earned the support of military hard-liners because it preserved prison as an option for the most egregious offenses, while providing the military with a more flexible way to both remove those with "undesirable traits" and retain those it judged "reclaimable." The new discharge policy, in some aspects more humane, enabled the military to broaden its operation beyond those who could be convicted of sodomy to police homosexual status much more expansively. Indeed, the war years provided the significant state infrastructure that processing homosexuals as people required. Soldiers suspected of homosexuality might be followed by vice patrols, observed in hospitals, diagnosed by psychiatrists, assessed by the Red Cross, and interrogated by military police, before finally having their fate determined before a military board.[45]

The army issued around five thousand undesirable discharges for homosexuality during World War II. Some four thousand sailors were undesirably discharged for homosexuality from the navy during the same period.[46] While the discharge was also given to drug addicts, bed wetters, alcoholics, and African American soldiers who challenged segregation, its association with homosexuality made it especially damaging to those who received it.[47] Soldiers who bear "the stigmatization of an 'other than honorable' discharge . . . face all the problems of explanation at home," reported an army captain, "especially when the reason [is] homosexuality."[48] "I am ashamed to let anyone know what has happen [sic]," one African American woman wrote to the National Association for the Advancement of Colored People (NAACP) on behalf of her son. Her sense of shame (and secrecy) may suggest that her son committed a homosexual offense, or perhaps it reflects the way that the sexual stigma of the discharge made challenges to the military's system of Jim Crow more costly. "Please forgive writing bad," she closed, "I am trying to rush before anyone comes in."[49] The Henry Foundation, a New

[45] Bérubé, *Coming Out Under Fire*, chapter 5.

[46] Between December 7, 1941, and June 30, 1945, the army issued 51,963 total undesirable discharges. U.S. Congress, House, *Blue Discharges*, 3; Bérubé, *Coming Out Under Fire*, 232.

[47] Generally, soldiers with psychoneurotic conditions were honorably discharged. U.S. Congress, House, *Blue Discharges*, 7.

[48] Wilson R. G. Bender, "Rehabilitation and the Returning Veteran," *Mental Hygiene* 29 (January 1945): 29.

[49] "We are a family never had any type of bad record of any kind," the woman continued. It is unclear if the discharge of this woman's son was for homosexuality, but the NAACP did advocate for soldiers who had been so discharged. Defense Department and War Department Correspondence, Change in Discharge Cases, 1948–1951, box 59, part I, Washington Bureau, NAACP Records, Library of Congress, Washington, DC.

York organization that assisted individuals in trouble with the law for homosexual offenses, stated that the undesirable discharge, "following a man through the years," was "too great a punishment." The organization reported that it had "been consulted on several occasions by citizens and [veterans' organizations] in their efforts to lighten what in many cases has been an intolerably unjust burden."[50] Congressman Rankin declared that he would rather come home with a *dishonorable* discharge than as "neither fish nor fowl," with an undesirable discharge that "I would have to explain for the rest of my life."[51]

While the VA had assumed responsibility for deciding which undesirables would be eligible for benefits, as a practical matter the agency was initially confused about how to adjudicate individual cases. "This office is having considerable difficulty in defining the term 'under conditions other than dishonorable,'" the VA Administrator Frank Hines wrote to Secretary of the Navy James Forrestal in 1944.[52] As a result of such initial confusion, the VA began to construct more explicit guidelines for adjudicating benefits. In October of that year, the VA used language from the World War Veterans' Act of 1924 to argue that any discharge for an offense involving "moral turpitude" would constitute a discharge under dishonorable conditions.[53] But in implementing this policy, the VA ignored the provision of the 1924 law requiring that a soldier be convicted by a civil or military court before being disqualified from benefits. A memo from VA headquarters expressed frustration that local VA offices were following the language of the 1924 legislation more literally, and were awarding benefits to blue discharges as long as they had not been convicted under civil or military law.[54] One adjudicator, facing numerous cases of soldiers given undesirable discharges for homosexuality, wrote in to ask whether "in the absence of any . . . convictions by court-martial" such discharges were to be considered as under dishonorable conditions.[55]

[50] George Henry, "Report of the Psychiatrist-in-Chief," April 15, 1949, box 62, Society for the Prevention of Crime Papers, Rare Books and Manuscripts Library, Columbia University, New York.

[51] U.S. Congress, House, Committee on World War Veterans' Legislation, *Hearings on H.R. 3749 and Related Bills*, 79th Cong., 1st sess., June 20, 1945, 159.

[52] Frank T. Hines to Secretary of the Navy James Forrestal, August 9, 1944, Policy Series 807, Records of the Department of Veterans Affairs, RG 15.

[53] Frank T. Hines, "Legal Bars under Section 300, Public No. 346, 78 Cong., and Character of Discharge under Public No. 2, 73 Cong., as Amended, and Public No. 346, 78 Cong.," October 30, 1944, Policy Series 800.04, volume 2, Records of the Department of Veterans Affairs, RG 15.

[54] Solicitor to Board of Veterans' Appeals, September 28, 1945, Policy Series 300.5, Records of the Department of Veterans Affairs, RG 15.

[55] Adjudication Officer W. F. Greene to Director, Veterans' Claims Service, April 21, 1945, Policy Series 800.04, volume 2, Records of the Department of Veterans Affairs, RG 15.

As the letter indicates, the VA's policy on eligibility for undesirables confused some adjudicators, because why wouldn't a discharge that was by definition *not dishonorable* fall into the category "under conditions other than dishonorable"? The apparent irrationality surrounding the VA's policy was compounded by the situation of service members discharged for homosexuality, only some of whom were charged with committing homosexual acts, and many of whom had stellar service records.[56] To some VA adjudicators, such soldiers must have seemed the sort Congress had in mind when it added to the GI Bill the liberalizing provision that those whose service had been "meritorious, honest, and faithful" were not to be deprived of benefits.[57]

In April 1945, Hines responded to such confusion by issuing an order that addressed homosexuality explicitly. The policy held that an undesirable discharge because of homosexual acts or *tendencies* "will be considered as under dishonorable conditions and a bar to entitlement."[58] Hines's order did not end debate on the issue, however. A letter from the American Civil Liberties Union (ACLU) challenged the new VA policy. The ACLU maintained that because a blue discharge was not a dishonorable discharge, it was awarded under conditions other than dishonorable and the denial of benefits was illegal. The VA's response to this letter was simply to reassert the text of the new policy on homosexuality.[59] Likewise, local VA offices, slow to catch on to the 1945 directive, continued to request clarification in adjudicating the eligibility of veterans discharged for homosexuality. The decentralized administration of benefits—devised to allow southern states to keep black veterans out of the program—thus may have ironically slowed homosexual exclusion for a time.[60] Headquarters dismissed these queries about how to handle sol-

[56] Homosexuals "may even turn out to be excellent soldiers," *Newsweek* admitted. "Soldiers and Sex," *Newsweek*, July 26, 1943, 70, 72.

[57] "Section 1503 amends section 1603 as passed by the Senate and, as amended, requires a discharge or release from active service under honorable conditions as a prerequisite to entitlement to benefits . . . but adds a liberalizing provision, to the effect that, except as to persons dishonorably discharged, benefits to which a person otherwise would be entitled but for a discharge under other than honorable conditions may be awarded if his service is shown to be otherwise meritorious, honest, and faithful." U.S. Congress, Senate, *Providing Federal Government Aid for the Readjustment in Civilian Life of Returning World War II Veterans*, 16.

[58] U.S. Congress, House, *Blue Discharges*, 8–9.

[59] Clifford Forster, American Civil Liberties Union, to Omar Bradley, Veterans Administration, January 18, 1946, Policy Series 800, Records of the Department of Veterans Affairs, RG 15; O. W. Clark, Veterans Administration, to Clifford Forster, February 2, 1946, Policy Series 800, Records of the Department of Veterans Affairs, RG 15.

[60] On the GI Bill's "provisions for the dispersion of administrative responsibilities that were designed to shield Jim Crow," see Katznelson, *When Affirmative Action Was White*, 124.

diers discharged for homosexuality with pronouncements that the policy was "fully comprehensive and sufficiently clear."[61]

Insisting on the clarity of the policy, the VA drew a line between homosexuality and heterosexuality to separate deserving veterans from undeserving ones. And while the military awarded the undesirable discharge for a variety of traits or behaviors, only the discharge for homosexuality led to a separate policy statement from the central office. For other undesirables, "decisions about who qualified [were] kept in state [administrators'] hands."[62] The policy of 1945, by contrast, exemplified federal leadership in the attempt at homosexual exclusion. As the policy was "one of the last orders of an outgoing administrator," some explanation for it may rest in Hines's biography.[63] Hines, a conservative Republican, was appointed to head the Veterans Bureau by President Warren G. Harding in 1923, and then reappointed by presidents Calvin Coolidge and Herbert Hoover. In 1930, the Veterans Bureau became the VA, and Hines was appointed its first administrator. He ran the agency tightly, "emerging with a [budget] surplus every year." During the Great Depression, he fought to block early disbursement of the bonus payment to World War I veterans, insisting that the government had already "dealt most generously with its veterans."[64] Even after the passage of the GI Bill, observed the *New York Times*, "under General Hines's administration, there were no complaints of extravagance."[65]

Hines also would have been at the helm when a handful of federal transient camps specifically for veterans—run jointly by the FTP and the VA—were established.[66] He would have seen them fail, and observed firsthand the way that this attempt at social provision was damaged by rumors about perversion among the beneficiaries. This experience also may have fortified his conviction, shared by other New Deal opponents, that too much social provision was degenerative for the recipients. One army official, for example, believed the damage had already been done with respect to "WPA types" in the service who lacked strong "masculine identification."[67] For Americans more generally, Hines

[61] George E. Brown, Director of Veterans Claims Service to Manager, "Instructions Numbers 1, 2, and 3, Sections 300 and 1503, Public No. 346, 78th Congress," May 11, 1945, Policy Series 800.04, volume 2, Records of the Department of Veterans Affairs, RG 15.

[62] Katznelson, *When Affirmative Action Was White*, 127.

[63] Cory, *The Homosexual in America*, 278–79.

[64] *Current Biography 1944* (New York: H. W. Wilson, 1945), 296–99. *Current Biography* was an encyclopedia with brief bibliographic essays on important Americans.

[65] "Brig. Gen. Hines, Ex-V.A. Head, Dies," *New York Times*, April 5, 1960, 37.

[66] On the Federal Transient Program, see chapter 3.

[67] Major Kilpatrick to Dr. Harry Steckel, October 24, 1942, Office of Surgeon General/Army Nomenclature folder, box 25, Papers of Superintendent Winfred Overholser, Records of St. Elizabeth's Hospital, RG 418, National Archives, Washington, DC.

"expressed fear that the moral fiber of the [citizenry] is in danger of being undermined through work relief and security programs," as a 1944 biographical sketch of the VA administrator elaborated. "He has . . . expressed the opinion that one hundred dollars a month from a Government relief or Social Security program would induce many citizens to give up all effort to get private employment."[68] The navy also echoed Hines's concern about the way that the GI Bill was implemented, particularly the "52-20 Club," which provided unemployed veterans $20 a week for up to fifty-two weeks. "Benefits should not encourage laziness," warned a navy report on the GI Bill. For "many *unmarried* servicemen without responsibilities [the 52-20 Club] offered a one year vacation with pay."[69] Implicit in such warnings was the idea that besides soldiering, the male citizen's other obligations were to get a job and have a family. If generous benefits freed men of those obligations, such benefits would create weak and dependent men.[70] Hines's overall frugality may have resulted in a specific policy barring soldiers suspected of homosexuality from benefits because of these broader cultural associations linking weakness, dependency, and immorality.[71] Moreover, in drawing on the association between overly generous entitlement and moral decline, the VA's antihomosexual policy justified the agency's dismissal of congressional intentions to distribute benefits broadly—a dismissal that some undesirably discharged soldiers would soon challenge.

The Veterans' Response

The VA's policy on blue discharges did not make sense to some undesirably discharged veterans and their families. One mother, whose son had told her that his undesirable discharge was on account of homosex-

[68] *Current Biography 1944*, 298. "Pensionitis" was the particular term coined by the VA to describe "debilitating dependence on the state" by those with psychiatric discharges. See Ellen Herman, *The Romance of American Psychiatry: Political Culture in the Age of Experts* (Berkeley: University of California Press, 1995), 120, 344.

[69] Commander-in-Chief Atlantic and U.S. Atlantic Fleet to Secretary of Defense, June 1946, decimal 292, box 800, decimal file G-1 Personnel, Records of the War Department General Staff, RG 165 (emphasis added).

[70] Related to this is Kessler-Harris's discussion of the opposition of trade unionists to universal entitlement programs because they believed such programs would create "cringing" and dependent men (*In Pursuit of Equity*, 68).

[71] Postwar culture tended to conflate effeminacy, weakness, and homosexuality. The connections between degeneration due to excessive social provision and the threat of same-sex sexuality in domestic policy have a strong counterpart in cold war foreign policy. See, for example, Robert D. Dean, *Imperial Brotherhood: Gender and the Making of Cold War Foreign Policy* (Amherst: University of Massachusetts Press, 2001); K. A. Cuordileone,

uality, called the War Department to ask for clarification. "They told me," she reported to her son, "that every soldier who does not hold a dishonorable discharge is entitled to the G.I. [Bill of] Rights." Trying to allay her son's fears that he would receive nothing for his time in the service, his mother incorrectly reassured him: "I think someone is trying to hand you a terrific line," she soothed. "No one can see how they can withhold [your benefits]."[72]

The economic value of the benefits was extremely important to many veterans. "If anything should prevent my future education," worried one veteran discharged for homosexuality, "I'd be sunk because the money to carry on myself is simply not available."[73] Going to college on the GI Bill, or buying a house or starting a business with a VA loan, were indeed critical steps toward occupational achievement as well as financial stability. But it was not the economic benefits alone that made the GI Bill so important to veterans. Collecting on the entitlements of the program also brought honor to many families who had never sent a son or daughter to college, or had never owned a home. Just as collecting benefits conferred honor on the recipient, the economic costs of being denied GI Bill benefits were not easily separated from the stigma of the discharge. "[My family is] not wealthy and without the aid of the government, school is practically out of the question," one soldier wrote another. "If [they] ever found out it would be awful, because Mother worships the ground I walk on and she could never take it."[74] The letter of another soldier discharged for homosexuality also conflated the stigma of the discharge with its economic penalties:

> Now I'm up against it. What is painfully embarrassing is that [blue] discharge. . . . What am I to do? Starve? Be kicked around because things got too much for me to bear? Because I really am in need, and unemployed, and willing and able to re-enlist, if only they will take me on, provisionally or otherwise, so I can disprove once and for all what nonsense appears in my case record.[75]

"'Politics in an Age of Anxiety': Cold War Political Culture and the Crisis in American Masculinity, 1949–1960," *Journal of American History* 87 (September 2000): 515–45; Robert L. Griswold, "The 'Flabby American,' the Body, and the Cold War," in *A Shared Experience: Men, Women, and the History of Gender*, ed. Laura McCall and Donald Yacovone (New York: New York University Press, 1998), 323–48.

[72] Mother to "Dear," 1944, box 4, World War II Project Records, Gay, Lesbian, Bisexual, and Transgender Historical Society, San Francisco. The World War II Project Records are largely comprised of primary source materials collected by Bérubé during the course of researching *Coming Out Under Fire*. I am grateful to him for making these sources available to other researchers.

[73] Milqui to Harold, March 6, 1945, box 4, World War II Project Records.

[74] Milqui to Harold, February 20, 1945, box 4, World War II Project Records.

[75] Francesco ——— to VA Administrator Omar Bradley, October 19, 1945, case no.

The humiliation of the blue discharge was more severe because of its association with homosexuality. But different families handled the stigma differently. "I really can't see where you can think that coming home would be anything desperate to face," one mother told her son. "We all know dozens of boys who are out of the service on psychiatric discharges." She attempted to calm her son's fears that friends and neighbors would discover his blue discharge. "Have you ever seen daddy's discharge? Did anyone important ever ask to see it? Are you sure that *it* was an honorable one?"[76]

Despite this mother's assurances, employers and universities did ask to see discharge papers, often with devastating results for veterans. "These 'blues' do hold a veteran back in so many ways," commented a soldier who had been denied his prewar position after an employer saw his blue discharge.[77] "I really am . . . determined to clear myself," another veteran wrote, "[The blue discharge] is an obstacle, and I can't tolerate it much longer."[78] Indeed, some policymakers began to worry that the denial of rights and benefits stigmatized undesirably discharged soldiers so severely that they were unable to reenter society. The "individual is not going to become a very useful citizen to society if he is walking around with a blue discharge," Congressman B. W. Kearney fretted during debate on the GI Bill.[79] A decade later, in 1957, the navy's own Crittenden Report warned that "the service is creating a group of unemployables by [issuing] the undesirable discharges."[80] Many World War II soldiers—especially those who were drafted—came home infuriated that their blue discharges were actually closing doors that were open to them before the war. "I cannot prevent myself from feeling outraged at the injustice of the government's returning me to a society with whose contempt I shall be in constant struggle," one man wrote in a letter, "and further burdening me with the stigma which is automatically attached to the person receiving a [blue discharge]."[81]

Faced with both social stigma and the loss of benefits, veterans had a variety of reactions. A few literally walked away, embarking on a "pat-

4217128, Veterans' Claims Service, obtained through the Freedom of Information Act, in author's possession. I have omitted this man's last name, and have made similar alterations in all postwar chapters to protect the privacy of individuals who may still be living. I have not altered the name of any individual involved in a federal court case.

[76] Mother to Harold, 1944, and November 1944, box 4, World War II Project Records (emphasis added).

[77] Soldier to Senator Lister Hill, August 28, 1946, box 6, World War II Project Records.

[78] Francesco ——— to Major Frederick Vater, May 6, 1945, case no. 4217128, Veterans' Claims Service, obtained through the Freedom of Information Act, in author's possession.

[79] Quoted in *Congressional Record*, 78th Cong., 2nd sess., May 12 1944, 4454.

[80] Crittenden Report, box 16, World War II Project Records.

[81] Harold to Blanche, November 18, 1944, box 4, World War II Project Records.

tern of wandering."[82] Some may have had nearly the opposite response (to settle down), as with one undesirable (discharged for homosexuality) who contemplated getting married "and demand[ing] things on that basis."[83] Others simply disregarded the blue discharge and applied for benefits anyway. "I filed an appeal at the Veterans Administration in Kansas City to claim compensation for a nervous condition sustained in the Service," one soldier told a friend, predicting that his claim would be rejected as a result of his blue discharge.[84] And receiving benefits in the first instance offered no assurance of keeping them. One Florida veteran, for example, was discharged from the navy in 1944 for engaging in consensual homosexual activities. Despite his blue discharge (which occurred before the VA issued its policy on homosexuality), he used GI Bill benefits to enroll at the LaFrance School of Beauty Culture in Miami. Things were going well for him—the school received $500 a year for tuition, and the veteran received an allowance of $50 a month—until he was featured in an article in the *Miami Herald*. An official in the navy (who apparently knew the sailor and was familiar with the circumstances surrounding his discharge) saw the article and wrote to the VA to ask "if all naval personnel discharged for [homosexuality] will receive the benefits of the laws administered by the Veterans Administration?" VA headquarters in Washington, DC, then notified the local office in Bay Pines, Florida, that the veteran was ineligible for benefits.[85]

Indeed, it was not at all uncommon for the VA to be aggressive in correcting mistakes it made during the years that the policy was being worked out. The agency had established its own "little FBI" to address "matters of personal interest" to VA administrator Hines.[86] "The VA is

[82] National Committee on Service to Veterans, *Veterans on the Move.*

[83] Milkie to Harold, June 30, 1945, box 4, World War II Project Records.

[84] Bob to Harold, November 28, 1944, box 4, World War II Project Records. In 1967, the Society for Individual Rights conducted a survey of soldiers discharged for homosexuality (which would have included World War II veterans). The survey asked if veterans had applied for veterans' benefits after their discharge—a question that suggests the practice was probably not uncommon. Confidential Survey, Society for Individual Rights, Military 1960s folder, ONE/IGLA Archives, Los Angeles.

[85] Bureau of Naval Personnel to Veterans Administration, "Enlisted Personnel Discharged with Undesirable Discharges—Veterans' Benefits," March 15, 1945, Policy Series 800.04, volume 2, Records of the Department of Veterans Affairs, RG 15; District Civil Readjustment Officer, U.S. Naval Reserve to Chief of Staff, 7th Naval District, February 21, 1945, Policy Series 800.04, volume 2, Records of the Department of Veterans Affairs, RG 15; Administrator of Veterans Affairs Frank T. Hines to Bureau of Naval Personnel, March 25, 1945, Policy Series 800.04, volume 2, Records of the Department of Veterans Affairs, RG 15.

[86] A. Rosen to the Director, November 28, 1945, "Investigative Unit of Veterans Administration," and "GIs Guarded from Fraud by 'Little FBI,'" November 26, 1945, *Washington Post*, both obtained through the Freedom of Information Act, in author's possession.

hep against these Blue bastards," observed one undesirable.[87] "My friend Louie is still going to school under his own power and simply takes things as they come," wrote one soldier to a friend. "He recently received a letter from the [VA] 'requesting' him to pay back to the United States Treasury the sum of $475 that he received under the GI Bill."[88] Another soldier who was undesirably discharged for homosexuality managed to qualify for GI Bill benefits and used them to obtain his bachelor's degree. After the VA discovered the error, the agency not only demanded repayment but also threatened the young man with a civil suit and imprisonment for receiving money under false pretenses. The soldier contacted the Henry Foundation, which then enlisted the help of a U.S. senator to obtain a waiver from the VA for the soldier.[89]

Faced with the specter of the VA coming after them, many veterans did not claim benefits directly but instead used established channels to protest the denial of benefits. In the text of the GI Bill, Congress had provided for the establishment of boards of review within all branches of the service. An undesirably discharged service member's only recourse was to go before a board of review to request that their discharge be upgraded to honorable. Some soldiers who decided to fight for an upgrade blamed the military for what had happened to them. "When I entered the army I had certain homosexual tendencies," one explained in a letter to a friend. "Army life developed them into traits of character which I will never be able to change. [This camp] has done the most damage to me and it was here that I fell into a clique of homosexuals that has brought me into the classification of 'confirmed.'"[90] The same soldier's mother concurred that the military was responsible for her son's state. "Since the army has had a large part in tearing down your health and mental abilities," she told him, "I see no reason why they should not assume at least part of the responsibility for building you up again."[91]

As such veterans went through the appeals process, they sought out other blue discharges for help and counsel. "I'd appreciate any concrete advice and procedure you can give on how to handle the Veterans Administration," one veteran wrote another.[92] Undesirably discharged soldiers monitored the situation, and kept each other apprised of legal or political changes. This same soldier told his friend of a newspaper story he had read about the blue discharges. "The article stated that none of the stigma of the dishonorable discharge is to go

[87] Bob to Harold, November 28, 1944, box 4, World War II Project Records.
[88] Milqui to Harold, September 20, 1945, box 4, World War II Project Records.
[89] George Henry, "Report of the Psychiatrist-in-Chief," April 15, 1949, box 62, Society for the Prevention of Crime Papers.
[90] Harold to Blanche, November 18, 1944, box 4, World War II Project Records.
[91] "Maw" to Harold, November 20, 1944, box 4, World War II Project Records.
[92] Milqui to Harold, April 12, 1945, box 4, World War II Project Records.

"Ex-Serviceman Seeks Answers." Travelers Aid partnered with the United Service Organization to provide services to return-ing soldiers, including those holding undesirable discharges and considered especially likely to "drift" after the war. Trav-elers Aid Collection, Social Welfare History Archives. Used with permission.

along with the blue" he reported, "and that we are to receive all the benefits of the G.I. Bill."[93]

Blue discharges reached out for assistance not only to one another, but to a range of organizations as well. The Veterans' Affairs Office of the NAACP devoted most of its resources to helping African Americans who had gotten blue discharges, some of whom had been discharged for homosexuality, upgrade their discharges to honorable.[94] Some blue discharges wrote to the ACLU—one man discharged for homosexuality contacted the ACLU to recommend himself as a "suitable plaintiff" should the ACLU decide to fight "Hines's arbitrary ruling which denies veterans' rights."[95] Social service agencies—to whom "veterans released

[93] Milqui to Harold, January 8, 1946, box 4, World War II Project Records.

[94] See, for example, Defense Department and War Department Correspondence, 1948–1951, box 59, part I, Washington Bureau, NAACP Papers.

[95] In this case, the ACLU declined to act. The ACLU's position was that it would not take action in cases where it appeared that homosexual acts had occurred. But the agency was sympathetic to the plight of veterans discharged for homosexuality. ACLU lawyers read Donald Webster Cory's book, *The Homosexual in America*, and expressed concern about possible VA discrimination. Edward ——— to Alan Reitman, November 28, 1951, box 1127, folder 1, "Military Discharges," American Civil Liberties Union Collection, See-ley G. Mudd Archives, Princeton University, Princeton, NJ.

with the blue discharge will . . . be well known"—also extended help.[96] In New York City, for example, the Henry Foundation helped undesirably discharged veterans directly and also corresponded with the American Red Cross and the American Legion on behalf of soldiers discharged for homosexuality.[97] Travelers Aid as well made its services available to blue discharges, providing help, for instance, to one soldier discharged for homosexuality and on the road because his mother "was not at all eager to have him at home."[98] Veterans "with various degrees of disturbance" made their way to desks in railway terminals set up jointly by Travelers Aid and the United Service Organization. (One army officer was incredulous that "any man would [go] to the United Service Organization in Grand Central Station and ask for help with an intimate personal problem.")[99] Finally, many undesirably discharged soldiers wrote to members of Congress, some of whom were becoming increasingly vexed by the situation of the blue discharges.[100]

Congressional Ire

When Congress enacted the GI Bill, members had expressed concern that soldiers who were undesirably discharged would be unfairly denied benefits. The final version of the legislation they passed—which created boards of review within each branch of the service—reflected

[96] William C. Menninger, "Psychiatric Social Work in the Army and Its Implications for Civilian Social Work," in *Proceedings of the National Conference of Social Work* (New York: Columbia University Press, 1945), 91.

[97] George Henry, "Report of the Psychiatrist-in-Chief," April 15, 1949, box 62, Society for the Prevention of Crime Papers; Alfred A. Gross to Charles Cook, November 3, 1949, box 62, Society for the Prevention of Crime Papers; George W. Henry, *All the Sexes: A Study of Masculinity and Femininity* (Toronto: Rinehart and Company, 1955), 372.

[98] Jules Coleman, "When People Move—Motives, Meanings, and Problems," Professional Papers-1 folder, box 24, Travelers Aid Association Records.

[99] Dorothy Elkund, "Psychiatric Social Work and Casework in the USO," Miscellaneous folder, box 25, Travelers Aid Association Records.

[100] See, for example, George E. Brown, Veterans' Claims Service, to Congressman Vito Marcantonio, January 1946, Policy Series 800, Records of the Department of Veterans Affairs, RG 15; Vito Marcantonio to General Omar Bradley, December 22, 1945, Policy Series 800, Records of the Department of Veterans Affairs, RG 15; Civilian Aide to Secretary of War and Marshall P. Patton, May 8, 1947, Subject File, 1940–1947, Records of the Civilian Aide to the Secretary of War, RG 107, National Archives, College Park, MD; Civilian Aide's Notes concerning Cases of Individual Blue Discharges, "Blue Discharges," Subject file, 1940–1947, Records of the Civilian Aide to the Secretary of War, RG 107; Letter to Honorable Michael Kirwin, file no. 949, box 86, AGO Legislative and Policy Precedent file 1943–1975, Records of the Adjutant General, RG 407; Soldier to Senator Lister Hill, August 28, 1946, box 6, World War II Project Records; Senator C. Wayland Brooks to Vice Admiral Ross T. McIntire, Navy Department, July 18, 1944, box 13, World War II Project Records.

that concern. While soldiers could attempt to upgrade their discharges through the boards, Congress did not have the foresight to establish an appeal mechanism within the VA itself. As members of Congress became increasingly aware of the number of blue discharges denied benefits by VA adjudicators, some members began to feel that the VA was violating the generous intent of the GI Bill. Resistance to the VA policy came not only from undesirably discharged soldiers, in other words, but from Congress itself.

Congressional frustration with the VA's policy on blue discharges first surfaced in the fall of 1945. Race, not sexuality, was the initial basis of congressional concern, as evidenced by Senator Edwin Johnson's reading into the *Congressional Record* a series of editorials on the injustice of the blue discharge from an African American paper, the *Pittsburgh Courier*. "There should not be a twilight zone between innocence and guilt," Johnson remarked on the Senate floor.[101] Congressional criticism of the VA's policy was centered not in the Senate, but in the Democratic-chaired House Committee on Military Affairs, where a seven-member subcommittee held hearings in the fall of 1945 and then drafted a remarkable report protesting the VA policy on blue discharges.[102] In explaining that the blue discharge targeted those who had committed misconduct, including "sodomy or sex perversion," and those who exhibited undesirable traits of character, including "psychopathic personality manifested by homosexuality," the authors of the report clearly considered both the situational offender and the "true" homosexual as among the victims of the VA's policy.[103] In contrast to the way that the VA singled out soldiers discharged for homosexuality, however, the committee made its case for the more liberal extension of benefits without sharply distinguishing between soldiers discharged for homosexuality and other recipients of the blue discharge.

Although the committee did not, like the VA, use sexuality to differentiate among veterans, its members seemed to recognize that the association between the blue discharge and homosexuality exacerbated its stigma. The language of the discharge, between honorable and dishonorable, gave the impression "that there is something radically wrong with the man in question," the committee wrote, "something so mysterious that it cannot be talked about or written down, but must be left to

[101] Quoted in *Appendix to the Congressional Record*, 79th Cong., 1st sess., 1945, A4778.
[102] The Special Committee of the Committee on Military Affairs that authored the report on blue discharges was comprised of Chair Carl Durham (D-NC), Robert L. F. Sikes (D-FL), Arthur Winstead (D-MS), Melvin Price (D-IL), Thomas E. Martin (R-IA), Ivor D. Fenton (R-PA), and J. Leroy Johnson (R-CA). Many of these men were veterans of either World War I or World War II.
[103] U.S. Congress, House, *Blue Discharges*, 2.

the imagination."[104] Homosexuality—which was actually becoming less visible as it was coming to be identified with sexual-object choice rather than gender inversion—was more likely on the minds of committee members when they made that assertion than the other offenses that led to a blue discharge (such as drunkenness or insubordination).[105] Likewise, the committee noted that the vagueness of the discharge meant that "moral suspicions are aroused."[106] The stigma surrounding the blue discharge was so powerful, the committee complained, that many of those facing an undesirable discharge "have been known to ask for an out-and-out dishonorable discharge."[107] The report expressed amazement at the numbers who had come forward to complain, thus "publicizing the stigma of having been discharged from the Army under circumstances which savor of disgrace." Still, those who complained surely spoke for thousands more, "who feel the same sense of injustice but prefer to bury their hurt in as much oblivion as possible."[108]

The report protested the unfairness of the blue discharge. Soldiers caught in its web were denied the procedural protections provided to soldiers who were court-martialed. The military refused legal counsel to candidates for blue discharges, and it did not give them a record of the hearing proceedings. Its victims were young, inexperienced men (and women) whose mistakes were often quite minor in nature.[109] The blue discharge would prevent them from receiving benefits, make post-war employment difficult, cause them to be denied admission to many colleges and universities, and as the report claimed, "depress and tor-

[104] Ibid., 6.

[105] On gender inversion, sexual-object choice, and visibility, see Regina Kunzel, *Criminal Intimacy: Prison and the Uneven History of Modern American Sexuality* (Chicago: University of Chicago Press, 2008), chapter 3. This notion that the offense cannot be named also seems to suggest "the love that dare not speak its own name" that originally appeared as a line in the Alfred Douglas poem "Two Loves." Douglas was the companion of Oscar Wilde, and the line was quoted during Wilde's trial in 1895 for homosexual offenses. The poem is reprinted in Stephen Coote, *Penguin Book of Homosexual Verse* (Harmondsworth, UK: Penguin Books, 1983), 262–64.

[106] U.S. Congress, House, *Blue Discharges*, 7.

[107] Ibid., 6.

[108] Ibid., 1.

[109] The report did refer to women soldiers, but rarely, and only in ways that highlighted their exceptionality as, for example, in the following passage: "In the event the 'enlisted man' is a woman, an officer of the Women's Army Corps serves on the board [of officers]." Women were not targeted to the same extent as men for homosexual offenses during World War II. They were, however, occasionally undesirably discharged—more often for gender inversion (mannishness) than for sexual acts per se. See chapter 5. Also relevant is Leisa D. Meyer, "The Myth of Lesbian (In)visibility: World War II and the Current 'Gays in the Military' Debate," in *Queer American History*, ed. Alida M. Black (Philadelphia: Temple University Press, 2001), 271–81; Meyer, *Creating G.I. Jane*, chapter 7.

ture them for the rest of their days."[110] The fact that many of these soldiers had been drafted made the members of the committee especially sympathetic. "Some succumbed to temptations they never met until they entered the Army," the committee wrote, referencing the opportunity that life in the military during World War II provided for homosexual activity.[111] The army should eject such men and women from the service, the report argued, but it should not make the "rest of their lives grievous."[112]

The committee was particularly incensed that the VA had usurped congressional authority in its refusal of benefits to blue discharges. The report argued that the law's awkward phraseology, "under conditions other than dishonorable," reflected a clear congressional desire to distribute benefits broadly. Congress "intended that all persons not actually given a dishonorable discharge should profit by this generosity."[113] By evaluating each undesirable discharge as either under honorable or dishonorable conditions, the VA refused to "take the discharge at its face value."[114] The committee called the VA policy "illogical" and "disingenuous."[115] Asserting that the VA had secured the support of the War Department, the report called the current policy a "squeeze play" by the two agencies. The VA exercised "something like court-martial jurisdiction" over soldiers whom the "Army has been unable or unwilling to subject to dishonorable discharge by court-martial." The 1946 report concluded with strong recommendations that the VA be stopped "from passing moral verdicts on the history of any soldier" and be required "to accept all veterans but those expressly excluded by Congress in . . .

[110] U.S. Congress, House, *Blue Discharges*, 10.

[111] Ibid., 11. Some within the military also believed that military life itself created conditions that encouraged homosexuality. "While there is no intention to compare army camps with prisons," stated a 1943 army report on homosexuality, "there is no gainsaying the fact that in many military establishments the interference with the soldiers' normal way of life is substantial. His reduced access to female companionship, his close association twenty-four hours a day with men of his own age and of all kinds of character, the complete change of his daily routine, and the accent on vigorous outdoor living, coupled in time of war with suppressed apprehension of the implications of the future, all affect his mental cosmos." "Notes on Homosexuality and Suggestions Concerning its Control and Punishment," circa 1943, decimal 000.51, box 5, decimal file 1918–1942, Records of the Judge Advocate General, RG 153.

[112] U.S. Congress, House, *Blue Discharges*, 10.

[113] Ibid., 8.

[114] Ibid. The NAACP raised a similar objection, noting in a report that the "Veterans Administration has ruled that the 'other than dishonorable' clause in the G.I. Bill eliminates most blue discharges, even though the interpretation of this phrase in army language would admit such persons." William H. Hastie and Jessie Dedmon to Walter White, March 9, 1946, box G-18, group II, NAACP Records.

[115] U.S. Congress, House, *Blue Discharges*, 8.

[the GI Bill]."[116] Moreover, the committee urged that the blue discharge be eliminated; instead, soldiers demonstrating "inaptness" or "inadaptability" should receive a discharge under honorable conditions.[117]

As a result of this congressional pressure, the military moved to correct past inequities. "The major difficulty resulting from the past use of the blue discharge is that causes for separations have ranged from honorable to dishonorable," Brigadier General John L. Pierce, the president of the secretary of war's Discharge Review Board, explained in a memo. "[Some] government agencies and some industries are attempting to determine whether the blue dischargee's separation was under honorable or dishonorable conditions as a prerequisite to either benefits or employment." But the general noted that often no such distinctions were made, and sometimes blue discharges were automatically considered dishonorable. "In some instances this same view of a blue discharge undoubtedly affects the individual's standing within his community," Pierce concluded.[118]

To address the issues that the Committee on Military Affairs had raised, the army replaced the blue discharge with a "general discharge" for unsuitability in 1947. The general discharge was considered under honorable conditions, "granted to those found unsuitable as inept but who otherwise meet all qualifications for an honorable discharge."[119] Those who received the general discharge were eligible for benefits. Simultaneously, for more serious offenses, the military preserved the undesirable discharge, to be awarded without benefits under dishonorable conditions "for unfitness or misconduct as a result of administrative action."[120]

The spirit of reform, however, only briefly included soldiers charged with homosexuality. From late 1945 to 1947, the military experimented with awarding honorable discharges (as distinct from the general discharge under honorable conditions) to soldiers who had committed no homosexual acts but had "tendencies." Officials stopped the practice after this short period of leniency. Thereafter, soldiers who had homosexual tendencies, as the next chapter will show, were occasionally awarded general discharges. They were also awarded undesirable discharges, as were soldiers who committed homosexual acts.[121] But

[116] Ibid., 9.

[117] Ibid., 14.

[118] Brigadier General John L. Pierce to War Department General Staff, May 13, 1946, file no. 949, box 86, AGO Legislative and Policy Precedent file 1943–1975, Records of the Adjutant General, RG 407.

[119] "New Discharge Plan Is Adopted by the Army," New York Times, May 21, 1947, 4; U.S. Congress, House, Blue Discharges, 14.

[120] U.S. Congress, House, Blue Discharges, 14.

[121] The military's discharge policy has changed several times since World War II. From

whether they were generally or undesirably discharged, the VA continued to treat soldiers who committed homosexual acts or were suspected of homosexual tendencies as ineligible for benefits.[122]

The Shift in Congressional Attitudes

Well into the 1950s, many members of Congress remained concerned
about soldiers who were undesirably discharged. "Congress has interested itself in the field of discharges, particularly undesirable discharges," noted a Department of Defense (DOD) memo from 1957.[123]
That interest rose in tandem with the increased use of the administrative discharge, which surged after the passage of the 1950 Uniform
Code of Military Justice provided more rights to soldiers who were
court-martialed.[124] In response, members of the Senate held hearings to
determine if the administrative discharge was being used to circumvent
the code. (The military viewed the hearings as congressional "molly-
coddling" of soldiers.)[125] The Senate's deliberation came in the midst of
a sustained effort by Congressman Clyde Doyle—in 1957, the representative from California drafted legislation to help those undesirably discharged soldiers whose punishment, he believed, was out of proportion
to their offenses while in the military. Doyle's proposed legislation

---

October 1945 to 1947, the War Department mandated that enlisted personnel with homosexual tendencies who had committed no in-service acts be granted honorable discharges. In 1947, this lenient policy was reversed: although soldiers with homosexual
tendencies who had not committed homosexual acts were technically eligible for an honorable discharge, most so charged received undesirable discharges, as did soldiers who
had engaged in consensual homosexual acts. See Louis Jolyon West and Albert J. Glass,
"Sexual Behavior and the Military Law," in *Sexual Behavior and the Law*, ed. Ralph
Slovenko (Springfield, IL: Charles C. Thomas Publisher, 1965), 254–55; Colin J. Williams
and Martin S. Weinberg, *Homosexuals and the Military: A Study of Less Than Honorable Discharge* (New York: Harper and Row, 1971), 26–29.

[122] Bérubé, *Coming Out Under Fire*, 230; R. J. Novotny, Assistant Deputy Administrator,
to Manager, VA Regional Office, Los Angeles, California, January 24, 1955, obtained through
the Freedom of Information Act, in author's possession.

[123] Ad Hoc Committee on Administrative Discharges, memo, circa 1957, file no. 211,
box 36, AGO Legislative and Policy Precedent file 1943–1975, Records of the Adjutant
General, RG 407.

[124] On the Uniform Code of Military Justice, see Elizabeth Lutes Hillman, *Defending
America: Military Culture and the Cold War Court-Martial* (Princeton, NJ: Princeton University Press, 2005). On the rise of undesirable discharge rates in the mid-1950s, see "Administrative Discharges: Policies, Procedures, Criteria," 9, file no. 211, box 36, AGO Legislative and Policy Precedent file 1943–1975, Records of the Adjutant General, RG 407.

[125] U.S. Congress, Senate, Committee on the Judiciary, *Hearings on the Constitutional
Rights of Military Personnel*, 87th Cong., 2nd sess., February 20–21, March 1, 2, 6, 9, and 12,
1962, 534.

would enable soldiers to upgrade undesirable discharges if they could prove that their "character, conduct, activities, and habits since [being] granted [the] original discharge [had] been good for . . . not less than three years."[126] The bill was intended to eliminate the stigma of an undesirable discharge for those who had acted as good citizens in civilian life. Because the bill stipulated that soldiers who had their discharges upgraded would receive no additional benefits, but only remove "unearned stigma [from] deserving men and women," the bill also preserved the military's fundamental principle that benefits would go to good soldiers rather than good civilians.[127]

In many ways an outgrowth of the 1946 House report, *Blue Discharges*, this later campaign to help recipients of undesirable discharges differed in one critical aspect. In the years immediately following the Second World War, lawmakers had been concerned with the fate of *all* blue discharges. The 1946 report included soldiers discharged for homosexuality as among those unfairly victimized by the VA's benefits policy; indeed, the report did not always distinguish between them and other blue discharges. The 1957 Doyle bill eliminated such blurriness. Its intent was to salvage the reputations of those who suffered from the association between the blue discharge and homosexuality—an association that had only become more stigmatizing as the linkage between Communism and homosexuality tightened during the red scare of the early 1950s.[128] Given that the legislation would have no impact on benefits, its only effect seemed to be to mark certain undesirably discharged soldiers as nonhomosexuals. The bill mimicked the VA's earlier use of sexuality to differentiate among citizens, and reflected the increasing salience of homosexuality and heterosexuality as constructs that not only divided the populace but also structured public policy.

Doyle and his colleagues saw the proposed legislation as addressing a long-standing inequity: "An admitted homosexual, or an admitted user of narcotics is awarded an undesirable discharge," noted a report by Doyle's special subcommittee on military discharges. "So, also, is the man who is discharged administratively for committing a series of petty offenses."[129]

[126] U.S. Congress, House, Committee on Armed Services, *Hearings before Special Subcommittee on H.R. 1108*, 85th Cong., 1st sess., June 24, 1957; *Congressional Record*, 85th Cong., 1st sess., August 5, 1957, 13666. After committee hearings, the Doyle bill was redrafted and introduced as H.R. 8722. The new legislation was substantially the same—only it made more explicit that the Armed Services were only required to consider good conduct in civilian life in tandem with the circumstances surrounding the original discharge.

[127] *Congressional Record*, 85th Cong., 1st sess., August 5, 1957, 13666.

[128] John D'Emilio, "The Homosexual Menace: The Politics of Sexuality in Cold War America," in *Passion and Power: Sexuality in History*, ed. Kathy Peiss and Christina Simmons (Philadelphia: Temple University Press, 1989), 226–40.

[129] U.S. Congress, House, Committee on Armed Services, *Hearings on H.R. 8722*, 85th Cong., 1st sess., July 23, 1957, 3217.

Was it reasonable, asked the committee's attorney John Blandford during hearings on military discharges, "this lumping together" of undesirably discharged veterans "with . . . homo[s]?"[130] Should a boy who had gone AWOL on several occasions, he inquired, "go through his life with the same stigma as one who is an admitted homosexual?" To make his point, Blandford asked a DOD official if in giving out dinner invitations, he would distinguish between homosexuals and other blue discharges. "I certainly would not be . . . anxious to invite homosexuals to my home," the official replied.[131] The House report on the legislation urged that "immediate steps be taken to differentiate by class among the various types of undesirable discharges."[132]

The method of differentiation varied. Initially, the legislation proposed to give soldiers an upgraded discharge, but the military balked at the idea that civilian conduct should have any bearing on one's military service record. In a gesture of compromise with the secretary of defense, Doyle later introduced legislation that would allow the original discharge to stand, but provided soldiers who demonstrated good civilian behavior with an "Exemplary Rehabilitation Certificate" that they could show to prospective employers.[133] (Doyle asked industry leaders if they would interview undesirably discharged soldiers, and the answer was "universally 'no'"; but with the Exemplary Rehabilitation Certificate the answer from the "great bulk" of employers was "yes.")[134] Both proposals aimed to provide a way to distinguish those individuals who were not "undesirables *in the accepted sense of the word* and who [had] established themselves in society following their separation from the service."[135] It was not lost on soldiers discharged for homosexuality that this "rehabilitation" would not extend to them, as with one vet who wrote a letter to the ACLU declaring Doyle's proposed certificate to be "the product of a cruelly warped sense of justice." Because "most people despise a homosexual," he elaborated, "it does not matter that I am a decent human being who fought for this country in Korea."[136]

Because the Doyle legislation was designed, in part, to give undesirably discharged soldiers a way to prove to prospective employers and community members that they were not homosexual, it is hardly surprising that settling down with a wife and children demonstrated the

[130] U.S. Congress, House, *Hearings before Special Subcommittee on H.R. 1108*, 2379.

[131] Ibid., 2366.

[132] U.S. Congress, House, Committee on Armed Services, *House Report to Accompany H.R. 8722*, 85th Cong., 1st sess., July 23, 1957, 6.

[133] *Congressional Record*, 86th Cong., 1st sess., January 27, 1959, 1213–14; *Congressional Record*, 86th Cong., 1st sess., June 2, 1959, 9575.

[134] U.S. Congress, Senate, *Hearings on the Constitutional Rights of Military Personnel*, 315.

[135] U.S. Congress, House, *House Report to Accompany H.R. 8722*, 6 (emphasis added).

[136] Frank —— to Rowland Watts, June 19, 1961, folder no. 27, box 1067, ACLU Collection.

sort of behavior that Doyle's committee pointed to as entitling a veteran to a fresh start. One undesirably discharged soldier, for example, was late returning from leave on several occasions. But "after getting out of the service, he has assumed the position of a man," one congressman explained, "and has done a very commendable job of providing for his family."[137] Another man, described during the hearings as the type that the proposed legislation could help, returned home with his undesirable discharge, "has accepted a position in a trucking firm, has a family of his own, and has become a very good citizen."[138] Yet another soldier "made a fool of himself on [liquor]" when he was in the service. After being given a blue discharge, though, the man married, obtained a decent job, and had two children. "He wanted to get a veteran's loan to acquire a home for his children, his wife, and himself," the author of the bill reported.[139] The legislation under consideration would not make a loan available to such a man, but it would restore to him a kind of symbolic first-class citizenship. The proposed legislation thus was designed to protect certain soldiers and their families from the stigma of the undesirable discharge. In this way, the Doyle bill stood in contrast to current discharge policy, which as one congressman pointed out, left young fathers holding discharge papers that their sons would not understand when they found them in "daddy's drawer." All "the 8 year old . . . sees," this representative concluded, "is undesirable."[140]

Forty members of Congress had introduced similar or identical bills, and the Doyle bill passed the House with nearly unanimous support. The military strongly objected to the bill, however, on the grounds that military discipline would be damaged if Congress violated the military's basic principle that "an honorable discharge should be given only for honorable military service."[141] Accordingly, when the Senate Armed Services Committee asked for the Pentagon's views on the legislation, the Pentagon stalled for over two months—long enough that the legislation died in Senate committee. But Doyle was tenacious, continuing to reintroduce a version of the bill in several following sessions of Congress. Each time, the bill received unanimous or nearly unanimous support in the House only to be blocked by military opposition on the Senate side.[142] Finally, in 1966, Congress passed a watered-down version of

[137] *Congressional Record*, 85th Cong., 1st sess., August 5, 1957, 13674.

[138] U.S. Congress, House, *Hearings before Special Subcommittee on H.R. 1108*, 2606.

[139] Ibid., 2476.

[140] Ibid., 2379.

[141] Ibid., 2359.

[142] A legislative history is provided in U.S. Congress, House, Committee on Armed Services, *Hearings on H.R. 16646, H.R. 15053, and H.R. 10267*, 89th Cong., 2nd sess., July 26, 1966, 10286.

the bill. It specified that the secretary of labor (rather than the DOD) would issue the Exemplary Rehabilitation Certificate, which would in no way affect the original military discharge.[143]

While the military took issue with Doyle's assertion that the undesirable discharge was often too punitive, the DOD and congressional proponents of the Doyle bill agreed about one thing: soldiers discharged for homosexuality did not deserve lenient treatment. An internal 1957 DOD memo that proposed administrative changes to the military's discharge policy to avoid "the necessity for legislation of the type represented by . . . [Doyle]" warned against any changes that would remove the military's authority to discharge homosexuals.[144] "Surely there can be no great disagreement," one DOD official ventured, "with the administrative separation under other than honorable conditions of the homosexual."[145] Doyle certainly did not disagree. On the floor of the House, the congressman explained that he had decided that the undesirable discharge had some value (and should not be eliminated entirely) when he thought of the situation, "true of homosexuals," where "individuals admit to having certain undesirable traits but cannot . . . be legally convicted by court-martial."[146]

The way the Doyle legislation proposed to rehabilitate certain soldiers itself suggests how the undesirable discharge had become even more stigmatizing than it was immediately after the Second World War. The greater stigma was the result of two factors. First, in response to the 1946 House report on blue discharges, the military had begun to give general discharges to some of those whose discharges fell between honorable and dishonorable. In continuing the World War II–era practice of using the undesirable discharge for soldiers discharged for homosexuality, the military increased the association between undesirability and homosexuality. "An undesirable discharge," one law professor told a Senate subcommittee, "carries with it the suspicion of homosexuality,

[143] The bill was enacted as Public Law 89-690, *U.S. Statutes at Large* 80 (1966) 1017. *Congressional Record*, 89th Cong., 2nd sess., October 4, 1966, 25083; *Congressional Record*, 89th Cong., 2nd sess., October 18, 1966, 27390.

[144] Proposed DOD Directive, May 6, 1957, file no. 211, box 37, AGO Legislative and Policy Precedent files 1943–1975, Records of the Adjutant General, RG 407.

[145] U.S. Congress, Senate, *Hearings on the Constitutional Rights of Military Personnel*, 10.

[146] *Congressional Record*, 85th Cong., 1st sess., August 5, 1957, 133667. Doyle's position on homosexuality did not stop the DOD from exploiting homosexuality to argue against the bill: "Should H.R. 1108 be enacted," the DOD wrote in opposition to the legislation, "a person administratively discharged as a homosexual . . . could demand that he be issued the same type of honorable discharge to which a combat veteran with a splendid record would be entitled, simply by establishing that his post-service conduct had been good." U.S. Congress, House, Committee on Armed Services, *House Report to Accompany H.R. 8722*, 11.

almost invariably."[147] Second, the increasing centrality of homophobia in 1950s' political culture—expressed most vividly in a congressional investigation in 1950 into "sex perverts" in the federal government—made the suspicion that homosexuality might lurk behind one's undesirable discharge even more damaging than it had been immediately after the war.[148] That the VA purged nearly as many suspected homosexuals from its employ as the Department of State did during the early stages of the "lavender scare," suggests as well that the agency continued to push the sexual stigma of the discharge well after the departure of General Hines.[149]

The impulse to protect some recipients of the undesirable discharge from the stigma of homosexuality was a major impetus behind Doyle's various attempts to sort veterans retroactively. After its enactment, the legislation helped to lessen the stigma of homosexuality for some undesirably discharged (presumably) heterosexual soldiers, while leaving them in a benefitless limbo of good citizenship. That legislators were not more concerned with restoring benefits to those soldiers is evidence of not only how much *closer* Congress had moved to the VA in its antipathy toward homosexuality, but also how much *further* it had moved from New Deal aspirations to distribute state resources broadly among the citizenry. As with the transients, one has to wonder if the two phenomena are related: Did the specter of perverse sexuality cast a shadow on the idea of universal social provision?[150]

[147] U.S. Congress, Senate, Committee on the Judiciary and Special Subcommittee of the Committee on Armed Services, *Hearings on S. 745-762, S. 2906–2907*, 89th Cong., 2nd sess., January 18, 19, 25, and 26, and March, 1, 2, and 3, 1966, 335.

[148] U.S. Congress, Senate, Committee on Expenditures in Executive Departments, *Employment of Homosexuals and Other Sex Perverts in Government*, 81st Cong., 2nd sess., 1950.

[149] Of the 574 cases of sex perversion documented in civilian agencies between January 1947 and November 1950, 143 were employees of the Department of State, and 101 were employees of the VA. The next highest number belongs to the Department of Commerce at 49 and then the Department of Agriculture at 32. Most agencies had no cases. See U.S. Congress, Senate, *Employment of Homosexuals and Other Sex Perverts in Government*, appendix III. On cold war homophobia and political culture more generally, see Cuordileone, "Politics in an Age of Anxiety"; D'Emilio, "The Homosexual Menace"; David K. Johnson, *The Lavender Scare: The Cold War Persecution of Gays and Lesbians in the Federal Government* (Chicago: University of Chicago Press, 2004); Randolph William Baxter, "'Eradicating This Menace'": Homophobia and Anti-Communism in Congress, 1947–1955" (PhD diss., University of California, Irvine, 1999).

[150] This is, of course, a highly speculative point, but one that I intend to suggest future avenues for research. Comparative work on this question might be especially useful. Is there a relationship between the universal social citizenship provided by the Beveridge plan in Britain and the government's 1957 Wolfenden Report, recommending the decriminalization of homosexual offenses (recommendations that were enacted in 1967, nearly four decades before the U.S. Supreme Court's *Lawrence v. Texas* decision)? What should historians make of the fact that the most socially democratic welfare states (in Scandi-

The Closet

Policy decisions by the military and the VA, and later by the Congress, drew on and helped strengthen an increasingly binaristic understanding of sexuality. As with other dualisms—man/woman, good/evil, light/dark—the two poles of sexual identity were not equally valued. Rather, as homosexuality began to crystallize as the opposite of heterosexuality in the postwar period, the latter was more explicitly connected to (while the former was more estranged from) first-class citizenship. That dynamic was readily apparent in the VA's reliance on sexual identity as the clearest criteria by which to adjudicate benefits to soldiers. But while the VA's reliance on a homosexual-heterosexual binary to separate the deserving from the undeserving helped to attach heterosexuality to the best class of citizens, it was only partially successful at channeling the flow of benefits toward them. A majority of the male and female soldiers who experienced or acted on homosexual desire during the Second World War *were* GI Bill beneficiaries.[151] "You know as well as I that there have been many 'homosexuals' in the Navy and the Army," one soldier frankly told Secretary of the Navy Forrestal, and "that many have been discharged 'under honorable conditions' because they were undiscovered."[152] The army's surgeon general conceded in 1946 that "following confidential research studies it is known that homosexuals were inducted into the service," and that "most of them served long and faithfully."[153] These soldiers were able to use GI Bill benefits to start businesses, buy homes, and attend college.[154] The down-payment that these soldiers made on their GI Bill entitlements

---

navia) have generally been the most progressive in providing rights for sexual minorities? Closer to home, is it only a coincidence that the first state to enact same-sex marriage (Massachusetts) followed that legislation with a pathbreaking plan to provide to its citizens the most universal health care in the nation?

[151] See, for example, Bérubé, *Coming Out Under Fire*, 245.

[152] Robert ———— to James Forrestal, July 16, 1946, box 15, World War II Project Records.

[153] Norman T. Kirk to Assistant to the Secretary of War, July 20, 1946, box 17, World War II Project Records.

[154] All of which may have furthered the development of urban subcultures, which were a precondition for the emergence of the gay rights movement. See John D'Emilio, *Sexual Politics, Sexual Communities: The Making of a Homosexual Minority in the United States, 1940–1970* (Chicago: University of Chicago Press, 1983). Bérubé argues as well that the gay rights movement was to some extent motivated by the unfair treatment of soldiers suspected of homosexuality by the military and under the GI Bill. "The GI Bill of Rights, which was meant to protect veterans from the inequities of the discharge system, together with the campaign against blue discharges, introduced the concepts of 'rights,' 'injustice,' and 'discrimination' to public discussions of homosexuality" (*Coming Out Under Fire*, 249, 253).

was remaining hidden while in the service.[155] "I have laid down an iron clad rule for myself that any[one to whom] I may be connected officially is 'off limits,'" one officer wrote, after a "section eight" case landed on his desk "with the ugly word [blue discharge] written across it. . . . Not if I can help it," he concluded.[156] For such individuals, the state's allocation of veterans' benefits may have been internally fragmenting—providing the possibility for a better life even while stigmatizing a central element of it.

In essence, the military establishment used the GI Bill to build a closet within federal social policy. The closet depended on the visible exclusion of certain soldiers believed to have engaged in homosexual acts or to possess homosexual tendencies. The closet simultaneously allowed for the inclusion of many soldiers who experienced homosexuality during World War II. Yet the invisibility of those soldiers was critical. It drove deeper the wedge separating homosexuality and citizenship by enabling military and VA officials to pretend that homosexual soldiers had not defended their country, and that they could not meet the obligations of good citizens. This sleight of hand in turn highlighted the masculinism of the citizen-soldier. "War is not a petting party," remarked one congressman during debate on the GI Bill, "it is not a powder puff affair."[157]

Such masculinism also helped conceal another type of soldier—women—and ensured that women's contributions to the war effort would also be minimized.[158] This made it more difficult for women veterans to claim their benefits as rights they had earned, and reinforced lawmakers in upholding the gender inequities that had been written into the GI Bill legislation. The GI Bill offered the most generous benefits to married men—shoring up their position as family providers

[155] Soldiers were made aware that in-service conduct would have an impact on their lives after discharge. The text of one "Armed Forces Talk" warned soldiers that homosexuality was one of the grounds for an undesirable discharge, and that "your eligibility for veterans' preference in federal employment, for payments for service-connected disability, for a pension, and for many other benefits and privileges . . . will depend upon the type of discharge you receive. . . . Therefore, it is of the utmost importance to your future life that you do all you can to earn a discharge under honorable conditions. To do so should be one of your major concerns throughout your service." "Armed Forces Talk," 288, file no. 211, box 36, AGO Legislative and Policy Precedent file 1943–1975, Records of the Adjutant General, RG 407.

[156] The discharge was for homosexuality. Sid to Hal, May 7, 1944, decimal 250.1, box 73, General Correspondence 1939–1947, Records of the Inspector General, RG 159, National Archives, College Park, MD.

[157] U.S. Congress, House, *Hearings on H.R. 3917 and S. 1767*, 203. The speaker was the committee chair, John Rankin.

[158] Women's military service was rendered invisible by devaluing women's actual military service as well as women's work in the war industries.

through dependency allowances and survivors' benefits.[159] Women's benefits—particularly allowances granted to care for dependents—were inferior to men's to begin with, and women veterans also faced hostility from the veterans' organizations that helped so many male veterans obtain their GI Bill benefits.[160] Most critically, the fact that the military capped women's participation in the military at 2 percent of the total force (until 1967) circumscribed women's overall access to the GI Bill, automatically directing 98 percent of state resources allocated for veterans toward men.[161] All of this ensured that most women would experience the expansion of welfare state provision primarily through their husbands' benefits.[162]

The GI Bill did more than just create a closet, then. It also institutionalized heterosexuality by channeling resources to men so that—at a moment when women had made significant gains in the workplace—the economic incentives for women to marry remained firmly in place. The

[159] For the way that military benefits for active-duty personnel also "structure the social relations of recipients, primarily in ways that promote the reproduction of dominant gender and familial forms," see Gifford, "The Camouflaged Safety Net," 388. On the GI Bill's selective generosity, see Cohen, *A Consumers' Republic*, 137–39; June A. Willenz, *Women Veterans: America's Forgotten Heroines* (New York: Continuum, 1983), 169. Legislators intended that widows of deceased male veterans receive their husbands' benefits (and the use of dead or disabled husbands' veterans preference points) as derivative of the men who had "earned" them, rather than as women's own entitlements. Ritter, "Of War and Virtue," 223. As Cott observed, "The G.I. Bill dispensed privileges to as much as one quarter of the population . . . and at the same time confirmed the rightness of a family model in which the male head was the most secure and best skilled provider in the household" (*Public Vows*, 191).

[160] According to Hartmann, the "assumption that women were economic dependents not supporters" undermined benefits for women veterans (*The Home Front and Beyond*, 44). Women veterans could not collect unemployment benefits until they demonstrated that they were not receiving support from a male wage earner. Male dependency distressed legislators; hence, women veterans attending college collected smaller allowances for dependent spouses than did male veterans. Cohen, *A Consumers' Republic*, 138. Similarly, unremarried widows, but not widowers, of veterans were eligible for GI loans for homes, farms, and businesses. Benefits for dependents of women veterans were equalized in 1972. Willenz, *Women Veterans*, 169, 193. On discrimination against women in benefits' counseling, see Cohen, *A Consumers' Republic*, 138.

[161] *New York Times*, July 26, 1946, 18; Kerber, *No Constitutional Right to Be Ladies*, 227. Hartmann explains that "the G.I. Bill . . . increased the gap between men and women in opportunities and status" (*The Home Front and Beyond*, 26). Not all women who served in the military during the Second World War were eligible for GI Bill benefits. It wasn't until 1980 that women who served in the Women's Auxiliary Army Corps (the predecessor to the WAC) and the Women's Airforce Service Pilots (the air force equivalent of the WAC) were awarded veterans' benefits. Willenz, *Women Veterans*, 169.

[162] Women were also incorporated into Social Security—the other major welfare state outlay—primarily through their husbands' benefits. See Kessler-Harris, *In Pursuit of Equity*, chapter 3.

institutionalization of heterosexuality in federal welfare policy was a two-part process that required the state to provide economic support for marriage (through male breadwinners) at the same time that it stigmatized homosexuality.[163] The way that sexual identity was used to differentiate among citizens both drew on and helped to preserve other axes of subordination, especially, in this case, that of gender.[164] Still, wives might collect benefits, and so might numerous soldiers who had expressed homosexual desire during the war. But the shakiness of their claims only underscored the dignified and easy access to benefits that the prototypical heterosexual male citizen-soldier enjoyed. The way that the GI Bill excluded certain soldiers from the benefits of citizenship must be understood in tandem with the way that it included them; that inclusion not only shored up male and heterosexual privilege, but simultaneously relied on those who differed from the normative to reveal the most deserving strata of the citizenry.

Benefits for veterans illustrate that establishing conditions for inclusion and exclusion in national citizenship also meant distinguishing homosexuality from heterosexuality. The homosexual-heterosexual binary visibly emerged in federal welfare policy during these critical years of American state-building. It seemed to happen quite suddenly, but federal officials for years had been gradually setting traits and behaviors that were coming to be associated with homosexuality in opposition to citizenship (in military, immigration, and welfare policy). The pace of change quickened during and after World War II, however, and the state's increased social provisioning was one impetus behind the speedup, as it provided officials with yet another reason to sort and evaluate the citizenry. The VA's implementation of the GI Bill in particular demonstrates how the state's distributive function sharpened iden-

---

[163] On the history of state economic support for marriage, see Cott, *Public Vows*; Kessler-Harris, *In Pursuit of Equity*; Peggy Pascoe, "Race, Gender, and the Privileges of Property: On the Significance of Miscegenation Law," in *Over the Edge: Remapping the American West*, ed. Valerie J. Matsumoto and Blake Allmendinger (Berkeley: University of California Press, 1999), 215–30.

[164] Implementation of the GI Bill also reinforced the whiteness of the normative citizen. Many black soldiers received dishonorable or undesirable discharges, making them ineligible for the GI Bill. But even black soldiers who were technically eligible experienced difficulty collecting their benefits; veterans' organizations denied them membership; those who approached the VA for help sometimes faced hostility; white colleges refused them admission; and housing loans were often useless for them because the VA required veterans to qualify at private banks, many of which refused to qualify black veterans for loans. Cohen, *A Consumers' Republic*, 167–73. David Onkst argues that the GI Bill was of limited use to black World War II veterans in the South because of both racial discrimination and poor administration. See David Onkst, "'First a Negro . . . Incidentally a Veteran': Black World War Two Veterans and the G.I. Bill of Rights in the Deep South, 1944–1948," *Journal of Social History* 31 (Spring 1998): 517–44. See also Katznelson, *When Affirmative Action Was White*.

tity categories in especially acute ways. With more resources to give out, the question of *who* would benefit became substantially more important (to those offering the handouts and to those with their hands out). What kind of person was deserving of state support? What kind of person was not? In the context of answering those questions, the federal government would come to penalize the homosexual, as one midcentury commentator put it, "less for what he does than for what he is."[165]

While homosexual status would begin to be explicitly targeted, the tools used for such policing across the federal bureaucracy would, paradoxically, remain vague. Such vague tools (like the undesirable discharge) absolved the state of having to provide hard evidence of homosexual behavior, *but not from having to produce the category that it simultaneously wanted to regulate.* In making its vague devices work with its explicit prohibitions—prohibitions against being homosexual—the federal government would help to constitute homosexuality. This production occurred not despite but through ambiguous instruments. The military's policy on homosexual "tendencies," as the next chapter will show, is an especially revealing example.

[165] Alfred A. Gross to George Rundquist, September 18, 1962, folder 4, box 1068, ACLU Collection.

CHAPTER 5

MILITARY

"Finding a Home in the Army"

Women's Integration, Homosexual Tendencies,
and the Cold War Military, 1947–1959

———◦———

While Alfred Kinsey's 1953 study of female sexuality is usually remembered for shattering several mid-twentieth-century myths about
women's sexual behavior, the volume also contained several important
observations about the American state, especially concerning the regulation of homosexuality among women. The relationship between the
state and female homosexuality, Kinsey concluded in *Sexual Behavior in
the Human Female*, was not a well-developed one. The state had, in fact,
a long history of indifference to homosexuality among women. Kinsey
observed that while state sodomy statutes had generally been drafted
in gender-neutral language that could encompass sexual acts between
women, his "search through several hundred sodomy opinions which
have been reported in this country between 1696 and 1912 . . . failed to
reveal a single case sustaining the conviction of a female for homosexual activity." Kinsey's survey of the more recent enforcement of sex law
in New York City revealed three cases from the 1940s or 1950s in which
women had been arrested for homosexuality. "But all of these cases
were dismissed," Kinsey noted, "although there were some tens of
thousands of arrests and convictions of males charged with homosexual activity" during those same years.[1]

Kinsey's assertion about government indifference to lesbianism is ac-
curate even when applied in contexts beyond the state-level regulation
of sexual behavior that he surveyed. In the early years of the twentieth
century that this study has documented, the federal government's concern with sexually degenerate aliens included effeminate men and male
sodomists, but focused on neither mannishness nor same-sex eroticism

[1] Alfred C. Kinsey, *Sexual Behavior in the Human Female* (Philadelphia: Saunders, 1953),
484–85. See also "The Consenting Adult Homosexual and the Law: An Empirical Study of
Enforcement and Administration in Los Angeles County," *UCLA Law Review* 13 (1966): 740.

among women. While World War I vice investigators occasionally identified "female pervertors" in and around military bases—one witness
even testified during 1919 hearings into the homosexual scandal at the
Newport naval training station that "there were a lot of queer women
in Newport"—such revelations seemed to have little impact on local,
state, or federal policing, which remained directed at men.[2] It was concern about male degeneration, moreover, that resulted in federal services for male transients. Female drifters—however closely associated
with psychopathy—were on their own.

Work on mid-twentieth-century America by historians of sexuality
supports Kinsey's insight as well. In his study of gays and lesbians during the Second World War, for example, Allan Bérubé argues that lesbians were often invisible to military authorities and women were
rarely discharged for homosexuality.[3] Even during the massive 1950s'
purge of homosexuals from the civil service, women (who comprised 40
percent of the federal workforce) were far less likely to be targeted than
men. "Of the initial ninety-one homosexuals fired from the State Department," historian David Johnson writes, "only two were women."[4]

Yet while generally true, Kinsey's conclusion about state indifference
to lesbianism does not hold in at least one time and place: the early cold
war military. Here one finds a state that did not ignore, conflate, or sub-
sume lesbianism, but was instead focused upon it. Although women
made up just 1 percent of the force during the late 1940s and early 1950s,
the military's efforts to purge soldiers suspected of homosexuality targeted women especially. Military officials maintained that homosexuality among women was more disruptive to morale and discipline than
homosexuality in men, and they attributed a far higher rate of homosexual activity to female than male personnel.[5] "I could have written a
supplement to the Kinsey report," declared the director of the Women's

[2] Testimony of Zipf, 19, March 18, 1919, file no. 10821-1, box 254, Proceedings of the
Court of Inquiry 1866–1940, Records of the Judge Advocate General (Navy), RG 125, National Archives, Washington, DC.

[3] Allan Bérubé, *Coming Out Under Fire: The History of Gay Men and Women in World War
II* (New York: Plume, 1991), 28.

[4] David K. Johnson, *The Lavender Scare: The Cold War Persecution of Gays and Lesbians in
the Federal Government* (Chicago: University of Chicago Press, 2004), 12. Johnson's finding
holds true for civilian employees of the Department of Defense (DOD). In 1957, the navy's
Crittenden Report observed that female employees of the DOD were terminated for homosexuality far less often than male civil servants in that agency. Crittenden Report, 54,
box 16, World War II Project Records, Gay, Lesbian, Bisexual, and Transgender Historical
Society, San Francisco. Relatedly, Elizabeth Lunbeck notes that male homosexuality has
almost always been more condemned by sexologists than lesbianism. See Elizabeth Lunbeck, *The Psychiatric Persuasion: Knowledge, Gender, and Power in Modern America* (Princeton, NJ: Princeton University Press, 2003), 410–11.

[5] Crittenden Report, 40, box 16, World War II Project Records.

Army Corps (WAC) in her report on the prevalence of lesbianism after the war.[6]

As with earlier moments of increased federal attention to homoerotic practices and desires, the process of state-building itself stimulated growing federal interest in homosexuality among military women. The coming of the cold war, as political scientist Bruce D. Porter has argued, gave an enduring "cast to the transmutations of World War II"—especially the increased size of the bureaucratic state, which remained "intact."[7] The postwar boom in military spending expanded the economy generally, paving the way for greater numbers of women to enter the civilian labor force.[8] Cold war expansion also created a lasting need for women inside the military. When Congress authorized a permanent peacetime force that was at least five times its 1939 size, it simultaneously provided for a stable nucleus of women who would attend to the military's growing clerical, administrative, and other needs. Legislation that permanently integrated women into the regular forces was passed in 1948.[9]

Homosexuality mattered most to state officials in the places where citizenship was defined, and if women's military service was becoming less peripheral, then so was their perversion. The cold war military thus reveals another federal arena in which the increasingly salient opposition between citizenship and homosexuality was forged, but one in which the lesbian was as meaningful in defining citizenship's outside as the figure of the male homosexual. Women's proximity to first-class citizenship helps to explain why the focus on lesbianism first became apparent inside the cold war military, but other factors were at work. The federal regulation of homosexuality among women also depended on the crystallization of a binaristic conception of homosexuality and heterosexuality, which as previous chapters have shown, developed gradually in the years before World War II, and then hardened during and immediately after the war. By the late 1940s and early 1950s, many

---

[6] Memorandum from Colonel Mary Hallaren to Major General G. E. Byers, "The Homosexual Problem," January–February 1950, box 86, Background Papers, Women's Army Corps 1945–1978, Records of the Army Chief of Staff, RG 319, National Archives, College Park, MD.

[7] Bruce D. Porter, *War and the Rise of the State: The Military Foundations of Modern Politics* (New York: Free Press, 1994), 286–91.

[8] Alice Kessler-Harris, *Out to Work: A History of Wage Earning Women in the United States* (Oxford: Oxford University Press, 1982), 303.

[9] Women's Armed Services Act of 1948, Public Law 80-625, *U.S. Statutes at Large* 62 (1948) 368. Two weeks after the enactment of women's integration, Harry S. Truman authorized the nation's first-ever peacetime draft (the Selective Service Act of 1948). Jeanne Holm, *Women in the Military: An Unfinished Revolution* (Novato, CA: Presidio Press, 1992), 129.

Americans (and certainly most state officials) believed that individuals were either heterosexual or homosexual, and that "normal" men and women were those who had sexual relations with persons of the opposite sex. As a result of this broad-ranging conceptual shift, and in contrast to the early twentieth century, men and women who were identified as homosexual were seen as fundamentally similar kinds of people, and this paved the way for a military policy that applied to both men and women "irrespective of sex."[10]

In drafting new guidelines after the war, military officials were adamant that a single policy would be used to deal with homosexuality among both sexes. Under that policy, women, like men, could be discharged for either committing homosexual acts or possessing homosexual tendencies. Yet while military authorities used the same regulation to handle male and female personnel suspected of homosexuality, the policy was implemented in ways that suggested gender difference. Unsure of how to define a homosexual act between women, military authorities often relied on the provision barring soldiers who had homosexual "tendencies" to eliminate women who were physically intimate with other women. Moreover, officials not only believed that sex among women was less easily defined than sex between men, but that women were more private in their sexual lives. As a result, and in contrast to the way that investigations of homosexuality among men often centered around the commission of an act, women's romantic attachments, social networks, and emotional ties were all scrutinized for evidence that a woman possessed homosexual tendencies. The provision on tendencies thus enabled military authorities to aggressively police what they believed to be a less public sexual culture, one in which "proof" would be harder to come by.

As relationships (rather than relations) became the focus of state policing, antilesbian investigations took on an unprecedented size. Such investigations encompassed not simply the parties to an alleged sexual encounter, but an expansive web of friends and acquaintances that sometimes extended far beyond a single base or unit. These ordeals—which represented a huge expansion of the state's investigatory power—were a manifestation of the military's own ambivalence about the women who served in the military after the war. In contrast to the women whose World War II service was understood as a heroically brief interlude before marriage, this later cohort signed up not to meet a temporary emergency but rather as part of a permanent nucleus of women

[10] Hubert E. Howard to the Secretary of the Army, the Secretary of the Navy, the Secretary of the Air Force, "Discharge of Homosexuals from the Armed Services," October 11, 1949, decimal 250.1, box 100, Assistant Secretary of Defense decimal file 1949–1950, Records of the Secretary of Defense, RG 330, National Archives, College Park, MD.

within the armed services. Because they were seen as choosing the military (as opposed to marriage) for a career, these soldiers were automatically suspect, considered overly ambitious and unlikely to be satisfied with the things that "normal" women wanted. The way that these soldiers were policed, then, was related to why they were policed: antilesbian investigations aimed not only to remove a few women from the service, but to employ the threat of lesbianism to secure the subordination of women soldiers as a class. Policing this vast network of relationships enabled military officials to touch the lives of virtually every woman in a unit under investigation, warning each not only to monitor her own relationships with other women on her base, but to avoid appearing too driven or exercising too much authority as well. The exclusion of women believed to be lesbians was, in short, closely related to the inclusion of women in the service in general. Lesbianism was constituted by military authorities to help maintain gender hierarchy after women's integration eliminated a historic barrier between male and female service.

The way that military officials policed lesbianism not only set limits on the career aspirations of women soldiers, it changed the very configuration of homosexuality. It was the policing of women that brought together into one regulatory framework all of the elements that have become the markers of homosexuality in the postwar era—a homosexuality that reveals itself not only through sexual acts and gender inversion, but in the architecture of relationships, culture, and community. Thus, while the military may seem distinct from the rest of the federal state—and its treatment of women especially anomalous—it more than any other institution of state power identified the attributes of lesbianism and brought that assemblage *into* homosexuality.[11]

The Increasing Focus on Lesbianism

Albeit in a temporary capacity, women first served in the U.S. military in significant numbers during the Second World War.[12] Approximately 350,000 women enlisted during those years in the WAC or its equivalent

[11] On "militarization"—the movement of military "ideas, values, and structures" into the broader culture—see Laura McEnaney, *Civil Defense Begins at Home: Militarization Meets Everyday Life in the Fifties* (Princeton, NJ: Princeton University Press, 2000), 6; Michael S. Sherry, *In the Shadow of War: The United States since the 1930s* (New Haven, CT: Yale University Press, 1995).

[12] Small numbers of women served during World War I. See Lettie Gavin, *American Women in World War I: They Also Served* (Boulder: University Press of Colorado, 1997); Susan Zieger, *In Uncle Sam's Service: Women Workers with the American Expeditionary Force, 1917–1919* (Ithaca, NY: Cornell University Press, 1999); Jean Ebbert and Marie Beth-Hall,

in the other branches of the armed services (the WAVES, WAF, WASP, or SPARS).[13] Women were drawn to the military for a variety of reasons—it offered excitement and independence, as well as a chance to serve the country. A portion of those who enlisted were also attracted by the emotional and perhaps sexual dimensions of working and living with other women. Some of these women continued in the military a lesbian life they had led before the war; some had their first romantic or sexual experiences with women after they enlisted. As long as they did not attract public attention, the military generally ignored "romantic friendships" among women. But women who drew suspicion of lesbianism to their unit—usually butch, often working-class women—presented a greater problem for military authorities. Such women were only rarely subject to formal regulations barring homosexuality, but historian Leisa Meyer argues that the military used "informal means" to deal with some women who were not conventionally feminine. They might be discharged for unsuitability (or for such general offenses as public drunkenness or insubordination), if they even made it past the initial screening procedures that "focused on class background, education, personality, and behavior . . . to eliminate women who demonstrated characteristics culturally associated with female homosexuality."[14]

While military officials occasionally acknowledged that "homosexuality occur[red] among women also," they did not develop explicit instructions for handling lesbianism until almost the end of the war.[15] In 1944, a manual for military psychiatrists advised that lesbians should be excluded and instructed psychiatrists "to be on guard against the homosexual who may see in the WAC an opportunity to indulge her perversity."[16] Yet despite growing official recognition that lesbian-

---

The First, the Few, the Forgotten: Navy and Marine Corps Women in World War I (Annapolis: Naval Institute Press, 2002).

[13] Most of the evidence for this chapter is from army records, because records are most available for that branch of the service. The Records of the Secretary of the Air Force at the National Archives, for example, have only been declassified recently. Because all branches were under the DOD after 1947, however, relatively uniform policies guided all branches, and wherever possible, I have included evidence from the air force and navy.

[14] Leisa D. Meyer, "The Myth of Lesbian (In)visibility: World War II and the Current Gays in the Military Debate," in Queer American History, ed. Alida M. Black (Philadelphia: Temple University Press, 2001), 272; Leisa D. Meyer, Creating G.I. Jane: Sexuality and Power in the Women's Army Corps (New York: Columbia University Press, 1996), 156, 161, and chapter 7 generally.

[15] Meyer, Creating G.I. Jane, 157 (quoting policy); Memorandum for Chief of Staff, October 25, 1943, decimal 250.1, box 438, G-1 (Personnel) decimal file 1942–1946, War Department General Staff, RG 165, National Archives, College Park, MD.

[16] Meyer, Creating G.I. Jane, quoting War Department manual TB MED 100 ("WAC Recruiting Stations Neuropsychiatric Examination"), 158.

ism existed among women soldiers, military officials continued to de-emphasize it. "During the war," WAC commander Mary Hallaren remembered, "we skirted the homosexual problem."[17] An army inspector general's report from 1944 found little evidence of homosexuality among women, contending that "the incidence seemed no greater and probably less than in the civilian population."[18] That assessment was echoed in military psychiatrist William Menninger's account of the war, in which he defined homosexuality in terms of sexual activity between men, and asserted that homosexuality among women was never a "serious" problem in the military.[19] Similarly, WAC psychiatrist Margaret Craighill described homosexuality as a "serious problem" for men during the war, but "much less of a problem than . . . expected" for women.[20]

Such attitudes stand in stark relief to those expressed in the years after the war. Women's entry into the armed services paralleled a broader movement of women into the labor market overall during these years, and women in the military generally performed the same kind of clerical work as their counterparts in the civil service.[21] But while many working women pushed up against the conservative gender ideology of the era, only women in the service threatened the special relationship between men, soldiering, and martial citizenship.[22] Hence, while the purge of homosexuals from the civil service did not target women, similar witch hunts in the military did. Widespread concern about lesbianism among women in the military, moreover, actually preceded the 1950s' "lavender scare" in the federal government.[23] What

[17]Memorandum from Colonel Mary Hallaren to Major General G. E. Byers, "The Homosexual Problem," January–February 1950, box 86, Background Papers, Women's Army Corps 1945–1978, Records of the Army Chief of Staff, RG 319.

[18]Mattie E. Treadwell, *The United States Army in World War II, Special Studies, the Women's Army Corps* (Washington, DC: Office of the Chief of Military History, Department of the Army, 1954), 626.

[19]William Menninger, *Psychiatry in a Troubled World: Yesterday's War and Today's Challenge* (New York: Macmillan, 1948), 225, 106.

[20]Margaret Craighill, "Psychiatric Aspects of Women Serving in the Army," *American Journal of Psychiatry* 104 (1947–1948): 228.

[21]On women's workforce participation during the 1950s, see Kessler-Harris, *Out to Work*, chapter 11; Susan M. Hartmann, "Women's Employment and the Domestic Ideal in the Early Cold War Years," in *Not June Cleaver: Women and Gender in Postwar America, 1945–1960*, ed. Joanne Meyerowitz (Philadelphia: Temple University Press, 1994), 84–100. On women's work in the military, see Holm, *Women in the Military*, especially 113, 175.

[22]On domestic ideology during the 1950s, see especially Elaine Tyler May, *Homeward Bound: American Families in the Cold War Era* (New York: Basic Books, 1988). On the tension between gender ideology and women's work, see Kessler-Harris, *Out to Work*, 300.

[23]The fullest account of the midcentury purge of civil servants suspected of homosexuality is Johnson, *The Lavender Scare*. See also John D'Emilio, *Sexual Politics, Sexual Com-*

one journalist referred to as the military's "project lesbian" instead co-incided with congressional debates on women's integration in 1947 and 1948.[24] During those hearings, military and congressional leaders argued that the services would only be able to meet recruitment goals for female personnel if women were given the opportunity to build a lasting career in the military.[25] Official interest in lesbianism arose in tandem with the military's growing need for women.

It was, for example, as Congress was making plans for women's permanent entry into the service in 1947 that the army drafted instructions for investigating homosexuality among female soldiers.[26] The creation of these guidelines suggests that such investigations were becoming widespread. In 1948, as integration was enacted, the military established the WAC Training Center at Fort Lee, and in response to what it then described as an extraordinarily high rate of homosexuality among women, included lectures on homosexuality in the curriculum for enlistees. (The approach may have backfired as a special 1950 report on Fort Lee noted that many of the WAC soldiers there were still "homo-sexually inclined.")[27] Leadership courses for noncommissioned officers and officer refresher courses introduced around the same time included segments on how to detect and handle abnormal conduct among female personnel. The approach was, the WAC director wrote, to bring homosexuality among women out from "behind a veil of silence and mystery." It was also obvious "from recent developments," she concluded, perhaps alluding to a growing number of investigations under her watch, "that what had been done [was] not enough."[28]

Some months later Lieutenant General Lutes reported to WAC director Hallaren that "the indications continue to grow that a condition of homosexuality is widespread in the army." Despite the outbreak of war

munities: *The Making of a Homosexual Minority in the United States, 1940–1970* (Chicago: University of Chicago Press, 1983), chapter 3.

[24] Sam Crown, "Do Lesbians Dominate Our WAC?" *SIR* (March 1956): 20, in vertical file "Homosexuals in the Military," Kinsey Institute, Indiana University, Bloomington.

[25] Janann Sherman, "'They Either Need These Women or They Do Not': Margaret Chase Smith and the Fight for Regular Status for Women in the Military," *Journal of Military History* 54 (January 1990): 72.

[26] Memo from R. L. Howze, "Investigation of WAC Personnel," October 14, 1947, decimal 321, box 843, "WAC Project," G-1 (Personnel) decimal file 1946–1948, War Department General Staff, RG 165.

[27] Report of President's Committee on Petersburg, Virginia, July 7, 1950, decimal 334, box 3653, "President's Commission," classified decimal file 1948–1950, Records of the Adjutant General, RG 407, National Archives, College Park, MD.

[28] Memorandum from Colonel Mary Hallaren to Major General G. E. Byers on "the Homosexual Problem," January–February 1950, box 86, Background Papers, Women's Army Corps 1945–1978, Records of the Army Chief of Staff, RG 319.

Psychiatrist Marion Kenworthy training officers on recruit selection methods at the WAC Training Center at Fort Lee in Virginia. Lesbianism would have been on the agenda. Marion Kenworthy Papers, Rare Books and Manuscript Library, Columbia University. Used with permission.

with Korea—which might have encouraged officials to look the other way—150 enlisted women and officers were implicated, Lutes told Hallaren, in investigations into homosexuality in the Fourth Army.[29] In 1951, a memo from the commanding officer of the Military District of Washington described the situation in more alarming tones. "The number of sexual perverts in the WAC who are assigned to this command is a matter of grave concern to me," he wrote. "This situation is steadily growing worse, although I have been cognizant of it for some time and have used every means at my disposal to cope with it." The command had already separated two officers and transferred four more; nine enlisted women had been undesirably discharged for homosexuality. Beyond that, the general claimed to have conclusive evidence that another thirteen WAC soldiers were perverts and stated that eleven others were under suspicion. The general's memo prompted a high-level meeting

[29] Lt. General L. Lutes to Colonel Mary A. Hallaren, November 22, 1950, decimal 333.9, "Fourth Army," box 1012, decimal file July 1950–June 1951, Records of the Inspector General, RG 159, National Archives, College Park, MD.

with seven other commanders a month later.[30] The numbers themselves were not unusual, but reflected a broader pattern. Investigations conducted at any given base during these years regularly involved up to twenty women and sometimes several times that number.[31]

The army's postwar focus on homosexuality among women existed with equal or greater intensity in the navy, air force, and marines. When he took command of his office, for instance, the head of the air force's special investigations unit did not believe the rumors concerning homosexuality among air force women because they were so incredible. He soon found that the "situation was actually more fantastic than the rumors." A major in the WAC described the air force's "mechanism" for investigating female homosexuals, noting that "large numbers of both the old timers and the newer crop," including one woman referred to as the "queen bee," had already been "clear[ed] out."[32] A 1952 report on the women's marine detachment at El Toro, California, observed that homosexuality among the women there was considered to be a "definite problem" that probably existed at other bases as well.[33] Yet it was the navy's 1957 Crittenden report that most clearly articulated that homosexuality was a special problem among women.[34] The report noted that "homosexual activity of female members of the military has appeared to be more disruptive of morale and discipline . . . than similar male activity," and it posited a higher rate of homosexuality for women than men in the navy.[35] The different rates might have resulted from a variety of factors, the Crittenden Board opined, including both greater surveillance and the attraction of military service to "females with

[30] Memorandum from Major General Thomas W. Herren, March 26, 1951, "Unsatisfactory Control," decimal 250.1, box 967, G-1 (Personnel) decimal file 1951–1952, Records of the Army Chief of Staff, RG 319; Memorandum from Colonel W. T. Moore, Chief, Personnel Actions Branch, April 24, 1951, "Homosexuality," decimal 250.1, box 967, G-1 (Personnel) decimal file 1951–1952, Records of the Army Chief of Staff, RG 319.

[31] See, for example, discharge files for homosexuality, decimal 220.8, boxes 3592–93, Classified decimal file 1948–1950, Records of the Adjutant General, RG 407; decimal 220.8, boxes 3776–78, Classified decimal file 1950–1951, Records of the Adjutant General, RG 407. See also decimal 333.5, "WAC," box 2401, Confidential decimal file July 1958–June 1959, Records of the Inspector General, RG 159.

[32] Major Robin Elliott to Colonel Lewis and General Lutes, "Air Force Investigation," November 20, 1950, decimal 333.9, "Fourth Army," box 1012, decimal file July 1950–June 1951, Records of the Inspector General, RG 159.

[33] Lt. Bowdre L. Carswell to Chief of the Bureau of Medicine and Surgery, October 22, 1952, file no. P13-1, box 503, Administrative Division General Correspondence 1952–1955, Bureau of Medicine and Surgery, RG 52, National Archives, College Park, MD.

[34] The Crittenden Board was a special committee assembled by the navy in 1957 to study homosexuality in the military.

[35] Crittenden Report, 40–41, box 16, World War II Project Records. Because the services did not break down overall discharge statistics by gender, there is not hard statistical evi-

latent homosexual tendencies."[36] That analysis suggested the military's own uneasiness with the women who chose the military rather than marriage for their career; it was also a harbinger of the incredibly broad way that the military's antihomosexual apparatus would be used against all women in the service. To understand the military's broadest purposes in regulating homosexuality, it is necessary to look at its most precise targets. Antilesbian repression in the military was *broadly* powerful against all women because it was *individually* devastating against a smaller number. How, then, was homosexuality in women defined, how was it policed in specific women, and how did those individuals who were directly targeted resist such policing?

Defining Female Homosexuality

In its discussion of the high incidence rate of homosexuality among women, the navy's Crittenden Board noted a strange paradox: the prevalence of female homosexuality was, the board wrote, "in contradiction to the fact that homosexual activity in the female is difficult to detect." That difficulty arose because military officials, as they admitted again and again, were unclear as to what characterized homosexuality among women. The Crittenden Board confessed to "uncertainties" about female homosexuality, noting that it was "impossible to provide a fixed and concise overall definition to all that constitutes homosexual activity in the female."[37] The commanding general of the Fourth Army concurred: "Little is apparently known about female homosexuality," he remarked.[38] Military officials contrasted the mystery of homosexuality among women to its relatively straightforward expression among men. "It is generally understood that homosexuality between males is manifested [by] . . . commonly known perverse sexual acts," wrote two military psychiatrists based at Fort McClellan. "On the other hand, there is practically no understanding . . . as to what is evidence of homosexual

---

dence available to back up this claim. Approximately 4,380 cases of perversion were handled by the armed services from January 1947 to October 1950. Another estimated 10,000 cases were handled by the armed services from November 1950 to December 1955. Louis Jolyon West, William T. Doidge, and Robert L. Williams, "An Approach to the Problem of Homosexuality in the Military Service," *American Journal of Psychiatry* 115 (November 1958): 400.

[36] Crittenden Report, 40–41, box 16, World War II Project Records.

[37] Ibid.

[38] Lt. General L. Lutes to Colonel Mary A. Hallaren, November 22, 1950, decimal 333.9, "Fourth Army," box 1012, decimal file July 1950–June 1951, Records of the Inspector General, RG 159.

activity between women." Homosexuality in women might consist of anything, the Fort McClellan psychiatrists stated, from the "bus station pick up . . . to a close emotional relationship extending over a period of years with no more than . . . casual physical contact."[39] As this broad range suggests, the ambiguity of homosexuality in women increased its scope.

Part of the confusion as to what comprised female homosexuality resulted from a greater cultural tolerance for homosocial intimacy between women than between men. Acts that were "indicative of homosexuality in the male" were thought "normal [in] the female." Women might, the Crittenden Board reported, "kiss and embrace . . . and live together and occupy the same bed without any connotation of homosexuality," while "similar acts on the part of males would immediately be branding." In a military context, where women had to adapt to male behavioral norms, such circumstances meant that "normal female propensities" might be misinterpreted as homosexual acts.[40] "It is very difficult to know where to draw the line on anything of this kind," commented WAC director Hallaren.[41]

But military officials did not attribute the high rate of homosexuality among women solely to such misinterpretation. Rather, as the WAC director conceded of the women in her branch, there might be "some fact among the fancy."[42] Indeed, widespread acceptance of the expression of affection between women could conceal actual homosexuality in the service. Relationships among women, army psychiatrists wrote, could be "more easily covered" than relationships among men.[43] A homosexual act between two women "leaves no physical evidence of its commission," an army manual on female homosexuality noted, "and seldom if ever is committed in the presence of an innocent person."[44] Relatedly, the Crittenden Board noted that female homosexuality was difficult to

[39] M. D. Hogan and R. E. Anderson to CG, Third Army, "Fort McClellan, Mental Hygiene Consultations Service Report," September 14, 1956, box 64, Background Papers, Women's Army Corps 1945–1978, Records of the Army Chief of Staff, RG 319.

[40] Crittenden Report, 40–41, box 16, World War II Project Records.

[41] Colonel Mary Hallaren, Interview by Colonel Donald Hargrove and Lt. Colonel Milton Little, March 7, 1977, box 86, Background Papers, Women's Army Corps 1945–1978, Records of the Army Chief of Staff, RG 319.

[42] Mary Hallaren to Marion E. Kenworthy, April 17, 1950, "WAC Conference June 1950" folder, box 26, Marion Kenworthy Papers, Rare Book and Manuscript Library, Columbia University, New York.

[43] M. D. Hogan and R. E. Anderson to CG, Third Army, "Fort McClellan, Mental Hygiene Consultations Service Report," September 14, 1956, box 64, Background Papers, Women's Army Corps 1945–1978, Records of the Army Chief of Staff, RG 319.

[44] "Female Homosexuality," 1950, decimal 333.9, "Fourth Army," box 1012, decimal file July 1950–June 1951, Records of the Inspector General, RG 159.

detect because women were "more secretive" and "more seclusive" than men.[45] Because women were thought more likely to engage in sex in private, and because military officials were unclear about how to define sexual activity between women even when it was witnessed, the regulation of female homosexuality could not rest primarily on homosexual acts.

The perceived differences between how homosexuality would manifest itself in women and men were dwarfed, however, by the differences presumed to exist between homosexuals and heterosexuals. As the latter binary hardened, military officials insisted that male and female homosexuals were basically alike, and that one policy should govern homosexuality among both sexes. There was "consensus" that there should be "no difference in the handling of male and female homosexuals."[46] The navy acted first to update its guidelines on homosexuality for the postwar period, releasing in July 1949 a policy instructing military officials to consider homosexuality among personnel, whether "male or female." The navy policy then guided the work of a Department of Defense (DOD) committee charged with creating a uniform policy for all branches of the service. The DOD committee—in what was a harbinger of rising homophobia throughout the federal government—firmly broke with World War II policies that permitted some personnel charged with homosexuality to be rehabilitated and returned to the service. "Prompt separation of homosexuals from the military is mandatory," the DOD policy of October 1949 read. The committee, which included a representative from the WAC to cover "women's interests," wrote women into the hardening opposition between homosexuality and martial citizenship. Homosexuals were not to be allowed to serve in any capacity, these officials mandated, and "the character of separation" would be, moreover, "without distinction as to sex."[47]

In addition to eliminating the possibility that soldiers who engaged in homosexual activity might be reclaimed for duty, the new policy es-

[45]Crittenden Report, 40–41, box 16, World War II Project Records.
[46]Ibid.
[47]Elmer Wohl to Ralph Stohl, "Study to Revise Regulations for the Handling of Homosexuals in the Armed Services for Both Sexes," June 20, 1949, decimal 730, box 153, Assistant Secretary of Defense, decimal file 1949–1950, Records of the Secretary of the Defense, RG 330; Hubert E. Howard to the Secretary of the Army, Secretary of the Navy, and Secretary of the Air Force, "Discharge of Homosexuals from the Armed Services," October 11, 1949, decimal 250.1, box 100, Assistant Secretary of Defense decimal file 1949–1950, Records of the Secretary of Defense, RG 330; file M-46, box 1481, Assistant Secretary of Defense Subcommittee Studies 1948–1951, Records of the Secretary of Defense, RG 330; Manfred S. Guttmacher, *Sex Offenses: The Problem, Causes, and Prevention* (New York: W. W. Norton, 1951), 132–33; Bérubé, *Coming Out Under Fire*, 260–62.

tablished three classes of homosexual offenders. Class I homosexuals, as with the World War II–era policy, were violent offenders who were to be court-martialed. Class II homosexuals, also a carryover from the war years, were to be undesirably discharged for consensual homosexual acts. Finally, the new policy inaugurated the category of the Class III homosexual, who had homosexual "tendencies," and was to be either generally or undesirably discharged.[48]

To be clear, the idea that a person could have homosexual tendencies was not entirely new—during World War II the term referred to a soldier (generally male) who declared himself homosexual but had committed no in-service acts.[49] But the new policy's denotation of such persons as a separate class indicated a growing emphasis on the category of tendencies by the end of the 1940s. "The only major change prescribed by [the DOD policy]," wrote Under Secretary of the Navy Dan Kimball, "is the establishment of the Class III category of personnel."[50] As deployed by the new guidelines, the concept of tendencies paved the way for more aggressive policing, capturing, as one air force captain put it, "the complexity of the homosexual problem."[51] When applied to men, the designation of Class III was used to discharge a soldier who was suspected of homosexual activity despite a dearth of evidence, as well as one who confessed homosexuality but admitted no sexual acts. With women, too, the category could designate (a physically) unexpressed homosexuality. Yet in contrast to the way it was used with men, the provision barring soldiers with tendencies also helped military offi-

[48] File M-46, box 1481, Assistant Secretary of Defense Subcommittee Studies 1948–1951, Records of the Secretary of Defense, RG 330.

[49] Bérubé, *Coming Out Under Fire*, 141–48. From 1945 to 1947, the army made honorable discharges available to soldiers with homosexual tendencies who had committed no homosexual acts in the service. In 1947, the policy changed such that a soldier who had tendencies but had committed no acts would be given either an undesirable discharge (for unfitness under AR 615-368) or a general discharge (for unsuitability under AR 615-369). See Colonel Robert J. Carpenter to the Assistant Chief of Staff, G-1, July 13, 1945, decimal 250.1, Classified decimal file 1943–1945, Records of the Adjutant General, RG 407; War Department Circular No. 85, March 23, 1946, decimal 250.1, box 437, decimal file 1942–1946, Records of the War Department General Staff, RG 165; and AR 615-368, 1948, decimal 220.8, box 267, decimal file 1946–1948, Records of the Adjutant General, RG 407.

[50] Under Secretary of the Navy Dan A. Kimball to Chairman of the Personnel Policy Board, "Discharge of Homosexuals from the Armed Services," December 16, 1949, file M-46, box 1481, Assistant Secretary of Defense Subcommittee Studies 1948–1951, Records of the Secretary of Defense, RG 330.

[51] Colonel Robert R. Gideon Jr. to Director of the Staff, "Preliminary Survey of Separation Procedures for Homosexuals in the Armed Forces," March 15, 1949, file M-46, box 1481, Assistant Secretary of Defense Subcommittee Studies 1948–1951, Records of the Secretary of Defense, RG 330.

cials cope with the fact that, despite their best efforts, they still did not understand how homosexuality in women was expressed. The concept of tendencies absolved military officials of the responsibility of drawing a line between sex and what was considered normal female intimacy. In so doing, the designation of the Class III homosexual enabled military officials to extend the apparatus they used to police women far beyond sexual acts. The label of tendencies not only penalized mannish women for "the way they walk[ed], talk[ed], or dress[ed]," but also brought a sprawling web of women's friendships and associations under state surveillance.[52] Military authorities, in short, had begun to identify a new set of attributes as evidence of homosexuality, revealing the power of the state to not only regulate but constitute identity as well.

Some policymakers objected, however, to the way that lesbian identity was being constituted—the meaning of tendencies was overly broad, they argued, when applied to women. "With male personnel the regulation has worked well enough," one military report opined, but with women it led to "misinterpretation" and even "witch-hunts."[53] As a result of several such large-scale investigations, a group of WAC psychiatrists suggested that "homosexual tendencies" be defined sexually as "genital play" between women.[54] Subsequently, Dr. Marian Kenworthy, a leading expert on homosexuality in the military and a member of the Defense Advisory Committee on Women in the Service (DACOWITS), recommended that the policy on tendencies be reviewed by the DOD. She complained that the policy was not an effective way to handle the problem of the "so-called homosexuals," and that the directive did not "properly delimit the term 'homosexual tendencies.'" The director of personnel policy for the secretary of the defense noted that because DACOWITS had recommended the review, "it is presumed that they were considering the policy as it pertains to females." Yet the personnel director concluded that "the Department of Defense policy applies equally to both sexes [and] . . . should apply to both."[55] A few months

[52]M. D. Hogan and R. E. Anderson to CG, Third Army, "Fort McClellan, Mental Hygiene Consultations Service Report," September 14, 1956, box 64, Background Papers, Women's Army Corps 1945–1978, Records of the Army Chief of Staff, RG 319.

[53]Ibid.

[54]Report of Psychiatric Consultants' Conference on Women's Army Corps Program, June 27–28, 1950, WAC Conference June 1950 folder, box 26, Marion Kenworthy Papers. In the same box, a fifty-two page transcript of this meeting can be found in the back of a photo album labeled "Women's Army Corps 1944–1950."

[55]Rear Admiral J. P. Womble Jr., "Memo for Record," March 18, 1952, decimal 334, box 265, Assistant Secretary of Defense decimal file 1952, Records of the Secretary of Defense, RG 330.

later—a culmination of these broader concerns about ongoing investigations into tendencies among women—Assistant Secretary of Defense Anna Rosenberg authorized a committee to review the "identification and disposition of Class III homosexuals for both sexes."[56]

The committee designated to study the problem of homosexual tendencies was divided as to whether the policy "arbitrarily stigmatize[d] some individuals as homosexuals when in fact they are not."[57] Despite this division, the committee's work led to some further clarification of the DOD policy in 1955. Class III cases were to be defined as "overt confirmed homosexuals" who had not engaged in homosexual acts in the military, and "individuals who possess homosexual tendencies to such a degree to render them unsuitable to military service."[58] While homosexual tendencies would continue to be defined broadly, commanding officers were to be given discretion to decide which sorts of tendencies would truly hamper military service. But in practice there seemed to be little difference in the way that Class III investigations were carried out after this directive was issued. As before, the provision on homosexual tendencies generated enormous witch hunts that were used not just to police sex, but female personnel more generally.

Far from being invisible or even an afterthought, women soldiers were centrally considered in the debates surrounding the development of the military's policy on homosexuality during these years. The idea of homosexual tendencies encompassed a vague concept of female homosexual activity—something that was not quite homosexual sex—but simultaneously expanded the scope of state policing to include appearance, relationships, and associations. Despite the new policy, the longstanding disjuncture between homosexuality and women did not immediately evaporate. This was illustrated, for example, by the inspector general's 1950 opinion that perversion among women should be handled not as an issue of homosexual tendencies, but under a separate policy for "immoral and abnormal sex tendencies."[59] This lingering no-

[56] Anna Rosenberg to the Secretary of the Army, the Secretary of the Navy, the Secretary of the Air Force, and the Chairman of the Armed Forces Medical Policy Council, "Committee to Review Policy on Discharge of Homosexuals," July 2, 1952, decimal 334, box 265, Assistant Secretary of Defense decimal file 1952, Records of the Secretary of Defense, RG 330.

[57] Rear Admiral J. P. Womble Jr., "Memorandum for Record," undated, decimal 334, box 265, Assistant Secretary of Defense decimal file 1952, Records of the Secretary of Defense, RG 330.

[58] West, Doidge, and Williams, "An Approach to the Problem of Homosexuality in the Military Service," 68–69.

[59] Major General Edward Witsell, "Investigation and Separation of Homosexuals," August 1, 1950, decimal 250.1, box 567, decimal file 1949–1950, Records of the Assistant Chief

tion that homosexuality was fundamentally male makes the extent to which numerous military policymakers conceptualized homosexuality as also pertaining to women all the more remarkable. Still, if the way that the DOD policy was constructed collapsed gender distinctions, the way it was implemented preserved them. In short, the cold war military not only brought women under the purview of state policing, but in broadening the very definition of what homosexuality was, it also singled them out.

Policing Tendencies

How, then, did military police and administrative discharge boards enforce the DOD's policy on homosexuality against individual women? Military discharge files for *male* soldiers from the early 1950s follow remarkably clear patterns. Most cases involved two or perhaps four men, who either admitted or were observed in acts of sodomy or fellatio. (Often the admissions followed being caught by other men in their units.) The investigation, while undoubtedly painful to those accused, was a contained and relatively straightforward inquiry: Did two men engage in sexual relations together? How, when, and where? Who saw it?[60] When male soldiers were processed as Class III (for tendencies), the investigation still generally revolved around the commission of acts, albeit ones with fewer witnesses. In one case, for example, a lieutenant reported that he suspected one of his men of homosexual tendencies. After an investigation, it was found that the man "did engage in *acts* of sodomy."[61] In another instance, a male soldier wrote a letter to the pres-

---

of Staff, RG 319; Colonel Rosser L. Hunter, September 1, 1950, "Investigation and Separation of Homosexuals," decimal 250.1, box 567, decimal file 1949–1950, Records of the Assistant Chief of Staff, RG 319.

[60] See the thirty-two discharge files for homosexuality involving men, decimal 220.8, boxes 3592–93, Classified decimal file 1948–1950, Records of the Adjutant General, RG 407; decimal 220.8, boxes 3776–78, Classified decimal file 1950–1951, Records of the Adjutant General, RG 407. Based on the available statistics, this cannot be a complete collection of discharge files for men from these years. Nevertheless, the strength of the pattern demonstrated by these files leads me to believe that they are a representative sample reflecting the implementation of military policy vis-à-vis male soldiers during this time period.

[61] ———— Case, decimal 220.8, box 3777, Classified decimal file 1950–1951, Records of the Adjutant General, RG 407 (emphasis added). In order to protect the privacy of individuals who may still be living, I have omitted surnames in case file citations. (Most case files involve investigations of multiple women.) The surnames that appear in the text are pseudonyms. I have not changed the names of individuals (in the citations or text) in court cases because of the public nature of those documents.

ident stating that he was a homosexual and asking for help to cope with his condition. After this admission, the army commenced an investigation into the soldier's homosexual tendencies. Again, the investigation focused on sexual acts. "Based on the evidence," the investigator wrote, "the undersigned feels that the offense did in fact take place." The soldier received a general discharge for homosexual tendencies "after the investigation disclosed that [the accused] committed acts."[62]

Policing homosexuality among women was not as clear-cut. While military police sometimes encountered two women hugging and kissing in cars on base, and were aware that many of the women "[went] steady" together, military authorities did not expect to observe acts between women that could clearly be identified as homosexuality. When they did, they were not well equipped to deal with such situations. In one episode from 1952, a military police officer (MP) spotted one WAC member performing oral sex on another in the front seat of a parked car. He watched for about thirty seconds, before the two women (having recognized the MP vehicle behind them) drove off. Although he had identified the two women, he did not make a report because, as he admitted subsequently, "I wouldn't know how." He further explained that "there never were any orders given to me to cover anything like that." A few months later, two different MPs stopped to investigate a "shaking" car because they saw a woman's leg thrown over the rear of the front seat. Inside the car, the same two women who were involved in the earlier incident were engaged in an act of oral sex, which the two MPs discovered when they shined their flashlights into the backseat. "Bewildered by it all," as they later explained, the two MPs neither arrested the women nor filed a report. When the issue later came to light, these MPs were also questioned as to why they failed to respond. One admitted during questioning that he would have arrested two men if he found them in a similar position, but treated the two women differently because "it was such a shock to me," and something "that MP training [didn't] cover."[63]

One could conclude, based on the way that these MPs responded to the two WAC soldiers, that military authorities were uninterested in policing sexual activity between women. But that was not the case. Military authorities sought evidence of physical involvement between women suspected of being lesbians. Yet MPs simply did not expect that women would routinely engage in homosexual acts where they could be observed. "It was just one of those things you read about and hear

[62]———— Case, decimal 220.8, box 3776, Classified decimal file 1950–1951, Records of the Adjutant General, RG 407.
[63]———— Case, decimal 220.8, box 3776, Classified decimal file 1950–1951, Records of the Adjutant General, RG 407.

about," declared one of the MPs who had spotted the two women together in the car, "but never *see*."[64] Accordingly, in most cases the policing of women relied more on interrogation, through which investigators induced women to confess and corroborate sexual activity with
other women, sometimes quite successfully.

Military authorities seemed to take pornographic pleasure in such
work, as in one case when several female soldiers were apprehended at
the "wedding" of two women at a Washington, DC, hotel.[65] During the
subsequent investigation, one soldier was asked if the woman with
whom she was alleged to be involved was "pretty in the nude." Another was asked if a woman she had been intimate with had "come,"
and if that felt "good to you." Investigators seemed particularly interested in determining whether women had engaged in oral sex—a practice that marked them as especially perverse. "Do you engage in div-
ing?" one investigator asked, clarifying, "That is when you use your
tongue." Another soldier was asked if anyone "dove on a woman when
she was drunk." Women soldiers sometimes resisted being placed on
the furthest end of the continuum. "I take it you were fingering her," an
investigator stated, and then added that he assumed that the accused
had used her tongue as well. "I didn't say anything about my tongue,"
the soldier snapped back at him. "I specified my hands and nothing
else."[66]

Despite this soldier's insistence—hands rather than tongue—military officials lacked hard and fast rules about which behaviors would be
considered overt acts.[67] The lack of clarity routinely led military authorities to categorize most sexual activity between women as indicative of
tendencies. This was particularly true when investigators failed to produce strong corroborating testimony, as well as in cases that involved
something akin to foreplay—those "latent tendencies to engage in a homosexual act which are expressed by kissing, caressing, or . . . verbal
manifestations."[68]

[64] Ibid. (emphasis added).

[65] ——— Case, decimal 220.8, box 3778, Classified decimal file 1950–1951, Records of
the Adjutant General, RG 407. Lesbian weddings appear with some frequency in military
discharge case files involving women. They seemed to be important events in the cultural
lives of some military women and were taken quite seriously. In the case described in the
text above, one woman was asked during the investigation, "Why do you girls get married?" She replied, "Just to make things a little better."

[66] ——— Case, decimal 220.8, box 3778, Classified decimal file 1950–1951, Records of
the Adjutant General, RG 407.

[67] Neither were there clear-cut guidelines about which acts corresponded to which
types of discharge, and cases seem not to be uniform in this regard.

[68] "Female Homosexuality," decimal 333.9, "Fourth Army," box 1012, decimal file July
1950–June 1951, Records of the Inspector General, RG 159.

Even incredibly public displays of same-sex eroticism could fall under the rubric of tendencies rather than overt acts—for example, when two African American WAC soldiers were discharged as Class III after an incident in the unit dayroom that occurred in front of other recruits. One woman started getting "real low down . . . kissing [the other woman's] neck, closing her eyes, moaning and carrying on." According to another account:

> Rct [recruit] Jackson was dressed in a field coat, white T-shirt, and panties, with loafers on. Rct Smith was asked by Rct Jackson to dance with her and Rct Smith got up and slipped her arms around Rct Jackson and they started dancing in an unladylike manner. Rct Smith then pulled Rct Jackson's pants down and inserted her finger in Rct Jackson's vagina and they continued dancing in . . . this manner . . . for approximately ten minutes.[69]

In addition to encompassing a range of sexual behaviors in women, homosexual tendencies were also attributed to women who exhibited gender inversion, or as one military guide to homosexuality among women put it, "the wearing of the clothes and the desire to assume the role of the opposite sex."[70] In the preceding investigation—which grew to include nine WAC soldiers—some of the subjects were accused of homosexual tendencies not only because of salacious dancing, but also because they were considered mannish. "If I didn't know there weren't any men in the area," one recruit testified, "I would have sworn [Jackson] was one." Williams was another "queer one" in the same unit who had "masculine ways." She would announce her presence in the barracks by calling out, "There's a man in the house!" She wore mannish clothes, "combed her hair in a mannish way," and women appeared to be drawn to her. She had, the investigation revealed, "magnetism."[71]

The investigator's mention of recruit Williams's apparent ability to attract women demonstrates that in identifying the attributes of homosexuality in women, military officials were attuned to not only sexual activity and gender traits but also women's relationships with one another. Indeed, the bonds between women were commonly scrutinized for evidence of homosexual tendencies—an assessment that rested on intimacy as much as sex. Moreover, including relationships within their scope meant that investigations among women often took on an enormous

---

[69]——— Case, decimal 220.8, box 3593, Classified decimal file 1948–1950, Records of the Adjutant General, RG 407.

[70] "Female Homosexuality," decimal 333.9, "Fourth Army," box 1012, decimal file July 1950–June 1951, Records of the Inspector General, RG 159.

[71]——— Case, decimal 220.8, box 3593, Classified decimal file 1948–1950, Records of the Adjutant General, RG 407.

scale. An investigation that began with evidence of a single homosexual incident might lead to every woman in a unit being called in for questioning. As women were pressured to name their associates, investigations thus expanded to massive proportions involving a complex web of women, sometimes spreading across several bases in different regions of the country. One "mushrooming" air force investigation was even "going forward world-wide with the undeveloped leads stemming from Lackland [Air Force Base]."[72] A 1955 army study to determine if there was an international organization of homosexuals within the armed forces further indicates the military's interest in female networks. The study found evidence of only one such cabal. Not surprisingly, it was a women's organization: "The United Association of Gay Girls in the Armed Forces."[73] Relatedly, the provost marshall's glossary of terms pertaining to homosexuality included "queen mother," described as "an established lesbian who is a leader of a female homosexual ring." The queen mother—who "may or may not have [sex] relations with other members of the ring"—was defined relationally rather than sexually. There was no equivalent term listed for men.[74]

In contrast to investigations involving male soldiers, then, a focus on relationships and associations could supplement or even supplant questions about sexual activity when women were the subjects of official scrutiny. One such large-scale probe at Fort Meyer, Virginia, began when one woman admitted to her commanding officer that she was a homosexual and had "performed acts of cunnilingus." A comparable admission by a male soldier most likely would have resulted in his discharge and that of his sex partner(s). The scope of the WAC investigation's final report was much broader: "Baker has told Armstrong, that she, Baker, loves Duffy. It is known that Duffy visits Baker at Ft. Meyer, and vice versa." Mitchell and Tracey were "co-owners of a Nash two-door sedan automobile," and the investigating officer explained, "this partnership was consummated to strengthen their friendship." These two women also exchanged Christmas presents; two others, Abel and McNeil, exchanged letters. Hale and Taylor were constantly together,

[72]Major Robin Elliott to Colonel Lewis, "The Air Force Investigation," decimal 333.9, "Fourth Army," box 1012, decimal file July 1950–June 1951, Records of the Inspector General, RG 159.

[73]Harry O. Paxson to Assistant Chief of Staff, G-1, "International Organization of Homosexuality," October 10, 1955, decimal 706, box 2213, Confidential decimal file July 1955–June 1956, Records of the Inspector General, RG 159 .

[74]The provost marshall's office was responsible for military policing. "Homosexuals—A Command Problem," decimal 250.1, box 23, General Correspondence 1955–1962, Records of the Provost Marshall General, RG 389, National Archives, College Park, MD.

and "Hale wears a ring of Taylor's." Warren and Schneider had also exchanged rings, and so had Baker and Simonides, which "undoubtedly hurt Edwards." Baker knew "Edwards to be extremely jealous of Simonides." But the latter woman also dated Jones. Edwards wanted to exchange rings with Jones, but "Jones denied this offer for fear of consequences which had developed after having exchanged rings with Simonides." And on and on it went.[75]

Military authorities did not just police sexual acts or gender traits; they policed a culture of women. That broad focus involved, despite official "consensus" that one policy on homosexuality govern both sexes, the development of an entirely separate and quite elaborate methodology for investigating homosexuality among women. This methodology borrowed extensively from loyalty and other anticommunist investigations (which also uncovered a network among women, although one allegedly connected by political ideology rather than sexual desire).[76] One manual described army procedure to handle the "widespread condition" of "female homosexuality": in addition to "scientific" interrogation, unit commanders were instructed to set up a cross-reference file (with information from the FBI and civil vice squads as well as military intelligence agencies); "secure a . . . roster of the unit concerned [and] a list of all automobiles owned or operated by suspects"; "secure and maintain informant-informer systems"; "arrange for mail cover"; and finally, that the most valuable information would come "through surveillance, the secretive and continuous watching of persons, vehicles, and places." Should such surveillance reveal female homosexuals, commanders were instructed to "plan and conduct a detailed search of their personal effects, automobiles, and any known 'off post' residences, for the purposes of obtaining correspondence, literature, or pictures of a homosexual nature."[77]

In carrying out their duties, agents went through wastepaper baskets looking for notes. They conducted "shakedowns" of the barracks, searching for letters, photographs, and books with lesbian themes.[78]

[75] ——— Case, decimal 220.8, box 3776, Classified decimal file 1950–1951, Records of the Adjutant General, RG 407.

[76] On women's networks and the way they were uncovered during loyalty investigations, see Landon R. Y. Storrs, "Red Scare Politics and the Suppression of Popular Front Feminism: The Loyalty Investigation of Mary Dublin Keyserling," *Journal of American History* 90 (September 2003): 508–9.

[77] ——— Case, decimal 220.8, box 3776, Classified decimal file 1950–1951, Records of the Adjutant General, RG 407.

[78] The 1950 pulp novel *Women's Barracks*—which sold three million copies and was singled out during a congressional investigation in 1952 into pornographic materials—must have enjoyed considerable circulation among military women. See Martin Meeker,

196 THE STRAIGHT STATE

They set up wiretaps and took polygraphs.[79] Investigators planted informants within units to report on the complicated textures of women's lives together. They uncovered evidence of lesbian weddings, and noted which women had arrived in men's formal wear. Agents recorded the names of women who lived with "notorious homosexuals," as well as those who expressed tolerance for or curiosity about such women. They knew which soldiers did not date the men on base, and they kept a record of which women gave each other gifts, shared a bank account, participated in a business venture, traveled together, or did each other's grocery shopping.[80] "They knew the times I was [with a lover], the buses that I took, how long I stayed, my mode of transportation home, [and] what I wore," one woman in the air force recalled of the painful investigation she experienced. "They knew every damn move I made. It was mind shattering."[81]

Such intensive techniques were in some measure the result of the military's belief that homosexual acts among women were more obscured and less clear-cut than similar acts between men. They were also a result of fierce misogyny. Simply put, there is little evidence in the documentary record that male soldiers went through anything like what their female counterparts did.[82] "The methods used by these investigators," one WAC major wrote in a complaint to the inspector general, were "calculated to embarrass and humiliate the women involved."

Contacts Desired: Gay and Lesbian Communications and Community, 1940s–1970s (Chicago: University of Chicago Press, 2006), 87, 118.

[79] Women could not be forced to take a polygraph test, but a refusal to take a polygraph was seen as evidence that the accused had something to hide. Complaint to Inspector General from Major Florence M. Packard, June 18, 1957, decimal 333, "Ft. McPherson," box 2283, Confidential decimal file July 1957–June 1958, Records of the Inspector General, RG 159.

[80] For these investigatory techniques, see cases involving homosexuality among women in decimal 220.8, boxes 3592–93, Classified decimal file 1948–1950, Records of the Adjutant General, RG 407; decimal 220.8, boxes 3776–78, Classified decimal file 1950–1951, Records of the Adjutant General, RG 407. See also Colonel John E. Ray, "Basis for Reply to Congressional Inquiries," decimal 333.5, "WAC," box 216, Classified decimal file 1953, Records of the Provost Marshall General, RG 389; decimal 201.23, box 2281, Confidential decimal file July 1957–June 1958, Records of the Inspector General, RG 159; decimal 333, "Ft. McPherson," box 2283, Confidential decimal file July 1957–June 1958, Records of the Inspector General, RG 159; decimal 333.5, "Ft. McClellan," box 2375, Confidential decimal file July 1958–June 1959, Records of the Inspector General, RG 159; decimal 333.5, "WAC," box 2401, Confidential decimal file July 1958–June 1959, Records of the Inspector General, RG 159.

[81] Interview with Loretta "Ret" Coller, in Mary Ann Humphrey, *My Country, My Right to Serve: Experiences of Gay Men and Women in the Military, World War II to the Present* (New Yorker: HarperCollins, 1990), 13.

[82] This is evident even from the physical heft of the discharge files. Most of the files involving men are a quarter- or a half-inch thick. Women are not only disproportionately represented among the extant files; the files themselves are huge (relative to most of the

The major described how investigators searched the belongings of a woman "not even 20 years of age" by opening "the woman's box of Tampax" and going "to the extreme of ripping the tissue paper from each of them." She asked, "What could possibly have been gained by this action except to perpetrate an indignity on this young woman in front of her Commanding Officer?"[83] Another woman compared the tactics of the army's Criminal Investigation Division to those of "Chinese communists." Women were picked up for questioning at all hours, held under guard, and not allowed telephone calls or visitors. MPs, rather than the woman under investigation, were sent back to the company to pick up all her clothes.[84] And the interrogation itself was a humiliating experience that could approximate psychological rape. One woman, for example, was asked if she was not "missing a lot of fun" because she had never had intercourse with a man. "You are the same as a little girl that didn't like cake because she had never had any," the investigating officer chided her.[85]

Women investigated for homosexuality went through ordeals that could last months. It was "psychological warfare," one WAF member recalled of her investigation by the air force's Office of Special Intelligence. "They opened my mail . . . they'd look under my mattress . . . they'd get me up in the middle of the night for questioning." She recalled being questioned once or twice each day for four months. "They'd come to the mess hall and get me in the middle of a meal. They knew no bounds." But the worst part was the isolation. "There was no way I could tell [my lover] what was happening and explain to her that my whole relationship with her was something of value, not some tawdry affair." Other women on base avoided this soldier too, "for fear of their own careers." She remembered that she kept to herself, afraid of incriminating others. "I had no outlet."[86]

When her discharge finally came—an undesirable, not a general one—it was soul destroying. "I left that base feeling like a real piece of shit." Fired twice when employers learned of her discharge, "for the next six years, I felt like a real loser. . . . I had no ego left, no self-image,

---

men's files)—two or three inches thick. By making this statement I do not mean to suggest that men did not suffer from military homophobia during this time.

[83] Complaint to Inspector General from Major Florence M. Packard, June 18, 1957, decimal 333, "Ft. McPherson," box 2283, Confidential decimal file July 1957–June 1958, Records of the Inspector General, RG 159.

[84] Letter to Senator Wayne Morse, decimal 333.5, "Ft. McClellan," box 2375, Confidential decimal file July 1958–June 1959, Records of the Inspector General, RG 159.

[85] ——— Case, decimal 220.8, box 3778, Classified decimal file 1950–1951, Records of the Adjutant General, RG 407.

[86] Interview with Coller, in Humphrey, *My Country, My Right to Serve*, 13–14.

no confidence, no surety-of-self." For years, the WAF member "never told a soul about it."[87] Evidence suggests that other women were equally tormented by these witch hunts. One woman stated that she was so scared during her interrogation that "she would sign anything."[88] "I just hung myself out of fear," said another.[89] The stress of the interrogation had physical manifestations, with the Criminal Investigation Division sometimes leaving women in a "severe state of health."[90] One woman submitted to a polygraph, but her "blood pressure rose from 88 to 120 and she became very shaky and her breathing . . . erratic," so that the test had to be discontinued.[91] "I have steadily lost weight," another WAC member stated, "[and] I have had to go on 'sick call' for a nervous condition caused by this aggravation."[92] Some women committed suicide.[93] The scale of these investigations, moreover, made even those who were not targeted feel vulnerable. "If you were so accused, how would you prove your innocence?" one WAC major asked herself, in the midst of a destructive investigation in her unit. She concluded that this was a "precarious and untenable position to occupy. How does one prove the absence of tendencies?"[94]

Resistance and Identity

This was precisely the problem: most women could not prove the absence of tendencies. That fact, combined with the incredible scope of military policing in these types of cases, put all women, as the WAC major said, in a precarious position. Yet while these ordeals affected women very broadly, they did not touch them all in the same way. Women who were actually accused (as opposed to those who were

[87] Ibid., 16–17.
[88] ——— Case, decimal 220.8, box 3592, Classified decimal file 1948–1950, Records of the Adjutant General, RG 407.
[89] B. S. to ACLU, February 15, 1951, in folder 1, box 1127, American Civil Liberties Union Collection, Seeley G. Mudd Archives, Princeton University, Princeton, NJ.
[90] Congressman Bob Casey to Lt. Gen. Clark L. Ruffner, decimal 333.5, "Ft. McClellan," box 2375, Confidential decimal file July 1958–June 1959, Records of the Inspector General, RG 159.
[91] ——— Case, decimal 220.8, box 3778, Classified decimal file 1950–1951, Records of the Adjutant General, RG 407.
[92] B. L. to Senator Spessard L. Holland, decimal 201.23, box 2281, Confidential decimal file July 1957–June 1958, Records of the Inspector General, RG 159.
[93] Allan Bérubé and John D'Emilio, "The Military and Lesbians during the McCarthy Years," *Signs: Journal of Women in Culture and Society* 9 (Summer 1984): 775.
[94] Complaint to Inspector General from Major Florence M. Packard, June 18, 1957, decimal 333, "Ft. McPherson," box 2283, Confidential decimal file July 1957–June 1958, Records of the Office of the Inspector General, RG 159.

questioned as witnesses or who merely observed the events unfolding on their base) had to have incredible fortitude to get through the investigation. Some women did fall apart, but many others had "some place deep down," as one soldier surmised, "*something* that kept the survival instinct intact."[95] The subjects of these investigations could be remarkably tough under questioning as, for example, one woman who demonstrated a "complete absence of anxiety" during her interrogation.[96] In another episode, a suspect was reported to be "belligerent" toward investigators. "She states that she can be affectionate with another female—kissing and exchanging gifts—and that is her own affair," a major working on the case recorded.[97] In yet another instance, an army psychiatrist remarked on his subject's aggression and hostility. "This girl entered the interview situation rather snappily," he observed. "She . . . flatly refused to discuss anything sexual."[98]

Some women refused to answer questions; others simply denied that they were homosexual. When air force recruits Fannie Mae Clackum and Grace Garner were asked by a fellow soldier to accompany her and another WAF member on a trip to visit the woman's aunt in a bordering state, they reluctantly agreed. They arrived in Dallas only to find that there was no aunt, and when the woman who had initiated the trip suggested that the foursome stay over in a motel at her expense, Clackum and Garner might have been a little suspicious. But the woman's role as an informant was only apparent when the Office of Special Intelligence later called them in for questioning. Despite the fact that Clackum, Garner, and the third woman along on the trip denied that anything had happened in the motel room, the two women were asked to accept undesirable discharges. They refused and demanded to be court-martialed. The military discharged them anyway. The two women then moved in together in Marietta, Georgia—not because they were lovers, they said, but to fight their case in federal court. Clackum's case file included statements by employers and other associates testifying to her "lady-like manner," and expressing disbelief that anyone would call her an "undesirable or homosexual." She denied that she was or ever had been a homosexual. The Court of Federal Claims eventually awarded the two recruits back pay, finding it "unthinkable" that the air force should have the "raw power, without respect for even the most

[95] Interview with Coller, in Humphrey, *My Country, My Right to Serve*, 17.

[96] ——— Case, decimal 220.8, box 3776, Classified decimal file 1950–1951, Records of the Adjutant General, RG 407.

[97] Resume of Proceedings, June 27, 1957, decimal 333, "Ft. McPherson," box 2283, Confidential decimal file July 1957–1959, Records of the Inspector General, RG 159.

[98] ——— Case, decimal 220.8, box 3593, Classified decimal file 1948–1950, Records of the Adjutant General, RG 407.

elementary notions of due process of law, to load [them] down with [the] penalties" of an unfavorable discharge.[99]

Clackum and Garner were the first soldiers (male or female) discharged for homosexuality to sue for denial of due process.[100] Yet while soldiers rarely fought their discharges in the federal courts, it was not unusual for military women to refuse to be discharged administratively and to demand a court-martial proceeding.[101] Perhaps women did so out of desperation. What better career option than the military existed in the early 1950s for working-class women who wanted to avoid marriage and family, or who did not conform to conventional gender stereotypes? "I went into the service to be a career woman . . . and I'd have stayed there," remembered one woman who was devastated by losing everything "that was air force" right down to her boots.[102] "I request that I be allowed to stay in the army [to] prove that I can be a good soldier," another wrote.[103] Alternatively, women may also have demanded trial by court-martial because they were politically savvy, insisting that the military prove a case that was often based on tenuous evidence regarding emotional ties and loose associations (rather than well-documented accounts of homosexual acts). While military regulations allowed the secretary of each branch to administratively remove a soldier without a court-martial who refused a discharge for homosexuality, in practice a demand for a court-martial could derail the entire process. Officials sometimes just dropped a case, in other words, when a discharge was refused and conviction by court-martial seemed unlikely.[104]

[99] *Fannie Mae Clackum v. United States*, 296 F.2d 226 (Ct. Cl. 1960), trial records at the National Archives; Rhonda R. Rivera, "Our Straight Laced Judges: The Legal Position of Homosexual Persons in the United States," *Hastings Law Journal* 30 (March 1979): 841–42.

[100] See appendix in U.S. Congress, Senate, Committee on the Judiciary, *Hearings on the Constitutional Rights of Military Personnel*, 87th Cong., 2nd sess., February 20–21, March 1, 2, 6, 9, and 12, 1962, 827–967.

[101] It is unclear as to how women knew to do this; it seems plausible that word traveled among women being investigated from base to base. In any event, the air force wondered the same thing, and asked Clackum who advised her to refuse her discharge. Clackum replied that she made that decision on her own. *Fannie Mae Clackum v. United States*, 296 F.2d 226 (Ct. Cl. 1960), trial records at the National Archives. For other examples of cases in which women refused an administrative discharge, see Bérubé and D'Emilio, "The Military and Lesbians during the McCarthy Years," 773; ——— Case, decimal 220.8, box 3776, Classified decimal file 1950–1951, Records of the Adjutant General, RG 407; ——— Case, decimal 220.8, box 3777, Classified decimal file 1950–1951, Records of the Adjutant General, RG 407.

[102] Interview with Coller, in Humphrey, *My Country, My Right to Serve*, 11–12.

[103] ——— Case, decimal 220.8, box 3592, Classified decimal file, 1948–1950, Records of the Adjutant General, RG 407.

[104] *Fannie Mae Clackum v. United States*, 296 F.2d 226 (Ct. Cl. 1960).

A different strategy taken by women under investigation was to try to control the type of discharge they received by admitting to homosexual tendencies but not to homosexual acts.[105] In a more unusual scenario, two female soldiers *asked* to be discharged for homosexuality when one corporal's Estimated Time of Separation was approaching and the other, her lover, had been reassigned to the Far East Command. It was a calculated move to stay together, but not without risks—the WAC soldiers had to avoid confessing too much in order to prevent a court-martial or an undesirable discharge. Carefully, the two women wrote a letter to their commanding officer in which they admitted "no specific, provable homosexual acts," but explained that they had been "inseparable" since they arrived at Fort Lee. "Although our actions in public certainly have never been censurable insofar as homosexuality is concerned," the two women wrote, "any intelligent person having any contact with us would arrive at the conclusion that here was a case in which more than ordinary friendship figured." And in case this admission was not enough to earn the women a general discharge, they ended their letter with a threat: if the army went ahead and recommended that one be separated under her normal Estimated Time of Separation while the other be sent to the Far East Command, "there would be nothing to prevent" the first from volunteering for service in the Far East Command to be with her lover. "We would assume from such a recommendation," the two women asserted, "that two people experiencing a homosexual relationship in the service is condoned."[106]

The couple's attempt to use the military's antihomosexual policy to advance their own interests succeeded. The two women were discharged simultaneously with general discharges. In obtaining their desired outcome, the two corporals emphasized their happiness and their commitment to one another. One told investigators, for example, that she planned to live with the other "indefinitely." The other, declining treatment, announced that she was "quite happy" as she was.[107] Like these two WAC soldiers, other women refused to pathologize their sexuality during the investigatory process. One soldier, for instance, described her relationship as "beautiful" and told investigators that her "life in the future [would] be centered around [her] relationship."[108] Another woman told investigators that she did not consider her homosexual activity to be

[105]——— Case, decimal 220.8, box 3776, Classified decimal file 1950–1951, Records of the Adjutant General, RG 407.
[106]——— Case, decimal 220.8, box 3777, Classified decimal file 1950–1951, Records of the Adjutant General, RG 407.
[107] Ibid.
[108]——— Case, decimal 220.8, box 3777, Classified decimal file 1950–1951, Records of the Adjutant General, RG 407.

unnatural.[109] Perhaps most remarkably, one woman wrote in a detailed confession for the Criminal Investigation Division, "I am not ashamed of what I have done, for it was something which has been born with me."[110]

As such declarations indicate, state repression was productive of identity in complicated ways—women's attempts to manage the antilesbian apparatus within the military frequently led them to articulate a lesbian identity in much sharper terms. "The patient declares that she has been homosexual all her life," one psychiatrist reported, but "did not realize [it] until . . . the investigation into this problem at Ft. Lee stimulated her interest."[111] Just as historian Landon Storrs argues that "it was the red scare that forced people to adopt tidy labels" regarding political identity, being officially labeled as a lesbian by the military could lead one to regard homosexuality not merely as an attribute, but in the words of sociologists Colin Williams and Martin Weinberg, as a "master status."[112] "Knowing about [homosexuality] now," one woman informed authorities during an investigation at her base, "I look back into my childhood and feel that I have been gay all my life."[113]

Not surprisingly, then, many women centered the military experience in the confessional statements that they drafted for military authorities. Even those who first encountered homosexuality as civilians described the military as clarifying their sexual feelings, and it was common for women to attribute their initial discovery of homosexuality to the military. "Prior to my arrival here at Ft. Bliss," one such soldier declared, "I had never known what a homosexual was nor what the term meant." Another wrote that she first became aware of homosexuality when she "noticed that certain members of the WAC detachment wore fly front trousers, and [had] . . . mannish and peculiar characteristics." Many soldiers described an educational process whereby those more experienced not only initiated them sexually, but culturally as well. One woman remembered that she had to look up the word homosexual in the dictionary when she first heard it used in her detachment, but soon after a more experienced soldier took her on as a project. The younger woman was taught the vernacular ("butch," "fluff,"

[109]——— Case, decimal 220.8, box 107, decimal file 1953–1954, Records of the Adjutant General, RG 407.

[110]——— Case, decimal 220.8, box 3777, Classified decimal file 1950–1951, Records of the Adjutant General, RG 407.

[111]——— Case, decimal 220.8, box 3777, Classified decimal file 1950–1951, Records of the Adjutant General, RG 407.

[112]Storrs, "Red Scare Politics," 516. Colin J. Williams and Martin S. Weinberg, *Homosexuals and the Military: A Study of Less Than Honorable Discharge* (New York: Harper and Row, 1971), 130–54.

[113]——— Case, decimal 220.8, box 3777, Classified decimal file 1950–1951, Records of the Adjutant General, RG 407.

and "gay"), how to recognize "other homos" (by hair length, sock color, and fingernails), and finally, courtship. "I told her I was very, very fond of Lt. Vance," this soldier recalled. "She told me that Lt. Vance was a 'fluff,' and that if I wanted to get her, I would have to be a 'butch.'" For that reason, the young private said, "I took all these lessons . . . to heart, and it didn't take me too long to learn."[114]

What is striking about these confessions—beyond the role that the writers assigned to the military in their own growing self-awareness—is their length and complexity. It was the rare writer who limited her statement to a straightforward (if graphic) enumeration of sexual "activities."[115] (More unusual still were those who gave up terse confessions that resulted in dismissal, but must have frustrated nonetheless the prurient interests of authorities: "I come from Beeville, Texas," read the text of one such woman's entire statement, "and I am a homosexual.")[116] Most women's statements were not so direct. Rather, women on one base referred to one's emergence as a homosexual as "making a person," and often women's confessions reflected this much more complex narration of all the elements that had led them to be involved in the investigation, to be, as some women confessed, homosexual. These more expansive statements of identity mirrored the broad scope of the military interrogation—self-explorations of emotion, personality, and culture. The statement of the accused often started with a discussion of early childhood. One woman attributed her "beginning in homosexuality" to a "lack of proper teaching into such things on the part of my parents."[117] Another simply began, "Ever since I can remember I have always been a tom-boy." One woman's confession—which ran on for six, single-spaced typed pages—included an involved description of her years in art school.[118] The adolescent/young adult coming-of-age story was a central element of many confessions that then led up to what were sometimes steamy and sometimes sweet depictions of the barracks romance.

Such detail suggests that many women turned the tables on military authorities in drafting their statements. Forced to confess, the statement became about each woman's need to tell. Was it the explicit na-

[114] Ibid.
[115] _____ Case, decimal 220.8, box 3777, Classified decimal file 1950–1951, Records of the Adjutant General, RG 407.
[116] _____ Case, decimal 220.8, box 3776, Classified decimal file 1950–1951, Records of the Adjutant General, RG 407.
[117] _____ Case, decimal 220.8, box 3592, Classified decimal file 1948–1950, Records of the Adjutant General, RG 407.
[118] _____ Case, decimal 220.8, box 3777, Classified decimal file 1950–1951, Records of the Adjutant General, RG 407.

ture of the information sought by the investigator that provided an un-usual opening for a soldier to talk about the intimate details of her life? Consider, for example, how vividly one woman described her first sex-ual encounter with Private Finn, "a beautiful lover." She portrayed the place ("McKelligan's Canyon," in "my car, a coupe, the windows were open"), the weather ("it was very hot, perspiration was streaming down our faces"), the line ("Bonnie, we are both soaking wet"), and eventually, the results ("Finn is extremely passionate, and suddenly she got me that way").[119] The detail here seems less about providing authorities with the necessary facts to close the investigation than about recording a powerful memory. The same soldier's account of a date at a drive-in after the two women had officially broken up is even more evocative:

> When [Finn] is tight, she is the cutest thing you ever saw. It was raining, and I mentioned the song "Pennies from Heaven." She said, "Bonnie, you always did like rain didn't you?" We got dreamy eyed. We were parked at the side of the Drive-In, and we moved to the middle of the car seat. I put my arm around her shoulder, and she leaned her head down on my shoulder. Boy it hit me, I just bent over and kissed her.[120]

Is this a criminal investigation or a pulp novel? Did the authorities need to know that it was raining, that the rain made the women think of the song "Pennies from Heaven," that they got "dreamy eyed"? The excess of detail was a way for the writer to construct a mood, to remember an affair, perhaps to make it something good rather than shameful. Yet to say that some women sometimes found their own purposes in drafting their confessions is not to deny the presence of the state in the manufac-ture of such statements. "State officials can often make their categories [into ones] that organize people's daily experience," the anthropologist James Scott writes, "precisely because [individuals] are embedded in state created institutions that structure that experience."[121]

Scott's formulation is perceptive and useful, but does not fully cap-ture the extent to which state officials were also dependent on the women they investigated. Unsure of what defined lesbianism, military investigators listened intently to women themselves for an answer. The process was not terribly distinct from the way that state officials, going back to the turn of the century, had crafted homosexuality in reaction to their repeated encounters with certain kinds of difference. The unique-

---

[119]——— Case, decimal 220.8, box 3592, Classified decimal file 1948–1950, Records of the Adjutant General, RG 407.

[120] Ibid.

[121] James C. Scott, *Seeing Like a State: How Certain Conditions to Improve the Human Con-dition Have Failed* (New Haven, CT: Yale University Press, 1998), 82–83.

ness here may be how involved the conversation was between the regulator and the regulated, how much women themselves worked with the state to produce the category of lesbianism. It was, to be sure, a forced and unpleasant collaboration, but also extremely far-reaching in that it did not just affect the women who had begun to think of themselves as homosexual, the women who literally and figuratively *found themselves* in front of military boards. From the beginning, the lesbian witch hunt had a much broader audience and purpose.

Women's Integration: Marrying the Military

In every case this study has so far examined, it has been argued that the state did not simply discover and immediately react to homosexuality. Rather explicit regulation occurred after state officials came across evidence of sex and/or gender nonconformity, decided they cared about it, and then developed the conceptual and legal apparatus to respond. That process—like so much policymaking—normally stretched on for years. The state's pace in this chapter is faster—the cold war military mobilized against lesbianism with incredible speed and intensity. Military officials seemed to police lesbianism almost before they knew what it was, and they did this so aggressively that investigations affected (directly or indirectly) women in the service in general.

One suspects, of course, McCarthyism, but that is not the answer to this puzzle. It doesn't explain why lesbianism continued to be mostly ignored outside the military. Moreover, the timing is wrong: the lesbian witch hunts both preceded and outlasted the federal lavender scare. But neither were the witch hunts an attempt to remove women in general from the military after the Second World War. Military recruiters struggled throughout the 1950s to attract more women to the service.[122] Concern about low enlistments, however, offers an important clue. The

[122] "At no point, not even during the build up for the Korean War, was the two percent limit [on women in the armed forces] ever reached," writes Holm. "Until the late 1960s, women rarely exceeded even one percent of the services' strengths" (*Women in the Military*, 122). The perennial shortage of female inductees led to the formation of DACOWITS. Personnel Policy Board, Conference on Civilian Women Leaders, "Historical Background on Women's Military Services," June 21, 1950, decimal 291.3, box 115, Assistant Secretary of Defense decimal file 1949–1950, Records of the Secretary of the Defense, RG 330. The formation of DACOWITS is discussed in Charlotte Seely Palmer, *American Women and the U.S. Armed Forces: A Guide to the Records of Military Agencies in the National Archives Relating to American Women* (Washington, DC: National Archives and Records Administration, 1992). Other documentation of the military's shortage of womanpower and efforts at recruitment includes Vicki L. Friedl, *Women in the United States Military, 1901–1995: A Research Guide and Annotated Bibliography* (Westport, CT: Greenwood Press, 1996), 99.

witch hunts were, in fact, closely related to women's permanent integration into the regular force (enacted in 1948), as well as to the military's continuing need for female personnel during the cold war era.[123] Here as before, the state's exclusionary imperatives were closely bound together with its inclusionary ones.

What *kind* of women would be brought into the force? A permanently mobilized peacetime military would draw on a somewhat narrower demographic pool. During the war, women had volunteered in an unprecedented national emergency for what was assumed to be a relatively short interruption of their lives. After the war, by contrast, the military sought a small but permanent nucleus of women who would make the military a career. And the nucleus of women who would be willing to do so, especially as domesticity took on greater cultural salience, was comprised of those women who rejected the career of marriage.[124]

Military officials knew this; they saw themselves, quite explicitly, in competition with marriage for the country's best women. "As you can see, marriage is our chief competitor," wrote one WAC captain. Another WAC officer worried about the "losing battle with marriage."[125] A 1952 DOD study of reenlistment among women urged a focus on those "not anticipating marriage" in order "to get a clearer picture of re-enlistment intentions" of women with the most potential for long careers. The same report asked if negative experiences in the service *caused* women to marry—a fascinating query that reveals a subtle hostility toward marriage as something other than a natural or normative condition for women.[126]

The recognition that the armed services would lose some of its potential womanpower to marriage sometimes provoked a more explicit hostility toward the venerable institution. "The Government is not realizing a return on its investment in the case of many WACs," one general snapped, alluding to the numbers of female personnel who married and then left the service. Even married women who stayed on were

[123] On the Women's Integration Act of 1948, see Holm, *Women in the Military*, chapter 10; Sherman, "They Either Need These Women or They Do Not."

[124] Even "if you snare them, you can't keep them," fretted one expert of military "manpower" in 1956, "because the number of women who marry is at an all time high." Dr. Eli Ginzberg, quoted in Holm, *Women in the Military*, 162.

[125] Captain Lorraine Schultz to Colonel Lillian Foushee, February 10, 1956, and Lt. Anna K. Goffar, "Comments," February 9, 1956, decimal 342.06, "Re-Enlistments—Decline In," box 4, WAC Director's files 1952–1956, Records of the Army Chief of Staff, RG 319.

[126] Attitude Research Branch, Office of Armed Forces Information and Education, "Attitudes of Enlisted Women in the Regular Service toward Reenlistment," April–May 1952, decimal 324.5, "WAC," box 720, decimal file 1951–1952, Records of the Army Chief of Staff, RG 319.

likely to become pregnant, others opined, and then be required (by the military's own policy) to separate. Because of such unreliability, this general advocated that women who married be immediately discharged and that married women be refused induction in the first place (this latter provision was already official policy).[127] The WAC director similarly mandated that no special arrangements be made to accommodate service personnel who married; the married couple would not be treated like "Siamese twins," she asserted with some venom.[128]

The attrition of married women was thus exacerbated by the military's own policymaking, which did not contemplate that a woman could have a "dual career" as soldier and wife (even as numerous married women were entering the civilian labor force).[129] When women who were forced to choose opted for marriage and family, some military officials expressed bitterness. An equally narrow-minded response to the problem was to try to woo women away from marriage. DOD materials during these years offered recruiters advice, for example, on "how to meet the eligible young woman."[130] And guaranteeing women stability—part of the rationale for the establishment of a *permanent* women's force—made the military more viable as an alternative to marriage. This, it was hoped, would help to draw attractive candidates rather than "second-rate" women.[131] For the best women would not respond to a "peacetime call in which their status is ambiguous," opined Secretary of the Navy James Forrestal. They needed the "appeal of co-equal status" to "attract" and "hold" them.[132]

Women were to be offered, in other words, something similar to marriage. This partnership would free male soldiers from the burdens of "women's work" in the service. Women would be, General Dwight D.

[127] Major General Thomas W. Herren to Deputy Chief of Staff, March 23, 1951, and Lt. General Edward H. Brooks to the Commanding General, Military District of Washington, March 30, 1951, decimal 324.5, "WAC," box 720, decimal file 1951–1952, Records of the Army Chief of Staff, RG 319.

[128] Colonel Mary A. Hallaren, "Marriage of Service Personnel," October 20, 1949, decimal 334, "Personnel Policy Board," box 155, G-1 (WAC) Central decimal file 1949–1950, Records of the Army Chief of Staff, RG 319. Hallaren was not married. Tom Brokaw, *The Greatest Generation* (New York: Random House, 1998), 139.

[129] Kessler-Harris, *Out to Work*, 301. See also Alice Kessler-Harris, *In Pursuit of Equity: Women, Men, and the Quest for Economic Citizenship in 20th Century America* (Oxford: Oxford University Press, 2001), 205–6.

[130] "Manual of Selection," May 18, 1954, "Manual of Selection" folder, box 24, Marion Kenworthy Papers.

[131] *Appendix to Congressional Record*, 80th Cong., 2nd sess., 1948, 2153.

[132] Quoted and paraphrased in Sherman, "They Either Need These Women or They Do Not," 72. "Having a critical nucleus of women in place in the event of a remobilization," stated Forrestal, "depended on those women making a career of the military" (ibid.).

Eisenhower told the House Committee on Armed Services, "your efficient filing clerks, your stenographers, your telephone centrals."[133] The military also got a labor force that was cheap and continually on call.[134] With a civil service employee, "when 5 o'clock came they started to go home," Representative Johnson stated during subcommittee hearings on women's integration. With a permanent women's force, "you . . . get better work," he said, "cheaper work." Eisenhower agreed. Just like wives, military women were "on duty," he said, "24 hours a day."[135]

Clearly, women's integration was considered more a "pragmatic necessity" than the "righting of any great societal wrong against women."[136] But the proponents of integration believed that women who married the military, for their part, at least got to feel desired: "I want them . . . to feel that the army wants them badly," Eisenhower said. "By including them in the Regular Establishment first you show [them] that they are valuable, that you are perfectly delighted to get hold of them." Women also got security out of the arrangement. "Make them feel that they have something to look forward to," Eisenhower advised. "They will stay with you for thirty years."[137]

Despite Eisenhower's seductive tone during the hearings, military officials were generally realistic about which women would accept these terms. "Unfortunately," two military psychiatrists concluded, it was the "masculinized female" who found "*a home in the army*" and "stay[ed] on for a career." The military's growing brutality toward women it perceived to be lesbians, then, was a manifestation of the ambivalence of its leadership toward the women who would make a permanent home in the military after the war. This was the "career type . . . generally hostile toward men," who made the women's branches, officials complained, into a "literally hard corps."[138]

[133] Quoted in Congress, House, Committee on Armed Services, *Subcommittee Hearings on S. 1641, to Establish the Women's Army Corps in the Regular Army, to Authorize the Enlistment and Appointment of Women in the Regular Navy and Marine Corps and the Naval and Marine Corps Reserve, and for Other Purposes*, 80th Cong., 2nd sess., February 18, 1948, 5563–70.

[134] Rates of pay for enlisted women were less than rates for women in the civilian labor force; enlisted women were also less expensive to the military than enlisted men, especially because the latter had more dependents. Holm, *Women in the Military*, 163–64.

[135] Quoted in Congress, House, *Subcommittee Hearings on S. 1641*.

[136] Linda Witt, Judith Bellafaire, Britta Granrud, and Mary Jo Binker, "*A Defense Weapon Known to Be of Value": Servicewomen of the Korean War Era* (Hanover, NH: University Press of New England, 2005), 25.

[137] Quoted in Congress, House, *Subcommittee Hearings on S. 1641*. Eisenhower was also anxious not to portray himself as antimarriage. Most young women would inevitably leave the military to marry, he said, "and thank heaven." Quoted in Holm, *Women in the Military*, 162.

[138] M. D. Hogan and R. E. Anderson to CG, Third Army, "Fort McClellan, Mental Hygiene Consultations Service Report," September 14, 1956, box 64, Background Papers,

Yet the most "undesirable" personnel could have been purged—as a few DOD officials pointed out during these years—without such intensive and far-reaching investigations. Indeed, some policymakers worried that the witch hunts jeopardized the respectability of the institution and actually hurt recruitment efforts.[139] Perhaps the point of the investigation was not removal as much as submission—to train those who survived the purge, in other words, to be junior partners in the military marriage that Eisenhower and others envisioned. For military officials were uneasy not only about a particular type of woman who would choose the military for a career once the force was made permanent (among whom lesbians probably were well represented). They worried as well about maintaining gender hierarchy as formal barriers separating men's and women's service fell.

Prior to the Women's Integration Act, women's service was always differentiated from men's in such a way as to highlight its lesser character, to set it apart from the kind of sacrifice that produced first-class citizenship.[140] Women's service was auxiliary, quasi-auxiliary, or temporary. After 1948, only the provision keeping women out of combat demarcated women's service as different—a distinction that was becoming less and less meaningful in the nuclear age. "The more we progress toward this so-called future push-button war, everybody is going to be a target," Eisenhower told the Senate Armed Services Committee during hearings on women's integration. "Everybody in the United States is going to be a target just as much as if they were within fifty miles of the battle."[141] This increasingly blurry boundary between soldier and

---

Women's Army Corps 1945–1978, Records of the Army Chief of Staff, RG 319 (emphasis added).

[139] Lt. Colonel Lillian F. Foushee to Colonel Irene O. Galloway, February 17, 1956, decimal 342.06, "Re-enlistments—Decline In," box 4, WAC Director's files 1952–1959, Records of the Army Chief of Staff, RG 319; Lt. Colonel Nora Springfield to Colonel Irene O. Galloway, October 1956, file no. 312, "General-WAC Activities Survey, 1956," box 1, WAC Director's files 1952–1959, Records of the Army Chief of Staff, RG 319.

[140] While the WAC was "full military" during World War II, its temporary status set it apart. Legislation that created the women's branches provided for their disbandment six months after the end of the war. Sherman, "They Either Need These Women or They Do Not," 70. "Gender lines" were maintained by keeping women "not-quite military," argues Francine D'Amico in "Citizen-Soldier? Class, Race, Gender, Sexuality, and the U.S. Military," in States of Conflict: Gender, Violence, and Resistance, ed. Susie Jacobs, Ruth Jacobson, and Jen Marchbank (London: Zed Books, 2000), 111.

[141] Quoted in Congress, Senate, Committee on Armed Services, Hearings on S. 1103, S. 1527, S. 1641, 80th Cong., 1st sess., July 2, 9, and 15, 1947, 12. The cold war's emphasis on nuclear technology rather than combat in general "suggested that the military technologists' gender might be irrelevant," and that "'the old dividing line between a man's job and a woman's job' might someday disappear." Witt, Bellafaire, Granrud, and Binker, "A Defense Weapon Known to Be of Value," 25.

civilian was highlighted by advocates of women's integration, but in some respects this dynamic only made the potential for women's authority in the military more threatening. A provision was written into the integration bill, for example, restricting women's command authority to other women and creating "grade ceilings" that "limited each [women's] service to only one full colonel."[142] More remarkable was a 1950 report by the army's chief of staff, suggesting that the "integration of women into the Regular Army" would be advanced by placing women at the WAC Training Center under male rather than female commanders "to accustom" female personnel to working under men.[143] This remarkable assertion—that women would need to be *trained* to take orders from male superiors—reveals the extent of official concern about maintaining women's subordination in the postintegration period.

That concern is perhaps nowhere more obvious than in the hostility directed at women officers across the service branches, and the way in which lesbian baiting worked especially to rein in those marked as deviant by their own career ambitions. (The vitriol directed at women officers, usually older women, was also expressed via concerns about the potentially harmful impact of having menopausal women in the service.)[144] So a psychiatrist noted the "drive" of one officer under investigation for homosexuality. She desired independence, the psychiatrist said, positing that her homosexuality was the result of "competitive feelings toward men."[145] Moving up the ranks was itself a sign that an officer bore watching. One navy memo, for instance, noted that female homosexuals achieved "rapid advancement" because they worked hard to "compensate for or to avoid suspicion of [their] sexual weakness."[146]

Women officers were regularly blamed when lesbianism was seen as flourishing within their commands. It was women officers who allegedly opened the floodgates to lesbian recruits, or who turned a blind

[142]Moreover, the senior grade could be held for only four years. "The sole purpose of the grade ceilings was to prevent the possibility of women becoming top-level policy or decision makers in the military, except on women's matters." Holm, *Women in the Military*, 118–20.

[143]"A Survey of Women's Army Corps, Continental U.S.," December 11, 1950, decimal 321, "WAC," box 616, G-1 (Personnel) decimal file 1949–1950, Army Chief of Staff, RG 319.

[144]Menopausal women were discussed during hearings on women's integration. See Sherman, "They Either Need These Women or They Do Not," 69. The irony is, of course, that they, along with lesbians, were a perfect solution to the military's pregnancy problem.

[145]——— Case, decimal 220.8, box 3777, Classified decimal file 1950–1951, Records of the Adjutant General, RG 407.

[146]Lt. Bowdre L. Carswell to Chief of the Bureau of Medicine and Surgery, "Prophylactic Measures for Control of Homosexuality among Women Personnel of the Armed Services," October 22, 1952, file no. P13-1, box 503, Administrative Division General Correspondence 1952–1955, Bureau of Medicine and Surgery, RG 52.

eye on sexual misconduct because "there but for the grace of God go I."[147] Sometimes such complaints were registered by enlisted women, perhaps as a way of turning the tables on an authority figure.[148] But it was the male command structure that viewed women officers with the most animosity. "I cannot depend on WAC officers to command even a small detachment," one general wrote in a scathing memo on perversion among women. He advocated that both the WAC Training Center and WAC units over a certain size be placed under the control of male officers. It was also proposed that "male officer inspection teams make periodic inspection of all WAC installations," during the course of which enlisted women be granted confidential interviews to discuss their concerns on the subject of "leadership" and "homosexuality."[149]

For enlisted women as well but especially for officers, the closer women moved to power, to first-class citizenship, the more homosexuality seemed to matter.[150] Indeed, the air force was the first service to feature coeducational officer training and a single gender-integrated officer promotion list.[151] It was also "far ahead of the army in investigating and discharging female homosexual personnel."[152] The extent to which the air force carried both gender integration and lesbian persecution only makes clearer their interconnection across the service branches.[153] Women knew at what cost their own ambition came—Assistant Secretary of Defense Anna Rosenberg was derided as "Mr.

[147] Resume of Proceedings, June 27, 1957, decimal 333, "Ft. McPherson," box 2283, Confidential decimal file July 1958–June 1958, Records of the Inspector General, RG 159; M. D. Hogan and R. E. Anderson to CG, Third Army, "Fort McClellan, Mental Hygiene Consultations Service Report," September 14, 1956, box 64, Background Papers, Women's Army Corps 1945–1978, Records of the Army Chief of Staff, RG 319.

[148] ———— Case, decimal 201.36, box 52, General Correspondence 1939–1947, Records of the Inspector General, RG 159.

[149] Memorandum from Major General Thomas W. Herren, March 26, 1951, "Unsatisfactory Control," and Colonel T. J. Hartford, "Recommendations regarding WAC Enlistment and Utilization," March 29, 1951, decimal 250.1, box 967, G-1 (Personnel) decimal file 1951–1952, Records of the Army Chief of Staff, RG 319; M. D. Hogan and R. E. Anderson to CG, Third Army, "Fort McClellan, Mental Hygiene Consultations Service Report," September 14, 1956, box 64, Background Papers, Women's Army Corps 1945–1978, Records of the Army Chief of Staff, RG 319.

[150] This point would not have been lost on Kinsey, whose study of female sexuality attributed overall state indifference to lesbianism to women's lack of social and cultural power. Kinsey, *Sexual Behavior in the Human Female*, 485.

[151] Witt, Bellafaire, Granrud, and Binker, *"A Defense Weapon Known to Be of Value,"* 36.

[152] Lt. General Lutes to Colonel Mary A. Hallaren, November 22, 1950, decimal 333.9, "Fourth Army," box 1012, decimal file July 1950–June 1951, Records of the Inspector General, RG 159.

[153] This nexus is buttressed in the civilian world by what appears to be the somewhat exceptional case of Miriam Van Waters, whose life is beautifully documented in Estelle Freedman, *Maternal Justice: Miriam Van Waters and the Female Reform Tradition* (Chicago:

Rosenberg"—and how carefully they had to manage it.[154] Perhaps this was part of what led the women service directors (all unmarried) to personally fight congressional legislation that would have allowed them each to obtain a rank higher than colonel. "They were afraid of appearing 'grasping.'"[155] It was similarly what motivated these same women to stop saying, as their counterparts had during World War II, that female personnel could "replace" men, and instead talk about how well female soldiers "complemented" male personnel.[156] Just like a marriage. This was knowledge that also moved down the ranks, where the fact that women officers were not especially protected must have registered a warning to all. For "who among us" was without the homosexual tendencies of which careerism was a sign, one enlisted woman asked, noting, "they have [even] discharged married girls for this."[157]

The way that women's integration intensified antilesbian repression makes citizenship seem like a zero-sum game: as one group wins, another must lose. A parallel observation may be made with respect to racial integration, which was also occurring as the armed forces adopted increasingly homophobic policies more generally.[158] Yet while this substitutionist logic dominates the rhetoric of citizenship, one need not probe far beneath it to see that every new inclusion was deeply sedimented by past exclusion. Women's integration, in short, did not neuter the tradition of martial citizenship, which remained male. To preserve

---

University of Chicago Press, 1996). Van Waters—the warden of Framingham Reformatory—was lesbian baited in the 1950s. It is not clear from Freedman's account if Van Waters's experiences might have exemplified more general trends in prison administration during these years. Yet the attack on Van Waters seems to have had much to do with her own authority at the moment when the gender-segregated world of women's reform was becoming integrated into a more professionalized state bureaucracy. This has strong parallels to the case I lay out for the military.

[154] "Washington gagsters" called her "Mr. Rosenberg" because "she always walks ahead, pushes open the doors, and sits down last." Jack Lait and Lee Mortimer, *U.S.A. Confidential* (New York: Crown Publishers, 1952), 350.

[155] Witt, Bellafaire, Granrud, and Binker, "*A Defense Weapon Known to Be of Value*," 8. Colonel Mary Hallaren (army), Colonel Mary Jo Shelly (air force), Colonel Katherine Towle (marines), and Captain Joy Bright Hancock (navy) were all unmarried at this time. Hancock was widowed and later remarried.

[156] Ibid., 93.

[157] B. S. to ACLU, February 15, 1951, folder 1, box 1127, ACLU Collection.

[158] In 1945, military officials suggested the increasing separation of policies on race and sexuality in a statement that there was "less reported homosexuality among colored troops then white"; and again, in a claim in 1957 that homosexuality "could not be correlated with any other characteristic." Lt. Colonel Lewis H. Loeser, "The Sexual Psychopath in the Military Service: A Study of 270 Cases," *American Journal of Psychiatry* 102 (July 1945): 100; Crittenden Report, 11, box 16, World War II Project Records. This contrasts to the army's statement during World War I that "the colored show a higher percentage of

gender hierarchy in citizenship, though, the state had needed to constitute lesbianism. The incredibly broad way it did so meant that so many
women were touched during the course of any given investigation that
it was not individual women who were policed, but women in the service as a class. It stood in contrast to the way that homosexuality was
policed among male soldiers. Men too were brutalized by the military's
antihomosexual apparatus during these years, but it was a targeted and
contained brutality that did not undermine the claims of most men to
the military institution.

The policing of homosexuality in women in the cold war military was
in some ways then *anomalous*, and not only because of its reach and cru-
elty. In contrast to the other cases examined, there was no administrative lag in the regulation of female homosexuality; rather, widespread
awareness and concern coincided with an immediate regulatory response. If anything, the federal policing of female homosexuality was
actually ahead of bureaucratic knowledge about the condition such that
state policy was at its most constitutive in the case of women. And it
was, in sum, the regulation of women, not men, that united all the elements that would today look to contemporary viewers "like" homosexuality—appearance, relationships, sex, and culture.

When explored from a different angle, however, the regulation of
women was not anomalous but in fact *paradigmatic* of the way that the
state policed homosexuality more broadly at midcentury. During these
years (and in contrast to the early twentieth century), the state crafted
tools to explicitly target homosexuality, but the tools were not in themselves explicit. What, after all, was a homosexual tendency? That ambiguity could be harnessed in the production of a precise category (in this
case, lesbianism), that it might enhance rather than hamstring state
power, was one of the central tenets of postwar policing. It will appear
again in the immigration law's murky advent of the psychopathic personality in the next and culminating chapter.

---

sexual psychopathy than the whites." Pierce Bailey et al., *The Medical Department of the United States Army in the World War* (Washington, DC: U.S. Government Printing Office, 1929), 230. Also intriguing in this regard is an enormous witch hunt in 1947 concerning fifty African American WAC soldiers at Camp Beale, California. Because the service feared "probable publicity concerning racial discrimination," the women were "sur-plused" rather than being given undesirable discharges for lesbianism. ——— Case, dec-imal 201.36, box 52, General Correspondence 1939–1947, Records of the Inspector General, RG 159.

CHAPTER 6

IMMIGRATION

"Who Is a Homosexual?"

The Consolidation of Sexual Identities in
Mid-twentieth-century Immigration Law, 1952–1983

———$\ominus$———

States are powerful, according to the anthropologist James C. Scott, because they simplify complex social facts into a set of categories that are easily "legible."[1] Some of Scott's examples include imposing standard weights and measures or uniform naming practices on a people, but he just as well could have considered the way that state practices make a variety of gender codes and sexual behaviors legible as homosexuality. Such simplification not only makes a state more powerful, but it also takes a powerful state to render complex social facts legible in the first place. Nowhere is the process more clear than in the case of immigration—the arena where the state had the greatest administrative discretion to act against a subject population, noncitizens who lacked basic rights of due process.[2] There, the state created and articulated some of its most far-reaching rules defining homosexuality.

In creating these new rules—codified in the omnibus McCarran-Walter Act of 1952—the state built on patterns already begun by military officials at midcentury. Just as the military had adopted tools to police homosexuality as an act or a status (supplementing the court-martial with the administrative discharge), so other state officials devised ways to exclude and deport immigrants not only for engaging in homosexual activity but also for being homosexual. While an alien could be excluded or deported before 1952 for committing crimes of moral turpitude (i.e., homosexual acts), a prohibition barring aliens afflicted with psychopathic personality was enacted in 1952 to explicitly prevent ho-

---

[1] James C. Scott, *Seeing Like a State: How Certain Schemes to Improve the Human Condition Have Failed* (New Haven, CT: Yale University Press, 1998).

[2] On procedural rights for aliens, see Mae Ngai, *Impossible Subjects: Illegal Aliens and the Making of Modern America* (Princeton, NJ: Princeton University Press, 2004), 77.

mosexual aliens from entering or remaining in the country. The moral turpitude provision continued to be a backup throughout the 1950s and 1960s, and it is far too crude to describe the application of the psychopathic personality provision as evidencing a shift from the policing of acts to the policing of status. Midcentury immigration policy instead reveals a consolidation of formerly competing paradigms into a single model in which homosexual identity or status could be deduced from homosexual acts, or by other related markers of psychopathy that revealed to immigration officials a propensity to commit a homosexual act.

A vague status charge, the provision on psychopathic personalities might seem to resemble the public charge clause that was used against sexually degenerate aliens at the turn of the century. (The public charge clause had generally fallen out of favor by the late 1930s, and was no longer likely to be used against aliens suspected of perversion.)[3] The new provision was entirely different, however: not a preexisting device that officials tried to retrofit to police homosexuality, it was rather designed with that purpose in mind. Yet just like the military's policy on tendencies, this finely honed tool relied on ambiguity to do its work. This was not an accidental ambiguity, it was an instrumental one. "Loosely written laws" were called for because they widened the net as to what kinds of evidence could be "read" by state officials as homosexuality.[4] If the process itself seems messy and uncertain, the results were clear and predictable. Think of a huge laboratory vat into which a myriad of ingredients are being dumped; with enough heat and the right fixing agents, it will cook down into a chemically simple, pure substance.

Ultimately, though, it was not medical professionals who stirred the pot. Despite the fact that homosexual exclusion relied on the psychiatric category of psychopathy, the medical consensus about what defined homosexuality was breaking down just as a bureaucratic consensus was solidifying. Many psychiatrists were reluctant to equate homosexual acts with homosexual people, or to tag the latter with the label of psychopathy. Because the law required Public Health Service (PHS) psychiatrists to certify aliens as psychopathic prior to deportation, the increasing defection of medical experts left federal officials in a difficult position. When aliens facing deportation pointed strategically to scientific uncertainty surrounding the definition of both homosexuality and psychopathic personality, moreover, courts countered that these were, in fact, legal rather than medical terms. According to the law, they insisted, one who had homosexual sex was a homosexual person and a

[3] Ibid., 80–81.
[4] Karl M. Bowman and Bernice Engle, "A Psychiatric Evaluation of the Laws of Homosexuality," *Temple Law Quarterly* 29 (1956): 315.

psychopath. With homosexuality defined as a nonmedical category, however, the PHS relinquished all responsibility for certification, and the Immigration and Naturalization Service (INS) was left as the primary arbiter of homosexuality among aliens. By the late 1970s—with different political investments in the issue—the PHS, the INS, and the federal courts had thus all converged on the idea of homosexuality as a *legal* construct.

This was the culmination of nearly a century of federal regulation of homosexuality—a consolidation that definitively made homosexual sex (and a variety of markers that were seen as proxies for actual sex) irrefutable evidence of homosexual identity. In thereby defining homosexuality, the simple taxonomy of the immigration law eliminated earlier complexities: gone not only was an older conception of perverts and normals, but also men with feminism, cross-dressers, weak sisters, punk boys, muff-divers, female perverters, vicious wolves, and mannish social workers—the entire "galaxy of . . . freaks."[5] In their place, the courts, Congress, and the INS perfected in immigration policy the homo-hetero binarism that federal policymakers had been fashioning for several decades. Quite simply, the human race was divided; one was either heterosexual or one was homosexual. But even if heterosexuality and homosexuality were two sides of a binary, they were not symmetrical. While homosexual sex made one homosexual, heterosexual sex did not prove heterosexuality. Aliens who attempted to resist the state's definition of them by claiming heterosexuality found out how much more elusive it was.

The McCarran-Walter Act

Midcentury immigration reform cannot be understood apart from the "cold war civil rights" paradigm that legal historian Mary Dudziak has used to describe the postwar period.[6] Racist provisions in the nation's immigration laws were a liability to cold warriors who proclaimed to the world that American democracy valued racial equality. In 1952, Congress attempted to remove these warts from the national image in its first major revision of immigration law since Congress passed the Immigration Act of 1917. The McCarran-Walter Act ended racial bars to naturalization and established "for the first time," Mae Ngai writes, "the gen-

[5] S. J. Smith to Harry Hopkins, May 2, 1935, Box 116, "State" Series (Louisiana), FERA Central Files 1933-1936, Records of the WPA, RG 69.
[6] Mary L. Dudziak, *Cold War Civil Rights: Race and the Image of American Democracy* (Princeton, NJ: Princeton University Press, 2000).

eral principle of color-blind citizenship."[7] But like other cold war civil rights measures, the McCarran-Walter Act was more antiracist in appearance than in substance. The legislation preserved the national origins quota system, which continued the preferences of the Johnson-Reed Act of 1924 for aliens from northern and western Europe.[8]

For half a century, American state-building had resulted in increased federal interest in the constellation of traits and behaviors that, by the 1950s, comprised homosexuality. That pattern was in evidence once again as American policymakers erected a legal edifice to fight the cold war: paired with McCarran-Walter's shallow commitment to racial inclusion was an explicit assurance of homosexual exclusion.[9] Immigration law—like the civil service's lavender scare and the 1950s' military purges—targeted the homosexual as an excluded figure against which a citizenry supposedly unified along racial and class lines could define itself.[10] "The ties among the non-deviant citizens," observed attorney Gilbert Cantor, "are strengthened by their common opposition to the rejected and excluded."[11] And as the law imposed more explicit penalties on homosexuality, it heaped greater rewards on heterosexuality. Indeed, besides racial liberalism, one of the major thrusts of postwar immigration law was family reunification. Under the 1952 act, husbands and wives were permitted quota-free entrance for the first time.[12] Im-

---

[7] Ngai, *Impossible Subjects*, 238.

[8] Ibid., 237–39. The McCarran-Walter Act was enacted (Public Law 82-414, *U.S. Statutes at Large* 66 [1952] 163) over President Truman's veto. Truman objected to the bill's renewal of national origins quotas. After Congress overrode Truman's veto, the president appointed a special commission on immigration. The commission's report *Whom Shall We Welcome?* laid the groundwork for revisions in immigration law enacted by the Immigration Act of 1965 (the Hart-Cellar Act). See Michael LeMay, *From Dutch Door to Open Door: An Analysis of U.S. Immigration Policy since 1820* (New York: Praeger, 1987), 104–7.

[9] That legal edifice included the Voting Rights Act, the Civil Rights Act, and immigration reform, which together comprised what Ngai calls "the highpoint of postwar liberalism" (*Impossible Subjects*, 227). For a broader consideration of the racial and sexual dynamics of the McCarran-Walter Act, see Siobhan B. Somerville, "Sexual Aliens and the Racialized State: A Queer Reading of the 1952 U.S. Immigration and Nationality Act," in *Queer Migrations: Sexuality, U.S. Citizenship, and Border Crossings*, ed. Eithne Luibhéid and Lionel Cantú (Minneapolis: University of Minnesota Press, 2005), 75–91.

[10] On the way in which the ideology of the liberal consensus concealed racial and class differences, see Gary Gerstle, "The Protean Character of American Liberalism," *American Historical Review* 99 (October 1994): 1043–73. On the civil service purge, see David K. Johnson, *The Lavender Scare: The Cold War Persecution of Gays and Lesbians in the Federal Government* (Chicago: University of Chicago Press, 2004).

[11] Amicus Curiae Brief of the Homosexual Law Reform Society of America, 16, Supreme Court Records and Briefs for *Boutilier v. Immigration and Naturalization Service*, 387 U.S. 118 (1967).

[12] See "Legislative History" in Oscar M. Trelles and James F. Bailey, *Immigration and Na-*

migration law, like other federal policies at midcentury, inscribed the homosexual-heterosexual binary in the architecture of the liberal state.[13]

It did so, however, in ways that harkened back to the past. The McCarran-Walter Act contained two antihomosexual provisions, the first of which was simply a carryover from some of the earliest federal laws regulating immigration. Occasionally used against immigrants who were found to have engaged in homosexual activity—as well as other crimes of immorality—some version of the moral turpitude provision had been on the books since 1891.[14] In the 1930s, courts more precisely defined moral turpitude as "an act of baseness, vileness, or depravity in the private and social duties which a man owes to his fellow men."[15] Under the McCarran-Walter Act, the moral turpitude provision excluded from admission aliens convicted of a crime of moral turpitude, or "who admit having committed a crime involving moral turpitude or acts which constitute the essential elements of such a crime." Additionally, aliens could be deported if they were convicted within five years of entry of a crime of moral turpitude and sentenced to confinement for a year or more, or convicted of two crimes of moral turpitude at any time after entry, regardless of the sentence.[16]

The moral turpitude provision was an imperfect tool for deporting homosexual aliens for several reasons. Like the military's court-martial, the moral turpitude provision required a criminal conviction for committing a homosexual act. If an alien had been in the country for more

tionality Acts, Legislative Histories, and Related Documents (Buffalo, NY: William S. Hein and Company, 1984).

[13] This dynamic (and the tension between racial inclusion/homosexual exclusion) was even more pronounced in the Hart-Cellar Act of 1965. LeMay has called the 1965 act a "civil rights" bill because it eliminated many racist provisions in immigration law, including the national origins quota system (*From Dutch Door to Open Door,* 14). But the new law further tightened the ban on the entry of homosexual aliens while continuing to support the principle of family reunification. A major goal of the 1965 act was to "preserve the family unit" (ibid., 111).

[14] *Jordan v. DeGeorge*, 341 U.S. 223, 230, n.14 (1951).

[15] *Ng Sui Wing v. United States*, 46 F.2d 755, 756 (7th Cir. 1931).

[16] Shannon Minter, "Sodomy and Morality Offenses under U.S. Immigration Law: Penalizing Lesbian and Gay Identity," *Cornell International Law Journal* 26 (1993): 784–85. Homosexuality was also a factor in naturalization cases. In order to be eligible for naturalization, an alien must have legally entered the United States and lived in the United States for five years. During that period of time, the petitioner must have demonstrated that they were a person of "good moral character." A conviction for a crime of moral turpitude during the five-year period would bar a finding of good moral character, as would evidence of homosexuality. For a discussion of homosexuality and naturalization issues, see Eric Sedlak, "*Nemetz v. INS*: The Rights of Gay Aliens under the Constitutional Requirement of Uniformity and Mutable Standards of Moral Turpitude," *International Law and Politics* 16 (1984): 881–912.

than five years, a single conviction would not suffice. Moreover, criminal statutes—whether they were for sodomy or offenses like disorderly conduct or lewd vagrancy—were defined by state and local governments. Not only did this make the federal regulation of immigrants dependent on state and local laws, but such laws were said to be a "crazy quilt" that stood in the way of a uniform national policy. (A person convicted of private, consensual adult sodomy might pay a small fine in one state and be sentenced to life in prison in another.)[17] And in some quadrants, change was in the air. As soon as Kinsey published his 1948 study documenting the prevalence of homosexual activity among American men, the liberalization of sex laws was open for discussion.[18] Indeed, between 1951 and 1965, nine states liberalized sodomy laws.[19] Within a few years of Kinsey's study, moreover, the American Law Institute advocated the decriminalization of consensual homosexual behavior among adults.[20]

Congress therefore sought to add a status charge to the new immigration law—a charge, in other words, that was not bound up with state criminal laws but vetted the homosexual alien as a class of person. Accordingly, the Senate Committee on the Judiciary proposed legislation that explicitly barred immigrants who were psychopathic personalities or "homosexuals and sex perverts."[21] But the new provision raised the problem of detection. "Apparently a homosexual or sex pervert is afflicted with a physical or mental disability which can be discovered by a medical examination," the general counsel for the INS commented. "Query: Is this so?"[22] Representative Emmanuel Cellar was even more skeptical during hearings on the immigration bill. "How in the world," he asked, "is the inspector going to determine that the person before

[17] "The Consenting Adult Homosexual and the Law: An Empirical Study of Enforcement and Administration in Los Angeles County," *UCLA Law Review* 13 (1966): 662–63, 657.

[18] Bowman and Engle, "A Psychiatric Evaluation of the Laws of Homosexuality," 307.

[19] Gilbert M. Cantor, "The Need for Homosexual Law Reform," in *The Same Sex: An Appraisal of Homosexuality*, ed. Ralph W. Weltge (Philadelphia: Pilgrim Press, 1969), 83.

[20] Institute for Sex Research, "The Challenges and Progress of Homosexual Law Reform," vertical file, "Legal Aspects of Homosexuality," Kinsey Institute, Indiana University, Bloomington. This was also part of an international trend. As early as 1949, a British report advocated the decriminalization of homosexual behavior. Bowman and Engle, "A Psychiatric Evaluation of the Laws of Homosexuality," 304.

[21] U.S. Congress, Senate, Senate Report 1515, 81st Cong., 2nd sess., April 20, 1950, 345. The provision was introduced by Senator Patrick McCarran, who was one of the Senate's most vigorous homophobes. On McCarran's antihomosexualism, see Robert Dean, *Imperial Brotherhood: Gender and the Making of Cold War Foreign Policy* (Amherst: University of Massachusetts Press, 2003).

[22] File no. 56190/113, box 2825A, Records of the Immigration and Naturalization Service (INS), RG 85, National Archives, Washington, DC.

him is homosexual?" Cellar made a tongue-in-check suggestion that immigration inspectors bring the Kinsey volume along with them as they carried out their duties, or that they employ the services of "test boys" and "test girls." "How could you find out?" He exclaimed, "It is a hard nut to crack."[23]

When Congress consulted with the PHS on the issue, the agency agreed that detection posed an obstacle. It was easy enough, the PHS reported, when homosexuality manifested itself in unusual dress or behavior. More typically, however, a history of homosexuality had to be obtained from the individual—"which he may successfully cover up." Psychological tests might help uncover homosexuality, the report noted hopefully, even when individuals were unaware of the condition in themselves. But the PHS report lamented that there were no reliable tests that could determine homosexuality in every case.[24]

The psychopathic personality provision offered a solution to the dilemma, PHS officials advised. Psychopathic personalities, the PHS told Congress, were those who were "ill primarily in terms of society and the prevailing culture," and included those "suffering from sexual deviation." The psychopathic personality clause made the task of the INS a little easier, because "in those instances [where] the disturbance in sexuality may be difficult to uncover, a more obvious disturbance in personality may be encountered which would warrant a classification of psychopathic personality or mental defect." While conceding that the psychopathic personality terminology was "vague and indefinite," the PHS concluded, it was "sufficiently broad" to cover homosexuals.[25]

The INS registered "no objection" to the new terminology, but predicted that its lack of clarity would result in "considerable litigation."[26] Congress was not dissuaded. It kept only the psychopathic personality terminology, dropping the words homosexual and sex pervert from the final bill, but noting that "this change of nomenclature is not to be construed in any way as modifying the intent to exclude all aliens who are sexual deviates."[27] As passed, the relatively uncontroversial psychopathic personality provision provided for the exclusion or deportation of any person who at the time of entry acknowledged being or was later

[23] U.S. Congress, Senate and House, *Joint Hearings before Subcommittees of Committees of Judiciary*, 82nd Cong., 1st sess., March 6–21 and April 19, 1951, 360–62.

[24] "Report of the Public Health Service on the Medical Aspects of H.R. 2379," in U.S. Congress, House, *House Report 1365*, 82nd Cong., 2nd sess., February 14, 1952, 46–47.

[25] Ibid.; U.S. Congress, Senate, *Senate Report 1137*, 82nd Cong., 2nd sess., January 29 and March 13, 1952, 9.

[26] File no. 56190/113, box 2825, Records of the INS, RG 85.

[27] U.S. Congress, Senate, *Senate Report 1137* (9).

found to be homosexual.[28] The law required that aliens suspected of homosexuality be examined by a PHS psychiatrist. After the examination (usually an interview), the PHS doctor issued a "Class A" certification to the INS, which then "constituted the sole evidence for exclusion or deportation" at the subsequent hearing.[29] The certification exemplified state simplification—medical officers transcribed complex social facts about an alien's life onto a short form, "static and schematic" for efficient processing.[30] Yet the procedure by which aliens were thus rendered legible did not begin in front of government boards. It often started in public bathrooms.

Bathrooms and Borders

In the 1950s and 1960s, immigration officials (like their turn-of-the-century predecessors) encountered sexually deviant aliens in one of two ways: through inspection prior to entry or, in the words of one immigration official, because aliens "brought attention to themselves" after being in the country.[31] Because inspection procedures moved abroad to foreign consulates after 1926, the deportation process is more visible to the historian than is inspection and exclusion. One midcentury commentator noted, for example, that while three thousand immigrants were excluded for medical reasons at the port of New York alone in 1906, only twenty-three immigrants were excluded for medical reasons at all U.S. ports of entry in 1962.[32] Despite this evaporating trail, it is still possible to sketch out the rough outlines of the exclusion process at midcentury.

The Division of Foreign Quarantine of the PHS was charged with examining aliens at U.S. consulates for excludable conditions, including

[28] I have found only one published federal court case involving the psychopathic personality provision that did not concern homosexuality. It concerned exhibitionism. Moreover, it is revealing that records pertaining to the deportation of mentally ill aliens in the 1950s and 1960s do not reference psychopathic personality in any way. C.O. no. 243.55, Central Office Subject Correspondence files, 1957–1995, box 5, Records of the INS, RG 85.

[29] Minter, "Sodomy and Morality Offenses under U.S. Immigration Law," 778.

[30] Scott, *Seeing Like a State*, 46.

[31] Interview with Betram M. Bernard, district director of the INS, 1967, quoted in Thomas R. Byrne Jr. and Francis M. Mulligan, "'Psychopathic Personality' and 'Sexual Deviation': Medical Terms or Legal Catch-Alls—Analysis of the Status of the Homosexual Alien," *Temple Law Quarterly* 40 (1967): 342.

[32] U.S. House of Representatives, *Study of Population and Immigration Problems: Inquiry into the Alien Medical Examination Program of the U.S. Public Health Service* (Washington, DC: U.S. Government Printing Office, 1963), 24.

psychopathic personality.[33] This was a more intensive inspection than an alien would have been subject to at Ellis Island in 1910: aliens could expect to be interviewed for signs of mental aberration, tested for syphilis, and x-rayed, before being given a complete physical examination.[34] The latter was thought to be especially revealing. For males, resistance to examination of the genitals might "suggest homosexual traits." Women were considered harder to read, but for those who came from cultures where modesty was not emphasized, a female alien's reluctance to expose her breasts to a male physician "should be an indication for more intensive study."[35] Any abnormal findings were then investigated by further psychological or physical testing. The burden of proving normalcy rested with the alien. "If at any point, it becomes necessary to make the medical decision without benefit of further information, the decision is that the suspected condition is present," the PHS declared.[36] Because the McCarran-Walter Act authorized fines for any person who knowingly brought a psychopathic personality into the United States, the ship captain and airline steward served as another checkpoint.[37] Finally, all aliens were examined once more on arrival at U.S. ports of entry.[38]

It is impossible to know how many aliens suspected of homosexuality were turned back at U.S. consulates or crossing U.S. borders. There are some limited statistics available. The INS reported that between 206 and 534 aliens were excluded each year between 1952 and 1955 for criminal reasons. While aliens who admitted convictions for sodomy, solicitation, lewd vagrancy, or the like would be included in the criminal classes, the fact that the category of crimes is not disaggregated in any way makes these statistics somewhat hard to interpret. A bit more helpful is the INS's estimate that between 9 and 22 aliens were excluded as psychopathic personalities for each of those same years—but the official number no doubt vastly undercounts those actually turned away.[39] Telling in this regard are INS statistics from the 1970s, when only 31 persons (in total) were reported to be medically excluded for homosexual-

[33] Ibid., 21. In some locations, examinations were performed by local physicians appointed by a visa-issuing consular authority.

[34] Ibid., 28–29.

[35] Public Health Service, *Manual for the Medical Examination of Aliens* (Washington, DC: Public Health Service, 1963), 2–6.

[36] U.S. House of Representatives, *Study of Population and Immigration Problems*, 29.

[37] File no. 56190/113, box 2825A, RG 85; Albert E. Reitzel, "Procedures in the United States for the Admission, Exclusion, and Expulsion of Aliens," *INS Monthly Review* 7 (1949): 10.

[38] U.S. House of Representatives, *Study of Population and Immigration Problems*, 3.

[39] *Annual Report of the Immigration and Naturalization Service* (Washington, DC: U.S. Government Printing Office, 1955), 78.

ity, but the National Organization of Women (NOW) reported that "private conversations with INS officers have indicated a figure closer to 2,000 per year." That incredible disparity existed, NOW explained, because of the INS's practice of intimidating aliens into "voluntarily" withdrawing their applications for entrance. "The victims," NOW asserted, "never surface in the numbers compiled."[40] Also revealing is the 1963 testimony before Congress of a psychiatric consultant for the PHS in Europe that he was *frequently* asked to rule on written evidence, police evidence, and quasi-admissions . . . by applicants for visas as to whether they [were] homosexuals."[41]

And what of the aliens who "brought attention to themselves" as U.S. residents? Hard figures here are equally vague, and also likely to be underrepresentative. In 1959, an article in the *Yale Law Journal* on the deportation of psychopathic personalities noted, for example, that just fifty-nine aliens were deported for physical or mental defects out of more than five thousand total deportations in 1957. The article elaborated that "in evaluating these figures it must be born[e] in mind that many aliens are permitted to depart voluntarily"—more than sixty thousand that same year—and would therefore not be recorded in deportation statistics.[42] Indeed, voluntary departure was to deportation (and voluntary withdrawal was to exclusion) what the administrative discharge was to the court-martial: "it allow[ed] the rapid removal of large numbers of aliens who could overwhelm the immigration system should they demand [formal proceedings]."[43] Because aliens who were formally deported were barred from ever again emigrating legally, many of those ensnared were easily convinced to quietly disappear, slipping out of both the country and the historian's grasp.[44] A mere handful had the resources and wherewithal to seek formal relief, first through the INS's Board of Immigration Appeals (BIA), with an even smaller number going on to sue in federal court. Because formal proceedings thus repre-

[40] "NGLTF to Oppose Justice Department Move to Bar Homosexual Aliens," *National NOW Times* (1980), 9, vertical file folder, "Immigration," at ONE/IGLA Archives, University of Southern California, Los Angeles. See also Larry Bush, "Borderline Homophobia," *Inquiry* (June 9 and 23, 1980): 8.

[41] U.S. House of Representatives, *Study of Population and Immigration Problems*, 15 (emphasis added).

[42] "Limitations on Congressional Power to Deport Resident Aliens Excludable as Psychopaths at Time of Entry," *Yale Law Journal* 68 (April 1959): 931–32.

[43] Chicago Regional Hearings, Papers of the Select Commission on Immigration and Refugee Policy, April 21, 1980, part II, reel I, University Publications of America.

[44] Ibid. Aliens who were formally excluded had to wait a year before attempting to enter again; aliens who voluntarily withdrew could attempt to reenter at any time. Boston Regional Hearings, Papers of the Select Commission on Immigration and Refugee Policy, November 19, 1979, 1980, part II, reel III, University Publications of America.

sent the tip of the iceberg in immigration regulation, the existence of thirteen published administrative-level hearings and twelve published federal court cases involving homosexuality from the 1950s and 1960s is itself important evidence of the reach of postwar policing.[45] The anti-homosexualism of the INS during these years was fierce.

The arguments and outcomes in these cases are significant for the way they reveal the logic of state simplification in the manufacture of homosexuality. These sources also suggest the contours of state polic-ing. Some patterns are remarkably clear. Most of the deportees were male aliens. They came—as did most aliens during these years—from Canada, Latin America, and Europe. All but a handful of the deporta-tions resulted from arrests. Most of the arrests occurred in public bath-rooms. In many of these arrests, aliens were victims of entrapment—through the use of police decoys "who are young, attractive, and seductively dressed, and who engage in enticing conversations."[46] A typical scenario is the "Matter of G," in which a police officer alleged that alien G loitered in a public toilet, "soliciting men for the purpose of committing a crime against nature and other lewdness, at which time the defendant did move from another urinal and stand at the right of the urinal which deponent [police officer] was using, and did reach over and place his left hand on deponent's penis."[47]

Such incidents captured aliens in the same legal traps that vetted huge numbers of native-born men—San Francisco, Washington, DC, Los Angeles, and Miami Beach were some of the centers of harassment arrests, as was New York. In 1949, the New York Police Department ar-rested 931 men for degenerate acts in bathrooms, and another 2,213 for "loitering in comfort stations."[48] Punishment for such offenses (usually disorderly conduct or loitering) might be minor—as little as a $25 fine—but for aliens the consequences could be severe. In the best-case sce-nario (municipalities that did not automatically contact the INS in the event of arrest), the incident might simply mean that an alien would live "under the tension of legal insecurity."[49] After his arrest, one alien

[45] Also relevant here is the fact that immigration was an arena of limited judicial review. See Daniel R. Ernst, "Law and the State, 1920–2000," in *The Cambridge History of Law in America*, ed. Christopher Tomlins and Michael Grossberg (Cambridge: Cambridge Uni-versity Press, 2008); Ngai, *Impossible Subjects*, 78, 88–89; Lucy Salyer, *Laws as Harsh as Tigers: Chinese Immigrants and the Shaping of Modern Immigration Law* (Chapel Hill: Univer-sity of North Carolina Press, 1995).

[46] Cantor, "The Need for Homosexual Law Reform," 92.

[47] File no. 56363/792, box 3421, Records of the INS, RG 85.

[48] Cantor, "The Need for Homosexual Law Reform," 92; Morris Ploscowe, *Sex and the Law* (New York: Prentice-Hall, 1951), 208. On the policing of homosexual offenses at mid-century, see especially, "The Consenting Adult Homosexual and the Law."

[49] "Matter of LaRochelle," *Administrative Decisions under Immigration and Nationality Laws of the United States* 11 (December 1, 1965), 442.

stated that he "felt that the United States Immigration might be looking for me because I heard that such things were reported to Washington, so I have been very careful."[50] In these cases, it was usually leaving the country for a short period and then reentering that led the INS to discover the arrest and begin deportation proceedings.[51] Occasionally, aliens applied for naturalization and confessed to an arrest (or sometimes to having homosexual desires) during the proceedings.[52] Sometimes a "tip" from a hostile neighbor or relative alerted the INS to an arrest record.

In some vicinities, however, local and state police (or local and state penal institutions) had a more active and direct relationship with the INS. (The INS also tightened its relationship with the FBI during these years, and FBI records were included in many case files.) G's entrapment (above) was described as part of a "pilot" program—and because New York (even that particular bathroom at Duffy Square) yielded so many deportations, it seems likely that the New York Police Department was particularly vigorous in looking for aliens. Detroit, too, was another city that seemed to have a direct line to the INS. There and elsewhere, investigators from the INS might go to city jails to interview immigrants who were serving even short sentences. Usually unrepresented by counsel, immigration officials secured admissions of homosexual behavior or desire that would render an alien deportable regardless of conviction. "Homosexuality . . . was thrown at me," one alien later protested. "I was ready to cry. I was all broken up."[53] But such confessions usually stuck. "There is not a right to counsel during the taking of a statement in the investigative stage," opined one official.[54] "The fact that an alien can make an admission which, in itself, renders him deportable, even though he may not have been convicted of the precise

[50]Complaint for Declaratory Judgment and Review of Administrative Action, 75, Supreme Court Records and Briefs for *Rosenberg v. Fleuti*, 374 U.S. 449 (1963).

[51]See "Matter of G.R.," *Administrative Decisions under Immigration and Nationality Laws of the United States* 5 (April 30, 1952), 18–22. Leaving the country made aliens especially vulnerable—and not only those who were technically deportable when they left the country. Under immigration law, returning after even a short trip constituted an entry. Because exclusion provisions were more far-reaching than deportation provisions, those immigrants "reentering" after a trip abroad experienced heightened vulnerability. On the related phenomenon of "delayed exclusion," see "Limitations on Congressional Power to Deport." See also "'Psychopathic Personality' and 'Sexual Deviation.'"

[52]Such was the case in *Matos Jordan v. P.A. Esperdy*, 290 F.2d 879 (2nd Cir. 1961) and with Clive Boutilier, the Canadian immigrant whose case is discussed below. See also "Canadian Not Good Enough for U.S.," *Advocate* (May 26–June 8, 1971): 12 (concerning the deportation of a man who applied for citizenship in 1967).

[53]Brief for the United States, 48a, 41a, *United States v. Roberto Flores-Rodriguez*, 237 F.2d 405 (2nd Cir. 1956), trial records at the National Archives.

[54]"Matter of Steele," *Administrative Decisions under Immigration and Nationality Laws of the United States* 11 (July 11, 1967), 303.

crime which he admits . . . has been part of the immigration statutes for many years."[55] When aliens were invited to "discuss [their] problems" with psychiatrists from the PHS, the government created another opportunity to secure admissions in cases where the evidence was too weak to sustain a conviction.[56]

After the INS had secured a certification from the PHS, a special inquiry officer would issue a finding in the case. (In these matters, the special inquiry officer functioned as "clerk, prosecutor, judge, and jury.")[57] Aliens facing deportation had the right to appeal these decisions administratively to the BIA.[58] The small number of aliens who appeared before these boards were only slightly better protected than they had been during their initial contact with INS and PHS officials. Deportation hearings—which could last days—were exempted from coverage under the Administrative Procedures Act.[59] They were not criminal proceedings, and the "rules of evidence applicable in courts of law need not be followed."[60] It is not surprising, in the absence of these procedural protections, that the INS would try one charge (usually moral turpitude), and if that failed, try another one (usually psychopathic personality). The INS could "explore any charge it deemed applicable," one official explained. "The alien cannot dictate to the government the charge which will be used in his case."[61] Moreover, when review boards found in favor of aliens, high-level meddling sometimes ensued, and cases were reopened. The findings were then preordained. "Examining once more the record of these proceedings," one such board wrote, "we

[55] "Matter of S," *Administrative Decisions under Immigration and Nationality Laws of the United States* 8 (July 21, 1959), 417.

[56] Opening Brief for Petitioner, 7, *Gerald Lavoie v. United States Immigration and Naturalization Service*, 360 F.2d 27 (9th Cir. 1966), trial records at the National Archives. "The manner in which the psychiatrist's interview was procured raises disquieting questions about how the service operates" (ibid.).

[57] Allan van Gestel, David S. Barnet, and Edward J. Hawie, "Immigration—Exclusion and Deportation, Proceedings and Review, under the McCarran-Walter Act of 1952," *Boston University Law Review* 41 (1961), 211.

[58] Aliens denied entry by a special inquiry officer also had a right to appeal to the BIA, but these cases are rare. A case from 1945 in which an excluded alien appealed to the BIA is "Matter of Z," *Administrative Decisions under Immigration and Nationality Laws of the United States* 2 (June 9, 1945), 316–18.

[59] On the length of deportation hearings, see "Boards of Special Inquiry—Port of New York," *INS Monthly Review* (March 1952): 117. "It is highly questionable as to whether or not the objectives of the Administrative Procedures Act are satisfied by the provisions of the Immigration and Nationality Act." Van Gestel, Barnet, and Hawie, "Immigration—Exclusion and Deportation, Proceedings and Review," 211.

[60] Van Gestel, Barnet, and Hawie, "Immigration—Exclusion and Deportation, Proceedings and Review," 221, 225.

[61] "Matter of LaRochelle," *Administrative Decisions under Immigration and Nationality Laws of the United States* 11 (July 11, 1967), 442.

find certain elements present to which we perhaps did not attach sufficient significance when we previously considered the case."[62]

Being caught in a bathroom, in short, usually meant an eventual ejection at the border. That trajectory—from bathroom to border—suggests what the federal government could do with the raw material of state and local enforcement (which was usually directed at homosexual behavior, not homosexual status).[63] Using the psychopathic personality provision as an instrument that "compounded vagueness with vagueness," federal officials perfected the art of manufacturing homosexual acts into homosexual people.[64] Because the courts are one of the arenas in which the state "speaks" (as well as the fact that aliens turned back at the agency level tend to disappear into the historical ether), this process can be best seen in a series of court cases where aliens attempting to prevent their deportation were rendered legible as homosexual. The cases, to be clear, are not typical. Yet to the extent that these aliens forced the state to explain and justify the way that it policed homosexuality among immigrants, the logic of state policing is laid bare. The obstacles are also exposed. Despite the centrality of the psychopathic personality clause in this process, psychiatry turned out to be enormously problematic.

The Sea of Psychiatry

As would be true with most federal cases involving homosexuality among immigrants, the first of these cases appealed to the federal courts shifted clumsily between conduct and status provisions of the immigration law. Roberto Flores-Rodriguez, an unmarried Cuban, was arrested for disorderly conduct on a visit to New York City in September of 1950. According to the police report, Flores-Rodriguez loitered at a men's toilet, and moved "from one urinal to several others," "manipulate[d] the exposed and naked parts of his person," and "motion[ed] . . . in the direction . . . of several others in said toilet." As a result, Flores-Rodriguez was sentenced by the City Magistrate's Court to thirty days of imprisonment, but the sentence was suspended and Flores-Rodriguez was allowed to return to Cuba.[65]

---

[62] "Matter of W," *Administrative Decisions under Immigration and Nationality Laws of the United States* 5 (December 23, 1953), 580.

[63] "The Consenting Adult Homosexual and the Law," 658.

[64] "Petition for a Writ of Certiorari to the United States Court of Appeals for the District of Columbia Circuit," 15, *Wyngaard v. Kennedy*, 295 F.2d 184 (D.C. Cir. 1961), trial records at the National Archives.

[65] *United States v. Roberto Flores-Rodriguez*, 237 F.2d 405 (2nd Cir. 1956).

Two years later, Flores-Rodriguez appeared at the consulate in Havana to apply for an immigration visa. When asked if he had ever been arrested or convicted, Flores-Rodriguez said no. His visa was granted, and he entered the United States as a permanent resident, settling in New York City. In June of 1954, Flores-Rodriguez was again arrested and convicted of disorderly conduct. The thirty-day sentence he received was of minor consequence except that it brought his case to the attention of immigration officials, who then ordered Flores-Rodriguez deported on the ground that his entry had not been valid because he failed to disclose his 1950 conviction for a crime of moral turpitude.[66]

Flores-Rodriguez appealed his deportation to the BIA, making a technical distinction between a "crime" of moral turpitude and, as it was classified under New York State law, the "offense" of disorderly conduct for which he had been convicted. Flores-Rodriguez argued that he could not have been excluded for a crime of moral turpitude, because he had been convicted under the New York statute only of an offense. Therefore, he maintained, his failure to disclose the conviction was not a material omission invalidating his entry. The BIA initially agreed. The INS then filed a motion for reconsideration, bolstering the original conduct charge with a status charge. Because Flores-Rodriguez had applied for his visa before the passage of the McCarran-Walter Act, the INS argued that the alien's arrest indicated that he was a "constitutional psychopathic inferior" under the terms of the Immigration Act of 1917. His conviction, therefore, was material to his entry. The BIA accepted this subsequent argument and upheld the deportation.[67]

Ultimately, Flores-Rodriguez appealed to the Second Circuit Court of Appeals, which heard his case in 1956. In its opinion, the Second Circuit first determined that Flores-Rodriguez had, in fact, committed a crime of moral turpitude under the immigration law. Despite the holding of New York State courts that an offense of disorderly conduct was neither a crime nor a misdemeanor, the Second Circuit held that "an Act of Congress should not be necessarily circumscribed" by the New York courts. How odd it would be, the court reasoned, for an alien convicted for the *crime* of disorderly conduct in another jurisdiction to be deported while an alien convicted for the *offense* of disorderly conduct in New York be allowed to remain. Congress, the Second Circuit wrote, had clearly expressed its disapproval of the behavior ascribed to Flores-Rodriguez, and could not have intended such a result.[68]

[66] Ibid.

[67] Brief on Behalf of Dependent-Appellant and Brief for the United States and Appendix, *United States v. Roberto Flores-Rodriguez*, 237 F.2d 405 (2nd Cir. 1956), trial records at the National Archives.

[68] *United States v. Roberto Flores-Rodriguez*, 237 F.2d 405, 410 (2nd Cir. 1956).

The Second Circuit could have stopped there, and decided that Flores-Rodriguez might have been excluded on that basis alone. Notably, the court pressed on to opine on the second argument advanced by the government—that had Flores-Rodriguez revealed his 1950 arrest to the consulate, he might have been excluded as a constitutional psychopathic inferior. The court observed that the government, in lodging the charge of psychopathic inferiority, had "offered no evidence whatever . . . to the effect that a homosexual who solicits unnatural acts in a public place comes within that category." Nevertheless, the Second Circuit reasoned that because Flores-Rodriguez had admitted being a homosexual to the investigating INS officer in 1955, "together with the fact of [the] defendant's conviction which in itself was evidence of homosexual tendencies of an extremely offensive and exhibitionistic nature," Flores-Rodriguez was potentially subject to exclusion as a psychopathic inferior. On this basis as well, the court held that the alien's failure to disclose his earlier arrest was therefore material to his entry.[69]

In his concurring opinion, Judge Frank voiced his discomfort with the majority's ruling as he feared that the intent of the 1952 act was being read back into the 1917 legislation.[70] Before coming to the conclusion that the constitutional psychopathic inferiority clause was meant to include homosexuals, Judge Frank argued, "we should have asked

[69] Ibid. Flores-Rodriguez later retracted his admission of homosexuality, attributing his misstatement to nervousness. Brief for the United States, 41a, *United States v. Roberto Flores-Rodriguez*, 237 F.2d 405 (2nd Cir. 1956), trial records at the National Archives.

[70] Some historians and legal scholars have fallen into a similar trap. Legislators in the 1950s claimed that they were updating the 1917 provision barring constitutional psychopathic inferiors by enacting the psychopathic personality clause. Scholars have therefore concluded that the constitutional psychopathic inferiority provision was used against "sexual perverts" in the early twentieth century. See, for example, William N. Eskridge Jr., *Gaylaw: Challenging the Apartheid of the Closet* (Cambridge, MA: Harvard University Press, 1999) 36, 70, and 383–84. Eskridge uses the psychopathic inferior clause as one index to the number of "sexual outlaws" barred from entering the country from 1917 until the provision was removed from the law in 1952. My own research, however, has shown that the psychopathic inferiority provision was regularly used against individuals for reasons unrelated to sex/gender deviance. Moreover, if "sexual degenerates" were to be excluded or deported, it was far more likely to be under the public charge or moral turpitude provisions (see chapter 1). The constitutional psychopathic inferiority clause was sometimes used in perversion cases against aliens (like Flores-Rodriguez) who entered the country before the passage of the McCarran-Walter Act, but came to the attention of the INS *after* the enactment of that legislation. In cases decided before 1952, "the BIA's use of the 'crime of moral turpitude' clause rather than the 'constitutional psychopathic inferiority' clause as a means of denying admission to aliens who had apparently engaged in homosexual activity may indicate that . . . homosexuality was not deemed a 'constitutional psychopathic inferiority.'" Robert Poznianski, "The Propriety of Denying Entry to Homosexual Aliens: Examining the Public Health Service's Authority over Medical Exclusions," *Journal of Law Reform* 17 (Winter 1984): 333–34.

the government to assist us by . . . supplying us with such data as, by diligent research, it might discover."[71] Because no such research was conducted, both the U.S. attorney and the Second Circuit emphasized the antisocial nature of Flores-Rodriguez's acts, thereby implying that the particular public expression of his homosexuality qualified him as a psychopathic inferior. This linkage between homosexuality and psychopathy rested on the long-standing notion that psychopaths were unable to control antisocial impulses and adapt to the norms of the communities in which they lived. Hence, the government's brief in the case noted that the defendant was "not merely homosexual," but that "his illness [had] twice manifested itself in public anti-social behavior."[72] The Second Circuit further observed that a deviate who solicited an unnatural act as Flores-Rodriguez had, "will find it extremely difficult to adapt himself and to become a useful member of the American community."[73]

This discussion of psychopathy and the related shift from conduct to status provisions of the law—the shift, in other words, from the notion that homosexuality was a behavior to the idea that the homosexual was a kind of person—thus introduced citizen motifs into the discussion of an alien's potential deportation. Psychopaths were problematic as citizens precisely because they flouted convention, according to William Alanson White, a leader of the American mental hygiene movement. "The individual who manifests a kind of conduct that is calculated to tear down the existing conventions, to deviate greatly from the normal conduct of the community," White remarked, "has to be relegated to some place other than a position of free citizenship."[74] Later, immigrants held for deportation under the 1952 act who more closely conformed to societal mores would use this same logic to challenge the notion that homosexuals were by definition psychopathic—and they would call on psychiatric expertise to bolster this claim. While this development still had yet to materialize in 1956, Judge Frank issued a prescient warning that anticipated the INS's eventual break with medicine: "I think it a mistake," he wrote, "for my colleagues needlessly to embark—without a pilot, rudder, compass or radar—on an amateur's voyage on the fog enshrouded sea of psychiatry."[75]

[71] *United States v. Flores-Rodriguez*, 237 F.2d 405, 413–14, n.4 (2nd Cir. 1956) (Frank, J., concurring).

[72] Brief for the United States, 23, *United States v. Roberto Flores-Rodriguez*, 237 F.2d 405 (2nd Cir. 1956), trial records at the National Archives.

[73] *United States v. Flores-Rodriguez*, 237 F.2d 405, 412 (2nd Cir. 1956).

[74] White, quoted in Henry Minton, *Departing from Deviance: A History of Homosexual Rights and Emancipatory Science in America* (Chicago: University of Chicago Press, 2002), 55.

[75] *United States v. Flores-Rodriguez*, 237 F.2d 405, 412 (2nd Cir. 1956) (Frank, J., concurring).

Frank's warning was based on the lack of clarity in the Immigration Act of 1917 concerning the definition of constitutional psychopathic inferiority. Perhaps heeding his warning, in several subsequent cases in which an alien's entry occurred before the enactment of the McCarran-Walter Act (and the adoption of the psychopathic personality provision), neither the INS nor the courts attempted to use the constitutional psychopathic inferior clause, relying solely on the conduct provisions of the law. Many of these cases involved, like the *Flores-Rodriguez* case, disorderly conduct convictions in states where that conviction was an offense and not a crime (and hence arguably not covered as a crime of moral turpitude). In these cases, the courts followed *Flores-Rodriguez* in asserting that "deportation is solely a federal power" and federal courts were not required to "slavishly follow state law."[76] Robert Wyngaard, a Dutch immigrant residing in Washington, DC, for example, had like Flores-Rodriguez been convicted for an offense of disorderly conduct in New York City. His counsel argued that it was unclear whether Wyngaard's conviction fell under the moral turpitude provision not only because it was an offense and not a crime, but also because of widely disparate reactions to homosexuality between state and federal governments as well as within society at large. Could Wyngaard have committed moral turpitude, his attorneys asked, "in view of the fact that consensual homosexual behavior is not a crime universally or in the District of Columbia . . . [and] in light of current knowledge [that such conduct] . . . is not regarded as necessarily vile or depraved, and the fact that under New York law the offense here is regarded as merely a minor breach of the public peace?"[77]

However lenient New York State was in its attitude toward homosexuality, the DC District Court and the DC Circuit followed the Second Circuit's decision in *Flores-Rodriguez.* "The Second Circuit very cogently argues that what constitutes a crime involving moral turpitude is a Federal question," the DC District Court contended, "and is not dependent on the manner in which State law classifies the violation of law."[78] But the repeated court challenges as to what constituted a crime of moral turpitude proved the point of one federal judge, who claimed that the moral turpitude clause "hamper[ed] uniformity."[79]

---

[76] *Babouris v. Esperdy*, 269 F.2d 621 (2nd Cir. 1959); *Babouris v. Murff*, 175 F. Supp. 503 (S.D.N.Y. 1958). See also *Hudson v. Esperdy and Matos Jordan v. Esperdy*, 290 F.2d 879 (2nd Cir. 1961).

[77] Brief for Appellant, 7, *Wyngaard v. Kennedy*, 295 F.2d 184 (D.C. Cir. 1961), trial records at the National Archives.

[78] *Wyngaard v. Rogers*, 187 F. Supp. 527 (D.D.C. 1960).

[79] Federal Judge Charles Wyzanski Jr., *Harvard Law Review* 43 (1929): 117, quoted in

The psychopathic personality provision did not share the same liabilities. Under the psychopathic personality clause, federal immigration officials and federal courts could decide—based on state convictions for offenses like disorderly conduct—that an alien was a homosexual, and therefore deportable as a psychopathic personality. As such, the clause enhanced the power of the federal government to remove aliens alleged to be homosexual from the country, regardless of how homosexual offenses were treated at the state level. Yet the status provision of the act did not only broaden the power of the federal government over immigrants by reasserting federal authority over state law. As with the military's policy on tendencies, the psychopathic personality provision offered a vague tool to capture a vague target.

That target, moreover, might sometimes be a woman. As in the military, female aliens were also the victims of federal antihomosexualism, although in smaller numbers than female soldiers. Of the twelve published federal cases dealing with homosexuality under McCarran-Walter during the 1950s and 1960s, just two dealt with women.[80] Women may disappear somewhat in court records because they were more likely to be vetted at the border for appearance (rather than arrested for sex offenses once in the country). This was a point at which aliens were less likely to have the economic and cultural resources to fight the charges against them. One female alien whose case survives in the historical record because, for whatever reason, she *was* able to hire a lawyer is that of Sara Harb Quiroz. The case is important because it is the first published case involving homosexuality in a female alien. It also foreshadows how right Judge Frank was to be apprehensive about the place of psychiatry in immigration law.

Quiroz had been stopped at the U.S.-Mexico border after a family visit, according to ethnic studies scholar Eithne Luibhéid, because her short hair and trousers made her look like a lesbian to the immigration official who stopped her.[81] In the Quiroz case, the alien's appearance suggested a propensity for homosexual behavior to immigration officials. She initially denied this association, stating that she was not a homosexual. But after interrogation, Quiroz admitted to the INS that she

Brief for Appellant, 12, *Wyngaard v. Kennedy*, 295 F.2d 184 (D.C. Cir. 1961), trial records at the National Archives.

[80] Besides the Quiroz case (discussed below), see also *Rose v. Woolwine*, 344 F.2d 993 (4th Cir. 1965). It is not certain that the "sexual perversion" that the alien is accused of in the latter case is homosexuality, but as the facts concern a suspicious friendship between two women, it seems likely. See also *In the Matter of Olga Schmidt*, 289 N.Y.S. 2d 89 (Supreme Court of New York 1968), which concerns the naturalization of a lesbian alien.

[81] Eithne Luibhéid, *Entry Denied: Controlling Sexuality at the Border* (Minneapolis: University of Minnesota Press, 2002), 80–81.

had felt "homosexual desires for at least a year, [and] had homosexual relations on numerous occasions over this period of time with two women."[82] Based on this admission, Quiroz's attempt to prevent her deportation failed at the administrative (BIA) level. When her case reached the federal courts in 1961, Quiroz asserted that her homosexuality did not make her a psychopathic personality. Quiroz's lawyer argued that Congress had not defined psychopathic personality, and even if Congress had the power to relegate the question to the PHS, the latter body had not stated that the psychopathic personality terminology *always* included sexual deviates.[83] "Since law is silent on the criteria or definition of a psychopathic personality," Quiroz's attorney wrote, "the only alternative to which law can turn is medicine." The brief cited the evidence presented at the INS hearing by two doctors, who maintained that while it was clear that Quiroz was a homosexual, it was not similarly obvious that she was a psychopathic personality. Remarkably, one of these doctors was a PHS surgeon who testified that while PHS regulations included all homosexuals as psychopathic personalities, he was not certain that Quiroz was "medically a psychopathic personality." The other doctor—a psychiatrist—testified that Quiroz's traits of "trustworthiness, conscientiousness, and hard work" indicated that she was not a psychopathic personality.[84]

Highlighting Quiroz's role as a useful member of her community was an attempt to reverse the discourse that associated psychopaths with those utterly devoid of the characteristics of good citizens. Perhaps because the psychiatrist's emphasis on strong work habits would not have carried as much weight in Quiroz's case as they might have for a male immigrant, the attempt failed and the Fifth Circuit rejected Quiroz's appeal. Presented with evidence from the two doctors that homosexuals were not necessarily considered psychopathic personalities by the medical profession, Judge Jones quoted Judge Frank's concurring opinion in *Flores-Rodriguez* that it was a mistake "to embark . . . on the fog enshrouded sea of psychiatry."[85] Ironically, courts cited Frank's opinion, according to legal scholar Shannon Minter, "to bypass the ambiguities of clinical discourse about homosexuality."[86] Almost as soon as the

[82] "Decision of the Special Inquiry Officer, 3–4," quoted in ibid., 89.

[83] Closing Brief of the Appellant, 5, *Quiroz v. Neelly*, 291 F.2d 906 (5th Cir. 1961), trial records at the National Archives.

[84] Brief of the Appellant, 3–5, *Quiroz v. Neelly*, 291 F.2d 906 (5th Cir. 1961), trial records at the National Archives.

[85] *Quiroz v. Neelly*, 291 F.2d 906, 907 (5th Cir. 1961).

[86] *Flores-Rodriguez* was cited in many of the cases that followed for an important reason. The court found Flores-Rodriguez excludable under two provisions: moral turpitude and as a constitutional psychopathic inferior. Judge Frank disagreed with the latter charge in his concurring opinion, arguing that it was not clear that the term included homosexuals

courts began to rule on cases that involved the psychopathic personality charge, then, they distanced themselves from the discipline of psychiatry. Judge Jones cited the legislative history of the act, which stated that the adoption by Congress of the PHS terminology "psychopathic personality" in no way modified congressional intent to exclude homosexuals. "Whatever the phrase 'psychopathic personality' may mean to the psychiatrist, to the Congress it was intended to include homosexuals and sexual perverts," Jones wrote. "It is that intent which controls here."[87]

Despite the court's ruling, Quiroz was not yet ready to give up. Two weeks before she was to be deported, Quiroz got married and then filed a motion to reopen her case. She requested that she be allowed to "present evidence of her marriage and full rehabilitation." Quiroz was, as her motion to reopen her case stated, "prepared to prove" that she was, at that time, "a normal individual and no longer a psychopathic personality." But Quiroz's attempt to claim heterosexuality failed. The INS ordered her deported, finding that her recent "rehabilitation" had no bearing on her original condition at entry. By its ruling, the INS suggested that heterosexuality was not so easily achieved.[88]

The Vagaries of Vagueness

From *Flores-Rodriguez* on, the point of moving through these cases is to see the state's evolving production of homosexuality as a legal status—*legal* rather than medical because of the growing reluctance of psychiatrists to equate homosexuality with psychopathy, which only became more evident in the cases that followed *Quiroz*; and as a *status* rather than a behavior because, as will be evident below, treating homosexuality as the latter opened immigration officials to charges that the psychopathic personality provision was "void-for-vagueness." That doctrine said that aliens were entitled to clear, adequate warning about

---

and that the court should not venture into the arena of psychiatry. Minter writes: "The disagreement between the majority opinion and the concurrence in *Flores-Rodriguez* allowed courts greater flexibility in interpreting the two Acts [of 1917 and 1952] and actually made the exclusion of homosexuals easier. In cases governed by the pre-1952 law, courts could cite the majority opinion's psychiatric rationale to authorize using a homosexual offense as evidence of 'constitutional psychopathic inferiority' under the 1917 Act." In cases governed by the 1952 act, as noted above, Frank's concurrence bolstered the court's rejection of any psychiatric opinion that complicated the relationship between homosexuality and psychopathic personality. See Minter, "Sodomy and Morality Offenses under U.S. Immigration Law," 790.

[87] *Quiroz v. Neelly*, 291 F.2d 906, 907 (5th Cir. 1961).
[88] Luibhéid, *Entry Denied*, 93–94.

behavior that rendered them deportable. If homosexuality was only a behavior, then the vagueness of the psychopathic personality provision was not an asset but rather a problem for the state, one that gave at least a few aliens a way to beat the INS.

George Fleuti—who sued to prevent his deportation in the early 1960s—was one such victor. Atypically, the Ninth Circuit in *Fleuti* treated homosexuality only as conduct, and in essence argued that had the psychopathic personality clause been less vague, Fleuti could have avoided the behavior that made him a homosexual.[89] Fleuti was a Swiss alien who had been living in the United States since 1952, and worked as the front office manager at the Ojai Valley Inn and Country Club in Los Angeles.[90] He was convicted in 1953 as "willfully and unlawfully a lewd and dissolute person," and in March of 1956 for an act of oral copulation.[91] It was not until another arrest (later dismissed) in November 1958 that the INS began deportation proceedings on the basis of moral turpitude.[92]

In the spring of 1959, an investigator from the INS obtained a statement from Fleuti that he had engaged in homosexual relations about once a month for twenty-two years.[93] Despite Fleuti's prior arrests, the examining officer concluded on a technicality that Fleuti was not deportable for moral turpitude. But the INS subsequently used testimony from the investigation to reopen the hearing on the ground that Fleuti was a psychopathic personality. During the new hearing, Fleuti denied the truth of the statement he had made to the INS investigator, but affirmed that he had been examined by a PHS doctor who had certified him as a psychopathic personality.[94] That doctor, who had no formal psychiatric training, noted that he had based that determination on "the history and documentation of the, shall we say, arrest." When pressed

[89] *Fleuti v. Rosenberg,* 302 F.2d 652 (9th Cir. 1962).

[90] Brief for Respondent, 4, Supreme Court Records and Briefs for *Rosenberg v. Fleuti,* 374 U.S. 449 (1963).

[91] Supreme Court Records and Briefs for *Rosenberg v. Fleuti,* 374 U.S. 449 (1963). According to court records from the 1956 conviction, Fleuti "did willfully, unlawfully and feloniously participate in the act of copulating the sexual organ, to wit, the penis of him, the said George Marcel Fleuti, with the mouth of" another man. Fleuti was fined $200 (43).

[92] "Matter of Fleuti," *Administrative Decisions under the Immigration and Nationality Laws of the United States* 12 (December 27, 1965), 308–11. Fleuti was also arrested as a lewd vagrant in November of 1958. That charge was dismissed, but it is probably what brought his case to the attention of INS officials, since he was first investigated in April of 1959. *People of the State of California v. George Marcel Fleuti,* 43, and *In Re: George Earnst Marcel Fleuti,* 47–49, Supreme Court Records and Briefs for *Rosenberg v. Fleuti,* 374 U.S. 449 (1963).

[93] Affidavit, 75, Supreme Court Records and Briefs for *Rosenberg v. Fleuti,* 374 U.S. 449 (1963).

[94] Decision of the Special Inquiry Officer, 79–86, Supreme Court Records and Briefs for *Rosenberg v. Fleuti,* 374 U.S. 449 (1963).

further, Dr. Dalhgren conceded that he had "'no strong feeling' as to whether, 'according to traditional medical terms,' respondent would be considered a psychopathic personality."[95] Fleuti also presented a letter from his own psychiatrist, a Dr. Harvey, stating that Fleuti's sexual deviation was under control and listing several attributes that suggested the opposite of psychopathy: "[Fleuti] seems to have traits of a better than average citizen, in the sense of hard work, general morality, and honesty." Harvey further noted that Fleuti had long recognized his homosexual interests and had his first homosexual experience at age twenty-six. "However," Harvey wrote, "his socio-economic relationships have been consistently good according to my history." The psychiatrist observed that Fleuti "did not frequent homosexual hangouts, had no evident interest in youths, manifested no irresponsible trends, and had his main social contacts with respected members of the community."[96] Fleuti had a greater interest in homosexual relations than was typical, but his overall sex drive was not strong. He had also engaged in heterosexual relations up to 1959, and he was not, according to Fleuti's doctor, "a sociopath, a psychopath, or a person of constitutional psychopathic inferiority."[97] In a remark clearly intended to highlight the PHS doctor's lack of psychiatric expertise, Harvey concluded, "I do not think that another psychiatrist with adequate training and experience will be likely to disagree with my findings."[98]

In ordering Fleuti's deportation, the special inquiry officer noted that the charge of psychopathic personality was supported by Fleuti's own admissions as well as the certification of the PHS.[99] The logic that made Fleuti a psychopathic personality was incredibly circular (and a typical example of state simplification). The INS cited the PHS certification, and the PHS doctor who made the certification had, when questioned by Fleuti's lawyer about medical disagreements surrounding the term, cited the authority of the PHS manual. "We have to use certain terminology—and the rest of the world may not agree," the doctor weakly explained. "We are so ordered; therefore we do."[100] The BIA

[95] Transcript of Hearing, 59–69, Supreme Court Records and Briefs for *Rosenberg v. Fleuti*, 374 U.S. 449 (1963).

[96] David R. M. Harvey to Richard F. Porter, 6-8, Supreme Court Records and Briefs for *Rosenberg v. Fleuti*, 374 U.S. 449 (1963).

[97] "Matter of Fleuti," *Administrative Decisions under the Immigration and Nationality Laws of the United States* 12 (December 27, 1965), 310 (quoting from psychiatrist's letter of August 1959).

[98] David R. M. Harvey to Richard F. Porter, 6–8, Supreme Court Records and Briefs for *Rosenberg v. Fleuti*, 374 U.S. 449 (1963).

[99] Decision of the Special Inquiry Officer, 79–86, Supreme Court Records and Briefs for *Rosenberg v. Fleuti*, 374 U.S. 449 (1963).

[100] Transcript of Hearing, 65, Supreme Court Records and Briefs for *Rosenberg v. Fleuti*, 374 U.S. 449 (1963).

upheld the order, Fleuti appealed his case to the federal courts, and lost at the district court level.

In his appeal to the Ninth Circuit, Fleuti's attorney argued that the deportation order was a violation of Fleuti's due process rights because the term psychopathic personality was void-for-vagueness—Fleuti could not be punished, in other words, for conduct that he could not be expected to understand as proscribed. The court observed that Fleuti's deportation had relied on conduct both before and *after* his entry to the country to determine that he was a psychopathic personality. Because Fleuti exhibited control over his postentry homosexual behavior, "it follows that if, by reason of vagueness, the statute failed to advise him that homosexual practices conclusively evidence a 'psychopathic personality,' Fleuti was substantially prejudiced." The Ninth Circuit observed that the PHS official and Fleuti's own doctor disagreed as to the meaning of the term psychopathic personality, that the PHS (in its report to Congress) conceded that the term was "vague and indefinite," and that experts in general disagreed about its meaning. Based on this confusion, the Ninth Circuit concluded that the psychopathic personality provision, "when measured by common understanding and practices, does not convey sufficiently definite warning that homosexuality and sex perversion are embraced therein." The court ordered Fleuti's deportation canceled on the ground that the statute was overly vague.[101] In doing so, it affirmed the narrowing premise of Fleuti's brief that homosexuality was a form of conduct, not a broader set of attributes—hence the notion that if properly warned, Fleuti would not have engaged in such behavior.

Fleuti's court battle was far from over. The government appealed the case to the Supreme Court, where its strategy was to reassert the idea that homosexuality was a condition or status, rather than a behavior. The government contended that the statute was not void-for-vagueness because Congress was "not seeking to regulate conduct but to prescribe standards for admission to the United States."[102] Fleuti was being deported, the government argued, not for postentry conduct but for his *condition at entry.* The void-for-vagueness doctrine, intended in the immigration context to ensure that aliens had adequate warning about conduct for which they could be deported, was inapplicable to Fleuti. The doctrine, government counsel claimed, "was not a device to enable

---

[101] *Fleuti v. Rosenberg*, 302 F.2d 652 (9th Cir. 1962). "The question of whether a statute is void-for-vagueness most frequently arises in criminal prosecutions. . . . But the Supreme Court has also applied this principle in civil proceedings, and in so doing has expressly ruled that a criminal penalty need not be involved" (655). The case of *Jordan v. DeGeorge*, 341 U.S. 223 (1951) examined a deportation statute for vagueness.

[102] Petition for Writ, 10, Supreme Court Records and Briefs for *Rosenberg v. Fleuti*, 374 U.S. 449 (1963).

persons having defined characteristics . . . or suffering from specified physical or mental diseases or defects, to conduct themselves so as to avoid making these conditions manifest."[103]

Although *Fleuti* was the first time the Supreme Court had heard a case involving an individual alleged to be homosexual, the Court declined to address the void-for-vagueness issue and instead vacated the district court's ruling on other grounds.[104] But in letting the Ninth Circuit's ruling stand, at least Chief Justice Earl Warren had been influenced by the ambiguity of the psychiatric testimony in the case. "It was conceded by the government doctors," Warren wrote in a note to himself, "that all homosexuals are not medically psychopaths."[105] After the Fleuti decision was remanded, the INS again ordered Fleuti's deportation, asserting that he had been a constitutional psychopathic inferior at the time of his entry in 1952. (Like Flores-Rodriguez, Fleuti's original entry occurred before the passage of the McCarran-Walter Act of 1952.) The renewed order for deportation was finally canceled in 1965 when the BIA ruled, in intriguingly broad terms, that it did not find compelling evidence that Fleuti was a homosexual:

> Respondent has been employed in a responsible position for the past 11 years by one employer who thinks very highly of him, that he has a history of devotion to family and interest in others, that he has sought psychiatric help and has his problem under control, that apart from these arrests resulting in convictions on two occasions, he has not been in trouble with the authorities, that he is well regarded by people who have known him over an extended period of time. . . . While the record reveals that respondent has an inclination toward homosexuality, it appears to be one respondent can control and that he had it under control before he entered. *Therefore, we cannot find that the record establishes that he was a homosexual at the time of that entry.*[106]

---

[103] Brief for Petitioner, 32, Supreme Court Records and Briefs for *Rosenberg v. Fleuti,* 374 U.S. 449 (1963).

[104] Joyce Murdoch and Deb Price, *Courting Justice: Gay Men and Lesbians v. the Supreme Court* (New York: Basic Books, 2001), 87; *Rosenberg v. Fleuti,* 374 U.S. 449 (1963). Under immigration law, leaving the country and returning after even a short trip constituted an entry. In Fleuti's case, when he was charged with being afflicted with psychopathic personality at the time of his entry, his entry comprised an afternoon visit to Mexico. The Supreme Court ruled that Fleuti's three-hour excursion from the country did not constitute an entry and vacated on that ground.

[105] Quoted in Murdoch and Price, *Courting Justice,* 93.

[106] "Matter of Fleuti," *Administrative Decisions under the Immigration and Nationality Laws of the United States* 12 (December 27, 1965), 308–11 (emphasis added). This was the last attempt that the INS made to deport Fleuti. In 1975, Fleuti became a naturalized citizen. Murdoch and Price, *Courting Justice,* 98.

What, then, according to the court, made one a homosexual? Fleuti's sexual acts—unlike Flores-Rodriguez's or Quiroz's—were mitigated by other facts that seemed to suggest to the BIA that Fleuti led an upstanding and moral life. In contrast to the image of the out-of-control psychopath, Fleuti's homosexual urges were held in check. Moreover, he had severed not only sexual but also social contacts with other homosexuals. Fleuti exhibited many of the traits of a good citizen—he was productively employed, a responsible family member who cared for his dependents, well thought of by his associates, and not least, both northern European and male. Interestingly, such traits did not suggest to the BIA that Fleuti was a good homosexual. Instead—the increasing opposition between homosexuality and citizenship made the former conclusion unlikely—they indicated that he was not a homosexual at all.[107]

Following *Fleuti, Lavoie v. Immigration and Naturalization Service* would initially seem to further destabilize government efforts to regulate homosexuality among immigrants. Lavoie, a Canadian alien, entered the United States in 1960. After Lavoie pled guilty to an arrest for a homosexual act in a Woolworth's store in 1961, the INS began an investigation. Lavoie told an INS investigator that he had first become aware of homosexual feelings when he was in the Royal Canadian Navy, and he admitted to frequent homosexual encounters, but to more than thirty "satisfactory" heterosexual acts as well. During hearings before a special inquiry officer, the government's own psychiatrist, PHS surgeon Beittel, testified that from a psychiatric point of view, Lavoie was not a homosexual but rather a "sexual deviate manifested by auto-eroticism and homo-eroticism." The testimony of Lavoie's own psychiatrist, a Dr. Diamond, was also vexing for the INS. He stated that the respondent was not a psychopathic personality, but suffered from a neurotic conflict over sex. Diamond initially testified that "homosexuality [was] not an appropriate medical term . . . [and] there [was] no such diagnosis as homosexuality." But then he reversed himself, arguing that while Lavoie clearly manifested sexual confusion, he bore none of the traits of a "true" homosexual:

> No molesting of children, no interest in adolescents, no sustained relationships "with some abnormal individual in any perverted way," no feminine characteristics, no love affairs with men. The homosexual "experience[s]" were "extremely superficial, extremely casual," and "in between the scattered homosexual contacts he has had perfectly normal relationships with women."[108]

[107] "Matter of Fleuti," *Administrative Decisions under the Immigration and Nationality Laws of the United States* 12 (December 27, 1965), 308–11.

[108] Decision of the Special Inquiry Officer (January 30, 1964), 1–6, and Opening Brief for

As evidenced by Diamond's testimony, then, there was such a diagnosis as homosexuality, but informed by a broad notion of psychopathy, its definition threatened to drift away from sex. What made one homosexual, according to Lavoie's doctor, was child molestation, effeminacy, and emotional attachments—but not casual sex with other men. The special inquiry officer rejected this notion, returning instead to the familiar argument that homosexual acts confirmed homosexual status. "A person who [has] engaged in homosexual acts twelve to twenty-four times a year for a period of at least eleven years," the special inquiry officer concluded, "[is] a sexual deviate within the definition Congress intended to apply to the term 'psychopathic personality.'"[109]

Lavoie then appealed to the BIA, which remanded the case so that the psychiatric issues could be reconsidered in light of the PHS's *Manual for the Medical Examination of Aliens*, and to take further testimony as to "what pattern determines a . . . homosexual." At the reopened hearing, the psychiatric testimony remained unchanged. "A good deal of their testimony only served to confuse me," the special inquiry officer wrote, "[but] I did get out of it that they agreed that the phrase 'psychopathic personality' has no precise medical meaning and that 'homosexual' is not a medical term." Having found in the PHS manual a reference to psychopathic personality as a "legal term," the officer firmly rejected the relevance of psychiatric testimony. "If, as testified to by the medical experts, 'psychopathic personality' and 'homosexual' are not medical terms," he reasoned, "any testimony concerning such conditions is without the scope of their special competence and is of little value in resolving the issue."[110]

While the INS may have felt that it had effectively dismissed the psychiatric testimony, Lavoie's lawyers resurrected it again when his case reached the Ninth Circuit. Lavoie's opening brief cited the testimony of the government psychiatrist in which he stated that Lavoie might be neurotic and not homosexual, and that he finally reached his "diagnosis" of psychopathic personality with "grave doubts" and "under [the] compulsion of a government manual" that he believed needed revision. "Like the government doctor in *Fleuti*," the brief argued, Beittel was "required to [so] certify anyone who is a sex deviate."[111] The govern-

Petitioner, 2–13, *Lavoie v. Immigration and Naturalization Service*, 360 F.2d 27 (9th Cir. 1966), trial records at the National Archives.

[109] Decision of the Special Inquiry Officer (January 30, 1964), 5, *Lavoie v. Immigration and Naturalization Service*, 360 F.2d 27 (9th Cir. 1966), trial records at the National Archives.

[110] Decision of the Special Inquiry Officer (March 11, 1965), 1–4, *Lavoie v. Immigration and Naturalization Service*, 360 F.2d 27 (9th Cir. 1966), trial records at the National Archives.

[111] Opening Brief for Petitioner, 5, 11, *Lavoie v. Immigration and Naturalization Service*, 360 F.2d 27 (9th Cir. 1966), trial records at the National Archives.

ment's case was clearly weakened by such testimony from within its own ranks, and the Ninth Circuit continued to hold that psychopathic personality was void-for-vagueness in its application to homosexuals.[112] But Lavoie's case would ultimately be settled after the Supreme Court's *Boutilier* decision, which follows next.

Like One Might Recognize a Redhead

Both *Fleuti* (a case "widely discussed" by consular officials in Europe) and the Ninth Circuit's opinion in *Lavoie* unsettled many of the givens on which the federal regulation of homosexuality among immigrants had come to rest.[113] In the *Boutilier* decision of 1967, immigration officials and the courts successfully reestablished those givens: first, the notion that homosexuality designated not merely a behavior but a kind of person, and second, that homosexual persons were psychopaths—incapable of being good citizens—and therefore excluded under the terms of the immigration law. In the face of psychiatric disagreement about the nature of homosexuality, the latter effort would require the court to find another foundation on which to establish homosexual identity. That foundation would be the law itself.

Canadian national Clive Michael Boutilier had been living in the United States for eight years when he applied for naturalization in 1963. During that process, Boutilier completed an affidavit that disclosed a 1959 sodomy charge that had been changed to simple assault, and then dismissed.[114] As a result of this admission, Boutilier was questioned by the INS in great detail about his entire sexual history, including the charge from 1959. Boutilier told the investigator that he had engaged in homosexual acts approximately four times a year both before and after his entry to the United States, and that he had also engaged in heterosexual acts. Immigration officials also obtained information from Boutilier that he had lived for some time with a man with whom he had occasional sexual relations, and that after a psychiatric examination, he was classified as "4F" by the Selective Service System.[115] Information from the investigation was submitted to the PHS, which reviewed the materials and certified that Boutilier was a psychopathic personality at the time of his entry. At his hearing, Boutilier declined to be examined

---

[112] *Lavoie v. Immigration and Naturalization Service*, 360 F.2d 27 (9th Cir. 1966).

[113] U.S. House of Representatives, *Study of Population and Immigration Problems*, 15.

[114] *Boutilier v. Immigration and Naturalization Service*, 360 F.2d 488 (2nd Cir. 1966).

[115] Record of Sworn Statement, 1–10, Supreme Court Records and Briefs for *Boutilier v. Immigration and Naturalization Service*, 387 U.S. 118 (1967). The 4F categorization indicated that one was unfit for military service.

by PHS doctors, but submitted evidence from two different psychiatrists who declared that Boutilier was not a psychopathic personality. The special inquiry officer ruled Boutilier deportable as a person afflicted with psychopathic personality at the time of his entry, revealing the conflict between INS and psychiatric definitions that would recirculate in various court rooms and legal briefs.[116]

When Boutilier's case made its way to the Second Circuit in 1966, the majority opinion supported the INS's attempt to label Boutilier (and all homosexuals) as psychopathic, regardless of medical opinion. The court asserted that homosexuals were defined by the legislative history of the McCarran-Walter Act as psychopathic personalities. "Congress utilized the phrase 'psychopathic personality' not as a medical or psychiatric formulation," the majority wrote in a by-then-familiar argument, "but as a legal-term-of-art designed to preclude the admission of homosexual aliens into the United States."[117]

In his dissent, Judge Moore argued that Congress could not have intended the psychopathic personality language to exclude *all* homosexuals. He pointed to Kinsey's finding that 37 percent of American men had at least one homosexual experience. "To label a group so large 'excludable aliens' would be tantamount to saying," Moore reasoned, "that Sappho, Leonardo da Vinci, Michelangelo, Andre Gide, and perhaps even Shakespeare were they to come to life again would be deemed unfit to visit our shores." Furthermore, Moore continued, "so broad a definition might well comprise more than a few members of legislative bodies." Moore raised the possibility that homosexuals (unlike psychopathic personalities) were not necessarily persons whose "sexual deviation put [them] into repeated conflict with the authorities." Rather, some homosexuals—not least legislators as well as famous writers and artists—might be contributing members of society, and were capable and potentially deserving of citizenship. The assertion certainly seemed true of Boutilier, who was, Moore observed, "young, intelligent, responsible," and "who has worked hard . . . and is respected in his work."[118]

The argument in the Supreme Court followed similar contours.[119] Boutilier's legal team employed a variety of legal strategies to make the case that the psychopathic personality provision did not apply to him. An amicus brief filed by the Homosexual Law Reform Society of America in-

[116] *Boutilier v. Immigration and Naturalization Service*, 363 F.2d 488 (2nd Cir. 1966).

[117] Ibid., 494.

[118] Ibid., 496–99 (Moore, J., dissenting).

[119] Solicitor General Thurgood Marshall urged the justices to take the *Boutilier* case to resolve a conflict between the Second Circuit's decision in the case and the Ninth Circuit's decision in *Lavoie* (on the void-for-vagueness issue).

cluded dozens of letters from prominent medical and scientific experts—Margaret Mead, Harry Benjamin, and John Money among them—maintaining that homosexuals were not by definition psychopathic.[120] The brief further charged the government with manipulating science. "In labeling the homosexual as . . . a psychopathic personality, we have not discovered a classification of disturbed persons," the amicus brief explained. "Rather, we have created such a classification in the purposeful but unscientific pursuit of certain non-medical ends."[121] Boutilier's lawyer strongly rejected the lower court's dismissal of scientific opinion, asserting that psychopathic personality was a medical term whose definition should be left to psychiatrists rather than administrators. As evidence, Boutilier's counsel observed that the clause was included in the statute in a section with other medical exclusions, such as epilepsy. And as Boutilier's brief explained, "Respondent and the court are . . . in the ambivalent position of denying that a medical opinion is required to find that petitioner was a psychopathic personality at the time of entry," and simultaneously basing his deportation on the "the pro forma certification" of the PHS. It was contradictory, in other words, to turn to the doctors of the PHS to legitimize the deportation of aliens for homosexuality, while ignoring the opinion of medical experts more broadly.[122]

In addition to the contention that Boutilier was a homosexual but homosexuals were not psychopathic personalities, Boutilier's legal team mounted the contradictory argument that Boutilier might not have been a homosexual at all. As evidence of this, Boutilier's heterosexual experiences were cited, as was the frequency of occasional homosexual contact among American men in general. "In no event can Boutilier be classed as homosexual without violating part of his history," concluded psychiatrist Clarence A. Tripp, "forcing him into a category that would include a sizable population of the whole white American population."[123] Like other aliens in court, Boutilier also challenged the INS's

---

[120] Appendix C of Amicus Curiae Brief of the Homosexual Law Reform Society of America, 27–96, Supreme Court Records and Briefs for *Boutilier v. Immigration and Naturalization Service*, 387 U.S. 118 (1967). The brief also pointed to similar positions taken in the writings of Kinsey, Evelyn Hooker, Sigmund Freud, and Richard von Krafft-Ebing. The Homosexual Law Reform Society was a homophile group. There were others—such as the Mattachine Society—that were also involved with Boutilier's defense. See Marc Stein, "*Boutilier* and the U.S. Supreme Court's Sexual Revolution," *Law and History Review* 23 (Fall 2005): 530.

[121] Amicus Curiae Brief of the Homosexual Law Reform Society of America, 14, Supreme Court Records and Briefs for *Boutilier v. Immigration and Naturalization Service*, 387 U.S. 118 (1967).

[122] Petition for a Writ of Certiorari, 1–11, Supreme Court Records and Briefs for *Boutilier v. Immigration and Naturalization Service*, 387 U.S. 118 (1967).

[123] Brief for Petitioner and Appendix C, 46, Supreme Court Records and Briefs for

construction of him as homosexual by distancing himself from psychopathy. In addition to his client's strong work record, Boutilier's psychiatrist testified that Boutilier had moved back home with his mother. Boutilier went to Mass and spent most nights at home. "He occasionally goes bowling," the doctor added.[124]

This attempt to problematize Boutilier's homosexuality was part of a larger strategy to disrupt the notion that homosexuality was a category of identity that could be deduced from homosexual behavior. Boutilier's brief asserted that "the source of the evil lies in an apparent belief that there is some kind of recognizable human being that is a homosexual, like one might recognize a red-head." This was, Boutilier's attorneys claimed, erroneous: "By and large homosexuality is a kind of behavior, evidently very wide spread, and not the manifestation of a particular kind of person."[125] Boutilier's writ to the Supreme Court adopted a similar tone. "Who is a homosexual?" the brief asked. One who engaged in both homosexual and heterosexual acts? One who engaged one time or many times? One who was drawn to such practices as experimentation? One who was drawn to such behavior compulsively?[126]

The facts in *Boutilier* raised such questions about the relationship between homosexual behavior and homosexual identity because while the petitioner had admittedly engaged in homosexual conduct, he did not *seem* like a homosexual. This disjuncture between conduct and status was itself an ironic effect of the much more expansive policing of homosexuality (not just in immigration law, but across the federal government) at midcentury. The figure of the psychopath in particular attached so many attributes to homosexuality that aliens (even those who had homosexual sex) had many points from which to resist the label. Boutilier's defense team mobilized from a variety of these different directions: Boutilier had heterosexual sex. Only rarely did he have sex in public places. He had no criminal record and had only come to the attention of the government by his own admission when he attempted to naturalize. And the alien bore many of the markers of a good citizen— he was a hard worker who lived with his mother, attended Mass, and even went bowling, a hobby so quintessentially American that political

Boutilier v. Immigration and Naturalization Service, 387 U.S. 118 (1967). Tripp probably limited his observation to white men because it was based on the Kinsey study, which surveyed the sexual experiences of white men.

[124] Report of Dr. Ullman, 15–17, Supreme Court Records and Briefs for *Boutilier v. Immigration and Naturalization Service*, 387 U.S. 118 (1967).

[125] Brief for Petitioner, 10, Supreme Court Records and Briefs for *Boutilier v. Immigration and Naturalization Service*, 387 U.S. 118 (1967).

[126] Petition for a Writ of Certiorari, 6–9, Supreme Court Records and Briefs for *Boutilier v. Immigration and Naturalization Service*, 387 U.S. 118 (1967).

scientist Robert Putnam has used it as a metaphor for engaged civic community.[127] Indeed, no other immigrant besides Fleuti so fully claimed the mantle of good citizenship. Fleuti did this so successfully that it entirely displaced his homosexuality (an outcome that enabled him to stay in the country while shoring up a rhetorical opposition between homosexuality and citizenship). That Boutilier could make a similar claim was not incidental to his whiteness and maleness—traits that, of course, he shared with Fleuti.

The contradictions that Boutilier posed as a homosexual man were consequential. They challenged the notion that homosexual aliens were an identifiable group that must be refused entry because they did not belong in the American body politic, and instead raised the possibility that homosexuality might be an occasional act among aliens who otherwise had the potential to become good citizens. The space that Boutilier had opened between homosexual acts and homosexual status, in other words, problematized sexual identity as a meaningful way to differentiate the citizenry, as well as the way that homo-hetero binarism had already been inscribed in federal policy. It is hardly surprising that the Supreme Court would move to close that gap, stabilizing homosexuality as an identity that could be deduced from sexual acts, and asserting the distance between that identity and one's capacity for citizenship. In the final view of the Court, homosexuality designated a type of people (psychopaths), not a set of free-floating practices from which no conclusions about identity could be drawn. "Congress commanded that homosexuals not be allowed to enter," the Supreme Court stated, collapsing all distinctions between psychopathic personality and homosexuality. "The petitioner was found to have that characteristic and was ordered deported." By forcefully rejecting the void-for-vagueness argument, the Supreme Court affirmed that Boutilier's deportation was not based on conduct but on his status at the time of entry.[128]

In so doing, the Court determined that the homosexual was a kind of person, but importantly it also rejected the medical terms on which homosexual identity had historically been based. The Court described homosexuality as a legal-political identity category. It did not care "what differing psychiatrists [thought]" because Congress had not laid down "a clinical test, but an exclusionary standard."[129] By its assignment of a legal rather than a medical valence to psychopathic personality cases, the Supreme Court thus made "the word of the bureaucrat supreme,"

---

[127] Robert Putnam, *Bowling Alone: The Collapse and Revival of American Community* (New York: Simon and Schuster, 2000).

[128] *Boutilier* thus resolved the void-for-vagueness issue from *Fleuti. Boutilier v. Immigration and Naturalization Service*, 387 U.S. 118, 124 (1967).

[129] Ibid.

regardless of what any given doctor might say about who a homosexual was.[130] Gerald Lavoie, whose case had been appealed to the Ninth Circuit Court of Appeals in light of *Boutilier*, was the first casualty. Weighing the alien's many homosexual experiences, the court ordered him deported as a psychopathic personality. The *Boutilier* decision rendered psychiatric testimony in the case irrelevant. Lavoie was someone who "in common opinion" would be a homosexual, the Ninth Circuit wrote, referencing the state's increasingly confident "common sense" of homosexuality.[131]

It's worth pausing here to say something about what these court cases can provide by way of evidence and what they cannot. In some respects, they offer limited insight into the experience of most aliens who encountered the state's antihomosexualism during these years. Indeed, *Flores-Rodriguez, Quiroz, Fleuti, Lavoie,* and *Boutilier* were all exceptional to the extent that they mounted defenses that exposed the contradictions of the government's strategy for regulating homosexuality among immigrants. Those acts of exposure have made the regulatory paradigm visible to the historian—they have left a trail to follow when agency records go cold—while doing relatively little for those individuals facing deportation.[132] In this latter sense, however, the experience of these aliens before the bar was not so different from that of a larger collective who never made it to court, but who (once vetted as homosexual) were more likely losers than winners. Federal authorities usually refused to recognize complexity in the sexual lives of the aliens they encountered—including those with extensive heterosexual experience. The INS and the courts instead imposed a simple (and simplifying) equation: homosexual act = homosexual person = psychopath = deportation. (Even homosexual behavior in women no longer seemed to mystify officials the way it once had.)

But following the arguments made in these cases, one question nags. Congress seems to have made the INS's work so much more complicated by giving psychiatrists such a large role to play in the deportation process as the arbiters of the psychopathic personality. In the 1960s, for example, the INS balked at the way that the condition was not uni-

[130] Ibid., 135 (Douglas, J., dissenting).

[131] *Lavoie v. Immigration and Naturalization Service*, 418 F.2d 732, 736 (9th Cir. 1969). The court's phrase "in common opinion" is revealing. In the early twentieth-century racial prerequisite cases (to determine if the petitioner was white and therefore eligible to naturalize), Ian Haney-López documents the rejection of a scientific rationale for one based on common knowledge. See Haney-Lopez, *White by Law: The Legal Construction of Race* (New York: New York University Press, 1996), 8.

[132] The relevant INS records from the mid-1950s onward are particularly difficult to access; as of this writing, many records are either unprocessed at the National Archives or still in the custody of the agency.

formly interpreted by PHS doctors. "Under the same facts," the INS complained, "doctors will certify at one location" but "not at another."[133] If Congress had wanted the INS to exclude homosexuals, why hadn't it explicitly written homosexuality into the law? Why had it relied instead on the psychopathic personality provision?

Casting an eye toward ground covered in earlier chapters suggests an answer: like the blue discharge, like the policy on homosexual tendencies, the psychopathic personality was *strategically ambiguous*, "knowingly conceived in confusion," as one commentator put it in 1959.[134] This was not a case, as one scholar wrongly surmised, of treating homosexuality as "the nameless crime," but rather the shaping of a "powerful weapon" when the "evidence [was] weak."[135] Not surprisingly, when Congress sought to replace the provision after the *Fleuti* decision, it found another term that was less rooted in psychiatry yet nearly as murky: in 1965, the law was rewritten to bar aliens who were "sexual deviates." The new terminology "does not appear to eliminate questions of vagueness as applied to homosexuals," one midcentury commentator groused.[136] "Rather than clarifying its original intention," another complained, "Congress has made it more obscure."[137]

Lifting the Engine out of the Mustang

In drafting the 1965 law, Congress responded to the potential weakness of the psychopathic personality provision by putting more distance between psychiatry and the legal definition of homosexuality. Yet Congress was shortsighted in neglecting to simultaneously remove psychiatrists from the certification process. Like psychopathic personalities, aliens suspected of the more sociological-sounding condition of sexual deviation still required PHS certification prior to exclusion or deportation. That psychiatrists remained procedurally central in the new law

[133] "The San Francisco immigration office informs me that the San Francisco United States Public Health office . . . is most reluctant to issue a Class 'A' certificate." Regional Counsel to General Counsel, May 14, 1965, memo obtained through the Freedom of Information Act, in author's possession.

[134] "Limitations on Congressional Power to Deport," 943. The same was true of the moral turpitude provision, but the latter had by the 1950s a settled meaning, it had "deep roots in the law." *Jordan v. DeGeorge*, 341 U.S. 223, 227 (1951).

[135] Robert J. Foss, "The Demise of the Homosexual Exclusion: New Possibilities for Gay and Lesbian Immigration," *Harvard Civil Rights–Civil Liberties Law Review* 29 (1994): 445; Ploscowe, *Sex and the Law*, 233.

[136] "Administrative Law—Deportation," *New York University Law Review* 42 (March 1967): 126.

[137] "Recent Cases: Aliens and Citizenship," *San Diego Law Review* 4 (1967): 153.

had something to do with the relationship between immigration officials and government psychiatry, which was long-standing. The INS
had partnered with the PHS in the enforcement of immigration matters
since the turn of the century.[138] And perhaps because the American Psychiatric Association (APA) had included homosexuality on its list of
mental illnesses (the Diagnostic and Statistical Manual, or DSM) as recently as 1952, Congress underestimated the extent to which psychiatry's liberalization was already under way.[139] Yet only a few years after
the publication of the 1952 DSM, the Group for the Advancement of
Psychiatry began to assert the problematic notion that homosexuality
and homosexual behavior were not synonymous.[140] A 1956 study
found, moreover, that it was not psychiatrists but *lawyers* who were the
most hostile of all the professions to homosexuality.[141]

Ironically, the *Boutilier* case itself may have contributed to a cultural
change within psychiatry in the late 1960s and early 1970s. The Mattachine Society and the Homosexual Law Reform Society—early gay
rights groups—worked on the case, which was widely reported in the
mainstream and homophile press.[142] Perhaps that inside perch helped
make clear to a fledgling gay rights movement both the diversity of
opinion on homosexuality among professional psychiatrists, as well as
the broad policy victories to be had by going after the APA. In 1970—
shortly after *Boutilier* was decided—gay activists commenced a campaign to pressure the APA to remove homosexuality from the DSM. Although that battle has been portrayed as a long and dramatic struggle,
what seems notable in retrospect is that victory was obtained in just
three years.[143] All told, homosexuality was formally defined as a men-

[138] The inspection process was not new in 1952. As early as 1891, Congress mandated
the medical inspection of all immigrants by the Marine Hospital Service (later called the
PHS). For a history of immigrant inspection, see Alan Kraut, *Silent Travelers: Germs, Genes,
and the "Immigrant Menace"* (Baltimore: Johns Hopkins University Press, 1994); Amy L.
Fairchild, *Science at the Borders: Immigrant Medical Inspection and the Shaping of the Modern
Industrial Labor Force* (Baltimore: Johns Hopkins University Press, 2003).

[139] Gerald Grob documents growing political and social liberalism within psychiatry in
the 1950s and 1960s. This liberal orientation affected mainstream psychiatry, and was ex-
hibited in such institutions as the Group for the Advancement of Psychiatry, the National
Institute for Mental Health, and even the American Psychiatric Association. See Gerald
Grob, *From Asylum to Community: Mental Health Policy in Modern America* (Princeton, NJ:
Princeton University Press, 1991), 275–77.

[140] Group for the Advancement of Psychiatry, "Report on Homosexuality with Particular Emphasis on This Problem in Governmental Agencies," report no. 30, January 1955.

[141] Bowman and Engle, "A Psychiatric Evaluation of Laws of Homosexuality," 312.

[142] See, for example, "U.S. Appeals Court Backs Order Deporting Alien as Homosexual," *New York Times*, July 9, 1996, 12; "Court Will Rule on Homosexuals," *New York Times*,
November 8, 1996, 24; "High Court Denies Homosexual Plea," *New York Times*, May 23,
1967, 49.

[143] The classic account is Ronald Bayer, *Homosexuality and American Psychiatry* (Prince-

tal disease by the establishment voice of professional psychiatry for a mere two decades.

Whether or not *Boutilier* can actually be linked to the APA's decision, the removal of homosexuality from the DSM directly affected immigration regulation. In July of 1974, then president of the APA John Spiegel sent a letter to the INS asking the agency "to refrain from the exclusion, deportation, or refusal of citizenship to homosexual aliens."[144] The INS ignored the letter, but for the next few years the INS, the PHS, the National Gay Task Force, and the American Civil Liberties Union "skirmished over the issue."[145] Decisive change only really set in when Jimmy Carter took office—the first president who (whatever his personal views) was at least aware of an organized gay constituency that was beginning to matter somewhat in the Democratic Party.[146] Although Carter himself was lukewarm on gay rights, some of his aides were not. Within months of taking office, Carter's public liaison Midge Costanza had organized meetings between gay rights advocates and representatives of federal agencies, including the PHS.[147] Given the stance of professional psychiatry, the agency only needed a slight push, and in November of 1977, Assistant Surgeon General William H. Foege (backed by Surgeon General Julius Richmond) sent a memorandum to INS commissioner Leonel Castillo. In light of the APA's recent decision, Foege wrote, "the Public Health Service should relinquish responsibil-

ton, NJ: Princeton University Press, 1987); see also Minton, *Departing from Deviance*, 256–62. More generally, Elizabeth Lunbeck argues that the hostility of psychiatrists (and other sexologists) to homosexuality has been exaggerated by historians. See Elizabeth Lunbeck, *The Psychiatric Persuasion: Knowledge, Gender, and Power in Modern America* (Princeton, NJ: Princeton University Press, 1994), 410–11.

[144] John P. Spiegel to Leonard F. Chapman, July 17, 1974, in *Lesbian/Gay Freedom Committee, Inc. v. I.N.S.*, 541 F. Supp. 569 (N.D. Ca. 1982), trial materials at the National Archives.

[145] Bush, "Borderline Homophobia," 9.

[146] See, for example, Allison Thomas to Anne Wexler, "Meetings in California with Leaders of Gay Community," May 8, 1980, in National Gay Task Force folder, Domestic Policy Staff (Malson), box 7, Jimmy Carter Presidential Library, Atlanta, GA; Tom Bastow to Martin Franks, "Impact of Gay Vote on Presidential Elections in November," Gays/Lesbians 2-8-79 to 6-30-80 folder, Domestic Policy Staff, (Malson), box 7, Jimmy Carter Presidential Library; Bob Malson to Administrative Staff, "Talking Points on Gay Issues," May 20, 1980, Gay Issues folder, Sarah Weddington files, box 68, Jimmy Carter Presidential Library.

[147] See National Gay Task Force/Agency Meetings folder, Office of Public Liaison (Costanza), box 27, Jimmy Carter Presidential Library. On Carter's policies on gay civil rights more generally, see William B. Turner, "Mirror Images: Lesbian and Gay Civil Rights in the Carter and Reagan Administrations," in *Creating Change: Sexuality, Public Policy, and Civil Rights*, ed. John D'Emilio, William B. Turner, and Urvashi Vaid (New York: St. Martin's Press, 2000), 3–28. On gay lobbying to change immigration policy during these years, see William B. Turner, "Lesbian/Gay Rights and Immigration Policy: Lobbying to End the Medical Model," *Journal of Policy History* 7 (1995): 208–25.

ity for the administration of the portion of the U.S. Code authorizing the exclusion of persons with a 'sexual deviation' insofar as this relates to homosexuals without other mental abnormalities." Foege invited the INS to participate in discussions prior to the PHS's abdication of its role in certifying homosexual aliens.[148]

The INS was determined to fight the PHS's move "tooth and nail."[149] After a series of interagency meetings, INS general counsel David Crosland responded by denying the PHS's authority to make such a move. "Medical officers of the Public Health Service have a legislative mandate to execute," Crosland barked.[150] Surgeon General Richmond's desire "to get out in front of the issue" was then stalled until a British alien named Carl Hill appeared at the San Francisco port of entry in June of 1979 wearing a gay pride button.[151] Hill was detained by INS officials, but he later secured a temporary restraining order and was paroled into the country. When he was ordered by the INS to a PHS hospital for an examination, he (and attorneys with the San Francisco–based Gay Rights Advocates) brought suit against Surgeon General Richmond to prevent the exam.[152]

Richmond was for Hill a dream adversary, and they and their attorneys met within weeks to settle the case, despite the INS's own threat to sue Richmond if he did so.[153] A week after the settlement, Richmond issued a memo stating that the APA considered homosexuality a "form of sexual behavior" and not a medical defect. The "determination of homosexuality could not be made through a medical diagnostic procedure," Richmond stated plainly. He advised the INS that "they should no longer refer aliens suspected only of being homosexual to the PHS for certification."[154] Because the law required certification, the PHS's action was, as one lawyer put it, like "lifting the engine out of the mustang."[155]

[148] William H. Foege to Leonel J. Castillo, November 7, 1977, in *Lesbian/Gay Freedom Committee, Inc. v. I.N.S.*, 541 F. Supp. 569 (N.D. Ca. 1982), trial materials at the National Archives.

[149] C. F. Brydon and Lucia Valeska to Bob Malson, July 13, 1979, in Gay Rights folder, Domestic Policy Staff (Malson), box 7, Jimmy Carter Presidential Library.

[150] David Crosland to Carl J. Wack, October 31, 1978, in Gay . . . Homosexuals 7/20/79 folder, Domestic Policy Staff (Malson), box 7, Jimmy Carter Presidential Library.

[151] Telephone interview with Dr. Julius Richmond, October 19, 2007. Richmond's assistant, Dr. Juel Janis, remembers that Richmond was spurred by the fact that another version of the DSM was about to be released (the DSM-III), which also did not list homosexuality. Telephone interview with Dr. Juel Janis, October 31, 2007.

[152] *Hill v. Richmond*, No. C-79-1405 SAW (N.D. Ca. 1979); *Hill v. I.N.S.*, 714 F.2d 1470 (9th Cir. 1983), trial materials at the National Archives.

[153] Bush, "Borderline Homophobia," 10.

[154] Julius B. Richmond to William H. Foege and George I. Lythcott, August 2, 1979, *Interpreter Releases* 56 (August 17, 1979): 398–99.

[155] Deposition of William O. Dillingham, June 11, 1984, 43, *Hill v. I.N.S.*, 714 F.2d 1470 (9th Cir. 1983), trial materials at the National Archives.

Yet the INS would not concede defeat.[156] The day after the Richmond memorandum, "almost to prove its mettle, the INS tried to turn back two [male] Mexican immigrants" because one wore an earring.[157] Some INS officials began to advocate the use of state sodomy statutes to bar homosexuals as presumed criminals.[158] On August 14, 1979, the INS sent out a cable to field offices ordering them to allow suspected homosexuals into the country with inspections "deferred" only as long as it took to resolve the legal issues at stake.[159] Despite that order, ten days later hundreds of women coming into the country for the Michigan Women's Music Festival were grilled. Fifty other individuals whom the INS admitted on deferred inspection from various ports of entry had, a year later, almost all voluntarily departed—suggesting that informal tactics were effectively deployed against aliens even as the formal policy was uncertain. Meanwhile, the State Department held the line even more fervently. Secretary of State Cyrus Vance announced "that since medical determinations no longer could be made, consular officials were given the authority to gauge from a person's appearance whether 'appropriate questions' should be asked to 'determine' homosexuality."[160]

With the standoff among various agencies at a heightened pitch, it was up to the Department of Justice (DOJ) to resolve the crisis. The agency's tactical position was not strong, for if there was some "cretin" within the PHS who would say that homosexuality was a disease, the DOJ could not "dust him off and find him." Rather, as one DOJ lawyer put it, "The doctors did their thing on medical grounds and ignored the law . . . and the [INS] followed the law and ignored the medicine."[161] Because the DOJ did not want to see "a portion of the immigration act [thus] rendered unenforceable," it sided with the INS, arguing that the surgeon general had no authority to stop certifying aliens. But in the face of the surgeon general's refusal (however illegitimate), Assistant

[156] INS commissioner Leonel Castillo seemed willing to compromise on the issue. Gay rights advocates referred to Castillo's "fight with the INS," indicating that he was somewhat alone in his position. Tom Bastow to Martin Franks, "Impact of Gay Vote on Presidential Elections in November," in Gays/Lesbians 2-8-79 to 6-30-80 folder, Domestic Policy Staff (Malson), box 7, Jimmy Carter Presidential Library. Reporter Larry Bush referred to David Crosland, who became the acting commissioner after Castillo resigned, as one of the agency's "Anita Bryants" ("Borderline Homophobia," 10).

[157] Bush, "Borderline Homophobia," 10.

[158] C. F. Brydon and Lucia Valeska to Bob Malson, July 13, 1979, in Gay Rights folder, Domestic Policy Staff (Malson), box 7, Jimmy Carter Presidential Library.

[159] Policy Cable from Carl Wack to INS Field Offices, August 14, 1979, *Interpreter Releases* 56 (August 17, 1979): 387.

[160] Testimony of Lucia Valeska, Boston Regional Hearings, Papers of the Select Commission on Immigration and Refugee Policy, November 26, 1979, 1980, part II, reel III, University Publications of America.

[161] Deposition of George C. Stoll, June 20, 1984, Lesbian/Gay Freedom Committee, Inc. v. I.N.S., 541 F. Supp. 569 (N.D. Ca 1982), trial materials at the National Archives.

Attorney General John Harmon asserted that the engine in the mustang was not psychiatry, it was law. Even without the PHS, Harmon mandated in December of 1979, "the INS was required nonetheless to enforce the Act's exclusionary provisions," and he urged the INS to develop a uniform procedure for going forward.[162]

From this unenviable position, the INS came up with a policy that appeared to be a "partial concession."[163] In September of 1980, the INS issued new operating instructions that restricted its officials from directly questioning aliens about homosexuality. Only if an alien made an "unsolicited, unambiguous oral or written admission of homosexuality," or if a third party informed immigration officials that an alien was a homosexual, was that individual to be referred for further inspection. During the secondary inspection, as long as the alien denied homosexuality, they were to be admitted into the country without further question.[164] Yet the new immigration policy was far more lenient on paper than in practice. The State Department specifically asked aliens whether they were afflicted with sexual deviation, and lying on a visa application was grounds for subsequent deportation.[165] Moreover, removing recalcitrant psychiatrists from the process of certification enhanced the power of border guards, who seemed to behave as if the policy had not changed at all. The legal director of Gay Rights Advocates informed the INS of "numerous complaints from various ports of entry where, apparently, immigration officials are failing to comply with the new regulations."[166] In 1982 litigation the INS conceded, in addition, to using arrest reports to determine homosexuality for aliens coming into the

[162]Memorandum for David L. Crosland, December 10, 1979, Hill v. I.N.S. 714 F.2d 1470 (9th Cir. 1983), trial materials at the National Archives. Here too, the State Department agreed with the INS: "The policy change by the Public Health Service does not alter the law," one Consular official opined, "but merely shifts the burden of determination from the panel physician to the Consular office." Donald R. Trembley, American Consul, to Mr. R. Duff, National Gay Rights Coalition, August 1, 1980, letter obtained through the Freedom of Information Act, in author's possession.

[163]Transcript of Hearing before Judge Hornbach, November 7, 1980, Hill v. I.N.S., 714 F.2d 1470 (9th Cir. 1983), trial materials at the National Archives.

[164]"Guidelines and Procedures for the Inspection of Aliens Who Are Suspected of Being Homosexual," Hill v. I.N.S., 714 F.2d 1470 (9th Cir. 1983), trial materials at National Archives.

[165]"Memorandum of Points and Authorities in Opposition to Plaintiff's Motion of Summary Judgment," and "Plaintiffs' Memorandum of Points and Authorities in Support of Motion for Order to Show Cause in re Contempt and for Preliminary Injunction," June 20, 1985, Lesbian/Gay Freedom Committee, Inc. v. I.N.S., 541 F. Supp. 569 (N.D. Ca. 1982), trial materials at the National Archives.

[166]Donald C. Knutson to David L. Millhallan, May 18, 1981, Hill v. I.N.S., 714 F.2d 1470 (9th Cir. 1983), trial materials at the National Archives.

country.[167] Perhaps most remarkable was the case of a gay alien whose bag was searched by immigration officials in New York on a pretense. "I turned to the desk behind me," the man later wrote, "and stood in complete amazement at what I saw: One person was reading a letter from my parents; one person was reading a letter from my friend in Toronto; . . . [and] one person was reading my own private journal." "*Jackpot*," said one of the officials.[168]

This kind of policy "liberalization" would have a strong parallel in the military's "Don't Ask/Don't Tell" policy, which came a little more than a decade later (and actually increased the number of soldiers purged for homosexuality). In that arena too homosexuality would be, as the legal scholar Janet Halley has written, "determined in the public sphere by law" via a series of state simplifications.[169] As defined by federal law, homosexuality was forged not only by a consolidation of acts and status, but also by a convergence of other markers as well (such as mannishness in women and effeminacy in men) that demonstrated a propensity to commit a homosexual act. Having the propensity was as damning as performing the act, which was then the same as being a homosexual person. "Making pro-gay statements, cutting your hair a certain way, not fitting the gender stereotype of the sex you belong to," Halley observes of the modern military, "can be an inference that you have engaged or might someday engage in homosexual conduct."[170] Halley's sharp analysis belies the military's defense that it only punishes homosexual conduct but not status.[171] So too does a longer view in which conduct and status are revealed to be historically intertwined in federal policing. Just a few years before Don't Ask/Don't Tell, the INS (to take the example closest at hand) had acknowledged treating homosexuality as not limited to behavior but also inseparable from a more persona-laden "way of thinking."[172]

[167] "Defendants' Answers to Plaintiffs' First Set of Interrogatories," *Lesbian/Gay Freedom Committee, Inc. v. I.N.S.*, 541 F. Supp. 569 (N.D. Ca. 1982), trial materials at the National Archives.

[168] "Exhibit E," *Lesbian/Gay Freedom Committee, Inc. v. I.N.S.*, 541 F. Supp. 569 (N.D. Ca. 1982), trial materials at the National Archives (emphasis added).

[169] Janet E. Halley, *Don't: A Reader's Guide to the Military's Anti-Gay Policy* (Durham, NC: Duke University Press, 1999), 33.

[170] Ibid., 2.

[171] The conduct/status distinction was (ironically) a litigation strategy pursued by gay rights advocates after the *Bowers v. Hardwick* decision in 1986 upholding state sodomy laws. President Bill Clinton saw Don't Ask/Don't Tell as a compromise in part because it appeared to uphold the conduct/status distinction. The reality has been entirely different. See Patricia A. Cain, *Rainbow Rights: The Role of Lawyers and the Courts in the Lesbian and Gay Civil Rights Movement* (Boulder, CO: Westview Press, 2000), 188–202.

[172] Bush, "Borderline Homophobia," 10.

Yet if the federal regulation of homosexuality toggled between status and act—sometimes relying on state and local policing of sexual behavior to author homosexual people into existence—so too did national citizenship. Indeed, it is not just an odd coincidence that scholars who study citizenship usually understand that category as connoting either an *act or a status*.[173] This similarity may be suggestive, rather, of the way that the federal state defined homosexuality and citizenship in relation to one another over the course of the twentieth century. In setting the terms of inclusion and exclusion in citizenship policy, in sum, federal officials also helped to set the terms for homosexuality. Sometimes they used medical knowledge and sometimes they dismissed it, but homosexuality was never something like tuberculosis: a problem to be discovered by the state and then simply reacted to. Homosexuality was much more like race: a certain set of rules produced out of the state's own murky encounter with difference.[174] That encounter was forceful and rarely benign. Still, an increasingly invasive state would in time also help to create rights consciousness for some queer individuals who, embracing the state's own emphasis on legal rather than medical categories, began to ask not whether they might be sick, but whether they might be citizens. They came to agree with the state's simple common sense definition of homosexuality, then, but could see less and less that was commonsensical about its placement outside national citizenship. This is, of course, an unavoidably ambivalent beginning for gay politics—the crafting of individual identity and state centralization, across the twentieth century, had gone hand in hand.[175]

[173] Will Kymlicka and Wayne Norman, "Return of the Citizen: A Survey of Recent Work on Citizenship Theory," in *Theorizing Citizenship*, ed. Ronald Beiner (Albany: State University of New York Press, 1995), 283–322.

[174] See, for example, Haney-López, *White by Law*; Peggy Pascoe, "Miscegenation Law, Court Cases, and Ideologies of 'Race' in Twentieth Century America," *Journal of American History* 83 (1996): 44–69.

[175] For a related point, see William Novak, *The People's Welfare: Law and Regulation in 19th Century America* (Chapel Hill: University of North Carolina Press, 1996), 240.

Conclusion

————⊖————

At the close of the nineteenth century, the federal state barely existed and national citizenship was, in historian Nancy Cott's words, "inchoate."[1] During these same years, homosexuality made its first appearance in American sexological writing, referring not to persons who engaged in sexual activity with persons of the same sex but to those whose "general mental state" was that of "the opposite sex."[2] During the better part of the next century, the federal state would grow exponentially, taking on the size and function of its modern form. So too would the meaning of national citizenship be clarified by Congress, the courts, and administrative agencies. Homosexuality would also come to be seen during these years—in the way that we now understand it—as an identity defined by sexual acts. Homosexual identity and modern citizenship crystallized, in other words, in tandem with the rise of the federal bureaucracy. That timing was not coincidental. Rather, homosexuality and citizenship are both a type of status that is configured (even, to some extent, conferred) by the state. Moreover, the definitional processes for citizenship and homosexuality are entangled. The federal government did not define homosexuality in the abstract, but always as part of drawing the boundaries around national citizenship. It is precisely because citizenship is a national category that the federal government (rather than states or localities) has played the predominant role in defining homosexual personhood.

While the federal state has never acted entirely alone in shaping homosexuality, its role has been fundamental. But the historical production of homosexuality is also, conversely, a story about the state's own development. State-building provides a way to talk about state institutions (who do the building) and what they actually build. With respect to homosexuality, what was built over the course of the twentieth cen-

[1] Nancy F. Cott, "Marriage and Women's Citizenship in the United States, 1830–1934," *American Historical Review* 103 (December 1988): 1444

[2] James G. Kiernan, "Responsibility in Sexual Perversion," *Chicago Medical Recorder* 3 (May 1892): 185–210, quoted in Jonathan Ned Katz, *The Invention of Heterosexuality* (New York: Plume Books, 1995), 19–20.

tury was less a completely reliable apparatus to police it than the *idea* of sexual citizenship.[3] The state defined the category, in short, without ever fully capturing its subject. Yes, some were squarely caught; some were even destroyed. But many of those who experienced homoerotic desire or engaged in homosexual behavior simply walked across the border, served out their enlistments, and collected their benefits. That so many went undetected suggests less the limitations of state power than the law's light touch in realizing its aims. The closet, after all, was a deliberate state strategy that became increasingly explicit toward the end of the century. Its brilliance was in inviting people to pass and then suggesting that they suffered no harm because they could hide.[4] Yet the incitement to pass was part of the harm, and so much more effectively did the state shape the citizenry by letting people in under certain conditions than by keeping them out absolutely. Whether one was ambivalently included or forcefully excluded by the modern regime of sexual citizenship, sexual citizenship turns out to be something that everyone has. Some people, of course, know this more than others.

The personal costs of this regime, however, may seem a bit muted in some of the foregoing chapters, and this is an unavoidable by-product of my approach. I have tried to see homosexuality through the state's eyes, to understand it as federal officials understood it, and to vest individual agency in bureaucrats rather than simply seeing the state as an unyielding peopleless structure. I have engaged in that exercise—bringing social/cultural and political/legal history together—because I think there are intellectual payoffs in both directions. For historians of sexuality, state-building as an explanation for postwar antihomosexualism offers an alternative to standard culturalist accounts of cold war anxiety. The rhetoric of McCarthyism has been made to do too much in the historiography, and it has obscured how the state actually works. McCarthyism can help explain the quickened pace of state homophobia after World War II, but it needs to be situated in terms of a much longer, quieter, and more incremental story of state officials coming to know and care about sex and gender nonconformity. Furthermore, once we are down on the ground with state officials, peering through their eyes, the story is at every phase more complicated than what McCarthyism heretofore has allowed. Citizenship has not only been defined by the steady nexus of inclusion and exclusion; state policy has at every mo-

[3] "Ideational and institutional components" work together in regimes of governance. See Rogers M. Smith, "Which Comes First, the Ideas or the Institutions?" in *Rethinking Political Institutions: The Art of the State*, ed. Ian Shapiro, Stephen Skowronek, and Daniel Galvin (New York: New York University Press, 2006), 92.

[4] This is precisely the argument mobilized by contemporary opponents of gay rights legislation.

ment been characterized by both repression and toleration. Repression is not surprising, but toleration is, especially in the postwar years that are usually characterized as the nadir of gay life in America. Historians of sexuality have to come to terms with the likes of Marion Kenworthy and Anna Rosenberg, who questioned the military's policy on tendencies, as well as the congressional representatives who stood up for those with blue discharges, or the Public Health Service psychiatrists who resisted calling homosexuality a disease. As much as the antihomosexual Marcus Braun or Frank Hines, they too are part of the state. Their voices help comprise the multiple registers in which the state speaks.

If part of my ambition in writing this book has been to hope to contribute to the emergence of a new gay political history, I want to suggest as well that mainstream political and legal historians should pay more attention to sexuality. The history of sexual regulation works against notions of the federal state as monolithic. This study has shown how the desire to regulate moved around in an expanding state, developing situationally in tandem with the state's need to do something else—process newcomers, go to war, or distribute resources, for example. In all of these venues, sexual regulation illustrates what the historian Ellis Hawley has identified as a more general pattern of growing federal involvement in social issues across the twentieth century.[5] But federal officials didn't simply assume tasks from their counterparts in state or local governments. Rather, they performed them in different ways. In the case of homosexuality, for instance, federal officials policed homosexual personhood where states and localities had mostly concerned themselves with homosexual behavior. Homosexuality is therefore an ideal case to explore how state institutions shape identity—a question in which legal and political historians have expressed interest.[6] The process here was not totally dissimilar from the way that race was constituted by legal-political structures (over a much longer period of time).[7] Yet the dynam-

[5] Ellis W. Hawley, "Social Policy and the Liberal State in Twentieth Century America," in *Federal Social Policy: The Historical Dimension*, ed. Donald T. Critchlow and Ellis W. Hawley (University Park: Pennsylvania State University Press, 1988), 118.

[6] Karen Orren and Steven Skowronek, *The Search for American Political Development* (Cambridge: Cambridge University Press, 2004), 17.

[7] "Racial identities in America have been extensively structured by laws and by the politics that has generated those laws," Rogers Smith writes, citing antebellum state laws as one early place where this work was done. Rogers M. Smith, "Black and White after *Brown*: Constructions of Race in Modern Supreme Court Decisions," *University of Pennsylvania Journal of Constitutional Law* 5 (2002–2003), 712–13. The legal adjudication of gender is, by contrast, especially distinct from that of race or homosexuality. Late in the twentieth century, when transsexuals went to court to legally change sex, courts had, Joanne Meyerowitz writes, "few precedents to follow. . . . [T]hey had never before had to spell out a legal definition of sex. They had simply assumed that male and female were readily ap-

ics may be even more clear with homosexuality, because of the latter's unique temporal relationship to federal state formation. Unlike race, homosexuality went from a total nonentity to a commonly understood category in the same years that the federal government went from a fledgling to a full-service bureaucracy. That timing helps to explain why the American bureaucracy was so much more homophobic than its corollaries in western Europe, where bureaucracies reached their modern form well before sexologists began talking and writing about sexual perversion.[8] Homosexuality was a novel concern in the years that the American bureaucracy took shape, and so it was etched deeply into federal institutions, giving us a state that not only structures but is itself structured by sexuality.

Does this unique timing—and the related deep inscription of homophobia into federal institutions—also help to explain why the federal government has been so reluctant to help advance gay civil rights even up to our own moment? The contrast to federal intervention on behalf of African American civil rights may be instructive on this point. I don't want to overstate the case for progressive change in terms of race. Civil rights historians have been critical of the belated and often anemic intervention of the federal government in the struggle against Jim Crow, and articulate as well about the limits of formal equality.[9] Yet a fascinating contrast remains: as a national policy of second-class citizenship for homosexuals was constructed across the federal bureaucracy, an administrative apparatus dedicated to racial (and sometimes gender) equality was simultaneously being built up over those same years.[10] And while it was federal authorities who finally stepped in to dismantle state and locally created systems of legal segregation for African Americans, it

parent and immutable." Joanne Meyerowitz, *How Sex Changed: A History of Transsexuality in the United States* (Cambridge, MA: Harvard University Press, 2002), 241.

[8] Philip Nord makes a similar argument in his discussion of John Carson's comparative study of intelligence testing, suggesting that professional social science was utilized more by the American bureaucracy than the French because of the timing of state development. "State-building in the U.S. accelerated at the very same historical moment that the social sciences were professionalizing and making a bid for public legitimacy. The consequence may have been a deeper social-science involvement in policy-making in the U.S. as compared to European countries, like France, where the state-building process had gotten a much earlier start." Philip Nord, review of *The Measure of Merit: Talents, Intelligence, and Inequality in the French and American Republics, 1750–1940*, by John Carson, *H-France Review* 7, no. 5 (September 2007).

[9] On the latter, see especially Nancy MacLean, *Freedom Is Not Enough: The Opening of the American Workplace* (Cambridge, MA: Harvard University Press, 2006).

[10] The centerpiece of this administrative apparatus is represented, of course, by the advent of the Equal Employment Opportunity Commission (EEOC) and the Office of Federal Contract Compliance Programs (OFCCP). But it has earlier roots as in, for example, Franklin Roosevelt's Committee on Fair Employment Practice (FEPC) or the Civil Rights Section within the Department of Justice. On the latter, see Risa L. Goluboff, *The Lost*

has been state and local governments that in the later-twentieth century have in practice ameliorated somewhat the federally created system of second-class citizenship for LGBT persons.

On gay rights, states and localities certainly have not been uniformly progressive, especially as evangelicals and other conservatives have effectively mobilized grassroots campaigns to block gay rights. Yet where progress has come, it has been predominantly at subnational levels of governance.[11] Starting in the 1970s, for example, numerous states and localities passed laws and ordinances prohibiting discrimination based on sexual orientation. In a few states, these new provisions protecting LGBT people from discrimination sat awkwardly alongside older and by then rarely used statutes prohibiting homosexual practices.[12] Many states also began to remove sodomy laws from their books. Some states and localities went further, offering select benefits for domestic partners.[13] In a remarkable extension of this trend, there are currently two states that offer same-sex marriage, and several others that offer the equivalent of state-level spousal rights to same-sex partners.[14] And some of the jurisdictions that have strongly opposed gay marriage have nonetheless, as Michael Klarman observes, "continued to expand gay rights in other contexts."[15] Moreover, local- and state-level political

---

Promise of Civil Rights (Cambridge, MA: Harvard University Press, 2007). On the EEOC, OFCCP, and FEPC, see especially Hugh Davis Graham, *The Civil Rights Era: Origins and Development of National Policy, 1960–1972* (Oxford: Oxford University Press, 1990).

[11] I would maintain that this is true even after a bitter defeat in the state of California on "Proposition 8" in the 2008 election. There voters narrowly passed a ballot initiative eliminating the recently won right of same-sex couples to marry. Yet even after Proposition 8, California (a state with expansive domestic partner benefits and strong anti-discrimination laws) remains light years ahead of federal policy on LGBT issues. So do numerous other states. Thirty-one states, for example, now have hate crimes laws that include sexual orientation; twenty states now prohibit employment discrimination based on sexual orientation. See http://www.hrc.org/about_us/state_laws.asp.

[12] Such was the case in Wisconsin, the first state to prohibit discrimination based on sexual orientation. See William B. Turner, "The Gay Rights State: Wisconsin's Pioneering Legislation to Prohibit Discrimination Based on Sexual Orientation," *Wisconsin Women's Law Journal* 22 (Spring 2007): 91–131.

[13] James Button, Barbara A. Rienzo, and Kenneth D. Wald, "The Politics of Gay Rights at the Local and State Level," in *The Politics of Gay Rights*, ed. Craig A. Rimmerman, Kenneth D. Wald, and Clyde Wilcox (Chicago: University of Chicago Press, 2000), 269–89.

[14] Massachusetts and Connecticut offer same-sex marriage (and a decision is pending from the Iowa Supreme Court). New York recognizes marriages by same-sex couples entered into in other jurisdictions. Vermont, California, New Hampshire, New Jersey, Oregon, and Washington, DC, offer the equivalent of state-level spousal rights to same-sex couples. Additionally, Hawaii, Maine, Maryland, and Washington State offer some statewide spousal rights to same-sex couples. See http://www.hrc.org/documents/Relation ship_Recognition_Laws_Map.pdf.

[15] Michael J. Klarman, "*Brown* and *Lawrence* (and *Goodridge*)," *Michigan Law Review* 104 (December 2005): 484.

gains—while still just patchwork protection—have helped to pave the way for better corporate practices, as many businesses have also adopted antidiscrimination policies, and offer health insurance, retirement, and other benefits to same-sex partners.[16] Some have done so explicitly to compete for state and local contracts.

The relative recalcitrance of the federal government on gay rights issues, by contrast, has led gay activists to sometimes focus on change at the state and local levels, with campaigns like "Equality Begins at Home," or coalitions such as the Federation of Statewide Lesbian, Gay, Bisexual, and Transgender Political Organizations.[17] "Achiev[ing] policy change requires shifting efforts away from the federal arena," wrote political scientist Rebecca Mae Salokar during the Clinton years.[18] The National Gay and Lesbian Task Force concurred that the "opportunities to move forward" were "at the state level."[19] This attitude has been prevalent not only among those who seek change through legislatures but through the courts as well. Indeed, legal scholar William Rubenstein has observed that while it is a truism that civil rights lawyers generally prefer to litigate in federal rather than state court, such is not the case for gay rights advocates. Gay rights litigators often choose to argue their cases in state courts, and have generally done better there. Sometimes this has even been true, Rubenstein points out, in socially conservative ("red") states.[20]

The gay experience thus confounds the overall narrative of twentieth-century civil rights history, in which the achievement of federal protection is seen as constituting a key moment of arrival.[21] That historical pattern further reveals protected groups, at some later point, inevitably

[16] Button, Rienzo, and Wald, "The Politics of Gay Rights at the Local and State Level," 287. The federal government will tax such benefits as income for same-sex but not for heterosexual married couples. David L. Chambers, "What If? The Legal Consequences of Marriage and the Legal Needs of Lesbian and Gay Male Couples," *Michigan Law Review* 95 (November 1996): 475. Furthermore, federal ERISA regulations discriminate against same-sex couples in pension benefits accessed through state/local/corporate domestic partnership programs. George Chauncey, *Why Marriage? The History Shaping Today's Debate over Gay Equality* (New York: Basic Books, 2004), 119.

[17] Donald P. Haider-Markel, "Lesbian and Gay Politics in the States: Interest Groups, Electoral Politics, and Policy," in *The Politics of Gay Rights*, ed. Craig A. Rimmerman, Kenneth D. Wald, and Clyde Wilcox (Chicago: University of Chicago Press, 2000), 291.

[18] Rebecca Mae Salokar, "Beyond Gay Rights Litigation: Using a Systematic Strategy to Effect Political Change in the United States," *GLQ* 3 (1997): 398.

[19] Quoted in Craig A. Rimmerman, *From Identity to Politics: The Lesbian and Gay Movements in the United States* (Philadelphia: Temple University Press, 2002), 34.

[20] William B. Rubenstein, "The Myth of Superiority," *Constitutional Commentary* 16 (Winter 1999): 599–625.

[21] "The civil rights laws of 1964, 1965, 1968, 1972, together with supporting court decisions and administrative enforcement," Hugh Davis Graham writes in his study of na-

discovering some limitations of federally bestowed formal equality. So advocates of African American, Latino, and women's rights (among others) eventually concluded, as Nancy MacLean has recently shown, that "freedom [was] not enough" and went on to push for more substantive reform.[22] But LGBT people in this country still have not yet achieved "freedom" as MacLean defines it. With the gains made at state and local levels—as well as broader cultural change—does it matter that second-class citizenship for sexual minorities remains inscribed in federal policy? Can the freedom that MacLean describes—formal legal equality backed by the federal government—simply be skipped over?

The answer that this history of the straight state offers is emphatically no. As much as we might chafe at how citizenship in practice almost never lives up to the ideal, what exactly does it mean to be written out of the nation's ideals altogether—to be deprived of what the historian William Chafe has called the "legal rights" to full citizenship?[23] States and localities can certainly make life better for LGBT people, but they cannot bestow equal citizenship upon them. Only the national government can do that. This is in part because citizenship in this country is, since Reconstruction, a national category. It is also because, as this book has argued, government homophobia has operated with the greatest force at the federal level. Any action taken by the federal government, after all, carries symbolic weight as a statement of our national values. So if discrimination by government (rather than a private actor) actually enhances the harm, then federal-level bigotry has cut deepest of all.[24] Moreover, while states and localities may have participated in homophobic policymaking, it was the federal government that initially developed the tools to police homosexual status rather than behavior alone, that employed sexuality to create a stratified citizenry, and that had the "raw power" to make its categories "stick."[25] In the words of one federal

tional civil rights policy, "broke the back of the system of racial segregation and destroyed the legal basis of denying minorities and women full access to education, employment, the professions, the opportunities of the private marketplace and public arena" (*The Civil Rights Era*, 3).

[22] The phrase, of course, was Lyndon Johnson's. MacLean, *Freedom Is Not Enough*, 5. The push for substantive equality has gained more political traction because of the *federal* commitment to the formal equality of racial minorities, women, the disabled, and so forth.

[23] William H. Chafe, "One Struggle Ends, Another Begins," in *The Civil Rights Movement in America*, ed. Charles W. Eagle (Jackson: University of Mississippi Press, 1986), 128.

[24] The argument that governmental action enhanced the psychological stigma of discrimination was mobilized in *Brown*. See Goluboff, *The Lost Promise of Civil Rights*, 245.

[25] James C. Scott, *Seeing Like a State: How Certain Schemes to Improve the Human Condition Have Failed* (New Haven, CT: Yale University Press, 1998), 82; *Fannie Mae Clackum v. United States*, 296 F. 2d 226 (Ct. Cl. 1960).

judge—ordering the deportation of a Dutch alien who had been arrested for disorderly conduct in a New York City bathroom—"the nomenclature or the label attached by state codes did not govern" nearly as much as "the nomenclature and the definitions [at] the federal [level]."[26]

Because of this, gay rights advocates began with and have never fully abandoned the hope of federal-level change, despite the obstacles. That notion was reflected in the earliest of homophile protests, when a handful of activists picketed the White House, and some years later, when gay activists organized the National March on Washington in 1979. During the 1960s, the Mattachine similarly made calls for the federal government to be at the "van, not in the rear," to "lead not lag," in making change.[27] In 1974, the top priority of the newly formed National Gay Task Force was a federal gay rights bill, which the organization expected to be enacted within five to ten years.[28] The original bill was modeled on the Civil Rights Acts of 1964 and 1968, and included provisions concerning employment, housing, federally funded programs, and public facilities. Twenty years later—and stripped down to cover employment alone—the Employment Non-Discrimination Act was finally heard by congressional committee. Despite the fact that "employment" did not include the military and the legislation skirted the issue of partner benefits, the bill did not make it to the floor for a vote.[29] Remarkably, my hometown of Cedar Rapids, Iowa, has had a fairly comprehensive gay rights ordinance for ten years, but the federal Employment Non-Discrimination Act has not been enacted.[30] To enclave issues facing sexual minorities as state and local matters is to deny that such questions merit the attention of federal policymakers, or that LGBT Americans are "legitimate participants in a national world."[31]

[26] *Wyngaard v. Rogers*, 187 F. Supp 527 (D.D.C. 1960).

[27] Mattachine Presentation to the Civil Service Commission, September 8, 1965, in "Homosexuals—Civil Liberties" vertical file, Kinsey Institute, Indiana University, Bloomington.

[28] *It's Time: Newsletter of the National Gay Task Force*, in Gay Rights Publications folder, Office of Public Liaison (Costanza), box 4, Jimmy Carter Presidential Library, Atlanta, GA.

[29] Chai R. Feldblum, "The Federal Gay Rights Bill: From Bella to ENDA," in *Creating Change: Sexuality, Public Policy, and Civil Rights*, ed. John D'Emilio, William B. Turner, and Urvashi Vaid (New York: St. Martin's Press, 2000), 149–87; Gregory B. Lewis and Jonathan L. Edelson, "DOMA and ENDA: Congress Votes on Gay Rights," in *The Politics of Gay Rights*, ed. Craig A. Rimmerman, Kenneth D. Wald, and Clyde Wilcox (Chicago: University of Chicago Press, 2000), 197.

[30] Chapter 69, Cedar Rapids Municipal Code (providing civil rights protection based on sexual orientation in employment, public accommodations, housing, credit, and education). Even the most targeted state or local ordinance tends to underprotect because the public associates the very concept of civil rights with the federal government. Nan D. Hunter, "Sexuality and Civil Rights: Re-Imagining Anti-Discrimination Laws," *New York Law School Journal of Human Rights* 17 (2000–2001): 572–73.

[31] This is an argument that feminist legal scholars have made about a related enclaving

The relationship of gays and lesbians to the national government, in short, stands apart from the parallel relationship between the federal government and most others who can also claim long histories suffering discrimination and prejudice. Yet our new century may be different. Indeed, legal scholars point out a recent exception in the courts: *Lawrence v. Texas*, the 2003 Supreme Court decision decriminalizing state sodomy laws, is regularly seen as analogous to *Brown v. Board of Education*.[32] Each decision was made possible by broader political and cultural changes, drew on unique kinds of evidence (social science in *Brown*, and history and international law in *Lawrence*), and built on rather than inaugurated a social movement. (*Brown* occurred earlier in the African American civil rights movement than did *Lawrence* in the gay rights movement.)[33] If the analogy holds true, then the immediate backlash experienced after *Lawrence* should, as with *Brown*, give way to greater long-term acceptance and eventually pave the way for federal gay rights legislation.[34]

When that happens, how should it occur? Homosexual exclusion and heterosexual privilege have been written into many different elements of federal citizenship policy—this study has only begun to sketch the contours—and there isn't one sweeping act of Congress that can undo what's been constructed over the better part of a century. Rather, the architecture of exclusion will have to be taken down in the same deliberate way it was put up: piece by piece. That dismantling actually began before *Lawrence*, in 1990, with the removal from immigration law of the ban on homosexual aliens.[35] This means that in the twenty-first century, matters of sexual citizenship are no longer primarily "threshold questions" about access to the nation-state, but rather "internal questions" about the substantive character of citizenship for existing members of the political community.[36] One of those internal questions has to do

---

of women's issues at the state and local levels. Judith Resnick, "'Naturally' without Gender: Women, Jurisdiction, and the Federal Courts," *New York Law Review* 66 (1991): 1749–50, 1766. See also Jill Elaine Hasday, "Federalism and the Family Reconsidered," *UCLA Law Review* 45 (June 1998): 1297–1400; Reva Siegel, "She the People: The 19th Amendment, Sex Equality, Federalism, and the Family," *Harvard Law Review* 115 (February 2002): 947–1046.

[32] Lawrence H. Tribe, "*Lawrence v. Texas*: The 'Fundamental Right' That Dare Not Speak Its Name," *Harvard Law Review* (2004): 1895.

[33] Klarman, "*Brown* and *Lawrence* (and *Goodridge*)," 443–45.

[34] Ibid., 431–89; Nan D. Hunter, "Twenty-First Century Equal Protection: Making Law in an Interregnum," *Georgetown Journal of Gender and the Law* 7 (2006): 145–46.

[35] See Barney Frank, "American Immigration Law: A Case Study in the Effective Use of the Political Process," in *Creating Change: Sexuality, Public Policy, and Civil Rights*, ed. John D'Emilio, William B. Turner, and Urvashi Vaid (New York: St. Martin's Press, 2000), 208–35.

[36] Linda Bosniak, "Universal Citizenship and the Problem of Alienage," *Northwestern University Law Review* 94 (Spring 2000): 963–82.

with the right to secure residency for a noncitizen same-sex partner in the same manner that heterosexuals who marry foreigners currently may. (A version of the "Permanent Partners Immigration Act" has been introduced in every Congress since 2000.) Other places that the federal government might begin are similarly obvious. Ending the military's ban on gay soldiers, equalizing federal benefits for same-sex partners (in social security and veterans' benefits, among many other federal programs), and enacting a federal antidiscrimination law would strike a heavy blow at the straight state.

Looking back on the past hardly equips one to predict the future, and yet I believe these changes are coming. I expect that well before my old age, I will live in a nation that allows LGBTs to share equally in the obligations and benefits of national citizenship. Given the enormous and well-documented generational change in attitudes toward homosexuality, it seems plausible that these changes could come much, much sooner.[37] Indeed, I take it as a positive sign that some have thought to warn me about writing a conclusion like this, about how quickly it could become dated. I can only say: the quicker, the better. How perfectly timed it would be, in fact, if closing the chapter that this book represents in my life could also mean closing the chapter on some of the injustices that have compelled me to write it. In the meantime, I find no better way to express my own impatience than to borrow the words of one young soldier who, accused of lesbianism, found herself in front of a military board in 1958. "I don't feel that I am being treated like an American citizen," she bravely implored. "I would like to know why."[38] It was such a simple question, and some fifty years later, from lawmakers, judges, and bureaucrats, it now deserves an answer.

[37] Klarman, "*Brown* and *Lawrence* (and *Goodridge*)," 485.
[38] File 333 (Ft. McPherson), box 2283, Confidential decimal file, July 1957–June 1958, Records of the Inspector General, RG 159.

Index

Note: Page references in italics indicate illustrations.

Federal Transient Program. *See* FTP

Federation of Statewide Lesbian, Gay, Bisexual, and Transgender Political Organizations, 260

feminism, conceptions of, 35, 35n.70, 71, 71–72n.75

Fenton, Ivor D., 159n.102

FEPC (Committee on Fair Employment Practice), 259n.10

FERA (Federal Emergency Relief Administration), 92, 102–3, 102n.49, 106, 106n.68, 109, 128–29

52-20 Club, 152

First World War. *See* World War I

Fisher, William, 125

Fleuti (George) case, 235–41, 235nn.91–92, 237n.101, 238n.104, 238n.106, 245, 245n.128, 246, 247

flophouses, 98, 98n.25, 103, 110, 130

Flores-Rodriguez (Roberto) case, 227–31, 229n.69, 233–34n.86, 246

Flynt, Josiah, 100

Foege, William H., 249–50

Food Administration, 59n.14

Forrestal, James, 208, 208n.136

Fort Lee Training Center (WAC), 181, *182*, 210–11

Fosdick, Raymond, 61, 73

Foucault, Michel, 10–11

4F classification, 241, 241n.115

France, state-building in, 259n.8

Frank, Judge, 229–33, 233–34n.86

Fraser, Nancy, 27

Freedman, Estelle, 211-12n.153

Freud, Sigmund, 29n.39, 69n.64, 243n.120

Frydl, Kathleen, 143–44

FTP (Federal Transient Program), 102–18; camps/shelters created by, 92, 102–3, *104*, 108–17, *111*, 116n.120; vs. CCC, 117–19, 122–23; creation of, 92; ending of, 128–30; female vs. male social workers for, 114–15, 114nn.108–09; funding for, 102–3; number served by, 118n.129; on old vs. new transients, 103–6; perversion policy of, 113; racial segregation in facilities of, 105n.64; stigma of supporting unattached single men, 92–94;

transients publicized as normal people by, 103–8; women/families vs. men in, 126–28, 128n.192

Fuel Administration, 59n.14

Furner, Mary O., 23n.14

Garden of Allah (Baltimore), 71

Gardner, Martha, 26–27

Garner, Grace, 199–200

gay life's visibility, Prohibition's role in, 69n.64

gay rights: antidiscrimination laws and business policies, 259–60, 259n.11–12, 260n.16; citizenship, 261, 264; at the federal level, 261–63; opposition to, 256n.4, 260; same-sex marriage/partners, 259, 259n.11, 259n.14, 264; sodomy laws removed, 259, 263; at the state/local level, 259, 260, 263, 262n.30

Gay Rights Advocates, 250, 252

gay rights movement: blue discharges as a cause of, 170n.156; on Leonel Castillo, 251n.156; on conduct vs. status, 254n.173; and exclusion of homosexual immigrants, 249–50; on homosexuality defined as mental illness, 248–49; Homosexual Law Reform Society of America, 242–43, 243n.120, 248; Mattachine Society, 243n.120, 248, 262; National Gay Task Force, 249

"gay," use of term, 110, 110n.93

gender: ambiguous, as perversion, 36–38; citizenship based on, 13, 13n, 180, 212–13; female vs. male social workers, 114–15, 114nn.108–09; inversion of, 12, 31n.54, 110, 193; legal adjudication of, 257n.7; military policies based on, 177, 180, 211–12; sexual relationships vs. gender traits/tendencies (*see under* homosexuality); welfare policies based on, 130–34, 131n.211, 134n.226. *See also* men; women

genitals, deformed. *See* arrested sexual development/small penis

Gentlemen's Agreement (1908), 23n.13

Gerber, Harry, 55n.2

GI Bill: for African Americans, 150, 150n.60,

women: dependency of, 26, 26n.27; GI Bill benefits for, 171–72, 171–72nn.160–163; in the military, 171, 171n.160, 172n.163, 178–79 (*see also under* military, cold war–era; WAC); perversion among, 61–62, 61–62n.25; prostitution suspected/assumed of, 26–27, 26n.30; single, as public charge aliens, 25–27; single, transient, 126–28, 127nn.187–88, 127–28n.191, 128n.193, 133; Social Security benefits for, 172n.162; as social workers, 114–15, 114n.108; sodomy arrests/convictions for, 174; traffic in, 20n.5; as witholding sex from unemployed husbands, 96, 96n.16. *See also* lesbianism
Women's Armed Services Act (1948), 176, 176n.9
Women's Army Corps. *See* WAC
Women's Auxiliary Army Corps, 171n.161
Women's Barracks, 195n.78
Women's Integration Act, 209–10
Works Progress Administration (WPA), 129–31, 130n.210
World War I: protests by veterans of (1932), 91, 142; state-building produced by, 59, 59n.14, 88–89; types of discharges during, 145, 145n.31; veterans benefits following, 142, 142n.16; vigilantism/violence in political culture during, 84–85, 85n.149. *See also* Bonus Armies
World War II: conscientious objectors during, 60n.17; military uncovers perversion during, 57; number of people serving in, 142n.18; number of women serving in, 178–79; size of military following, 88, 88–89n.166; state-building produced by, 59, 88; and state's relationship to homosexuality, 2–3; transiency during (*see* welfare, World War II–era). *See also* military, World War II–era
World War II Project Records, 153nn.73–74
World War Veterans' Act (1924), 149
WPA (Works Progress Administration), 129–31, 131n.211
Wyngaard, Robert, 231

Xilomenos, Nicolaos, 36

Yerkes, Robert, 64, 64n.32
YMCA, 70, 72–74

Zeiger, Susan, 62n.25
Zieger, Robert H., 59n.15, 60n.17

POLITICS AND SOCIETY IN TWENTIETH-CENTURY AMERICA

The Silent Majority: Suburban Politics in the Sunbelt South
by Matthew D. Lassiter

White Flight: Atlanta and the Making of Modern Conservatism
by Kevin M. Kruse

Troubling the Waters: Black-Jewish Relations in the American Century
by Cheryl Lynn Greenberg

*In Search of Another Country: Mississippi and the Conservative
Counterrevolution* by Joseph H. Crespino

*The Shifting Grounds of Race: Black and Japanese Americans in the Making
of Multiethnic Los Angeles* by Scott Kurashige

Americans at the Gate: The United States and Refugees during the Cold War
by Carl J. Bon Tempo

*School Lunch Politics: The Surprising History of America's Favorite
Welfare Program* by Susan Levine

Trucking Country: The Road to America's Wal-Mart Economy
by Shane Hamilton

The Straight State: Sexuality and Citizenship in Twentieth-Century America
by Margot Canaday